DATE DUE

79956645			nslating Empire
79956645			
MAY 07 2015		MAY 03 2015	

NEW AMERICANISTS

A Series Edited by Donald E. Pease

TRANSLATING EMPIRE

José Martí,

Migrant Latino Subjects, and

American Modernities

LAURA LOMAS

DUKE UNIVERSITY PRESS
Durham & London
2008

© 2008 Duke University Press
All rights reserved
Printed in the United States of America
on acid-free paper ∞
Designed by Jennifer Hill
Typeset in Minion Pro
by Keystone Typesetting, Inc.

*Library of Congress
Cataloging-in-Publication Data
appear on the last printed
page of this book.*

FOR MY PARENTS AND GRANDPARENTS
PARA MARTITA Y PUKAQUINDE

CONTENTS

Criticar es Amar:
Translation and Self-Criticism

> It is not by chance that we are born in one place and not another, but in order to give testimony.—**Eliseo Diego,** *Por los extraños pueblos*, 1958

> The world has expanded, the earth is not the center any more. It turns among the infinite multitude of worlds like it. —**Gustave Flaubert,** *Bouvard and Pécuchet*, 1881

      ᠀ AS A STATELESS, nonassimilating migrant, a colonized and a linguistically marginalized translator, José Martí elucidates an alternative to the modernity that serves imperial expansion. How does translation, rather than autonomy and originality in the tradition of U.S. American renaissance writers, become the means by which a migrant Latino writer elaborates an alternative modernity? How do Martí's inaugural experiments in modernist form in the Americas articulate the perspective of this journalist, poet, diplomat, and revolutionary born in Cuba, who resided in New York in the 1880s and 1890s? Through the daily labor of making translations of texts from English into Spanish and of interpreting North American culture, Martí developed a literary form adequate to capture the dynamic, sometimes shocking events that he read about and observed firsthand in New York.[1] This formal innovation merits more recognition in contemporary theorizing of American studies, of modernism in the Americas, and in the genealogy of alternative American modernities.

My work as a translator-interpreter between 1989 and 1992 for América Sosa and María Teresa Tula, two representatives of the award-winning Salvadoran human rights organization, the Committee of Mothers of the Disappeared, Assassinated and Political Prisoners (co-madres) made this book possible in many senses. Not only did I really become fluent in Spanish from these eloquent and courageous women; I learned from María and América and from the other members of a community of Salvadoran migrants who lived and worked together in the midst of the final phase of a twelve-year civil war to rethink the understanding of America I'd acquired while growing up in the United States. With their fearless and fierce eloquence in my mouth as I interpreted, or under my fingertips as I translated their analyses of the United States into English, I glimpsed the future of another American studies. In the post–cold war period, Salvadoran activists taught me that U.S. American studies would, sooner or later, have to rethink its relation to the other Americas. A new American studies— or scholarship about the United States and the other Americas—would prompt the United States to see itself through the eyes of people surviving and fighting long-standing policies of military, economic, and political intervention in Latin America and elsewhere. Immediately before joining the staff of co-madres in Washington, D.C., I visited Cuba as part of an international delegation of young people organized by the American Friends Service Committee. I harvested yams, interacted with politically privileged young Communists, marginalized poets, Christians, and disaffected adolescent critics of the revolution (or "freakies"), at a time when the winds of Tiananmen Square and perestroika were already beginning to whistle through the thirty-year old revolutionary regime. I, with my rudimentary Spanish skills during this two-month sojourn, concluded that layers of misconception rendered little hope for translation between Cuba and the United States. It was impossible not to encounter José Martí's remarkable poetry in Cuba, for little children walked around reciting his verses and his name and sculpted image were everywhere. I had the good fortune to bring home a weather-beaten anthology of his sylvan prose from that encounter with pre-special period Cuba, but I did not expect then to spend a decade writing a book about Martí and his interlocutors in the U.S.

It was only in 1991, when I was translating for two feminist academics in El Salvador, that I decided to study the other versions of the United States that emerge in the eyes of readers from Latin America. While undertaking research into the women's movement in El Salvador, our small group of two feminist academics, a Salvadoran feminist activist, her cousin, and I—the translator—were stopped by the Treasury Police, blindfolded and detained without charge for thirty hours. Upon our detention, we were stripped of our documents, but not our clothes (as was the case for our Salvadoran colleagues, whom I saw in ill-fitting military fatigues); we foreigners (two U.S. and one French citizen) had nothing with which to confront the U.S.-equipped and funded Salvadoran police but our tongues. I had been hired as a translator by the two academics, and I translated the entire interrogation of the U.S woman and then underwent interrogation myself through the night. That experience of interrogation in an underground prison by sixteen-year-olds who told me that they acquired their expertise at U.S. taxpayers' expense at the School of the Americas in Fort Benning, Georgia, and admonishment by the U.S. official upon whom our release depended for associating with "delinquent terrorists" (meaning, my colleagues, the Salvadoran feminist activists) prodded me to begin the research that led to this book. As I read more, I realized that José Martí saw the need for and successfully carried out translations of the not yet readily apparent imperial project of United States for Latin American, Latina/o, and eventually, for U.S. readers.

In one of the letters that the Cuban poet, novelist, and journalist Eliseo Alberto transcribes in his memoir of growing up in Cuba and participating in the 1959 Revolution, *Informe contra mi mismo* (Report against Myself) (1996), his correspondent defines "the true magnitude of *las patrias*" as "the planetary smallness of life."[2] This "planetary smallness," of which Gustave Flaubert, Benedict Anderson, and Walter Benjamin all write, becomes comprehensible through comparative imagining from a specific place in relation to the planet and in relation to a vast human history.[3] Although Alberto's memoir offers an unflinching critique of Cuba's bureaucracy, it also criticizes in no uncertain terms the government of the United States for entering Cuba uninvited in 1898, and for strangling Cuba's economy through its commercial embargo, which since 1961 has placed the island in "the last and most absurd straitjacket of the cold war."[4] Alberto's long history as a member of the cultural elite, and functionary within the Cuban Communist Party, his intense affection for the quotidian aspects of life in Cuba, and his willingness to publish his memoir—despite his friends' begging him not to—prevent his book from becoming reduced to the political agendas of either the official revolution or of Cuban exiles allied with the U.S. government. By this act of political suicide, Alberto

claims to have liberated himself—the person he abandoned when he became complicit with policies with which he profoundly disagreed. *Informe
contra mi mismo* expresses respect and love for Cuba's "given" culture
through criticism, and specifically, self-criticism.⁵ This kind of critical relationship to the nation informs my reconsideration of a selection of Martí's
major and minor writings as translations of empire.

   Alberto's memoir of his island and of the Cuban Revolution since 1959
represents a complex breaking down of the political divisions that continue to divide Cubans, by calling for a "necessary peace" (40) in the spirit
of Martí's "necessary war." Accordingly, he uses Martí's texts against the
official Martís on the island, without ceasing to challenge the official Martí
of the United States. Much as Alberto emphasizes the fact that Martí did
not live on the island for which he so intensely suffered, and that he
dignified, defended, and loved as he inscribed it into his prose and poetry,
so I, in *Translating Empire* focus on Martí's status as an extranational
migrant inside the United States. As Alberto criticizes a revolutionary
socialist ethic of "socialismo o muerte" that admits weaknesses of neither
mind nor body, so I call attention to the internally divided psychic condition and formal ambiguity in Martí's prose that records ambivalent responses to the culture of U.S. modernity and reveals shifting relations to
the veterans of the independence movement. Just as Alberto recalls the role
of the transamerican community of Mexicans, Nicaraguans, Venezuelans,
Argentines, Puerto Ricans, and New Yorkers who "offered bread and a roof
in hours of desperation, in the days when the veteran *mambises* [or soldiers
of Cuban independence] looked over [Martí's] shoulders with *militaris-
simo* disdain" (27), so I present Martí's writing as an expression of a newly
multiracial and transnational Latino/a community in the United States, at
a moment when the rhetoric of manifest destiny and scientific racism
joined forces to besmirch a Latin American grouping that Martí and others
referred to sympathetically during this period as his own "Latin" or "Latino" people.⁶ This book is thus indebted to Alberto's method, even though
my object of study necessarily diverges from his.

   How did Martí relate to the United States, to the politics and culture of
its mainstream and of its subcultures? While there is no question that Martí
absorbed ideas from the United States as he developed genres, literary innovation, and political practices, what interests me more are the ways that
through his work as a translator, in carefully measured arguments—and
against the recommendations of his editors and influential readers—Martí

critically reworked rather than simply embraced the Anglo-American U.S. culture all around him. In *José Martí: la invención de Cuba*, the exiled Cuban intellectual historian Rafael Rojas shows Martí's debts to models of republican government in Spain, France, Mexico, and, above all, to the post–Civil War United States in developing his political and cultural theory.[7] Whereas Rojas's interpretive emphasis makes sense for his Latin American, Spanish, and perhaps especially Cuban readership (who are unlikely to read Rojas's book and come to the conclusion that for Martí the United States represented the perfect paragon of self-government, democracy, and liberty), my different focus responds to lingering misperceptions about the United States in the United States, misperceptions that Martí's work prompts us to address. Although Martí's journalism, literary criticism, poetry, diaries, fragmentary pieces, epistolary writing, and oratory respect the founding principles of the United States, they also observe imperial modernity working hand in hand to stratify, exclude, and circumscribe access to modernity's key promises. In the context of imperial modernity, liberty had become a special privilege of the United States.

After spending a total of seven months in Cuba as a *Yuma* (U.S. citizen) researcher over the past decade, I could hazard guesses as to why Cubans call for reform and find it necessary to leave, like many other millions from Latin America who migrate to the United States. My forebears have willfully forgotten, in the course of several generations, the dilemmas and traumas of immigration and assimilation—that exile and migration have not cut my life nor my parents' lives in two, as has happened for so many Cubans since the nineteenth century. For this reason, this book does not pretend to marshal Martí's texts to address concerns about Cuba's struggling government and the range of its (disgruntled or enthusiastic) citizens and exiles. Instead, the accident of my birth and the language in which I learned to write demand that I bring Martí's insights to bear on contemporary research in and about the United States, at a time when work at the forefront of the field is at last taking up many of the preoccupations that Martí set out more than a century ago.[8]

Having proposed to read Martí from and for the United States, rather than in relation to Cuba or Latin America, I cannot, and do not wish to, assume a stance of cool, disinterested objectivity. A space for critical interpretation of Martí outside of Cuba is valorized and in fact demanded by Ottmar Ette's comprehensive narrative of the ideological battles over the symbolic capital that is contained in José Martí's writing and persona—

between politicians and literati, between those on the island and those in exile, between readers with socialist and republican commitments.[9] This is the perspective of *Translating Empire*, but such an outsider status, especially given my location in the United States, implicates rather than exempts me from the political networks that began to form in the late nineteenth century and that remain a defining tendency of our age. A U.S. perspective on Cuba that perceives itself as foreign to the struggle over the control of the island and its future neglects the historic assumption that "the law of our national existence is growth," as the New York transplant and Democratic senator of Louisiana, John Slidell, noted in 1859, in proposing legislation to facilitate the acquisition of Cuba. In defending this position, he claimed:

> The tendency of the age is the expansion of the great powers of the world. England, France and Russia, all demonstrate the existence of this pervading principle. Their growth, it is true, only operates by the absorption, partial or total, of weaker powers—generally, of inferior races. So long as this extension of territory is the result of geographical position, a higher civilization, and greater aptitude for government, and is not pursued in a direction to endanger our safety or impede our progress, we have neither the right nor the disposition to find fault with it.[10]

This long history shaped the struggle of Cubans in the 1880s and 1890s, and the sedimented assumptions of this position have not ceased to inform U.S. foreign policy toward Latin America and its migrants in the United States. The self-definition of imperial modernity as grounded on inexorable "natural" facts such as geographical position, "higher" civilization, and "greater" aptitude should still alarm us because such arguments still circulate.

Ette seeks to recontextualize Martí's writings in the historical period and cultural context to avoid reducing Martí's unwieldy and complex corpus to slogans, adages, and epigraphs (often reproduced without date or a textual citation). While I am sympathetic to Ette's goal of demystifying and desanctifying an untouchable, infallible, superhuman Martí, I cannot agree that readings of Martí "en el extranjero" (abroad; that is, in foreign, non-Cuban space) enjoy a privileged objectivity, above conditioning or orienting ideological interests. According to Ette, Martí's readers have erred in an attempt to show Martí's continuing relevance to one ideological agenda or another.[11] Martí's own translations refute this notion of objective interpretation, as I argue in the chapters that follow. Given that the United States has an especially long and involved relationship with Cuba, the idea that noninsular scholarship—in the United States and Europe—is less biased or somehow not complicit with imperial history and contemporary global politics tends to reinforce the occult artistry whereby empire parades behind a mask of democracy.

Translating Empire offers a critique of U.S. American studies from within North America, by recalling Martí's contributions to literary history of modernism and to transamerican literary studies. Against the long-standing construction of Martí as an ally of U.S. policy in the region, my book aims to show the indispensability of Latino migrant translations to the imagining of American cultural and literary history more broadly. If Rafael Rojas and Eliseo Alberto offer testimony that circulates clandestinely in Cuba and addresses a society bracing itself for a transition, underway officially as I write this preface in 2008, *Translating Empire* offers testimony about the United States, the *patria* that North American readers have the option and obligation to interrogate and narrate. I will have failed if the reader takes this book as a new weapon in the by now dusty and yet still overstocked arsenal aimed at Cuba's current government. Through the prism of Martí's translations, I seek to recast U.S. culture and letters, the history of transnational literary modernism, and imperial politics in the humbling light of their planetary smallness, which is to say, their mutability, comparability, heterogeneity, dependence, indebtedness, and responsibility to a larger community of the Americas and the planet.

I am greatly indebted to many friends, teachers, and colleagues whose encouragement, criticism, and support have enabled me to research and write this book. As Gabriela Mistral pointed out, José Martí's writings are an inexhaustible mine in which excavators have been fruitfully digging since he began to publish. Anyone who researches in this field feels an overwhelming debt to all the others who have dedicated years to reading and thinking about his work.

Indeed, this interdisciplinary field of Martí studies forms part of a rich, Latin American and migrant Latino intellectual tradition, my debts to which my bibliography and endnotes can make only inadequate acknowledgment. Seminars and conversations with Sylvia Molloy, Julio Ramos, Licia Fiol-Matta, and Jean Franco—exceptional readers and generous teachers—launched me on the project that eventually became this book. Each of these scholars' rigorous attention to the form of Latin American and Latino/a culture and politics, inside and outside the academy, has been an inspiration for me.

I have another set of debts to far-flung colleagues and friends who have engaged me in sustaining conversations while I was formulating this project. At the Universidade Federal de Santa Catarina in Florianópolis, Brazil, in 2005 and 2007, I was able to present parts of this book and engage in conversations with Eliana Avila, an astute interlocutor and exemplary practitioner of transamerican cultural translation, and with Sergio Bellei. I thank them both for these opportunities that fundamentally shaped my book. I wish also to thank my colleagues at the Centro de Estudios Martianos and Casa de las Américas, who offered suggestions, guidance, and signposts, and also facilitated access to research materials in the Sala Cubana of the Biblioteca Nacional José Martí, the Instituto de Literatura y Lingüística, and the Centro; among them I thank especially Pedro Pablo Rodríguez, María Caridad Pacheco, Enrique López Mesa, Javier Beltrán, and Luisa Campuzano. ¿Qué he de decir, a esta gente tan generosa que me ha hecho posible este trabajo—y con tanto gusto—en la Habana? A Eladio Moreno Heredia y Noel Martínez Hernández, quienes me brindaron tantas conversaciones, cenas y libros, gracias.

Numerous institutions have enabled me to write this book. I am grateful to Swarthmore College for making it possible for me to imagine writing a book, and to Columbia University for providing me with a remarkable library and an inspiring cohort of coresearchers and financial support. Although this book scarcely resembles the dissertation I wrote under his direction, I thank Robert G. O'Meally for endorsing and nurturing my intuition about where American studies was headed and for teaching me to listen before beginning to theorize.

A National Endowment for the Humanities fellowship released me from teaching during the year in which I completed the research and writing of this book. Through a National Endowment for the Humanities Summer Institute, I met an inspiring interdisciplinary cohort and benefited from meeting the greatest living Martianos, including the institute's director, Ivan Schulman, whose scholarly rigor, energy, and generosity evokes that of Martí himself. Thanks also are due to the Rutgers Research Council for defraying costs associated with research travel and publication, to my students and research assistants at Rutgers Newark, especially Spencer McGrath and Jeffrey González, and to many librarians, especially Ann Watkins and Joyce Watson, for help in accessing books, microforms, and periodicals.

I wrote this book over several years in two stimulating academic settings. I am grateful for the intellectual companionship, support, and friendship of my colleagues at Penn State University and Rutgers Newark, especially Djelal Kadir, Aníbal González-Pérez, Cecilia Novero, Barbara Foley, Fran Bartkowski, and Mara Sidney, who read and commented on portions of the manuscript. For incisive and encouraging comments at conference panels, in seminars, and in other settings as I worked through parts of this book, I thank Kristen Silva Gruesz, David Luis-Brown, Kevin Meehan, Jossiana Arroyo, Tovah Cooper, Chris Walsh, and Raúl Fernández. Lenny Cassuto provided indispensable suggestions, mentorship, and friendship at a crucial juncture in the publication process. I would like to thank my series editor, Donald Pease, the readers of my manuscript at Duke University Press, and my editor, Reynolds Smith, for bringing this project to fruition.

Finally, a project that has absorbed me for so many years would not have been possible without the sustenance, wisdom, and support of my family and friends, my most invaluable critics and teachers. To Sonia Baires and Tim Crouse, thank you for setting the unusual example of thinking without ceasing to pursue justice through political engagement. To my friends Martha Iris Rosas, Lisa Rohleder, Chrissy Fowler, Susanna Morrill, Irvin Moore, Rebecca Cota, and Elisa González, among others: thank you for easing forward the quotidian project of living and writing. I wish to acknowledge my enormous debts to my family, and especially my mother, who valued my education more than anyone else and who taught me at a young age that we are mongrels; my father, who instructed me to love my most demanding tasks by his own inimitable example; and my grandmother, Hildagarde, who is watching me fulfill her dream from beyond the grave. A mi familia lejana, Indan Yola y Gilbert Diogenes, y a mi Tía Elisa, no hay palabras para agradecerles los aportes naturales y supernaturales. A mi hija, Marta Zabina, y a Rubén, sólo les digo que la próxima estrofa del poema será construido y completado. Gracias por mantener la fé en sus pechitos que nadie ni nada sacará.

Metropolitan Debts, Imperial Modernity, and Latino Modernism

It gives us pleasure that with our Latino spirit [*espíritu latino*] we foresee and recommend months in advance what later appears very good to the cerebral and laborious neo-Saxons.**—José Martí,** "Exposición de productos americanos," *La América*, 1884

Small as they are, their historical origin and development have been such that these Caribbean islands can make highly significant contributions to the economics and politics of a world in torment.**—C. L. R. James,** *The Black Jacobins*, 1963

    THIS BOOK is about the translations—in the literal and figurative sense—through which José Martí and other Latin American writers resident in the United States conveyed to readers of Spanish inside and outside Latin America the Anglo-American empire's new phase of expansion in the late nineteenth century. More free than faithful, these translations of Anglo-American culture into a Latino idiom bring into focus aspects of nineteenth-century history that U.S. scholarship is only today beginning to acknowledge.[1] In the midst of truncated wars of independence and after the gradual abolition of slavery began in Puerto Rico in 1873 and in Cuba in 1880, the numbers of islanders and other Latino Americans in multiracial *barrios* in the eastern United States, especially Florida, swelled to the thousands.[2] Composed in another language (Spanish), but also in a distinct rhythm, style, and form, such texts parody Anglo conceptions of Latinness that were circulating in the North. However, under the sway of Englishcentered literary history, this Spanish-language critique has remained so marginal as to be practically invisible in U.S. American studies until recently. By provincializing the United States as a subculture within the Americas, the translations that are this book's subject stake a claim to define another American modernity beside that of the United States.[3]

Although in the decade of the 1990s critics began to single out José Martí's "Nuestra América" (Our America) (1891) as a touchstone for remapping the field of American studies, Latino migrant writing has helped to define North American culture since the 1880s and 1890s.[4] Since the late nineteenth century, these texts have defined a North-South axis of power. Within this late nineteenth-century map of the Americas, as Walter Mignolo has argued persuasively, the powerful North projected itself as modern and civilized in relation to a premodern, barbarous South.[5] Yet José Martí begins to elaborate a Latino modernist form in which to represent distinct American modernities from the heart of the new empire: New York City. Thus, some of the earliest modernist writing was insisting upon another America within earshot of North America's leading authors, and yet remained largely unknown to them. Among the handwritten notes on random sheets of paper that make up volume 22 of Martí's *Obras completas* (1963–73) is a response to a declamation made by a North American about America. In it Martí suggests that the observations of people like himself, a Cuban migrant, never register with the speaker: "He [i.e., the North American] speaks with pride of the American Union, alluding of course to his North America, without thinking that there might be another America" (*Obras*, 22:279).[6] Martí's quiet, obscure divergence from the unnamed North American's assumptions reveals the thinking process by which a modernist disruption begins. The possibility of another America ruptures the northerner's version of an American union.

In his work as office clerk, journalist, magazine and newspaper editor, translator, and later as a consul for Uruguay, Argentina, and Paraguay, Martí observed U.S. empire in formation from the "cold corner" of his office in lower Manhattan.[7] Immersed for nearly fifteen years in the Anglo-dominant culture of the United States, Martí ate, spoke, read, and wrote across at least two languages every day, and helped organize the Latino community at night. He made it his business for over a decade to translate the North American misrecognition of itself as the head of a continental body, which it believed itself to be destined to direct. In this book, I follow the course of these translations back to the social texts and scenes that

Martí chose to interpret, and translate them back into English, so that readers of English might apprehend the tactics of U.S. empire that a group of Latino migrants first observed with alarm in the 1880s.

⤳ A LATINO PRISM

Drawing on major and minor examples from Martí's voluminous corpus and from other late nineteenth-century Spanish-language migrants and travelers' texts, this book treats Latino writing as a prism through which to reexamine the definition of American literature and of modernity. To read the canonical literature and popular culture of the Gilded Age United States between 1880 and 1895 through Martí's eyes is to see afresh a trajectory of another modernity's emergence. Written from the perspective of a migrant intellectual worker who disidentified with the elite academicism and Eurocentric colonial culture into which he was born, these texts permit us to see the interrelation of a grassroots, anti-colonial movement and the modernist aesthetics that arose in its texts that respond to the threat of response to U.S. expansion.

I borrow the figure of subjectivity as a prism from *Autobiography of an Ex-Coloured Man*, by James Weldon Johnson, the African American novelist and legendary civil rights activist who also served as a diplomat in Latin America. In Johnson's fictive autobiography, the narrator, a light-skinned African American, fortuitously meets a light-skinned Cuban migrant, who invites him into the tobacco-rolling trade. Thus, the Cuban migrant becomes a lifesaving buoy to the narrator when he finds himself penniless and adrift in the segregated U.S. South. The novel's narrator describes a "dwarfing, warping, distorting influence" (21) that forces the person of color to view the world through the "prism of his relationship to society" (75)." This viewpoint measures the distance between the racialized subject and the ostensibly universal citizen equipped with full and equal rights. It also furnishes him with the gift W. E. B. Du Bois earlier described as "second sight": "the coloured people of this country know and understand the white people better than the white people know and understand them" (Johnson, *Autobiography*, 22). Imbued with this knowledge and insight, the narrator, finding himself adrift and penniless in the segregated U.S. South, finds in the Cuban migrant of the tobacco-rolling communities of south Florida a friend who helps him locate employment and a community. This encounter between two light-skinned people of color—a large-mustached, small-bodied, proindependence tobacco worker, whose physical description suggests Martí's own, and an African American pianist who discovers a trans-American range of black cultures in the South—evokes a solidarity that has not always endured into the twentieth century, either in the Cuban Republic or in south Florida. Nevertheless it documents an ephemeral historical reality and invites comparison and study of the African American, Latino, Caribbean, Latin American, and other postcolonial theories of subjectivity.[8] Situated in the midst of the racial violence, urbanization, immigration, and economic disparities of the post-Reconstruction period, Martí interpreted U.S. modernity from the perspective of a multiracial Caribbean political movement, which, in the U.S. North and South, did not conform to, and even openly resisted, practices of racial segregation, at least in the late 1800s.[9]

The relationship of Martí, a non-Anglo working migrant, to the society of the Gilded Age shaped the prism through which he interpreted the expanding modernity of the United States. Unlike Edgar Allan Poe's "man in the crowd," and Charles Baudelaire's flâneur, who studied with fascination and sometimes terror an urban crowd from a café window, Martí observed the imperial project in the guise of a democratic republic from the perspective of the streetcar passenger, a participant in a demonstration for the eight-hour workday, or a person amid the throngs watching a burning building from the street. His writing makes the effects of empire tangible to Spanish-language readers, who were predominantly, apart from the tobacco workers, a light-skinned, educated minority, who viewed the United States from a distance and in terms of the prosperity and comfort of illustrated catalogues that circulated in conjunction with its commercial expansion into Latin America. Viewing such shiny, novel objects without observing the imperial conditions of production exacerbated these readers' misperceptions. Martí's prolix phrasing and strange images attempted to translate the discrepancy between this "deceptive surface" (*Obras*, 6:22) or "mask" (antifaz) (6:52) and the hidden aspects of modernity in the United States. Martí alerted his readers to this tendency of U.S. modernity to hide one face behind the other, and to approach other American nations with "with friendship in one hand and a snake in the other" (12:206).[10]

After the annexation of half of Mexico in 1848 and William Walker's claiming of Nicaragua in 1855, U.S. imperialism in Latin America began to adopt less overt shows of force, employing instead such means as political pressure, loans, cultural narratives, and training in order to preserve these

countries' dependence on the United States. Because this tactic of imperialism advances at the invitation of the dependent nation's elite representatives themselves, it effectively claims to benefit the less powerful nation by
modeling an exemplary modernization, with the most humane intentions,
and in keeping with its God-given civilizing obligations.[11] Thus in the 1880s
and 1890s, the United States lurched into a new mode of economic and
cultural imperialism, with the emergence of what Donald Pease has termed
"global domination without colonies."[12]

ᯄ IMPERIAL MODERNITY AND AMERICAN ALTERNATIVES

I use the term "imperial modernity" to define a political and cultural
project in pursuit of political and economic expansion. Martí begins to
perceive and theorize this threat to his island shortly after his arrival to stay
in New York in 1881. In 1885, Martí observes imperial modernity at work in
a new economic agreement with Spain that "in such an absolute way binds
the existence of the island to the United States that it is only a step away
from the pouring of one country into the other, which may end up, to the
great suffering of many Latino souls [almas latinas], with Spanish America
losing the island that should have been its bulwark" (*Obras*, 8:88). The term
"imperial modernity" refers to just this state of penetration of a country by
a proximate and growing imperial power, the United States. We note how
Martí associates the experience of vulnerability with the adjective "Latino."
The cultural processes of imperial expansion laid the groundwork for
annexation of the still colonized islands of Cuba, Puerto Rico, and the
Philippines, among others. Perceiving that "modernity" in the singular
served to disguise a new U.S. empire, Martí begins to define an American
future in which Latin America's self-governing nations might coexist with
the powerful northern republic. This other American modernity spurs
aesthetic innovation that makes available conflicting and simultaneous
interpretations from the perspective of distinct modernities, examples of
which we will explore in the chapters that follow. In its literary form,
Martí's prose observed and commented on the nonuniversality of the
bourgeois individual's self-mastery as it criticized the protection of the
interests of a class of such individuals at the head of a national government
in the Americas. The formal aspect of Martí's texts, which many have
described as modernist, conveys the limited ability of European- or U.S.-
identified individuals to adequately recognize and value the heterogeneity

of Latin American cultures. As Raymond Williams has shown, unreflecting celebrations of mastery are inevitably bound up with imperial processes of exploiting material resources and human labor.[13] Thus, self-mastery and self-transparency are not readily available in Martí's American modernity. Critical self-study and constant translation are vital to the elaboration of another American modernity.

The phase of imperial modernity in the United States that concerns us here—the "ruinous times" in which Martí self-consciously launched his manifesto about modernist poetry in his prologue to Juan Antonio Pérez Bonalde's *El Poema del Niágara*—shaped Latino modernist form. In *Translating Empire* I adopt from a heterodox Marxist, poststructuralist, and postcolonial tradition the assumption that aesthetic and social processes are interrelated and mutually illuminating. If the U.S. Declaration of Independence in 1776 was signed on the backs of slaves—as Martí famously noted in "Madre América" (Mother America)—the radical ambiguity of Latino modernism emerges in conjunction with the foreign and domestic crises of the age. The time of Martí's sojourn in New York opens with the United States' botched embroilment in the War of the Pacific (1879–83) and concludes with the first Pan-American conferences (1889–91) and the start of the second strike for Cuban independence in 1895. It coincided with the failure of post–Civil War Reconstruction and lynch law's harvest of strange fruit across the South and Midwest; the economic stratification and political corruption of the Gilded Age; the exclusion of Chinese immigrants and the concomitant anti-Asian violence; massive immigration and anti-immigrant and anti-working-class violence, especially the hanging of labor activists who were leaders of the movement for an eight-hour workday and who demonstrated in Haymarket Square, Chicago; and the military subordination of Native Americans as part of the forceful appropriation of remaining Indian territory. *Translating Empire* rereads Martí's journalism and other writings in relation to the cultural, literary, and political material of this period with the hope that readers in the United States, cultural brokers and designers of curriculum, students of American literature and politics—in the broadest sense—may see how the writing and redefinition of America by Martí and his contemporaries seek to revise our understanding of the late 1800s. The gap between the original texts and Spanish translations, and between U.S. imperial modernity and another American modernity, invites new and sustained reading and interpretation, with an eye to how the migrant Latino text maps different possible futures.

Both Mary Louise Pratt and Frederic Jameson note that the term "modernity" is defined in contrast to a premodern realm of unfreedom, barbarian irrationality, slave mentality, backwardness, or incapacity for self-government, across a wide range of periods.[14] With decaying European monarchies and the barbarous "subaltern" as foils, modernity in the service of empire functions as a transhistorical identity discourse for a European-derived, bourgeois, "white world," without acknowledging its investment in either whiteness or empire.[15] In conceptualizing modernity as a parricidal rupture and a new beginning in a virgin land, European philosophical perspectives have historically interpreted colonization as a discovery that gently pushes "primitive" cultures or groups toward "advancement" and efficiency.[16] Martí questions this Hegelian, stagist understanding of history, and challenges the view of North America leading the continent with a European torch and generously extending its technology and saving ideals to immature, unfit, native and mestizo cultures.[17]

Latino/a migrants represent a threatening variable if they do not conform to the progress narrative associated with imperial modernity. The assumption held by those at the center of imperial power (the "metropolis") that non-European arrivants must desire to become absorbed into a "universal" European-identified culture obscures from metropolitan view the history of violence toward migrants. By contrast, migrants', especially Latinos', marginal texts and ironic reactions, often in popular genres, such as the newspaper column, bring into relief the tense relations between center and periphery, and thus make it possible to read these differences.[18]

The now commonplace spatial metaphor of a "contact zone" suggests a means by which peripheral cultures launch self-critical, self-interrogating alternative modernities. Mary Louise Pratt, in her theorizing of the "contact zone"—which (as I argue in chapter 1) is indebted to the Brazilian Silviano Santiago's concept of a Latin American "space in-between"—reveals how metropolitan literary history, institutions, and genres help blind the dominant culture to the multiple ways that, in fact, "the periphery determines the metropolis."[19] Pratt's groundbreaking essay on travel writing and imperialism notes that a European tradition of travel writing obsessively focused on the periphery and thus distracted the metropolitan culture from its dependence on the resources, techniques, and labor from such places as Latin America. As a Latino migrant in the North, Martí thwarts the notion of progressive radiation from center to periphery or through stages of upward development from the barbaric South to the

civilized North. In his reading, the North's impositions on the periphery in
the colonizing process become objects of critical inquiry. What often figure
officially as civilization's "gifts" to the colonizing world here appear as
products of the periphery's transformation of the metropolis.[20]

Martí regularly called his readers' attention to inversions of the assumed
vectors of imperial modernity in the Americas. He and the books he reviewed in his journalism gleefully demonstrate the colonial powers' belated
arrival to and appropriation of the ideas or practices of their peripheral
modernity.[21] In his 1880 review of Gustave Flaubert's posthumously published work *Bouvard et Pécuchet* (1880), Martí announces in English that
readers of the review will be indebted to him for the advance notice of the
work's publication: "[Flaubert's last work] may soon be translated and the
public will be obliged to us for noticing it beforehand."[22] According to
Martí, Flaubert's novel depicts two copyists in terms that suggest a "bourgeois Quixote" making his way through modernity, only to find the limits of
the march of progress and the evanescence of the master narratives of
enlightenment. The novel that Martí regards as a quintessentially modern
text interrogates a key assumption of such narratives: "Bouvard thought:
'Ah, progress, what a farce!' "[23]

In the realm of legal theory, we find similar evidence of belated arrival of
the colonial centers. The Argentine jurist and early crime fiction writer
Luis A. Varela argues that the American republics of Argentina, the United
States, and Chile can all claim the "glory" of having already put into
practice what the European capitals of the nineteenth century were merely
beginning to discuss in the 1870s. Varela's treatise *Democracia práctica*
(Practical Democracy) (1876) favors the safeguarding of minority viewpoints within the seat of government. Martí, in reviewing the book, would
have relished Varela's comment concerning European attitudes toward
South American nations: "The sages of Europe, who once looked upon
South-American Republics as savage because in their modest poverty they
could not send them large embassies, today react to these Republics' opinions, when they study political and constitutional law" (xv). Varela notes
his happiness at being able to make this point concerning South America's
exemplary role as model for Europe in Paris, the glorious City of Light,
where "everyone seems to be ignorant of this fact" (xv). After living in the
United States for a few years, Martí diverged from Varela's inclusion of the
United States as a model for Latin America (Varela 123), but he shared with
Varela the goal of correcting the misperception of Europe as autonomously

initiating modernity and generously extending its civilizing light to the rest of the world.[24]

Martí's goal is to provincialize not just Europe, but also the United States. He proclaims this agenda in New York, where many regularly demonstrated ignorance of Latin America's independent, creative aesthetic, theoretical and technological capabilities. Martí makes his review of Varela's book an occasion to celebrate the "ambitious imaginative faculties of America's sons" and to call for further theorizing from the distinct perspective of a "heterogeneous" America (*Obras*, 7:347). In his review, Martí associates liberty with acts of critical interpretation, especially self-interpretation. Varela's treatise, in his reading, defines a crucial condition of modern self-government as the "pacific practice of critique" (ejercicio pacífico del criterio) (7:347). The term "criterio," from the Greek noun *kriterion* and its root in the verb *krinein*, to judge, refers to a regularly repeated *exercise* or a *practice* in judgment. It suggests a critical subjectivity in formation. Martí was to engage in this practice and to enjoin others to develop this faculty throughout his life.

Against a common misreading of Martí as an uncritical celebrant of Euro-American modernity and technique, I hope in *Translating Empire* to demonstrate Martí's imagining of alternatives to the cultural models of progress available in the United States and Europe.[25] Martí in fact envisions an "alternative modernity" that acknowledges different cultural locations in the Americas, and rejects the idea that modernity is of strictly European origin. Dilip Parameshwar Gaonkar, in his edited collection *Alternative Modernities*, draws on Michel Foucault and Walter Benjamin's interpretations of Charles Baudelaire's essays to define modernity as an attitude of questioning the present, pertaining to an individual or a people. Alternative modernities follow from an attitude and a relative location rather than from a specific content or essence. Indeed, Martí's time and place, especially for a colonial subject in the ostensible cradle of democracy, led him to constantly pose questions about his present: "in this epoch of the renovation of the human world, disconsolate eyes turn full of questions toward empty skies and moan alongside the cadavers of gods" (*Obras*, 10:226). Even Martí's famously paradoxical definition of "patria" as "that portion of humanity that we see more closely and in which it was our fate to be born [nos tocó nacer]" (5:468) attributes the given quality of nationality to an attitude and a perspective rather than a fixed content. Following Gaonkar's formulation, we might say that Martí demands that his Latino community, the island of Cuba and Latin America as a whole, be able to "'make' themselves modern, as opposed to being 'made' modern by alien and impersonal forces," in keeping with their distinct culture and history.[26]

Like Gaonkar, Roberto Schwarz, in his essay "Pressupostos, salvo engano, de 'Dialética da Malandragem'" (commenting on Antonio Candido's essay "Dialectics of Malandroism"), nuances the relation between modernist literary form and politics. I will draw on Schwarz's argument in framing my book in terms of conflicting American modernities rather than in terms of a single hemisphere or a single modernity. On one hand, Schwarz concurs with most scholars of modernism that the social processes that most illuminate it are not national, even though nations then and now constitute the primary form of political and cultural representation. Imperial expansion and transnational exploitation provide the backdrop for the emergence of modernism in various parts of the globe, and the Americas are no exception. On the other hand, seemingly against this transnational political and economic frame, Schwarz stakes a claim and valorizes the knowledge available through a nondominant (national or regional) culture and literary tradition. Through "nossa literatura," says Schwarz in 1979, it is possible "to inaugurate a critical inquiry of the contemporary world."[27] To what does the "our" in "our literature" refer, so as to define a way of reading rather than an essential cultural content? This use of "our" stakes a Brazilian claim to read and define themselves in the world, as the Trinidadian historian C. L. R. James describes the West Indies as a quintessentially modern, sui generis culture that evades entirely the West's racial categorization.[28]

Similarly, Martí's "our" in "Our America" refers to heterogeneous, transnational migrant Latino and Latin American cultures that interpret and redefine America. In his essay "The Argentine Writer and Tradition," Jorge Luis Borges associates an Argentine perspective with an irreverent and intimate way of reading the Western European literary tradition. He takes the universe as the Argentine writer's subject and field, and does not restrict him or her to descriptions of a national picturesque, local color, or customs of the country (425–26). Martí similarly defines the collective Latino and Latin American subjectivity as amounting to nothing more— and nothing less—than constructions based on distinct historical conditions. Decades before the Martinican poet and political leader Aimé Césaire's influential assertion that "no race possesses the monopoly of beauty, of intelligence, of force," Martí declared that "no nation on earth has a monopoly on human virtue" (*Obras*, 8:381).[29] Like James, Borges, Schwarz, and Césaire, Martí strategically deploys antiessentialist concepts of nationality, *raza*, or group particularity to problematize and redefine Enlightenment claims to universality.

Because alternative modernities follow from a historically structured attitude rather than a fixed or pure essence, they suggest no fixed conception of what will constitute each modernity's end. Conflicts between American modernities begin, however, with the locked horns of dominant and peripheral societies in this hemisphere. So although there are multiple modernities, empire acts as the connective tissue that shapes the relations of force among them. The profit extracted through the interaction of metropolitan centers and their peripheries entices the builder of empire to the shift from colonization and slavery to the expansion of spheres of influence, which in turn brings industrialization, urbanization, and migration.

Can an alternative modernity exist without ejecting a radicalized abject "nonmodern" from its ranks? Like the Latin American and Caribbean theorists to whom I make reference above, Martí privileges ethical criteria over the physical criteria that predominated in nineteenth-century racial discourse in his definition of an alternative modernity. Martí's texts raise the question of who gets to define the modern and what counts among the formal qualities of modernist poetics. In raising these questions, he also seeks to wrest the future from imperial modernity. When did Caribbean postcolonial criticism begin to sound out the hollowness of Enlightenment narratives that read the story of capitalist expansion as progress? According to David Scott's *Conscripts of Modernity* (2004), C. L. R. James, in his book *The Black Jacobins*, presents Toussaint L'Ouverture's postcolonial predicament as a tragic one, in a self-critical revision of the 1938 edition of his history of the Haitian revolution's leader, which originally presented a romantic narrative of anticolonial redemption. According to Scott, in the wake of the conference of Asian and African nations in Bandung in 1955, a shift occurred whereby anticolonial nationalisms adopted a tragic, postcolonial skepticism toward Enlightenment narratives of progress. As James notes, this insight follows from Caribbean observation of a colonial power "more naked [there] than in any other part of the world" (*Black Jacobins*, 408). This instructive nakedness shapes what Scott calls the "Caribbean's modernity" (*Conscripts of Modernity*, 125). In James's revised version of his argument, Toussaint lives the tragic dilemma of postcolonial Caribbean modernity, including its revolutionary incompatibility with colonial power. This tragic practice of modernity represents the Caribbean alternative to the homogeneous empty progress of imperial modernity; it is a product of a "peculiar origin and a peculiar history" (*Black Jacobins*, 391). Caribbean modernity constitutes something new that these island cultures bring to the comity of nations. Although belatedly theorized by James and Scott, this condition helps explain the circumscribed revolutionary options available to Toussaint in the age of Enlightenment, and to postcolonial nations such as Cuba.

David Scott's analysis of C. L. R. James's revisions of the L'Ouverture story extends the time frame of Caribbean disenchantment with imperial modernity back to L'Ouverture. Although James excludes Martí and the great mulatto military strategist of Cuba's Wars of Independence, Antonio Maceo, from a tragic postcolonial modernity, a closer look at Martí's writings reveals his affinities with a tragically modernist—rather than a soteriologically romantic—postcolonial tradition.[30] Shakespeare's tragic figure captivated Martí. He translated *Hamlet* while studying in Cuba, and also offered dramaturgical comments on how to enact Shakespeare's character as internally divided. Hamlet, he said, ought to be played as wielding the dreadful curiosity that Martí attributed to several other thinkers and inventors, including Charles Darwin, Thomas Edison, and Wendell Phillips, as a daring Promethean who "turned to the sky in demand of its existence and of its secrets" (*Obras*, 22:280). Yet, the tragic hero's curious questioning begins with a sense of the immensity that escapes human knowing. In 1886, Martí admired Edouard Manet's *Portrait of Jean Baptiste Fauré as Hamlet*, 1876–77, because it revealed the "eye of someone who wants to know the immensity and does not know it" (*Obras*, 10:440). These phrases relate closely to Martí's own position. Martí died in the first skirmishes of the 1895 war of independence, without guarantees as to the future status of Cuba. Another reading in terms of the tragic postcolonial present in which he lived and died, rather than in terms of a triumphant romantic nationalist narrative, mitigates the smoothing over of vexed ambiguities related to his position as a migrant from a colonized culture who lived all his life outside the framework of national sovereignty.

Like Scott, Sibylle Fischer conceives of a single modernity with a double face that comes from its inception in Hegel, and she agrees that ambivalence about it arrives belatedly, "probably with World War II and Nazi rule," also in the wake of which James revised his *Black Jacobins*.[31] Underscoring the doubleness of modernity as both a project of genocidal European expansion and racialization, and as a means to emancipation and democratization, Fischer depicts radical black antislavery as a disavowed part of a whole, as the hidden face behind the smiling mask of a dialectical Enlightenment. Martí denounces precisely this masked, duplicitous quality of imperial modernity in order to make space for another practice of American modernity—and he does this in the 1880s, long before the time that Fischer suggests as the beginning of such ambivalence. His alternative America takes shape in intimate proximity to imperial modernity: his position is that of a translator inside the empire's belly.

☙ CREOLE MODERNIZATION AND BLACK ANTISLAVE INSURGENCY

In the racially charged environment of the post-Reconstruction U.S. South, and post-emancipation Cuba, the struggles between racism and anti-racism preoccupied Cuba's pro-independence movement, as Ada Ferrer has shown. What was Martí's relationship, on the one hand, to the light-skinned Creole elite in exile and in Cuba and, on the other, to black insurgent subjects? To what extent does Martí's revolutionary project resemble earlier Creole-led modernization and national integration movements that came into existence through the suppression of black aesthetic and political practices that carried forward the explosive effects of the Haitian revolution? In *Modernity Disavowed*, Fischer raises questions about white Cuban abolitionism of the early nineteenth century as she documents the autonomist, integrationist Creole elite's fantasies about and disavowals of a radical antislavery project commanded by black people themselves— the subjects that Toussaint L'Ouverture led to victory or inspired to revolt elsewhere in the Caribbean. These questions become especially urgent given assertions from various quarters that Martí's revolution was neither antiracist nor anticapitalist.

For example, in response to British historian Raymond Carr's laudatory review of Phillip Foner's multivolume edition of Martí in English, Carlos Ripoll claimed that "Martí's political writings give the lie to [Carr's] assertion and the notion that Martí gave 'social content' to the war."[32] Ripoll—a leading scholar on Martí—tells us that Carr, like many others, has been duped by the regime in Havana into endorsing what Ripoll calls the "Marxification of Martí." In Ripoll's view, a sustained ideological campaign on the part of Havana has implanted in Carr the "misconception" that

Martí struggled against racial and economic inequality. Ripoll's comments invite the reader to infer that Martí went so far as to promote racial inequality and that Martí envisioned an anti-Marxist revolution *avant la lettre*. Ripoll notes, for example, that Martí volunteered nights at La Liga, the night school for Afro-Antilleans founded by Afro-Cuban educator, independence movement leader, and journalist Rafael Serra during his final years of full-time revolutionary organizing—not, he claims, in order to train future citizens for participation in a self-governing, newly multiracial nation (which would have furthered the fight for equality) but with the "only purpose" of offering charity to "a small number of poor Cuban and Puerto Rican workers."[33]

Why does Ripoll insist that Martí did not have motives with social content in educating recently emancipated and working-class Afro-Antilleans? Why would he classify Martí's friend Rafael Serra, a member of Martí's revolutionary organization and a leader of a school designed to aid Afro-Antillean workers, as "ultra-conservative," on the one hand, and an object of Martí's pity, on the other?[34] This debate over the interpretation of Martí's relationship to a mostly black Cuban and Puerto Rican migrant working class becomes clearer if we examine his relationship to several generations of a light-skinned Creole elite.

Books by Kirsten Silva Gruesz, Anna Brickhouse, and Rodrigo Lazo illuminate the multilingual and deterritorialized routes and roots of Latino or trans-American writing in the work of mainly light-skinned Creole elites of early to mid-nineteenth-century Cuba. They shed light on the question of Martí's relationship to earlier generations of Latino and Latin American writers, and especially to former slaveholders from the islands. As Silva Gruesz has it, the earlier generations in New Orleans, Philadelphia, New York, and San Francisco were "ambassadors," well-heeled diplomats, translators, generals, and expeditionaries who advocated Cuba's freedom from Spain. However, with some important exceptions—among them Félix Varela, a Cuban Catholic priest, pedagogue and philosopher who lived in exile in the United States between 1823 and 1853, favored independence for Cuba, and called for indemnification of slave owners to end slavery—many newspaper editors, politicians, and statesmen did not see the danger of imitating or extending the United States and its racial system to the Hispanic Caribbean.[35] By contrast, in Martí's generation, the proindependence movement was constituted by a largely multiracial, working-class group of *tabaqueros*—crafters of Cuban cigars—who forged

José Martí in Jamaica, ca. 1892. Photograph by Juan Bautista Valdés. By permission of the Centro de Estudios Martianos, Havana.

an antiannexationist and antiracist opposition to the imperial modernity of the United States. In the 1880s, many migrant Latino texts and practices increasingly questioned progressive assimilation and naturalization to a bourgeois, Anglo cultural norm.

Different Latino migrant periodicals reflect successive generations' distinct political commitments. *La Verdad*, the longest running of the newspapers published by Cuban exiles in the United States in the 1850s, was founded through a $10,000 donation from an association of wealthy Cuban Creole planters, slave owners, and slave traders in conjunction with proannexation U.S. journalists. Although literary contributions by exiled Cuban poet Pedro Santacilia diverged from this view, and a competing short-lived Cuban exile newspaper, *El Mulato* (1854), attacked the New York leadership's frequently proslavery and proannexation positions, *La Verdad* reflected and disseminated the interests of its founders.[36] Planters such as the Cuban Gaspar Betancourt Cisneros, key U.S. ideologues of "manifest destiny" (including the phrase's author, the journalist John L. O'Sullivan, and the powerful newspaper editor Moses Yale Beach of the proannexationist newspaper *The Sun* in New York), joined forces to found and print *La Verdad*.[37] By contrast, the newspaper associated with the Cuban Revolutionary Party, *Patria*, began publication in 1892, in conjunction with a meeting of the party's founders in a New York–based, multiracial Caribbean Masonic lodge, one of whose members became renowned

Rafael Serra y Montalvo, Cuban migrant
and founder of La Liga, a night school for
Afro-Antilleans in New York, and editor
of *La Doctrina de Martí*. By permission of
the Centro de Estudios Martianos, Havana.

Sotero Figueroa. Puerto Rican Editor and
Printer of *La Revista Ilustrada de Nueva
York*, and of *Patria*. By permission of New
York Public Library, Schomburg Collection.

as a black historian and bibliophile, the Puerto Rican Arturo Schomburg.[38] Through tireless efforts of its Afro–Puerto Rican managing editor and printer, Sotero Figueroa, *Patria* raised money for its production largely through advertisements and subscriptions generated by proindependence clubs. Cuban and Puerto Rican members in around one hundred and fifty clubs rolled tobacco and lived in mixed-race communities in south Florida, and in metropolitan centers of Americas and Europe.[39]

Creole slaveholders and their allies found it difficult to welcome or even to envisage the possibility of Afro-Cubans' active participation or leadership in the revolution—except to imagine with horror the possibility of another Haitian revolution.[40] Unlike those in the later movement for independence, this earlier generation did not understand that annexation also racialized or stigmatized their position. Martí's own observation of the racialization of Chicano and Latino culture and his careful perusal of current events from the newspapers of the 1880s and 1890s led him to describe the mob killings of Africans, Asians, and European immigrants from the perspective of the victims. His translations of incidents of racial terror reveal the measured distance from the marauding lynch mobs and border vigilante groups made up of whites, who often tied their racial position to the status and honor of their expanding nation. By contrast, for those annexationist Cuban exiles in the United States who assumed the superiority of white national identity, conscious and politicized freedmen presented a threat.

Whereas the earlier generation had a difficult time shaking off the attitudes and assumptions of the slave owner, African-descended Cubans and Puerto Ricans such as Sotero Figueroa and Rafael Serra y Montalvo in New York, and Juan Gualberto Gómez in Havana, forged alliances and insisted on racial equality as they shared the podium with light-skinned Cubans such as Martí, Gonzalo de Quesada, and Rafael Castro-Palomino. In addition to working in African-centered projects such as La Liga, the night school founded by and for Afro-Caribbeans under the leadership of Rafael Serra, these activist writers were involved in cross-racial cooperation in the editing of newspapers and in the organizing of mostly working-class and multiracial Latino/a supporters of national independence, in violation of Jim Crow law in the South and segregationist practice in the North. Although many white Cuban leaders, especially Martí's successor as spokesperson for the Partido, Tomás Estrada Palma, maintained Martí's antiracist rhetoric while introducing a U.S.-style segregation system, the founders of the 1895 revolutionary movement made the preceding Creole generations' possessive investment in whiteness into a problem.[41] Although Martí could never escape the limitations that his own position imposed, a cross-class, multiracial nationalist movement forced Martí to problematize white privilege in the prevailing white-over-black racial stratification in the United States and in Cuba. Rather than accepting the corralling function of the color line of their day, Sotero Figueroa, Rafael Serra, and Martí analyzed key tensions in Cuba and Puerto Rico's heterogeneous societies as transpiring between annexationists and a revolutionary "race of freedom" that aspires to "absolute emancipation."[42]

In the first issue of New York's *Patria*, Figueroa published a manifesto in which he defines the "race of freedom" (raza de la libertad) of which Martí speaks as being in opposition to a "race for sale" (raza vendible), that is to say, persons willing to accept a colonial or imperial pay-off in exchange for compromised liberty: "we should not and we do not want to resign ourselves to the complete absorption of our race by another that does not seduce us to exchange for it, or to forget our language, customs, traditions,

sentiments—all of which constitute our Latin American physiognomy."[43]
Figueroa's position in *Patria* and elsewhere associate freedom with the
antiassimilationist preservation of distinctly Latino cultural practices. This
definition of race represents an alternative to an Anglo and white U.S.
pigmentocracy and refuses the reigning North American racial definitions
based on hypodescent or the "one drop" rule, by which a person of any
African ancestry was racialized as black under the law.[44] Insofar as Martí
adopted a critique of racism, he defined this "race of freedom" through
comparative thinking and in protest of the increasing incidence of white
working-class and state-sponsored violence against workers and immigrants of color during the 1880s and 1890s. Had Martí lived anywhere
besides the racially terrifying center of imperial modernity, Martí may not
have assumed the explicitly antiracist stance that Afro-Antilleans such as
Rafael Serra, Sotero Figueroa, Antonio Maceo, and Juan Gualberto Gómez
included at the heart of their proindependence organizing.[45]

In Rafael Serra's newspaper, *La Doctrina de Martí* (Martí's Doctrine),
Sotero Figueroa wrote a serialized article in defense of Martí and against
posthumous insinuations made by Enrique Trujillo in his book, *Apuntes
históricos* (Historical Notes) (1896). Figueroa's articles and Serra's newspaper suggest that Afro-Latinos attempted to use Martí's antiracist doctrine against the "myth" of the martyred saint who sought to prohibit
discussion of race and racism, a myth that, as Lillian Guerra has argued,
undermined antiracist efforts in the Cuban republic during Tomás Estrada
Palma's presidency. In the face of this myth, Rafael Serra and Sotero Figueroa sought to push the Cuban republic to resist policies of marginalizing
people of color and of pretending racism did not exist. In 1898, for example, Serra warned Cubans about the negative implications of annexation to
the United States and especially of the U.S.'s segregationist racial system, as
exemplified in the views of U.S. newspapers: "for the [New York] *Herald*,
the black does not belong to humanity. They should be deprived of the
protections of human rights. They are inferior to all others. Then, if Cuba
is a country of blacks, when it joins this people of whites, what hope for
happiness remains for us, when already the Americans announce the esteem that they have for us?"[46] Serra makes this argument about U.S. attitudes toward "them," the blacks, and the implications of such views for the
"us," as a country of blacks, among whom he includes himself and other
Cubans. Figueroa tumbled from his position as part of the Partido's leadership after Martí's death and also struggled to make ends meet as a printer
in the new republic despite his years of organizing the revolution and

publishing *La Revista Ilustrada de Nueva York* and *Patria*.[47] In January 1892, Serra defended Martí against attacks by the veteran Mambí Enrique Collazo by associating Martí with democratic participation and opposition to the disenfranchisement or exclusion of "disdained"groups.[48]

In the name of Martí's antiracist and pro-Latino doctrine, Figueroa similarly criticized Enrique Trujillo's portrayal of the Latino migrant community as sharing the predominant racial attitudes of the United States and Spain.[49] Figueroa implies that unlike Martí, Trujillo shared the Spanish consul's disdain for people of color in the independence movement. When the consul, Suárez Guanes, denounced a meeting to be held in honor of General Antonio Maceo to the U.S. authorities, he warned that it would be "a meeting of blacks, and that it would be disorderly [se iba a alterar el orden]." Figueroa notes that Trujillo reported on the meeting by noting the "absence of people of good appearance in the gathering" ("Calle la passión," 204). Similarly, in the March 2, 1897, installment of his vindication of Martí's doctrine, Figueroa specifically contests Trujillo's description of the Sociedad Literaria Hispano-Americano de Nueva York as an "oasis" that promoted the "union of our race in America," along with the independence of Cuba (*Apuntes históricos* 53). Martí—who for a period assumed the presidency of the Society in hopes of securing a source of support for the Cuban cause, and who in that capacity organized a series of meetings in honor of Latin American culture—had to step down in part because on the night the Society celebrated the Hispanic Caribbean, it refused to fly the flags of Puerto Rico or Cuba. Figueroa emphasizes the racist implications of the Society's affiliation with Spain: "The union of our race is not promoted where the presumption of Spanish habits imposes itself on virtue and modest knowledge, where the sovereignty of intelligence has no value if it is not accompanied by physical exteriorities, such as a certain miserable level of pigment in the skin" ("Calle la pasión," 223). Both Serra and Figueroa take pains to show Martí's divergence from other light-skinned leaders in the Cuban independence movement. Neither Serra nor Figueroa implies in his writings that Martí participated in La Liga or worked alongside them with the arrogance of someone engaged in mere charity for the "poor," as Ripoll's article suggests.

Although a complete discussion of the social content of Martí's revolutionary vision exceeds the scope of my argument here, I will briefly examine Ripoll's evidence and then consider one piece of counterevidence. Ripoll, in his effort to demonstrate a lack of commitment in Martí to social content in the war of independence, cites a letter from Martí to his childhood friend Fermín Valdés Domínguez in which Martí affirms his friend's respect and affection for "those Cubans who are sincerely searching, under one name or another, for a bit more cordial order and indispensable equality, in the administration of the things of this world" (*Epistolario*, 4:128). Implying, anachronistically, that Martí stood against the kind of revolution propounded by Fidel Castro, Ripoll's article quotes Martí as criticizing the "arrogance and hidden rage" of "socialist ideology," whose adherents, "in order to climb up in the world, pretend to be frantic defenders of the helpless."

In fact, Martí was writing to affirm an activity that his friend Valdés Domínguez had planned in relation to May 1, 1894—a day that like all subsequent May Days—commemorated the martyred Chicago anarchists of Haymarket Square, who led the protest of hundreds of thousands of workers in order to achieve better working conditions. Valdés Domínguez had written a letter to Gonzalo de Quesada that appeared in the Tampa newspaper *Cuba* in May 1894, outlining his proposal for the creation of a new club in support of both Cuban independence and a more equitable distribution of wealth. Martí's own letter of congratulations reveals not so much a total rejection of socialist ideas as a cautious openness to them. It acknowledges that despite the inevitable risks of socialism or other ideologies, the risks that might accompany socialism are not so great in Cuba as in other, more wrathful societies:

> For its nobility we should judge an aspiration, and not for this, that, or the other defect that human passion attaches to it. The socialist idea, like so many others, has two dangers: alienating, confused, or incomplete foreign interpretations, and the dissimulating haughtiness and anger of the ambitious, who raise themselves up in the world first by acting the part of the frenetic defenders of the homeless, in order to find shoulders on which to prop themselves up. Some go from pestering the queen—like [Jean Paul] Marat, when he dedicated to her his green-covered book—to Marat's bloody flattery, with its egg of justice. Others change from fanatics to charlatans, like those whom Chateaubriand discusses in his *Memorias*. But in our nation the risk is not so great, as compared to more wrathful societies, and those of less natural clarity. (*Epistolario*, 4:129)

The process of extracting and relocating passages always reorients a text's meaning. My fuller quotation shows that Ripoll's interpretation occludes the spirit of reconciliation with which Martí notes the risk of bad translations and of ambitious charlatans in order to applaud Valdés Domínguez's socially minded proposal. As Philip Foner and Carr both note, Martí never explicitly endorsed any existing forms of socialism, Marxism, or anarchism, despite his respect for Marx's commitment to remedying capitalism's effects on the poorest, and despite the fact that many others in the independence movement, such as Diego Vicente Tejera or Carlos Baliño, did openly advocate socialism and anarchism.[50] Nevertheless, the "social content"—or worker-identified and antiracist consciousness—of Martí's definition of an alternative American modernity becomes clear in this letter to Valdés Domínguez, as in many of the other essays that *Translating Empire* sets before the reader.

That Martí infused his Latino modernism with an uncompromising ethical or social content is supported by the assessment of a former classmate of Martí's, José Ignacio Rodríguez, in the years just after Martí's death. After studying with Rafael María Mendive and becoming a widely published teacher and scholar in Havana, Rodríguez traveled to the United States in 1860 and adopted U.S. citizenship in 1863. Rodríguez became the bilingual secretary of the Pan-American conferences, and continued thereafter as an employee of the U.S. government in the Bureau of American Republics. His study of and argument for the annexation of Cuba to the United States reveal a forceful animus against Martí, which indirectly underscores the fact of Martí's radical social commitments:

> Everyone believed that this improvised movement, made up only of Cuban migrants, the majority of whom were working-class, whites and blacks, from Key West, Tampa, New York, Philadelphia and several other cities of the Union, and possessing neither the money, nor the other elements that we had always believed to be indispensable to this sort of enterprise, was destined to miserably fail. . . . [Martí] hated the wealthy, cultivated, conservative man, and thus introduced into the Cuban problematic an element until then unknown, because all the country's movements had always been drawn from the upper and comfortable classes: and he hated the United States of America, which he accused of being egotistical and which he viewed as represented by an insolent race, against which the other race that dominated in the rest of the countries of continental America had to struggle unceasingly.[51]

Although Martí wrote amiable letters to and visited Rodríguez during his stays in Washington, D.C., in 1889, Rodríguez accused Martí of fostering a self-defensive pride in a group that constituted the majority in the other Americas but was a minority in the United States. Rodríguez goes on to define these two "races" as "la raza latina de América" (the Latino race of America), in contradistinction to the race of the "hombre del norte" (man of the North).[52] The elder Cuban could not believe that an integrated, multiracial, mostly working-class movement could actually succeed, especially because it differed so dramatically from the earlier political movements of the elite on behalf of the island. Even if Martí neither hated the United States, nor had the space to publicly express hatred for an elitist or white supremacist tendency therein, Rodríguez here tells us in no uncertain terms that Martí loathed this elitist tendency. Rodríguez also notes that Martí employed, with remarkable ease, an unusual figurative language characterized by sonorous, feverishly colorful words, replete with "monstrous strangeness" (extrañezas monstruosas).[53] In other words, someone who disagreed with Martí's political views, who was an employee of the United States, offers the soundest evidence to contest Ripoll's claim that Martí's politics had no social content; Rodríguez in fact demonstrates not only that its social content was well known but also that he used an innovative literary form to give it life on the page.

∽ LATINO MODERNISM

Martí's early, aesthetic innovations occur within the wide-ranging transnational literary movement that we know as modernism. My claims resemble Ramón Saldívar's argument to recognize Américo Paredes's border writing as modernist, Simon Gikandi's redefinition of Caribbean writing, Houston Baker's association of the Harlem Renaissance with modernism, and Roberto Schwarz's case for reading Joaquim María Machado de Assis as making an inaugural shift into modernist prose in 1880.[54] Octavio Paz, in his essay on the emergence of modern Latin American poetry, also affirms Martí's influence on twentieth-century poetry, though in an argument that appears to affirm a conventional definition of modernism, while troubling it at the same time. In his essay, Paz carefully distinguishes the symbolist-influenced poetics of late nineteenth-century Latin American *modernismo* from the transnational Anglophone modernism (parallel to *vanguardismo*) that emerges after 1910. He bases his distinction between modernismo and vanguardismo on the fact they are separated by the space of a few decades, but this distinction breaks down later in his argument when he attributes to Martí's poetry a harnessing of "the secret power of colloquial language."[55] Making this late nineteenth-century poet who initiated modernismo in 1882 into the harbinger of Latin America's modern avant-garde poetry in the twentieth century, Paz undermines his own strict temporal division.[56] In this light, Paz's reading prefigures Ivan Schulman and Evelyn Picón-Garfield's, which emphasizes formal and political continuities across the decades and schools of Latin American modernismo and the period ranging from the mid-nineteenth to the mid-twentieth century that we assign to European, Brazilian, and Anglo modernism.[57] The expansion of the temporal period of modernism makes it possible to see continuities between Latino migrant poetry and prose of the 1880s and 1890s, and a later, widely disseminated high modernism of the United States and Europe.

According to the first Spanish definition of the literary aesthetic of modernismo by the Salamanca-born editor of a collection of Martí's writing, Federico de Onís, Martí's distinct and innovative sensibility resulted from a profound consciousness of his historical moment and of the future, which imprinted itself in the modernism that gave "Hispanic form" to a global "crisis" beginning in 1885.[58] We traditionally associate modernismo with elaborate, carefully wrought language that focuses on the decorated aesthetic surface; I will comment on these associations by examining elements of Martí's combative mimicry of emergent forms of imperial expansion. My argument challenges the persistent exclusion of nineteenth-century Latino migrant writers from the history of modernism, and aligns itself with other critical efforts to debunk the view that modernism is politically regressive, as compared, for example, to realism.[59]

The Cuban literary critic Roberto Fernández Retamar lamented in 1995 that although Martí has received recognition and honors from the greatest poets and critics in Latin America, in the United States "the real Martí is almost forgotten."[60] Now a veritable renaissance of literary critical anthologies, translations, and studies that draw on Martí's "Nuestra América" and others of his texts in the new millennium is propelling Martí's literary contributions and historical interpretations into the forefront of a current remapping of American studies.[61] While I share Fernández Retamar's dismay with the amnesia that has limited or distorted our knowledge of Martí, I do not, however, presume to offer a definitive Martí, for his writing generates, and to an extent demands, different interpretations for each historical moment.

How would it possible to grasp the real Martí, when, as his contemporary and fellow revolutionary Manuel Sanguily observes, we find in Martí's "original prose, palpitating with life, scenes taken from reality that his powerful genius transformed into fantastic or quasi-Dantesque situations"?[62] Even while documenting quotidian events as a freelance journalist in New York, Martí's texts often represent scenes in figures that seem unreal. Gesturing with flourishes to what it cannot represent in the mode of a photographic reproduction or copy, Martí's modernism rebels against the dominant literary ideology of realism in the United States of the 1880s. Hermetic rather than transparent, Martí's writing conforms neither to romanticism nor to realism, decades before the official arrival of modernism to the Anglophone literature of the United States. Martí, who was familiar with the prose of the prominent and well-paid professional author William Dean Howells, notes with praise Howells's courageous letters in defense of the Chicago anarchists.[63] However, Martí refuses to imitate Howells's "false literary code" (falso código literario) of realism: "his novels are clumsy [burdas]. . . . To reproduce is not to create."[64] If realism only copies, naturalism "is nothing more than a pompous name for a defect: the lack of imagination" (*Obras*, 22:71). Instead, Martí's modernism uses willfully opaque, imaginative language that refuses to hand over a positive meaning and thus calls into question the very possibility of mimetic representation.[65] Martí's modernist form disproves assumptions that Latin America must follow the cultural example set by the United States. Moreover, it awakens his readers to their role in defining America through criticism of it.

Although it would be interesting to make a full comparison between Latin American modernism and other later modernism, such a project is beyond the scope of this book. Instead, I take Perry Anderson's and Fredric Jameson's indictments of a scandalous critical blindness to Hispanic modernism's historical antecedence in modernist studies as a point of departure for my consideration of Martí's form, tone, and style.[66] Martí's vatic prose and poetry grapples with the dynamics of reification in the rapidly modernizing metropolis and responds to the geographical dispersal of imperialism. According to Jameson, modernism records a constitutive absence in its form: the motor and the condition of modernity's economic existence—imperial exploitation of resources and lives—remain screened from the metropolitan subject's view. The modernist literary text, in Jameson's definition, formally mediates this absent, yet indispensable history:

modernism is "the new kind of art" that encodes "this formal dilemma."[67] Martí's texts call attention to unspeakable sources of imperial wealth from the peripheral angle of the still colonized and potentially annexed Caribbean islander.

Without a single national audience, Martí's modernism addresses and represents reading communities on the borders of the bourgeois industrial civilization that imperial modernity sought to extend throughout the hemisphere. The poet on the periphery creates extravagant metaphors to confound the logic by which liberty has begun to mean its opposite, especially for a large sector of workers and migrants of color. For example, the unexpected, shocking, or astonishing events that occurred in U.S. cities in May 1886 in the wake of the Haymarket affair pushes available forms of representation to their limit: "To put the events of these days into a newspaper chronicle is like trying to gather lava from a volcano into a coffee cup."[68] Similarly, the "modern poem," which Martí began to conceptualize in a prologue (published in 1882) to *El Poema del Niágara* by the Venezuelan poet Juan Antonio Pérez Bonalde, draws formal inspiration from the flowering of popular multilingual forms in the city.

What are the formal characteristics and rhetorical strategies of Latino modernist writing? Martí's prologue to Pérez Bonalde's poem, which Julio Ramos has taught us to read as a manifesto on "the relationship between literature and power in the modern age," invents phantasmagoric images that do not belong in realist or naturalist writing.[69] Addressed to a passenger in a modernizing metropolis, the prologue observes that instead of being enslaved to kings, the citizens of the imperial republic actually were "gilded cadavers" whose wings only appear to make liberty possible. In fact, the wings themselves are made of heavy chains, because the citizens had become degraded "slaves of Liberty" (*Obras*, 7:237–38; *Selected Writings*, 51). Although Martí adopts a favorite figure of the romantics, the enchained slave, his theory of modern poetry does not imagine it releasing the "empire of man over the external world," as Percy Bysshe Shelley did.[70] The modernist poet is not a lonely genius creating a single, culminating work; rather this poetry begins with many common people speaking, reading, and writing myriads of "small shimmering works" (pequeñas obras fúlgidas) (*Obras*, 7:227).[71] Martí listens for and gives form to the "dialogue of the large cities composed of fragments of sparks flying from everyone, and passing through common spaces . . . the public butterfly and flower of a common genius [mariposa pública y flor del genio común] that flits from mouth to mouth. From the common people and from life come the words that last" (*Obras*, 12:158). Fully aware of Baudelaire's celebration of the modern artist's need to distill the eternal within the transient, Martí draws on popular speech and hermetic imagery, which, in their zigzag dance, convey hope in a process of becoming: "the imperfection of human language to express with precision the judgments, affections and designs of a person is a perfect and absolute proof of the need for a coming existence" (*Obras*, 7:235–36). The colloquial, popular language that Octavio Paz identifies as a vanguardist, modern element in Martí's poetry is also what Martí makes into his own muse: the enduring element of the transient defines this peripheral modernist aesthetic.

Edward Said has noted that an emergent modernist sensibility responds to imperialism, and that it does so "not oppositionally but ironically."[72] Martí's literary style responds to the supposed progress of empire with an irony like that of Herman Melville and with witty puns reminiscent of Emily Dickinson. As with both of these U.S. writers, whose significance did not become visible in the mainstream of U.S. literary history until long after their deaths, Martí emerges in that same history belatedly, when imperial centers begin to take stock of themselves as hearts of darkness. Irony, satire, and farce undercut the center's triumphant self-projection as a force charged with liberating the rest of the world.

If a persistent coloniality resulted in an imitative copying in Latin American romanticism, Martí responded by appropriating masquerade to invert the Western claim to universality and mastery. To show how the United States "wears liberty as a mask for the conquest it nurtures in its bosom" (*Obras*, 3:48; *Selected Writings*, 323), Martí's texts make fun in the vernacular style of Cuban *choteo*, or merciless, playful ridicule. One local target of such joking is the Latin American elite's tendency to adopt foreign styles and repudiate the homegrown, provincial, or indigenous culture. Martí also attributed to modernist art this quality of postcolonial mockery. In a report on an exhibition of art on display to raise money to fund construction of the base of Frédéric Bartholdi's Statue of Liberty, Martí defines the indigenous art in the exhibition as thoroughly "modern" (*Obras*, 8:329; *Selected Writings*, 146). Characterized by abstract design of surfaces, these aesthetic objects confound European or North American claims that theirs is a superior civilization, for these Amerindian objects exhibit equal, if not superior, elegance, imagination, and intelligence. A small figurine entitled the *God of Pain*, with a flaxen mustache, naked body, and a large belly, reveals "extremely modern artistry" (de arte modernísimo). This object revises the myth that non-Europeans sat reverently in awe of Europeans, by offering a "sparkling and felicitous mockery of the white man" (*Obras*, 8:331; *Selected Writings*, 148). Enriched by Caribbean, African-diasporic, Amerindian, and Latin American popular forms, Martí's modernism too performs its own carnival of masks, in which subterfuge, mockery, camouflage, and biting wit play a role. The mask has the further advantage of providing cover for a rebellious Cuban community involved in clandestine organizing against absorption of the island by the United States.

ᘒ MODERNISM AS TRANSLATION OF IMPERIAL MODERNITY

My title, *Translating Empire*, cites the Uruguayan essayist and critic Angel Rama, who defines modernism in Spanish as a translation of late nineteenth-century imperial expansion.[73] In his neglected essay "La dialéctica de la modernidad en José Martí" (The Dialectic of Modernity in José Martí), which Rama developed and presented in the liminal space of Puerto Rico in 1971, he clarifies the relation between Latin American modernism and imperial modernity: "Modernism is nothing but the collection of literary forms that *translate* the different forms of incorporation of Latin America into modernity. Modernity is a sociocultural concept generated by the bourgeois industrial civilization of the nineteenth century, with which our America was rapidly and violently associated in the last third of the past century through the economic and political expansion of European empires, including that of the United States" (129). As a distinguishable set of literary forms, modernism developed an elaborately stylized technique in order to "translate" the economic and political prostration that resulted from the incorporation of Latin America into imperial formations of Europe and the United States. Martí's complex, sometimes hyperbolic figurative language and multilayered, labyrinthine sentences fit squarely in this pattern, by abandoning realism's pact of reporting on objective fact. Marked by a necessarily camouflaged radicalism inside the United States, Martí's modernism features an intensely self-referential, often self-deprecatingly ironic form that flaunts its literariness and unseats the authority of imperial modernity.

The long-standing and incompletely acknowledged imbrication of imperialism and modernity has deprived the abstract Enlightenment terms of

liberty, equality, and self-government of adequate referents in many postcolonial contexts, including Latin America, the Caribbean, and parts of the
United States.[74] The task of translating these terms becomes urgent in
order to highlight insufficiencies within the existing language of imperial
modernity. José Martí and others in his cohort aimed with precision an
intellectual blow to the conceptual structures they inhabited.[75] Upon recognizing the incommensurability between northern and southern cultural
systems and languages, Martí makes an antinomian claim to similarity and
difference in relation to the North American culture. For example, in
November of 1892, months after the founding of the Partido Revolucionario Cubano, a Key West newspaper summarized a speech that Martí
made in English, in Key West, Florida, before a mixed audience of some
seven hundred people, in which the "great majority" were North Americans (*Obras*, 4:333). On a stage filled with Anglo dignitaries in the enormous San Carlos lecture hall, Martí adapted Patrick Henry's call for liberty
or death to the circumstances of the Cuban war of independence. In decry-
ing colonial conditions in Cuba and proclaiming the island's destiny to be
as independent and sovereign as that of the United States, Martí sets his
people and island on par with the founding fathers of the United States.
But here is the antinomy: immediately after this claiming of the two peoples' equal standing, Martí calls attention to his own difference. He notes
how difficult it is for him to express himself in a foreign tongue.

In a no doubt accented English, Martí calls his listeners to account for
North America's "disdain of Cuba because she has not achieved what they
achieved a century ago."[76] In a brief article on this speech that appeared in
Patria, a statement by Martí attributes the North American misunderstanding of the Cuban's struggle to "language difference" (diferencia del
idioma) (*Obras*, 4:333). Based on this difference, North Americans had not
been able to see the continuity between the revolutionary war waged by the
United States against Britain and the new phase of the Cuban war of
independence then in preparation. The negative depiction of Cubans in
light of the small island nation's colonial status and cultural differences
reveals the long history of U.S. misunderstanding of its debts to Latino/a
migrant creativity.[77] Although the United States had not yet militarily
invaded and claimed a tutelary relationship to Puerto Rico, Cuba, Hawaii,
and the Philippines, U.S. politicians had repeatedly offered deals and cam-
paigned on the goal of annexing Cuba. Within the decade, the United
States achieved its goal of expanding into Asia and the Antilles. In his

speech, then, as in his other writings, Martí was taking on the peculiar task of translating this U.S. misprision of its empire as democracy for potentially and already annexed Spanish-language readers and audiences, but also for North Americans.

In the context of the Americas, translation replaces the outmoded concepts of autonomous originality and novelty as the basis of modern American literary technique. Translation in this sense refers to a creative transformation that enriches the North American text in keeping with limits imposed by the translator's cultural location and by a range of meanings available in the original. In addition to the labor of recreating an original text in another language, which was a common source of employment for educated nineteenth-century Latino/a writers in New York, including Martí, I use "translation" to refer to an unavoidable, absolutely necessary shuttling between cultures. These movements transform the source and the target language texts, and, in turn, reshape our understanding of their contexts. Although tied to the original, a translation opens hidden aspects of the source text's historically constrained and changing significance. Walter Benjamin defines the distance between languages (by extension, between cultures) as insurmountable in the same way that a universal history is impossible.[78] According to Benjamin, because translation will never be able to fully represent the incalculable, not fully translatable element that is lodged in the idiom and historicity of the text, the translator's task is to supplement the original's life.[79] As Martí puts it in his brief introduction to Gabriel Zéndegui's translation of Hjalmar Hjorth Boyesen's poetry in *La América*, "to translate is virtually the same as to create. . . . [T]he translator must go outside himself and put himself in the place the author occupied" (*Obras*, 28:243). Like the impossible and necessary task of seeing from another's point of view, the translator encounters on a daily basis formal elements that she or he is incapable of conveying in the target language. This untranslatable element stimulates the renovation of language and reveals the mutability of the original over time.

Translation by migrants from Latin America in the United States played a crucial role in articulating what Julio Ramos has called "divergent modernities." *Modernidad*, a key word in the title of Ramos's classic study, becomes plural in John D. Blanco's translation of it into English, a change that illustrates the generative potential of translating Spanish-language Latino theoretical formulations into English. Whereas Ramos's *Desencuentros de la modernidad en América Latina: literatura y política en el siglo XIX*

(1989) might literally be translated as "Missed Encounters [or Disagreements] in the Modernity of Latin America: Literature and Politics in the Nineteenth Century," Blanco's translation, *Divergent Modernities: Culture and Politics in Nineteenth-Century Latin America*, adds the sense of multiple modernities and their distinct possible routes through nineteenth-century Latin America. In keeping with Martí's influential references to "two Americas," in which "our" and "the other" America grate against each other, "divergent modernities" directs the reader to the implications of this debate not only for Latin America, but also for its powerful neighbor to the north.[80]

Translation has a special ability to register the complex responses of the Spanish-speaking migrant writer to an Anglo-dominant environment. Martí had a vexed relationship to the source language of most of his translations. Unlike some Latin American immigrants who adopted U.S. citizenship and effortlessly switched to English upon arrival, Martí and many Latino migrants never abandoned the language and culture that differentiated the group to and for which they spoke and wrote.[81] Even though by the end of his decade and a half in New York Martí became fluent in English as a result of diligent study, his acquaintances report that he rarely used what Martí described as his "barbarous" English.[82] Martí "trembled" when he first faced the task of writing an article in English, for up until 1882, he claims to have "never written in English," or to have written in it only in "extreme situations" (*momentos extremos*) (*Obras*, 22:285). This comment illuminates the economic necessity of the "friendless," "fresh Spaniard," as he undertook some twenty-nine articles for the New York weekly literary magazine *The Hour* between 1880 and 1881, on topics as diverse as Gustave Flaubert's novel *Bouvard et Pécuchet*, on Pushkin, and on modern Spanish poetry.[83] Unlike English—which he used out of necessity—Spanish represented a lifeline to the intellectual tradition and to the distinct culture of his America. To use it defied the common North American treatment of its speakers with disdain, ignorance, paternalism, or expectations of monolingualist assimilation.[84]

While my retransfer of Martí's interpretations from Spanish back into English necessarily departs from the Spanish and can never recuperate fully the original, this act of *untranslation* returns us to Latino interpretations of U.S. scenes and texts, which otherwise would have remained unrecognizable or lost to the literary historical record. Untranslation enjoins a North American audience to recognize its historical relationship to Latin

America through the eyes of the anticolonial Latino migrant. I adapt un-translation—the practice of retranslating back from Spanish into the original English—from Martí's German contemporary Friedrich Nietzsche. He claimed for himself the task of "retranslating man back into nature."[85] With this phrase, Nietzsche refers to a biological or organic origin of humans prior to language, which he paraphrases as "the frightful, basic text *homo natura*" (*Beyond Good and Evil*, 160). He is contemplating the idea that the human, which becomes imaginable through language, might trace its origins to a scientifically verifiable or intelligible state before language written in Latin. The original "source" text of *homo natura*, however, also calls attention to its cultural and linguistic construction. Thus Nietzsche does not imagine it possible to return to an unmarked and unmediated, freshly born human who exists prior to the archive.[86]

Translation thus mediates the reader's access to the human, including the English-language reader's relationship to Martí. Although Martí wrote for a transnational Spanish-speaking America throughout his residence in New York City, his texts also imagine, demand, and direct their critique to audiences in English and in the United States.[87] Despite a statement in one of his notebooks that he "would not like to have [his] works translated into English or French," I believe many of Martí's works speak to a possible future English-language audience, insofar as they propose to change the northern nation's imperial trajectory.[88] Martí derived "extreme pleasure" (gustazo) upon seeing his childhood friend Fermín Valdés Domínguez's name printed "in English letters" (en letras inglesas), in an article that Martí wrote about him in the [New York] *Herald*.[89] Martí also wrote under a pseudonym and under his own name in English, and spoke publicly in English on several crucial occasions, especially toward the end of his life. When these texts or performances are not available in the original language, we can and should reconstruct them through newspaper accounts or by translating them back into English from the Spanish-language newspapers that preserve versions of them in translation. Through untranslation, Martí's innovative acts of selection, framing, and translation in a Latino/a idiom become legible, and U.S. American studies may give appropriate credit to Latino migrant writers' contribution to the redefinition of the field.

Although Martí on a few occasions translated himself into English, he primarily translated English-language journalism or literature from English or French into Spanish.[90] This book presents many of my translations

from his writing in Spanish into English.[91] Metropolitan translation of the
peripheral text always potentially serves a disfiguring colonial imperative. I
keep this caveat in mind, sharing Alberto Moreiras's opinion that translation is useful above all for carrying out self-study and self-criticism. Translation's constant struggle with an untranslatable excess reminds us of the
opacity of what seems familiar and easily known. Across a temporal distance, what we think is "ours," just as much as what is not, demands
translation. In defamiliarizing the proximate and bringing near the foreign, translation has the potential to work against the repression of internal
homogeneity and to defy colonial or imperial stereotype.

Returning Martí's translations of U.S. culture to contemporary conversations about American studies in English is every bit as much a creative
remaking as translation is. Just as Martí added meanings to the social text
that many Anglo readers had ignored or disavowed, this book's work of
untranslation permits the generative friction of Martí's difference to bring
us back to certain unspeakable aspects of U.S. history and culture. This
detour through a Spanish-language Latino/a idiom challenges readers of
Martí to follow his mercurial movements back in time, in order to imagine
the tensions of his present through his eyes.[92] Martí's interpretations of
empire acquaint us with the history of a distinct (and still) possible future.

Given that translation involves a crossing of cultures, what is its relationship to the transnational, another paradigm that has transformed
American studies in recent decades? If Carolyn Porter advised us that U.S.
scholars don't know enough about external or internal Latin perspectives
on the United States, her other claim that "there is nothing inherently
socially progressive about transnationalist models, whether they be global
or merely hemispheric" bears repeating.[93] Translation's bringing into focus
the intangible gap between languages may push the reader to attend to
relationships among cultures and languages in a way that transnational
perspectives do not.[94] Attending to both translation and transnational
frameworks together will enable readers to avoid the pitfalls and shortsightedness of linguistic nationalism. Whereas transnationalism may focus
on the gaps and social circuits that straddle national borders as they are
traversed on the ground, translation has no choice but to do so. If a
transnational perspective makes it possible to read from both sides of the
border simultaneously, as if the reader could easily be in both places and
languages at once, as in an aerial view, translation can move in only one
direction at a time.[95] Translation forces the reader to traverse fissures,

points of contact and exchanges within the most intimate ligaments of culture. Like transnationalism, it reveals insufficiencies of any single national culture or of cultural nationalism, if accompanied by reflection on the dangerous activity of crossing and on what is inevitably lost or left behind. Attention both to the dynamics of translation and to transnational formations is necessary to reading Latino migrant translation of empire in a reconfigured American studies.

⟣ HEMISPHERIC AND TRANSNATIONAL FRAMES FOR AMERICAN STUDIES

In the post–cold war period of the 1990s, a veritable renaissance in comparative, inter-, trans-, and hemispheric American studies has brought relations among the Americas to center stage. However, even though the academic field and the object of study of "American studies" now refer to a transnational, multilingual crossroads of colonizers, displaced, or marginalized natives, people of various diasporas, settlers, and especially migrants, Martí is still claimed by scholars and politicians, including a president of the United States, as an authorizing figure for pan-American economic, cultural, and political programs.[96] Such hemispheric or totalizing proposals—annnounced as they were in English, in the United States, and often with the collaboration of unscrupulous Latin American elites—become key targets of Martí's critique. Fully thirteen years before 1898, the date usually associated with the U.S. emergence as an imperial power, Martí discerned that imposing influence through ostensibly friendly meetings and the promotion of hemispheric peace and "free" trade was a conjuring trick.[97] Some of Martí's most compelling and creative rhetoric translates a scheme to introduce a U.S.-led Pan-American system in the hemisphere. To make Martí a spokesperson of today's liberal, capitalist democracy, a free-trade area of the Americas, and against the current government and scholarship on Martí in Cuba diverts attention from the kind of unsettling and mind-opening self-criticism of imperial modernity and of U.S. literary history that Martí's writings model.[98]

In his report on "The Monetary Conference of the Republics of America" that appeared only a few months after "Nuestra América" in *La Revista Ilustrada de Nueva York*, Martí ridicules the idea that geographic proximity in America obliges a single political union.[99] Neither "geographic morality" nor laws of gravity and maturation, but the human-made history of

Pan-American political and economic relations determine the infeasibility of a single inter-American alliance.[100] The mistake of making Martí into a spokesperson for a hemispheric Pan-Americanism may follow from the eager interest in regionalism and transnationalism that arises as the nation-state wanes in comparison to increasingly powerful global forms of economic governance and administration. Gretchen Murphy's book on the imaginary of the Monroe Doctrine provides a useful warning against a too-quick embrace of Western hemisphericism as alternatives to U.S. nationalism, when Western hemisphericism in an English-dominant U.S. academy may well reproduce the imperialist dynamics it would criticize.[101] One of my tasks in this book is to call into question the association of Martí with Pan-Americanism and other forms of U.S.-led economic regionalization.

Although Latino writing has long been marginal in the place of its elaboration and publication, I do not propose to claim a place for these writings within U.S. multicultural canons. The now mainstream discourse of multiculturalism tends to imagine "minority" political and cultural projects inside the borders of the United States and in English. In keeping with ongoing efforts to recover literary texts in Spanish from the colonial period to the present in order to complicate a monolingual U.S. literary history, the Latino writing I consider here reveals the long-standing and influential presence of this migrant community in New York. But Martí's readings of the United States do not merely add to or diversify an existing U.S. national discourse, for they look past the limited goal of equal rights within national boundaries as a remedy for historical legacies of military and economic intervention that continue to prompt inter-American migration. I would not define Martí as a North American or even as a U.S. Hispanic author. In the crowning achievement of over a decade of archival recovery led by Nicolás Kanellos, *Herencia: The Anthology of Hispanic Literature of the United States*, Martí figures in sections entitled "The Literature of Immigration" and "The Literature of Exile." Yet neither of these categories, nor the volume's overarching rubric of "U.S. Hispanic," addresses the way Latino migrants such as Martí slip outside of and challenge the U.S.-derived paradigms for his America. Migrant Latino texts call upon the reader to acknowledge and to grapple with the omnivorous reading, multilingualism, and translations of this nomadic group, without reducing these writings to a detached cosmopolitanism.

ᐤ AMERICANS WITHOUT A COUNTRY

By reading José Martí within a tradition of economic migrants and non-citizen cultural workers that is also broadly American, this book contributes to a literary history of another America besides the United States. Living in the United States but with his eyes set on the dream of Cuban independence, Martí was, as he puts it in his grief-stricken reports on the Pan-American conferences, "an American without a country" (sin patria) (*Obras*, 6:102). Martí's America lies in and beyond the United States, both geographically and temporally. It is not hermetically separable from this nation of settlers, colonizers, diasporics, migrants, and "natives," nor is it fully containable within it.[102] The migrant Latino category does not exclude his other historical commitments to nationalism, Latin Americanism, and separatism from Spain. It permits a refusal of a long-standing and counterproductive mutual exclusion between the immigrant and the exile, between the admirer of Abraham Lincoln and critic of the annexationist leader Augustus K. Cutting, between the intellectual author of a Latin Americanist anti-imperialism and the first translator of U.S. literature for Latin American readers.

The term "migrant," without the inward moving and settling prefix of the term "immigrant," signals to the reader that not all alien residents in the United States inevitably identify with or yearn for naturalization in the United States, even when they may seek equal protections based on personhood and presence within the national jurisdiction where they work and live, and even when or if they find it necessary to adopt U.S. citizenship. I use the nomadic and unsettling term "migrant" to refer to a body of writing that is finally beginning to assume its proper place in contemporary discussions of the postcoloniality and planetarity of American cultures.[103] Following Mae Ngai's usage, "migrant" challenges the assumption that the only logical telos of migration is naturalization and U.S. citizenship, an enduring myth that obscures critical perspectives and trajectories of many migrants such as Martí, Serra, and Figueroa, all of whom left the United States.[104]

In addition to affiliating with a not-yet-formalized nation, Martí positions himself among a diverse group of migrants he refers to as "southern peoples." He claims that these migrants do not come by choice to the United States in order to acquire wealth or even to gain citizenship, but rather to defend the interests of their "South" in northern spaces (*Obras*,

13:394). Martí distinguishes broadly between "northern" immigrants who were arriving by the thousands each day in search of economic wealth, and those who left their countries reluctantly or unwillingly, through forced abduction and enslavement, as refugees from political persecution, bound by deceptive contracts, or impelled by stark necessity. The latter, which Martí refers to as the "faithful peoples of the South," would prefer "a shack on their piece of land to a palace in a foreign country" (*Obras*, 9:224). This capacious self-characterization of the "southern" migrant includes the disdained southern European or Jew, the displaced Amerindian, castoffs of colonized territories, formerly enslaved Africans, and Asian laborers. Prefiguring contemporary discussions of a global south, this identification with the south warns the Latino American reader of the perils of assimilation to a European-identified American culture.[105]

Rejecting English as a primary language and opting not to make the United States a final destination, some of the migrants of Cuba, Puerto Rico, and other parts of Latin America lived as political exiles yet also became profoundly entangled with their culture of residence.[106] Julio Ramos's essay "Migratories" acknowledges the extent to which Martí fits Theodor Adorno's descriptions of exile, but still he defines Martí as a migrant. Edward Said defines "exile" as a lonely foreignness, an impossibility of return, and as cause for a scrupulous subjectivity.[107] These are qualities that we certainly find in Martí's writings. To Martí the exile is a person who is out of place in an uncomprehending society and cut off from the possibility of home. Martí's interactions in English with neighbors and hotel employees who ridiculed his accent impressed upon him the stigma of being racialized in a xenophobic society.[108] While Martí left his island because the Spanish government deported him, he transgressed the stipulations of his exile and journeyed to New York from Spain and from Venezuela after temporary residences in Europe, and South and Central America. The term "migrant" acknowledges Martí's longing to engage critically in American cultural definitions and leaves open the possibility of a long-standing lack of affinity with U.S. politics and policies.[109] To refer, as I do, to nineteenth-century Cubans as migrants, not as immigrants or exiles or even émigrés, is to suggest that the United States did not offer an unbiased refuge or a society with only benevolent concern in the struggle over Cuba's future.

Noting how the concept of exile often represents only a temporarily interrupted narrative of return to the native land, Ramos's essay "Migratories" argues that to describe extended residence as exile diverts attention from significant interactions and invention that take place outside the nation.[110] For this reason, Ramos claims Martí as "one of the first intellectuals of the Latino community in New York" (281), and places him at the forefront of a migrant tradition in which home becomes a portable cultural tradition to be cited, sung, or constructed. These portable roots do not depend upon permanence in a single, solid, territorial space. I follow Ramos in privileging the term "migrant" over "exile," in order to read Martí's decade and a half in New York in relation to the cultural history that Latino migrants have built up in these metropolitan spaces since the nineteenth century.[111] In their bodegas, tobacco workshops, Spanish-language newspapers, volumes of poetry, boarding-house foyers, political speeches, and *veladas* (or evenings of speeches, poetry, *danzón*, and other Caribbean music), the labor and culture of Latino/a migrants have transformed the metropolitan cityscape.[112] Rather than limit our concerns to Martí's fathering of the national homeland, conceiving of Martí as a migrant reverses the erasure or marginalization of Latino migrant influence on the culture and theorizing of the United States and upon this country's narratives about itself.[113] As the field that calls itself variously comparative, trans-, or inter-American studies is taking form and scholars are struggling over its definition, this book highlights the way Latino migrant writers' interpretations reveal U.S. literature and culture to be subsets and effects, rather than defining models, of a larger field.[114] Without a nation-state that represents him—for he never exchanged his Spanish passport for a U.S. one—Martí has no option but to initiate his cultural and political rebellion within the compromised space of imperial modernity.

The chapters that follow proceed roughly in chronological order in order to convey to the reader a sense of the duration of Martí's residence and its accumulated effect upon him. Like the structures of feeling in a social formation that are haunted by residual and emergent sensibilities, the well-documented shift in Martí's consciousness toward a more openly critical view of the United States emerges through wide oscillations. Pécuchet (of Flaubert's *Bouvard and Pécuchet*, which Martí reviewed) saw progress as a wavy line; so also Martí wavered in relation to his place of residence: "Anyone who followed [this wavy line] would lose sight of the horizon every time the line dips."[115] A fierce mixture of attraction, ambivalence, and critical distance characterize Martí's readings of U.S. literature, culture, and politics. Never enjoying certainty about the outcome of his radical project, his tragic course made it possible—and unavoidable—for him to turn the literary journalism that served as a principle source of income into a venue for his most incisive critique.

Martí the prisoner, the deportee, and the migrant is the subject of my study, rather than the exile who loved Lincoln, the apostolic father of the Cuban nation, or the poet-politician who forged Latin American literary forms and identity. The first chapter of this book, "Latino-American Post-colonial Theory from a Space In Between," defines the theoretical frame-work through which this book reads Martí's translations and shows his inaugural contribution to postcolonial American cultural histories and theoretical frameworks. Drawing on Latin American, Caribbean, and es-pecially Brazilian cultural theory, I suggest how Martí's belated incorpora-tion adds to these fields. Chapter 2 focuses on Martí's first editorial enter-prise in New York and argues that Martí's translations of North American culture use the porous space of late nineteenth-century print culture to develop a strategy for reading imperial modernity in the United States. *La América*, the New York-based magazine of modern technology, culture, and ideas; a projected volume of critical studies entitled "Norteameri-canos" (North Americans); and Martí's neglected 1883 prologue to the Cuban migrant writer Rafael Castro-Palomino Jr.'s short fiction reveal the emergence of another America in between the lines of writings about North American authors and European cultural models. Martí differs from an older generation of Cuban migrants, including his editor at *La América* and compatriot Rafael Castro-Palomino. Unlike Martí's prologue, Castro-Palomino's little-known stories contrast the failure of Paris Com-mune revolutionaries' radical egalitarianism with the promise of New En-gland capitalism, in order to praise the latter as a model for Latin American development. Chapters 3 and 4 explore Martí's differences from such clas-sic U.S. writers as Ralph Waldo Emerson and Walt Whitman. Chapter 3, "The 'Evening of Emerson': Martí's Postcolonial Double Consciousness," questions the view that Martí identified totally with Emerson and teases out the Latino migrant's process of taking distance from the New En-glander over a period of several years. This divergence culminates with Martí's sense of the failure of Emerson's "Man Thinking" to address racial violence and legal exclusions of racialized migrant workers, including the Rock Springs, Wyoming massacre of Chinese laborers in 1885 in the wake of the Chinese Exclusion Act. In chapter 4, "Martí's 'Mock-Congratulatory Signs': Walt Whitman's Occult Artistry," I describe the Cuban's ritual eating

and regurgitation of the "angelic" poet of democracy Martí responds
to Whitman's naturalizing of imperial expansion with artfully duplicitous rhetoric. In the manner of Whitman's own self-parody with "mock-
congratulatory signs," Martí distances himself from the North American
poet by parodying the beatification of Whitman, who chanted the incorporation and annexation of the hemisphere to the United States. Drawing
on intertexts by the antiseparatist Cuban planter Ricardo Rodríguez Otero
and the Spanish literary critic Marcelino Menéndez y Pelayo, I suggest that
Martí's 1887 interpretation of Whitman problematizes this celebrated figure's complicity with U.S. expansion. Contemporary criticism that has
begun to address Whitman and Emerson's condoning of manifest destiny
retains an unacknowledged debt to Martí, who anticipates the use of "empire," "race," and "language" as categories of inquiry in American studies
research. Chapter 5, "Martí's Border Writing: Infiltrative Translation, Late
Nineteenth-Century 'Latinness,' and the Perils of Pan-Americanism," plots
the twinned emergence of the terms "Latino people" (gente latina) and the
"American imperial system." Martí's critical analysis of late nineteenth-
century popular culture, including travel writing, expositions, popular fiction, and politics, illustrated for his readers the vulnerable position of the
"Latino" in the U.S. racial and hemispheric system. Historically sedimented categories of displaced Native Americans, annexed Chicanas/os,
lynched or fleeing Africans and Italians reveal the racial logic through
which travel writers or people on the street "read" migrants from the
Hispanic Caribbean, including Martí. In his interpretations of Buffalo Bill
and other ritual reenactments of westward expansion, in his self-published
translation of Helen Hunt Jackson's popular romance novel *Ramona*, and
in his comments on travel writing and journalism about Latino/a Americans as inherently unfit for self-government, Martí undermined racialized
and sexualized representations of his America.

Unlike Herbert Bolton, who saw the Spanish borderlands as a new archive for U.S. scholarly exploration, Martí approaches this region by asking
his readers to imagine the United States from the position of the annexed
Mexican living in what used to be northern Mexico. In the aftermath of the
border's violent redrawing, he defines his America in terms of its cultural
difference from both Europe and the United States, and through its structural parallels or connections to Amerindian, African American, or Asian
diasporic and migrant cultures.

Translating Empire tells the story of Latino migrants' remarkable prescience about the United States' imperial future. It retells this story when U.S. scholarship across the disciplines is reckoning at last with the imperial trajectory of the United States. Latino migrant writers' critical foresight and formal bending of existing literary form to represent this imperial future derives in part from their location as translators in the space between American modernities, a space to which I turn in the first chapter.

Latino American
Postcolonial Theory from
a Space In-Between

> To what purpose did Cubans fly from Spanish tyranny if
> they were to find in an American republic its very horrors?
> **—José Martí,** "To Cuba!" *Patria*, 1894

❧ MARTÍ'S ACCOUNTS of his incarcera-
tion, deportation, and migration before the age of twenty, his translations and oratory in English from the end of his life, and his
manifesto on modernist poetry together demonstrate this Latino
migrant writer's contributions to Latino/a, American, and postcolonial studies. To include Martí within these fields of inquiry
pushes them to address the role that a subject on the edge of these
disciplines—the migrant Latino—had in shaping them. Beyond a
single national or linguistic tradition, Martí's travel writing, translation, and literary criticism illuminate the postcolonial urgency
of his final speeches to mixed Anglo and Latino audiences. He
writes from what Silviano Santiago calls the postcolonial "space in-
between" (*o entre-lugar*) of Latin American discourse. In this chapter I argue that Martí adopted tactics of subterfuge in his criticism
and translation because of his formative experiences as a deportee,
a political prisoner, and a migrant in an emergent empire. I define
the theoretical framework through which this book approaches
Martí's "translations," and consider the sizeable debts that critics

in the U.S. incur when drawing—sometimes visibly, sometimes invisibly—
on the rich, yet insufficiently acknowledged theoretical traditions of Latin
America.

ᔆᔆ "NOT AS A FOREIGNER DO I COME": INCARCERATION,
DEPORTATION, AND TRANSATLANTIC MIGRATION

Martí's divergence from either of the governing cultures in which he lived
for the longest periods—Spain and the United States—derives from his
intimacy with colonialism in Cuba and then as a postcolonial migrant
living and working amongst the fruit sellers, the newspaper urchins, and
boarding-house renters of Gilded Age New York. Migration between the
Caribbean, Europe, and New York helped Martí to claim histories of anticolonial Amerindian rebellion and African maroonage as legacies for urban
migrant organization and for postcolonial self-government. Latino migrant conditions make it possible for a light-skinned, professionally trained
Cuban to identify with displaced indigenous communities, harassed Asian
workers, and Africans in the grip of double consciousness in the Americas,
all of which Martí gradually became cognizant of while living in the United
States. The intersecting trajectories of these major cultures inform Martí's
definition of his Caribbean island as an American crossroads, traversed by
the world's cultures, but marginalized in New York.

Like Frantz Fanon's black Martiniquan, who travels to France and returns radically changed, or C. L. R. James, who said that "the first step to
freedom was to go abroad," Martí and other Hispanic Caribbean migrants
resident in New York shaped their perspective as translators for "the-ones-
who-never-crawled-out-of-their-holes" back on the island.[1] Making his
residence for over a decade in a boarding house run by the Venezuelan
Carmen Miyares for Latin Americans away from home, Martí did not
merely travel through the United States, as did the French aristocrat Alexis
de Tocqueville. In addition to the temporal extension of his residence,
Martí labored at a translator's desk crowded with dictionaries, stacks of the
day's newspapers from various countries, piles of magazines, and books in
various languages and half-finished speeches or correspondence.[2] The conditions and nature of his work as a translator and as a voracious reader
shaped Martí's critical angle and the form of his writing.

To read Martí as a colonial subject, a migrant, and a translator in New
York builds on a critical tradition that has focused on Martí's role in Latin

American and Cuban letters. It sheds new light on his contributions to U.S. Latino and American literary history broadly understood.[3] For acute logistical and political reasons, scholarship on Martí has faced practical political obstacles in linking Latin America to the history of exiles and immigrants in the United States. The Cuban exile community, from Martí's time to the present, has included individuals or groups ranging from José Ignacio Rodríguez in the late nineteenth century to Luis Posada Carriles in the late twentieth century, who have worked covertly or overtly in the service of representatives of the U.S. government to promote annexation or to undermine the island's self-government.[4] On the other hand, since the 1959 revolution, unauthorized departure from the island or criticism of the Cuban government's policies has often made would-be migrants into deserters. Whereas existing research on José Martí has demonstrated his contributions to the founding of Latin American literary forms, my reading adumbrates an alternative both to U.S. assimilation narratives and to Latin American national insularism.

Lacking official citizenship papers from any American nation and facing the xenophobia of earlier waves of immigrants, Martí nevertheless challenges the assumption that Latino migrants in the U.S. are foreigners, especially because Latino ancestry and culture are often partially indigenous to America. Martí augments his claim to America by likening Cuba's nationalist struggle against both Spanish and U.S. control of the island to indigenous military and cultural rebellion. For example, in the midst of an article on aboriginal American authors, Martí disidentifies with his Spanish and Canary Islander parents and, instead, affiliates with the submerged knowledges and historical resistance of pre-Columbian civilizations to the Spanish:[5] "What does it matter if we descend from parents with Moorish blood and white skin? The spirit of men floats on the land in which they lived and that breathes them [se le respira] still. Our fathers are from Valencia and our mothers from the Canary Islands, but in our veins rushes the warm blood of Tamanaco and Paracamoni" (*Obras*, 8:336). In this oblique reference to his immigrant parents from Valencia and Spanish colonies off the coast of Africa, Martí traces his skin color to Moorish or North African origins, and allies himself with the victims of European colonialism. According to his Colombian friend Román Vélez, Martí described Cuba as "a very large tomb, that guards an even greater cadaver: the murdered Amerindian race."[6] Breathing in the vigilant ghosts of indigenous leaders, and struggling to reclaim and honor the burial grounds of countless Amerindians, this Latino migrant writer affiliated with the continent's long aboriginal history rather than make filial claims to European ancestry.[7]

Martí and many of his interlocutors in the migrant community offer notes from native sons. A comparison of Martí to writers of the African diaspora who lived and thought outside a nationalist framework reveals the connections between racism, class exploitation, and imperialism that led Martí to disidentify with a white, Anglo, and imperial subject in formation in the United States. Like W. E. B. Du Bois, the African American interpreter of the souls of black and white folk, Martí positions himself as American while prophesying as a specter at the United States' extravagant banquet table. The historical suppression of radical postcolonial Americanist politics by the U.S. government shapes the planetary tradition of migrants, renegades, and castaways that C. L. R. James, during his predeportation imprisonment on Ellis Island in 1953, identified in Herman Melville's classic novel *Moby Dick*.[8] Martí's critical interpretations foreshadow this radical "outernational" Americanist tradition as he predicted and criticized an emerging U.S. empire in the public record of Latin America's major newspapers and in Spanish-language publications in New York.

Like Du Bois in "The Souls of White Folk" (453), Martí demonstrates unusual clairvoyance concerning the white imperial subjectivity in formation around him. Also, like the Black Atlantic from which Du Bois writes, Martí's America is more expansive than the United States, and his group spans cultural, national, and color-marked assemblages: Martí's is "the America that speaks Spanish" (*Obras*, 5:97), along with other languages, and is "composed of all Spanish-speaking countries" (in English; *Obras*, 22:286). Like Du Bois, Martí asserts his parity in the kingdom of culture. Unable to merge doubleness into a better and truer self, as projected by Du Bois, both of these writers arrive slowly and painfully at a sense of the radical heterogeneity and unsealable fissures within the Americas and within his own fragmented subjectivity.[9]

Martí became aware of this heterogeneity of the self and of the Americas through the extreme and interrelated experiences of colonization, incarceration, deportation, and migration. Economic necessity and conflicts with his volatile Spanish father, Don Mariano Martí Navarro, mirrored the turbulence of mid-nineteenth-century Cuba, which erupted into a ten-year civil war when Martí was fifteen. José Martí was the only son in an immigrant family of eight children, and his father had no education except working in his own father's rope factory in Spain. Don Mariano often suffered long periods of unemployment in Cuba, but mostly worked as a part of the Spanish Colonial Police. The young Martí won prizes for his studies and eventually took degrees in law, philosophy, and literature in Spain, but neither he nor his family owned their places of residence. Don Mariano struggled to support his eight children, and, after he died, his son worked to support his mother and sisters, in addition to his own small family. José Martí worked long hours at multiple white collar jobs for most of his life.[10] Those long hours explain his reference to striking workers in Key West in May 1894 as "my fellow workingmen," in a letter written in English to the union leaders George Jackson and Salvador Herrera.[11]

Working in colonial Cuba and living in Spain during that European country's brief experiment with republicanism sharpened Martí's anticolonialism. After the outbreak of the first Cuban war of independence, Martí became sympathetic to the separatist cause thanks to his observations of repressive conditions in the colony and through study with his proindependence high school teacher, Rafael María de Mendive. Martí complained in a letter to his teacher, then exiled in Paris: "I work from six in the morning to eight at night and I earn four and one half ounces which I hand over to my father."[12] Seven months of fourteen-hour days as an office boy for a Spanish merchant nearly drove Martí to suicide, he reports in this desperate letter. His experience of working in Cuba reiterated for him the contradictory nature of imperial modernity. Julio Burrel—a young Spanish journalist who met Martí briefly in Cuba while the latter awaited his possible deportation to Spain's African colony, Ceuta— recollects Martí's explanation of his radical politics: "I, who am among you an equal, a peer and a friend, am to be [in Cuba] nothing but a foreigner. I am to live in tutelage, subordinate, under suspicion. All doors are closed to my rights, were I to ask for justice, and to my ambitions, were I to legitimately pursue my ambitions."[13] Because Martí had lived and studied in Spain, the colonial abuses contrasted all the more intensely with the metropolitan rhetoric that informed the establishment of the Spanish Republic of 1873–74, precisely when Martí was studying in Zaragoza.[14] Martí observed firsthand the repression of the Republicans who resisted the return to monarchy in Zaragoza, among whom Simón—an Afro-Cuban who worked at the boarding house where Martí resided—stood out in Martí's mind because of his valiant fight against the anti-Republican forces (*Obras*, 4:391). The failure of reforms in Spain fed Martí's anticolonialism.

Martí identified himself, his parents, and his son, Pepe, publicly as workers in a draft of a speech amongst his fragmentary writings (*Obras*, 22:17), in keeping with his view that the vast majority of human beings are workers. He considered "vile" that small part of the world that exploits others' labor and refuses to work (*Obras*, 5:104). Describing himself as being of "humble origins" (*Obras*, 22:286), Martí claims his preference for those who work as he does: "It is nothing, but as I work, I love those who work: I too have quarried stone" (*Obras*, 22:252–53). This allusion to Martí's six months of forced labor as a political prisoner in Havana suggests the extent to which this experience marked him, even after decades of working more with his head than with his hands, as a journalist, consul, translator, and teacher.

The experience of quarrying stone occured in 1870, at the age of seventeen, after Martí was found guilty of being a "declared enemy of Spain." The six months of hard labor that he served in the Presidio de San Lázaro of Havana provided Martí with an intimate sense of the modern European state's investment of its reason with violent force.[15] Authorities had discovered a letter signed by Martí and his friend Fermín Valdés Dominguez, which criticized a classmate, Carlos de Castro y Castro, for agreeing to serve in the Spanish colonial forces. This unsent letter led to Martí's arrest and indictment. His experience in the prison, moreover, provided Martí with a reservoir of bodily memories for conceptualizing the abrogation of liberty.[16] His head was shaved, and he was fitted with a chain that ran up from his right foot to another chain around his waist. In these chains, he had to walk four miles every morning, work for twelve hours, and returned the same distance every day, under threat of the lash.

He recounts in his prison diary how his father visited him and was moved to tears by a suppurating wound in his son's leg, which had resulted from the chain rubbing against his flesh during these long workdays. For the Spanish empire, his injuries were a mere "detail," as he indicates with bitter irony:

> A repugnant detail [detalle], a detail that I also suffered, on which I, nevertheless, walked, and upon which my disconsolate father wept. And what a bitter day when he managed to see me, and I tried to keep from him the cracks in my body, . . . and when he saw at last . . . those purulent openings, those crushed members, that mixture of blood and dust, of matter and mud, upon which they made me prop my body and run, and run, and run! What a terribly bitter day! Clinging to that formless mass, he looked at me with

horror and he hastily wrapped the bandage, he looked at me again, and at last, feverishly squeezing the fragmented leg, he broke down weeping. His tears fell into my wounds. I struggled to dry his eyes. Heart-rending sobs knotted his voice, and at that moment the work bell rang and a rough arm dragged me from there, and he remained kneeling on the ground moistened by my blood, as a stick prodded me toward the tower of boxes that would be awaiting us for the next six hours. (*Obras*, crit. ed., 1:71–72)

This poetic prose builds up internal rhyme to figure the cracking of the subject under the weight of the enchained body. Deformed and suffering, the speaker bitterly decries this "detalle" (part, relation, fragment), his wounded limb. The first personal pronoun, "yo," echoes in words that refer to the broken body that his father mourns: "sin embargo" (nevertheless), "desconsolado" (disconsolate), "lloró" (he cried), "vio" (he saw), "rompió" (broke), and "llanto" (weeping). This insistent detail—the mangled, fissured, and suppurating body part—becomes the prop to the speaking subject that must serve him in walking and running before the prodding driver's stick. The subject becomes openings, used and broken parts, and mixtures of elements. Yet it must perform the work of an organized system.

In Martí's encounter with his father—who worked in the colonial police force—the son's bitterness is exacerbated by seeing his father weep in anger, disappointment, and frustration.[17] Furtively trying to bandage his child's leg, his father lets salty tears fall into the open wound, causing an inadvertently piercing sting that reminds the son of the father's complicity with the colonial bureaucracy that had imprisoned him. This image of the stooped father contrasts with the brutal anonymity of the prison, which forces the prisoner to labor by beating and pulling him with inanimate objects. A bell, a stick, and a rough arm drive the prisoner back to work and away from the father who remains kneeling in the mud of his tears, the Cuban soil, and his son's blood. The teenager's imprisonment for having written a letter he never sent at age sixteen provokes an experience of physical and mental brokenness that would continue to mark Martí's perspective as a writer and speaker throughout his life. Like Ralph Ellison's Invisible Man, Martí kept mementos of this period: a link of the chain lay on his work desk, and he wore on his left hand a ring forged from another of the links, as a physical sign of the prison's less visible marks on his subjectivity.[18]

The prison, which epitomizes Enlightenment reason through bodily discipline, breaks down political prisoners' reason. Martí attests to this reality in his prison writing. Witnessing the conditions of a twelve-year-old orphan who was condemned to ten years of hard labor in the Presidio, Martí contrasts the brokenness of the prisoners' bodies to Spain's appeal to the cause of Hispanic "national integrity," in the name of which Spain claimed the necessity of its colonial occupation: "before that innocent face and that delicate figure and those serene and pure eyes, reason was lost to me [se me extraviaba], and I could not find my reason . . . National integrity dishonors, whips, assassinates there [in Cuba]" (*Obras*, crit. ed., 1:76, 78). The foundation of the edifice of Western modernity, reason, loses its footing in Havana's Presidio.

Martí conceptualized his subjectivity in terms of broken and contradictory strivings. Deportation, incarceration, and migration lead him to privilege a "philosophy of relation," as he calls it in his early philosophical notebooks, over the Western philosophical tradition's conception of a self-present, transcendental, and universal subject. In response to his Spanish, Catholic introduction to Western philosophy in universities in Madrid and Zaragoza, Martí contrarily observes the sour staleness of these intellectual leftovers. In the margins of this tradition, he elaborates a definition of his "I" as "a part, and subject, and born" (*Obras*, 21:58). As partial, as subordinate and as the past participle of another's action, Martí writes in his early notebooks that he cannot subscribe to the notion of a transcendental science or intellectual truth (*Obras*, 21:55). Against the notion of a unified and harmonious order of being, Martí observes instead that "life is undoubtedly a contradiction" (*Obras*, 21:68).

In keeping with this critique of a transcendent, universal perspective, the young Martí articulates a relational alternative that helps explain why he might make translation into a cornerstone of his anticolonial project. Forming itself through critical practice and through the exercise of interpretive judgment, a relational subjectivity defines a proper set of criteria within the constraining legacy of empire. How is such self-study not merely solipsistic? The obsessive self-reflexivity parallels the rejection of an imposed, or foreign basis for judgment: "It is necessary that I, given my situation [puesto en mí], see myself through my viewpoint [me vea por mí a mí mismo]" (*Obras*, 21:68). What Martí takes away from his youthful study of Kant, Fichte, Schelling, Hegel, and Kant's friend Karl Christian Krause is a philosophical inquiry into "a Philosophy of relation" (*Obras*, 19:367). In this project, philosophy adopts the task of defining the relation between the "I," the "not-I," and "how I communicate with what is not I" (*Obras*, 19:369). If, as Martí writes elsewhere in his notebooks, "human life is the mutual and irrefutable relation between the subjective and the objective" (*Obras*, 21:54), then the task of translation takes on this larger philosophical significance of how to traverse the gulf of alterity that defines human subjectivity.[19] The constitutive exclusions of imperial modernity generate an intimate and quotidian sense of twoness, which erupted with force during Martí's years of immersion in U.S. culture and ideas. For example, in Martí's early philosophical notebooks, a passage beginning with the word "YO" (I) in capitals defines his first-person subjectivity in terms of contradictions: "energetic and impotent, entirely free and enslaved, noble and miserable, divine and extremely human, delicate and disgusting, night and day. This am I" (*Obras*, 21:68). Martí's philosophical observations in the wake of a six-month imprisonment represent his divergence from an integral and universal reason, which, in the Spanish context, brutally punished any expression of a desire for a separate, independent existence.

Martí's texts describe the debilitating effects of the Latino migrant's exclusion also from U.S. modernity. For example, in his essay on José María Heredia, a Cuban born to Dominican parents who lived most of his life as a migrant and who was in Martí's estimation the "first poet of America" (*Obras*, 5:136), Martí writes that Latino migrants suffer with the consciousness that "they appear ridiculous and intrusive, if, from a rudimentary country, they try to speak out in a loud voice on the issues facing humanity."[20] Exclusion from the discussion of what is modern may be tantamount to exclusion from the definition of humanity. Much as the postcolonial theorist Simon Gikandi defines a space "between nation and empire" in order to see how colonial cultural relations shape the definition of British imperial identity, Martí sets out how U.S. imperial subjectivity depends upon the exclusion of the "rudimentary" Americas for its self-definition.[21] Although Martí's changing relationship to the United States preserves a horizon of self-governing liberation on the other side of empire and enslavement, Martí imagines it from within the tenacious structures of coloniality, which, as Martí so fatefully asserts, tend to live on in the republic.[22] The Latino/a migrant has to straddle statelessness and an incipient nationality, empire and colony, and "early" and "late" temporalities assigned by timekeepers in the metropolitan center. Cherishing certain political ideals, they confront the jagged fragments of America's prior cultures strewn about on the ground. The sense of having to negotiate such differences places the Latino/a migrant simultaneously inside and outside of imperial modernity's frame.[23] Martí speaks of his errant predecessor

José María Heredia in terms that echo his own conflicted subjectivity and dissatisfaction with the existing forms of representation: "Heredia had a surplus of sighs and the world proved too small for him" (*Obras*, 5:138). Living within the plot of the center's developmental narrative, some Latino migrants find imperial modernity insufficient to define the world. Merely to extend Europe's unfinished modernity is not enough.[24]

Inextricably linked to his colonial status, Martí's experience of political imprisonment shadowed his experience of sea travel as a migrant. In addition to a two-year stay in Spain as a child, Martí crossed the Atlantic en route to America twice, and arrived at the port of Ellis Island several other times during his inter-American journeys. Memories of his transatlantic crossing as a lonely deportee transport him back to the physical abjection, to the imposed regime, and to his lack of control over his body in prison. Each time he was deported (the first, after his imprisonment, and the second, in 1879), Martí flouted the dictates of Spanish authorities by taking a ship to America, as did many other banished Cubans who promoted independence by organizing in New York. On the voyage from Paris, via Liverpool and Cobh (then Queenstown), Ireland, Martí traveled across the Atlantic in steerage, in a ship full of emigrants.[25] He was twenty-one years old. Martí recounted the experience to his childhood friend and classmate, Fermín Valdés Domínguez, who recalls anecdotally: "Martí said that they gave him a dirty plate and spoon, and he saw himself in that squalid place in which the smell of the dirt and misery was suffocating. Amidst hundreds driven by fate, there was a foul-smelling sump that reminded him of the mess hall at the prison in Havana."[26] Both the migrant and the political prisoner are driven into degrading, dirty conditions about which neither has any choice.

For this trip across the Atlantic, Martí assumed a different nationality, profession, and motivation for travel. In testimony concerning the passengers from the *Celtic*, on whose manifest Martí's signature appears, the captain reported to the immigration authority in New York that Martí swore before him that he was one of five Italian musicians, who had declared that "the Country of which they intended to become inhabitants" was the United States of America. Martí's Cubanness and his plan to make his way to Mexico—where his family had been displaced by the 1868–78 war—disappeared from this official U.S. record.[27] Martí's false testimony to the ship's captain reveals how easily Martí could pass as a European. It suggests the route of settlement into European-American identity, an option that Martí vociferously opposed but nevertheless most likely benefited from in the racially segregated United States.

Martí's twelve days in that storm-tossed ship from Ireland to New York found their way into the author's prose and poetry, in images that Carlos Ripoll associates with the romanticism of Heredia. It is also possible to locate elements of an incipient modernism in this writing, insofar as it stretches literary language to its limit in an attempt to represent the chronicler's reflection on his historical moment and seat of consciousness.[28] In keeping with Aníbal González's definitive work on the modernist *crónica*—the hybrid of essay and journalism and a genre in Spanish that Martí helped to define—Fina García Marruz distinguishes between romanticism and modernism by highlighting modernism's intense consciousness of its particular temporality. Modernism reveals a sense of being on the threshold of becoming something else, or "a leap into another order."[29] Martí's travel notes on his passage to the New World juxtapose the raging waves of the "Black Atlantic" with tranquil, blue water under a clear sky. He compares the ocean that divides Europe and America to the Caribbean Sea, with its intrahemispheric routes between Cuba, Mexico, and the United States. The two bodies of water suggest the discrepancy between two states of consciousness: in the first, a monstrous anger forms a limit to a European-inspired modernity and in the second, a simple tranquility accommodates the North-to-South flow of modernity across the sea. Martí's notes recollect the two functions of the sea as border space and cutting edge of contact:

> When I voyaged in the powerful *Celtic*, ship of immigrants and princes, where I saw—and not among the princes—more respectable heroes, the black Atlantic united all the force of its breast. Its dilated body did not fit in the implacable margins of its seas, and it twisted upon itself with mountainous trembling, begging the sky for strength, also black and obscure, like the face of a furious father who would detain with his ire the impatience of a rebellious son. The sea gazed at the sky, there in the immensity of the horizon. . . . And then, after two years, how blue this somber ocean, how unfurrowed the brow of this sky, what a stingy soldier has taken the place of that iron warrior! (*Obras*, 19:16–17)

With self-reproach, the passage refers to two distinct encounters with the sea and to two figures of the sea as consciousness: "iron warrior" and "stingy soldier." The figures also rework the encounter years before of the

Spanish father facing his rebellious son. For if Martí confronted his father as a political prisoner in 1870, by 1877 Martí traveled secretly to Cuba in order to arrange for his family's return to the island. Hiding his identity under his mother's patronym—he used the name "Julian Pérez"—Martí took care of his family's business and left for Guatemala at a time when Cuba was still in the midst of the Ten Years War. Traveling from the Old World to the Americas, the "Black Atlantic" comes face to face with the fury of a sky that would detain rebellion. Spilling over its own limits, the sea mimics the movements of consciousness under the fragmenting force of imperial modernity. A motif of migration, diaspora, and forced trans-plantation, the Black Atlantic here represents the divided, doubled con-sciousness of the migrant who feels uncomfortable with his paternal inher-itance. As the sea becomes impassive and blue, the subject's consciousness no longer writhes and twists upon itself; it no longer has the same power to transform the fate of the absent dead, especially those chained Africans who were lost in these crossings or who disembarked as slaves. A young Martí very likely witnessed the cargo of the transatlantic slave trade being unloaded, or strung up on a Cuban tree; in his poetry, he describes such scenes and swears to "wash those crimes with his life."[30]

Martí's candid and critical reflection on two distinct modes of con-sciousness during his trips acorss the Gulf of Mexico in these years informs his early contempt for North American culture, which he saw heading to an imminent collapse: "Oh! the North American nation will die soon, will die as the greediness, as the exuberance, as the immoral wealth will also die. North America will die shockingly, just as it has lived blindly"(Obras, 19:17). Although Martí nuances and historicizes this youthful, moralistic condemnation of North American greed during the next decade and a half, this early observation ties the turbulence of his literary form to states of consciousness formed in migration and in imprisonment.

Evocations of these two moods reappear in Martí's poem "Odio el mar" (I Hate the Sea). The poet condemns the tranquil portion of the Atlantic that fails to resist the tyrant's journey to his island, but finds beautiful the sea when it wildly howls "bajo la hendente quilla" (beneath the cleaving keel) of the arriving ship.[31] This comparison echoes the distinctions that Martí draws between his journey from Europe to America, and his journeys between Cuba, Mexico, and New York. The sea in its flat, placid form represents the now impassive somnolence of forgetting and suture. Its flatness and quietness suggest the page of a book, which represents the soldier/poet/reader's slumbering consciousness: "Vuelve un hombre impasible la hoja a un libro" (A man, impassively, becomes/turns the page of a book) (*Selected Writings*, 66, translation modified). This double sense returns us to the revolutionary's acute presentiment of the potential suppression of his own and his reader's rebellious consciousness in the quiet pages of history—as human aspirations and daring forms of writing become someone else's story. The poem meditates on how human acts—especially forms of insurgency—are remembered, distorted, or forgotten in historical, national, and literary critical narratives. As Martí later notes, with poignant pessimism about his future interpreters' acuity: "So much effort—to leave, in sum, as the record of our life, a confused phrase or an erroneous judgment, so that what were mountains of pain appear as grains of sand in the books of a historian" (*Obras*, 21:161). Against this deadening oblivion, Martí's fragmentary travel writing and his lines of poetry portray the deportee, the migrant, and the prisoner as they cultivate the rage of the sea beneath the writer's quill and below the ship's keel. The "I" of these early narratives, the philosophical notes of a former prisoner and the travel writing of a deportee, all map his divergence from a bourgeois universal individualism that his professional training and his light skin trained him to adopt.

"EN EL CRUCERO DEL MUNDO": CUBA AND THE CROSSROADS OF THE AMERICAS

Moving from south to north and from Old World to New World across several languages, cultures, and continents, Martí finally took up residence in New York in 1881. From the city, he began to send his cultural translations to Latin American newspapers. Martí envisioned Cuba in the Americas as a cultural crossroads. In a letter to his Afro-Puerto Rican collaborator Sotero Figueroa, Martí describes his vision of an America characterized by a distinct diversity, in opposition to caste hierarchies:[32] "After a disorganized war among a heterogeneous people, we have managed to put back together our souls. This was my message and my life: let us prove in time our virtue, in order to raise up *in the world's crossroads* [en el crucero del mundo] a republic without despotism and without castes" (*Epistolario*, 3:424–25, emphasis added). Martí does not call for "racelessness" per se. He calls instead for the abolition of regional, linguistic, and color hierarchies that derive from European and colonial legacies. In the late nineteenth century, this rhetoric marks a starting point for several influential discourses concerning distinctly hybrid or heterogeneous Latino cultures in the Americas.[33] We might judge Martí's vision of healing the wounds and fractures within Latin American nations to be utopian, but we should also credit him for perceiving the global significance of his region's—and his island's—heterogeneity.

Martí's letter to Sotero Figueroa sets in circulation a metaphor of the "American crossroads" that becomes a recurrent motif or organizing idea in his public revolutionary discourse. In the last public communiqué of the rebel leaders that addressed a North American audience and which appeared in the *New York Herald* on the day of his death, May 19, 1895, he declares the Caribbean an "estuary" of the Americas that belongs to the world and not to the United States.[34] Speaking for the Cuban insurgents from Guantánamo, Martí claims for the creative and intelligent Caribbean masses the task of redefining modernity's promises in order to shut down the last bastion of Spanish colonialism in the Americas and to block U.S. imperialism. Although some Cuban leaders pleaded with the people to accept the island's inevitable submission to a "Yankee" or a Spanish master in order to "subdue" the masses, Martí placed his hope precisely in Cuba's working people of color: "the powerful masses—mestiza, capable, earth-shaking—the intelligent and creative masses of whites and of blacks."[35] Having learned during the Ten Years War against Spain how to cut off the head of tyranny with a single *machetazo*, having mastered several languages and practiced the art of self-government during long migrations, this revolutionary movement of former slaves, *letrados*, and veterans was preparing to engage in a far-reaching battle over the very meaning of modern nationality and liberty.

As I suggested above, this proposal bears uncanny similarity to the ideas that C. L. R. James set forth in *The Black Jacobins* (1963). James repeats Martí's formulation by defining the Caribbean masses as the key to decolonization, primarily because of their firsthand knowledge of the naked power of imperial modernity. To James, Caribbean workers are "the most highly experienced in the ways of Western civilization, and the most receptive to its requirements in the twentieth century."[36] Although Martí's revolutionary vision did not find immediate fulfillment in the aftermath of the island's 1895 revolution, this project has continued to animate contemporary political and cultural strategies in the Americas into the present.

Martí's communiqué addressed to U.S. readers from Guantánamo was a startlingly current manifesto, which demonstrates what may be lost and what may be gained by returning to the scene of translation. Most likely dictated by Martí from his hammock in the Cuban army's camp to Eugene Bryson, a correspondent of the *New York Herald*, the text represents a specific geographic and historic juncture that includes, literally, the death of the author soon after it was submitted. Perhaps in keeping with a last request from Martí, Bryson delivered the original Spanish-language transcription to the editors of *Patria*, who published it in Spanish on June 3, 1895. Martí made some hand-written corrections to the manuscript before Bryson departed, so the English-language translators were working from a marked-up draft. Even so, the version created by the *Herald* staff only vaguely indicates the most critical arguments of the original Spanish version. The two versions merit careful comparison.

By returning to the Spanish original, it is possible to glimpse an aspect of the United States that the 1895 English translation occludes. Martí's contemporary Cuban biographer and critic, Luis Toledo Sande, reveals the extent to which the *Herald* suppressed key passages in preparing the English version. He compares the article in *Patria*, the original Spanish manuscript (now archived at the Center for Martí Studies), and the mangled English text. Comparing the versions makes it possible to excavate a message encoded in 1895, but which the Anglo readers whom Martí originally sought to address have not yet received.

As signaled by Toledo Sande, the English translation leaves out lengthy passages that call attention to the looming threat posed by the United States to the balance of power on the planet, specifically to the potentially disastrous implications of a U.S. alliance with a Spain-identified oligarchy in Cuba, rather than with the island's multiracial majority of working masses. Moreover, the *Herald*'s translation invents other passages in which the Cuban leaders appear to advocate not Cubans' economic and political self-determination, but foreigners' investment in and profit from the island's hidden treasures.[37] In the Spanish original it is argued that if the United States were to support the wealthy oligarchy in Cuba over and against the interests of the large, diverse working sector, that great North American republic would further betray a revolutionary American tradition. Martí alludes to this ominous possibility with the rhetorical device of litotes: "Certainly, it is not in the United States where men will dare to look for the breeders of tyranny."[38] Although still leaving space for the United States to disprove this prophetic description, this pithy and profoundly ironic sentence points to the opposite of what it says and suggests the United States' possible contributions to training tyrants in the hemisphere.[39]

Another passage that did not make it into the translation elaborates on black, white, and mestizo/a Cubans' shared capacity for their joint self-direction and self-government among the nations of the world. By alluding to the frequent nineteenth-century insinuations that it was Cuba's natural destiny to remain a colony, Martí implicitly refers readers to his more widely disseminated statement in English of 1889, "A Vindication of Cuba" (*Selected Writings*, 263–67).[40] The argument tackles the characterization of Cuba and Cubans in the U.S. press as unfit for self-government: "We are not the people of destitute vagrants or immoral pigmies that [the newspaper] *The Manufacturer* is pleased to picture; nor the country of petty talkers, incapable of action, hostile to hard work, that in a mass with the other countries of Spanish America, we are by arrogant travelers and writers represented to be."[41] Martí's "Letter to the *New York Herald*" on the eve of his death similarly seeks to refute arguments in favor of U.S. annexation that routinely appealed to such racializing rhetoric.

In keeping with the *Herald*'s endorsement of annexation—a view it held along with most U.S. newspapers—the English translation of the Guantánamo letter transformed or elided opaque aspects of the original text. The abridged passages reference concepts that were not yet acceptable for mainstream publication in the 1890s. The *Herald* distorted or excised segments containing radical methodological concepts that Martí sought to introduce. This letter exemplifies the two arguments that Martí contributes to American studies' contemporary reinvention. First, revolutionary pursuit of independence must begin with an active effort to dismantle racial and class hierarchies as legacies of imperial modernity; and second, imperial modernity's enrichment of the urban metropolis derives from and depends upon the undercompensated or unacknowledged labor, riches, and creativity of the periphery. Cuba—as a border space, a global crossroads, a submerged archive of another American modernity, and a key to the Americas' liberty—is precisely what was lost in translation.

Let us see how the passages in question reveal Martí's anticipatory labors in directing our attention to borders and spaces of crossing. With respect to postemancipation race and class relations, Martí's "Letter to the *New York Herald*" envisions more than the freed African "flying to his rifle" to fill the rank and file of the revolutionary army. Although this eager soldier does appear in the English version, the Spanish version speaks of a different sort of revolutionary culture, in which black leaders would command white soldiers and whites would march alongside blacks within integrated armies. In the Spanish version, we find the Afro-Cuban soldier looking on the faces that resemble his former master's without rancor, because "he [the white soldier] marches by his side, or behind him, defending liberty."[42] This radical notion of equality and integration does not appear in the English translation. Nor of course does this idea become a national policy in the United States until well after the centennial anniversary of the Emancipation Proclamation.

Martí and the generals Antonio Maceo and Máximo Gómez proposed with the 1895 revolution to invert the global map of modernity, as patterned on nineteenth-century discourses of purportedly natural national and racial hierarchies. Prefiguring James Baldwin's 1962 epistle on incomplete emancipation in the United States one hundred years after the official end of slavery, Martí's rhetoric in this letter challenges the misconception that the colony depends upon the metropole for its development. Baldwin describes the ground-shaking implications of a change in African American consciousness in the 1960s: "As [the African American] moves out of his place, heaven and earth are shaken to their foundations."[43] Likewise, the colonized island's decision to move out of its customary place within the constellation of imperial modernity represented to the United States an event as terrifyingly unnatural as the collapse of distinctions between night and day. Much like the African American subject's seemingly natural and foundational position in the white U.S. imaginary—as a fixed star, or immovable pillar—Cuba has had a pivotal role in giving both Spanish and North American imperial identity its bearings, and in sustaining the empire's elevated, privileged position. Martí says to the Herald's readers that imperial Spain is the product of her colonies in the New World: "Cuban earnings" (56) alone have sustained Spain, even in spite of the colonial bureaucracy's corruption. His argument serves as warning to the United States as it was seeking an imperial role on the world stage, for in exploiting colonized peoples, conquest always has "fatal" effects for the victors (55). Depending upon extraction of the peripheral country's resources, creativity, and skills, imperial modernity's lifeblood becomes intertwined with the abrogation of the liberty of other peoples and nations.[44]

In challenging the hierarchy between center and periphery, the combined effort of Latino/a migrants and Cubans on the island carries forward long-standing "ideas and practices of the New World" (57) and of its postcolonial tradition, according to Martí's Guantánamo letter. The "New World" tradition here refers to Cuba's continuation of centuries of revolution, in keeping with Martí's commemoration of indigenous and African rebels, including José Antonio Aponte and his eight coconspirators (*Obras*, 22:247), and Gabriel de la Concepción Valdés or Plácido (*Obras*, 20:359) from earlier in the nineteenth century. In his notebooks, Martí envisioned his revolution as a critical revision of the North American and French revolutions: "The upper class's intellectual revolution has been done: I have it all here. And from this have come more evils than goods" (*Obras*, 21:178). Whereas the revolutions of 1776 and 1789 in Europe ultimately represented the interests of an educated upper class, Martí proposes an alternative revolution "of those from below" (los de abajo). As an extension of a modern American revolutionary tradition that includes Toussaint L'Ouverture in Haiti, Gabriel de la Concepción de Valdés in Cuba, Tupac Amaru in Peru, and Benito Juárez in México, Cuba's war of independence aimed to remove color-based caste systems and embrace cultural diversity.[45] Social equality becomes a premise for moving beyond the existing bureaucratic structures that post-1848 revolutions would need to destroy and build differently, according to Marx. Martí's description of his long residence in New York as giving him intimate knowledge of "the monster's entrails" in his final correspondence echoes Marx's use of the figure.[46] In the *Eighteenth Brumaire of Louis Bonaparte*, Marx argues that the truly "monstrous shape" of France's "bourgeois republic" became apparent after Louis Bonaparte declared himself Emperor Napoleon III in a coup d'etat. As the French republic lost the semblance of respectability by suppressing the revolutionary press and popular meetings after 1851, the monstrous qualities of the United States similarly seem to spring forth in Martí's frank final piece of correspondence, a letter to Manuel Mercado that he wrote days after conversing with *Herald* correspondent Eugene Bryson.

Martí's characterization of the role of white and black working classes in the Cuban revolution also resonates with Marx's celebration of the proletarian revoution of Paris in 1871. Martí uses the expression "los de abajo" in an essay that was not included in the *Obras completas*, entitled "Escenas neoyorkinas" (New York Scenes), which depicts the arrival of European immigrants, including unaccompanied children, to Ellis Island. Unlike the arrogant "old" New Yorkers who denied their family's impoverished immigrant origins, the "living poetry" that washed up daily on New York's shores at Castle Clinton during these years of intense migration represented to Martí a heroic and liberatory force. Like the Communards of Paris in 1871, the migrants in "Escenas neoyorkinas" belonged to the "race of liberty" that "had decided to reach the gates of heaven."[47] Echoing

Marx's letter to Dr. Kugelmann of April 1871, in which he celebrates the Parisians of the Commune for "storming heaven," Martí uses the scenes of the immigrants of his time to characterize the Cuban revolution as a struggle between forces rising from below against those on high, setting this new group against a self-made feudal caste of established and willfully forgetful prior arrivants.[48] According to Martí the architecture of Castle Clinton expesses a "spirit of solidarity" that characterizes the experience of a modernity "from below": "Edifices are like the words and symbols of a people [. . .] form conveys the essence. Architecture is the common spirit. The age of war raised up fortresses; the age of shadow, convents. Our age builds structures for immigrants" ("Escenas neoyorkinas," 215). Having traveled in steerage amidst a throng of impoverished immigrants, Martí saw this shared history of necessity as a potential basis for dismantling racial enmity: "The races refuse to become enemies and already another is forming that unites them all and erases borders between them, and [this race] shines like an army of soldiers with armor made of light: the race of liberty" ("Escenas neoyorkinas," 215). This hopeful reflection on his age and its forms depicts immigrants' powerful potential to define an anti-racist modernity.

In proposing a radical equality among nations, cultures, and groups of people, Martí's Guantánamo letter to the *Herald* claims for the island in 1895 and for Martí's American modernity the special position and qualities of a "friendly ship or crossroads" (crucero amigo).[49] The *Herald*'s English translation entirely ignores this expression by rendering it a "home," when the multivalence of the term "crucero" more fully reflects the Cuban revolution's goals, as articulated in Martí's original letter. In addition to the first mention of the term, "crucero" reappears in the climactic point of the letter, when Martí indicts the United States for collaborating with Spain to undermine the revolutionary movement. (Only a few months earlier in 1895, the U.S. government had assisted Spain by confiscating three yachts bound for Cuba and filled with munitions.)[50] The letter depicts Cuba as a people positioned by nature to be "a pacific and prosperous *crucero* of the nations" (51). This use of the term, "crucero," resonates with the larger project of redefining American modernity that we discover in Martí's writings of the late nineteenth century.[51] Far from being inferior to the United States, Cuba, in its struggle for liberty and on behalf of the world, demonstrated that no nation may assume itself to be superior to any other country (70). The leaders' argument annuls the claim of the United States that it has the responsibility to take, to purchase, or to tutor islands or countries based on the color, language, or culture of its citizens.

The figure of a crucero brings to the fore Cuba's place within the Caribbean's diverse societies, in which cross-cultural contact among Amerindians, Africans, Europeans, and Asians had been the norm at least since the arrival of Europeans, if not before.[52] The figure of the crucero illuminates the claim that the island's position in the intersections of the world's oceanic routes and at the doorway of the Americas designates for it a role in guaranteeing each American nation's open access to all the world's nations (53). This sense of Cuba as a crossroads for the world and as a bulwark protecting a space of crossing, also evokes the etymological definition of "translation" —a carrying across. Translation points to a historic juncture of great opportunity and global need, "at the historic hour in which the earth opens and the seas embrace at its feet, and the planet widens its ports and its generative entrails to a world replete with unused capital and unemployed multitudes that would find in the fire of a strong Republic on the island the calm of prosperity and a friendly ship/place of crossing [crucero amigo]" (52).

The passage above begins with one of many temporal references that we also see in "Escenas neoyorkinas" and in Martí's other theoretical definitions of the revolutionary project. The Cubans' struggle to intervene in the definition and practice of another modernity responds to the "historic hour" when the United States imagined its future dominance on the world stage. Attuned to the specificity of the threshold moment of the revolution, the Cuban leaders allude to oppositional networks of transportation, translation, and communication that might undermine that imperial debut (50).

The text's consciousness of itself engaging in a spatial and temporal leap into another order reiterates a definition of the revolution's construction of another modernity that appeared in an essay entitled "El tercer año del Partido Revolucionario Cubano" (The Third Year of the Cuban Revolutionary Party), which appeared in *Patria* on April 17, 1894. Subtitled "El alma de la Revolución y el deber de Cuba en América" (The Soul of the Revolution and Cuba's Duty in America), this essay links Cuba, the Americas, and "modern humanity" (*Obras*, 3:143). With war imminent, the independence of Cuba would indicate the possibilities of balancing power in the hemisphere and in the world by proscribing U.S. expansion:

> The Caribbean occupies the site of the pointer on the balance scale of the Americas. If enslaved, they will be a mere pontoon in the war of the imperial republic against the superior, zealous world that is preparing to negate its

power. They will be merely a little fort of the American Rome. And if they are free and worthy of it—because of their level of equitable and working liberty—they will guarantee the continent's equilibrium. They will guarantee the still-threatened independence of Spanish America and the honor of the great Northern republic. For in the development of its territory—which sadly is already feudal, and divided into hostile sections—[the United States] will achieve a greater security than in the ignoble conquest of its smaller neighbors and in the inhuman fight that, with possession of the islands, it might open against the powers of the planet for the domination of the world. (*Obras*, 3:142)

This passage predicts that plans by the United States to take Spain's two remaining colonies and to make them into naval stations and arms storage— "pontoons" and "little forts" for the "imperial republic"—would pose an enormous threat to planetary security. By contrast, Cuba's and Puerto Rico's successful achievement of self-government, along with the fulfillment of the revolution's commitment to the island's diverse working masses, would force the United States to take stock of its inconsistency. Rather than continue in the trajectory of feudal relations, sectional divisions, and self-congratulatory narratives, this alternate approach—coming from a Latino migrant and islander—proposes to prevent impending forms of global aggression. Although this letter to *Patria* reflects Martí at the height of his powers as a war propagandist writing not only to mainstream U.S. readers but to potential Latino recruits, it is a prophetic contribution, pointing to the multiple global crises that would develop along fault-lines in the Caribbean in the twentieth century. The struggle to redefine American modernity has moved slowly from its beginnings in New York in the 1880s and 1890s, but it continues to bear traces of Martí's translations of empire.

Like a dog sniffing around at the roots of republics—a simile Martí uses in "El tercer año del Partido Revolucionario Cubano"—coloniality constantly returns to urinate on the slender young trees to which the revolutionary tradition of the Americas continues to give rise (*Obras*, 3:140).[53] The English translation of "crucero amigo" as "friendly home" in the *New York Herald* restricts the mobility and the charged historicity of this crossroads, this ship, and this site of intersection. Yet another applicable sense of the word "crucero" comes from the lexicon of printers and editors, with which Martí and many of his Latino readers who were printers, editors, and writers in the migrant press would have been familiar. In this register,

José Martí, ca. 1892, with a group of tobacco workers in Jamaica, West Indies.
By permission of the Centro de Estudios Martianos, Havana.

"crucero" signifies the fold or crease line in between the pages of a printed
publication or the cross mark that indicates the edges of the text page
within which the blocks of text are printed. This "crucero," a marginal
space at the center of the Spanish-language newspaper, evokes the position
of the Latino migrant voice in the empire city of Nueva York. The columns
of *Patria* provided the vehicle through which a vision of an alternative
modernity developed in the tobacco workshops and Latino/a migrant
communities that made the revolution possible by funding it and by sending people to fight in it. In the space between these columns and pages, the
fold along the center invites reflection, notes, conversation, and debate
among the working masses that funded and fought this revolution. By
taking a detour through translation to find this marginalized space, a
United States reader may encounter a body of theory that changed—and
may still change—the course of America.

How does Martí define this alternative set of relations in the hemisphere
and on the planet? While Martí lived in New York City, he would sometimes
go to the Catskills to recuperate his health. During those trips, he fre-
quented a village of cabins that belonged to the officers of the Twilight

Club.[54] An English-language speech that Martí made before New Yorkers who gathered weekly to eat supper for a dollar and discuss the issues of the day, formulates an alternative to expansion "in the name of liberty."[55] What Martí actually said in English that October evening in 1890 has been lost, but the Spanish-language New York newspaper *El Porvenir* published a translated fragment of the speech the week afterward. Here we catch a glimpse of the alternative modernity Martí intended to leave as a legacy for the United States and for his America: "There is a sympathetic and possible union, as attractive from this side of the border as it is from the other side, and it is the union that cannot avoid being born of mutual, unselfish, and just treatment of the men of one zone by the men of another" (*Obras*, 28:340). Binding this rhetoric to revolutionary self-determination, this vision of mutual respect across "zones" of cultural, linguistic, skin color, and national difference represented an alternative to the post–Civil War United States in its Gilded Age. First available through the Latino Spanish-language print journalism that has remained in dusty archives and largely unread until the last few decades, this vision portrays valiant small countries and migrant communities in the Caribbean crossroads or the estuary of the Americas as defining an alternative modernity.

METROPOLITAN AND PERIPHERAL READING: SANTIAGO'S "SPACE IN-BETWEEN"

How do Martí's translations inscribe the Latino migrant's difference from a U.S. literary and intellectual tradition? How do his texts define a U.S. literary tradition from a place within it but not of it, so as to make space for another American modernity? The Brazilian critic, translator, and novelist, Silviano Santiago, in his essay "O entre-lugar do discurso latinoamericano" (Latin American Discourse: The Space In-Between) (1978) offers a useful strategy for reading postcolonial literary relations in the Americas, and specifically Latino migrant translations of U.S. American literature and culture.[56] Written first in French in 1971 and published in English in 1973, five years before it appeared in Portuguese in Brazil, the essay traces the parallel significance of debt—both figuratively and literally—to colonial and neocolonial politico-economic and literary-cultural relationships. Neocolonialism exports obsolete or outmoded consumer objects, both physical and conceptual, from a powerful cultural context to a less powerful one, and it tends to devalue the local peripheral product. In the period my book focuses on, at the end of the nineteenth century, the colonial or imperial urban centers in Europe or the United States conceived of themselves as the powerful centers of knowledge and culture in relation to the distant, less powerful Latin American periphery.

Santiago claims that postcolonial literary relations linger in figures of economic or cultural indebtedness of the periphery to the center, even though, as Walter Mignolo has pointed out, whole economies and cultures in Europe acquired wealth, power, and in many cases technology through violent accumulation from Latin America. Neither in the current regime of foreign loans and trade agreements nor in the earlier colonial period is the center's indebtedness acknowledged. In other words, Santiago's essay anticipates Mignolo's and Pratt's influential arguments that call attention to the inverted vector by which the colonial regions grease the palms of brokers in the metropolis.

Santiago's essay calls into question a form of inquiry in comparative literature that resembles these economic and political relationships. He criticizes research that excavates proof of, for example, Zola's influence upon Brazil's most important nineteenth-century novelist, Eça de Queiroz.[57] In his essay "Eça, Author of *Madame Bovary*," Santiago notes that comparative research of this sort places the less powerful, peripheral writers in the position of parasites, precariously dependent upon the center for whatever light and life there may be in the colonial, or post–colonial country, because, it is often assumed, the colonized county has no cultural value, history, or capacity for creativity of its own (*Space In-Between*, 43). In the conventional search for European influences on Latin American writers, Eça's novel only interests in this mode of comparison because it confirms Brazil's—and by extension Latin America's—tutelary relation to France. In demonstrating Brazil's cultural inferiority and dependence, this method also tends to facilitate incrimination of the peripheral writer: Eça, in fact, faced charges of plagiarizing Zola's *La faute de l'abbé Mouret*.

As I set out in detail in the following chapters, scholarship on Martí's relationship to U.S. writers and its modernity has historically conformed to this traditional model of inquiry.[58] Martí's text becomes more palatable, more easily appropriated, and more visible in the literary historical record in the United States when his seduction by and identification with a North American intellectual tradition constitutes the salient truth of his literary contribution. To study North American influences on Martí tends to cast the Cuban migrant in the condition of cultural indigence; it suggests that

Martí uncritically embraced the model of an imported North American book. This construction of the Latino migrant limits his writings to echoes of the original authors' luminescence, or worse, as a plagiarized model for Cuban cultural independence. As the Latin American culture becomes more indebted to and more invaded by the U.S. culture, its transgressive difference appears in this kind of inquiry as the ideally silent copy.[59] Precisely when mainstream U.S. American studies begins to perceive Martí as an interlocutor and as a reader of North American cultural and political texts, the very possibility of the Cuban's difference seems to slip out of sight.

To the search for influences, the Latin American "space in-between" demands a reading strategy that pays close attention to what Santiago calls "the reactions of the dominated."[60] This strategy defines the reader's and the text's locations in terms of the relations of power that arose during centuries of colonization. If European appropriation of the culture of the New World works by projecting America as a copy, Latin American literature signifies upon, and subtly inscribes its difference in the act of consuming the metropolitan text. In the wake of colonization, a return to a pure or authentic precolonial voice is not an option. Neither is it possible for the dominated to react without regard for the definitions of culture and civilization that are the legacy of the colonial power.

In "The Space in-Between," Silviano Santiago draws on Jorge Luis Borges and especially his story "Pierre Menard, Author of the *Quixote*," to underscore the effects of distinct cultural-historical locations on writing and interpretation.[61] Language constitutes a crucial component of these distinct subjective locations. Thus, we may consider the interpretation of the metropolis's powerful cultural texts by the "dominated," to use Santiago's term, as a kind of translation. If George Steiner has called Borges's story "the most acute, most concentrated commentary anyone has offered on the business of translation," Santiago's appropriation of Borges draws out the significance of "Pierre Menard" as a commentary on Latin Americanist resignification of imperial modernity (*After Babel*, 73). According to Efraín Kristal's astute paraphrase of Borges's statements on translation, Borges conceived of translation "not as a transfer of a text from one language to another," but as "a transformation of a text into another" (32). Similarly, Martí's translations of U.S. literary texts and of imperial modernity's cultural contexts engage in transformative creation of another American modernity. Because Borges's story explains why the reactions of the dominated tend to be clandestine or invisible within the literary historical record, let us briefly turn to his definition of "visible" and "invisible" work. The distinction will prove fruitful in understanding the work of Martí.

ᨒ LUCRATIVE AND IMPOVERISHED INVISIBILITY IN COMPARATIVE AMERICAN LITERARY HISTORY

In Borges's short story, the "visible" and "invisible" differences between texts—and between writers and readers of distinct historical, geographic, cultural, or linguistic locations—record the relations of power that condition what becomes legible and credible in literary history. Like many of his other writings, the story narrates a theory of interpretation without developing a plot. The first-person narrator recounts his efforts to reconstruct the literary history of the story's titular character—Pierre Menard— who is a contemporary of William James, a so-called "old Turk," and who is "in the last analysis, a foreigner" (53). Menard, who refuses to merely copy or update *Don Quixote*, intends to "produce pages which would coincide" with those of Miguel de Cervantes (49).[62] Menard reveals his style or writerly voice to the narrator in the way he selects and paraphrases other texts, as for example, in his incorporation of Ovid's "mournful and humid Echo in *his* Quixote."[63] The narrator proposes to elucidate this "invisible" work of Menard against the unscrupulous omissions and interpolations that marred the catalogue compiled by a prior, Protestant-leaning critic, Madame Henri Bachelier. Bachelier saw only the "visible" work, and her obtuse misprision of Menard's remarks (comments that the narrator is convinced that Menard in fact intended as a joke) leads her to take Menard's "invective" against his old friend Paul Valéry at face value, and thus, to draw conclusions about Menard that are "the exact reverse of his true opinion."[64] By contrast, the narrator perceives the conditions that circumscribe what Menard can say about Valéry. He gets Menard's jokes. The invisible works, elided in the literary historical record of the story, cannot yet figure there as evidence of a radical divergence or of originality. Similarly, in Martí's case, literary historical and political pressures have produced a writer who—rather perversely—has become the mouthpiece and eponym of ideas and institutions that are the strict reverse of those he supported.[65]

Cervantes's theory of history as a witness of the past and a warning to the future fascinates the fictional Pierre Menard. As Borges's narrator observes, history is the mother of truth. But her fickleness makes truth's origins difficult to determine. Historical investigation therefore must, in a Nietzschean fashion, decipher the possibly murky origins of texts. Giving the reader a vital role, the narrator of this story concludes that historical truth "is what we think took place" (53). The narrator in Borges's story works with unreliable sources. Angered by the misrepresentation of Menard by biased interpreters, he proposes to reconstruct a literary history that draws on both "visible" and "invisible" works. In addition to revealing other interpreters' biases, the story affirms the possibility of recuperating invisible or forgotten texts. The inevitable bias of the translator or critic becomes most palpable when he or she does not acknowledge it and pretends that the "visible" works constitute a definitive literary history. In the very text that Menard is rewriting word for word, *Don Quixote*, the narrator makes the patently absurd claim that he is giving a disinterested, unbiased interpretation of the story of "the man of La Mancha," and then he promptly attributes any distortions in his narrative to the fact that the source text's translator, who made the history of Don Quixote available to him, "was an Arab."[66] Like the translation from the Arabic source, the foreign perspective that Menard brings to his task makes possible and reinvigorates his version of the *Quixote*. Similarly, Martí's less visible work —largely unexplored in the United States because of his status as a foreigner from Latin America—nevertheless makes possible a new turn in U.S. literary history.

By the "invisible" works of Menard, Borges's narrator evokes a never conclusively knowable realm of literary creation—the realm of the archives from which literary histories are fashioned. The "invisible" work is what does not yet figure in the literary historical record. It is, in Menard's reader's words, "subterranean, interminably heroic, and unequalled. . . . [It represents] the most significant [work] of our time."[67] Borges argues against a parasitic, total identification of Menard with the great authors whom he paraphrases, translates, interprets, or resignifies (including Cervantes). That would be too easy. Borges's text offers a model for rethinking the relationship between the relatively unknown, belated, and foreign critic and the great author, an apt description of Martí's position in relation to Emerson and Whitman in the late 1880s.

The inevitable disjuncture between the periphery and center, and between the metropolitan translator's cultural position and that of writer, reader, and critic in the less powerful original language facilitates the harboring of hidden assets that enrich metropolitan reading at the expense of the periphery. As Pratt posits, the metropolitan reader is often unable to perceive or strategically ignores her or his debts because of "the emanating glow of the civilizing mission or the cash flow of development."[68] The real danger arises when the diminishment of the foreign original and of its theoretical and historical context gives rise to interpretations in the center that, in eager pursuit of a product, minimize the complicated or transgressive reactions of the dominated.

In contrast to the periphery's *impoverished invisibility*, the center's *lucrative invisibility* enables metropolitan theory to incompletely acknowledge sources from a geopolitically, culturally, and linguistically peripheral context. In the center's process of incorporating peripheral texts in different languages, the source culture negotiates from a weaker position; it trades on less favorable terms. In the case of the United States, predominant monolingualism means that translation mediates the entry of the peripheral perspective into circulation in English. The English monolingualism that predominates in American studies means we depend on translations, and U.S. Americanists may have limited mastery of a Latin American intellectual tradition.[69]

Because this book involves extensive translation of Latin American and Latino texts, I wish to make explicit my debts to a Latin American theoretical tradition. I also propose that we attend to what Martí's essays can and cannot say, or must say indirectly by drawing on the tactics of subterfuge such as figurative language, irony, allusion, parody, and mimicry. Martí does not merely repudiate or applaud U.S. cultural models; he translates them, and in a collective revolutionary process, his and others' impoverished invisibility becomes a protective space for clandestine action.[70]

By lucrative invisibility, I refer to the biases, blindnesses, and passions that inevitably impinge upon metropolitan translations of Latin American texts. The narrator of Cervantes's *Don Quixote*—who admits that he obtained the account of the great knight, his partner, his horse, and his lady by paying an unnamed Spanish-speaking Moor some pounds of raisins and wheat to translate an obscure text originally written in Arabic—attributes any falsehood in his text, as I noted above, to the original source and its translator's bias. With clear irony Cervantes first notes his narrator's failure to acknowledge the anonymous labor of the unnamed translator: "when he could and should have let himself go in praise of so worthy a knight, he seems deliberately to have passed on in silence; an ill deed and malicious, since historians are bound by right to be exact, truthful, and absolutely unprejudiced, so that neither interest nor fear, dislike nor affection, should make them turn from the path of truth, whose mother is history, rival of time, storehouse of great deeds, witness of the past, example and lesson to the present, warning to the future."[71] Cervantes's tongue-in-cheek evocation of the myth of the "absolutely unprejudiced" historian suggests that the only means by which that fickle mother, history, and her progeny, truth, are accessed is through politically mediated and inevitably biased interpretations. Turning to the storehouse and archive of history, the poorly paid Moorish translator and the original writer of the Arabic text reappear among the interpretive agents who make possible the text the reader has in hand. By placing in the foreground the blindnesses and insights concomitant with a position in the center, and by highlighting the reactions of the dominated, I wish to make plain the difference between my work as a researcher-translator and the insights of the nineteenth-century migrant Latino subject, Martí, for which I cannot take credit.

Herein lies a key distinction between *lucrative* and *impoverished* invisibility: the former has the power to interpret or embrace at will without accounting for its debts, while the latter responds heroically from a position of relative weakness, with little hope of recognition or compensation. To give one example, we might consider an essay on Martí and Whitman (Doris Sommer's "José Martí, Author of Walt Whitman") that presents a disconcerting scenario for Martí's "productive" embrace of Whitman: "Productive embraces tend to be mutual, even when they are not desired."[72] In other words, a powerful embrace will be mutual and reciprocal, whether effected by agreement or by force. In the name of productivity, the dominant may well force an undesired groping and a violation of the nondominant partner's will. Like a loan that extenuating hierarchies of scarcity and wealth make impossible to refuse, and yet undermine the borrower, such embraces impose themselves by force and ostensibly with the "consent" of the dominated.

Although both lucrative and impoverished·invisibilities are subterranean and inconclusive, there are key distinctions between them. In contrast to the lucrative invisibility of metropolitan theory, *impoverished invisibility* is the condition of the postcolonial, peripheral text as it bears the burden of economic and cultural debt and has little choice but to respond to the metropolis's looting of the periphery in secretive, unacknowledged forms. Silviano Santiago ominously closes his essay "Latin American Discourse:

The Space In-Between" with a description of the emergence of the "anthro-
pophagist" school of Brazilian modernism: "Somewhere between sacrifice
and playfulness, prison and transgression, submission to the code and
aggression, obedience and rebellion, assimilation and expression—in this
apparently empty space, its temple and its clandestinity, the anthropopha-
gous ritual of Latin American discourse is constructed."[73] For Santiago,
Latin American discourse must perforce define an alternative to a stark
binary of clearly delineated identities, of either total assimilation or pure,
autochthonous expression. Such a position demands tactics of camouflage
and clandestinity.

The following chapters examine the points of tension in Martí's writing
that disturb what seems to be—or is read as—his identification with North
American authors. Martí's divergence from these writers resonates with
recent scholarship on the complicity of Emerson, Whitman, and Helen
Hunt Jackson with empire and white racism. What happens when the
disembodied "seeing-man"—Pratt's allusion to Emerson's "transparent
eyeball"—is the articulator of both American cultural independence *and*
Anglo-Saxon cultural or imperial dominance?[74] How does the proximate
Latino migrant resident in New York transform this diffusionist model of
metropolitan culture? As peripheral Latino/a cultures begin to remake
urban centers into increasingly heterogeneous spaces, Martí's semiclandestine intervention eloquently gestures to innovative, peripheral practices
inside metropolitan culture. What would it mean for Martí, in the midst of
a paean to their memory, to cannibalize Emerson, Whitman, Helen Hunt
Jackson, and Buffalo Bill, and to counter their claims to the hemisphere or
to the West? The camouflaged location "in-between" makes these translations into a pivot and a point of departure for another America.[75]

Following Santiago, I suggest that despite—or perhaps because of—a
relatively weak position in relation to the triumphant, expansionist, and
exclusionary system of the United States in formation during the decades
of the Gilded Age, Martí's translations mark a defining moment in a Latino
American tradition and for "U.S." literature as such. Migrant Latino readings of metropolitan precursors have supplemented a colonizing logic, in
spite of their long-standing subordination, especially in texts awaiting entry into the visible record of literary history. The attention readers have
rightly directed to "Nuestra América" (1891) occludes a wider frame of
texts. See, for example, Martí's explicit repudiation of Latin American
cultural assimilation to or imitation of European and "Yankee" cultures:

"In our America there abound, out of pure spinelessness, out of pure ineptitude and second-handedness, out of pure impatience and tendency to imitate, the iberophiles, gallophiles, yankeephiles, those who know not the deep pleasure of kneading greatness with their own hands, those who have no faith in the country's own seeds, and those who order their souls ready-made from abroad, as they do their shoes and suits."[76] The neologisms "iberophiles," "gallophiles," and "yankeephiles" pertain to a fully formed and unstinting self-critique that Martí directs toward the Creole political and intellectual elite of Latino America, not out of despair, but in a spirit of exacting hope. Rather than propose a return to a pure autochthony, it relates a subjective cultural and aesthetic condition directly to the labor of kneading, cultivation, and confection. Martí includes North American "Yankee" modernity amongst the overdeveloped and expanding metropoles that desperately sought to export its mountain of surplus products to his America as part of an emerging neocoloniality. His critique of an imitative and otiose Creole elite represents the terminus of a critical arc that began a decade earlier and seeks to transform relations between the United States and Latin America.

The exporting of theory and consumer products (including literary styles and criticism) from Europe and the United States, as Brazilian Marxist critic Roberto Schwarz notes, imposes a condition of receptivity.[77] This idea emerges in Schwarz's influential essay "Nacional por subtração" (translated as "Brazilian Culture: Nationalism by Elimination"), which notes the influences of French philosophers and literary critics (he mentions Michel Foucault and Jacques Derrida) upon Santiago's concept of a "space in-between." The intellectual of the periphery on the receiving end of a constant diffusion of European or North American theory is distracted from thinking in a sustained fashion about processes and traditions in which Brazilian culture defines the center. To Santiago's claim that Latin American writers have been participating in the Latin Americanization of the center—which is one of the claims that I find most generative—Schwarz counters: "It remains to be seen whether this conceptual break with the primacy of origins would enable us to balance out or combat relations of actual subordination."[78]

Reading Martí as an ancestor to Santiago proves useful for responding to this specific concern, because Martí's literary form and his intervention in history record the vicissitudes of a spirit impelled to engage in direct action: this is what Julio Ramos has called Martí's "gift of poetry to war."[79]

The extended engagement with U.S. literature and culture that sets in motion the Latin Americanization of New York does not function only at the level of a conceptual break with origins. It feeds Martí's theorizing and organizing of a grassroots social movement for Cuban liberation that embraced decentralized cultural production, popular education, and the ideal of an antiracist participatory government. While Schwarz raises an urgent question about the weak link between poststructuralist theory and practice and rightly calls for Brazilian theory of and about Brazil's cultural history (nossa literatura), he also minimizes the potentially radical implications of the poststructuralist critique of origins as part of that program. Santiago's and many other postcolonial and Marxist appropriations of deconstruction and of Foucault reiterate the potential of these ideas for challenging relations of subordination.[80]

If the wave of popular rebellions and subsequent repression in Europe during 1848 forced a bourgeois class of Europe and North America to glimpse the nonuniversality of its perspective, as Schwarz claims, military and economic aggression toward Mexico the same year similarly exposed the specific interests of an emerging "white" and "middle-class" imperialist subject in the United States. According to Schwarz, the modernist text arises in Europe to represent bourgeois normality in a "state of siege," where words and texts house incompatible meanings, and thus present the social antagonism between the hopeful promises of Enlightenment and the very different, often clandestine, exceptions that such a narrative held for the enslaved, the annexed, and the working classes.[81] The profoundly insulting ridicule of the bourgeoisie that characterizes the modernism of Charles Baudelaire and Gustave Flaubert recurs in a new form with the simultaneous availability of these contrasting readings in a single, radically ambiguous text. For example, the *Memórias póstumas de Brás Cubas* (The Posthumous Memoirs of Brás Cubas) by the Brazilian novelist Joaquim María Machado de Assis, published in 1880 incorporates the conflicting perspectives and merciless yet precise mockery of the bourgeois culture that we see in Baudelaire and Flaubert's responses to the counter-revolutionary violence of their era. Similarly, Martí's condition as a deportee, as a Spanish-dominant speaker in an Anglo-dominant context, and as an economically vulnerable migrant with no guarantees that his life's work would not be in vain, mark his text and demand his reader's complicity in a still clandestine project. In the spirit of Flaubert, Baudelaire, and Machado de Assis, Martí's modernist writing seeks to awaken the reader.[82] This modernist alarm defines the tone of wonder and tragic despair that inspires his repeated figures of divine cadavers and of writers wandering alongside and occasionally peering into a proximate abyss, demanding of life its secret.

In his critique of the condition of receptivity, and of the overproduction in the United States that fuels it, Martí seeks to counteract John Quincy Adams's 1823 characterization of Cuba as an overripe fruit, "incapable of self-support" and inexorably bound to fall by the laws of physical gravitation into the lap of the United States. He also acknowledges the structural effects of Adams's imperial discourse on individual subjectivity and on a national culture. Intermixed within the current of information and advertisements flowing from New York to Latin America during this period, Martí's manuscripts moved centrifugally from the industrializing metropolitan center to readers throughout the hemisphere and beyond. His translations brush against the grain of the structure that enabled him to circulate his message, by making the center's viewpoint and imperfect self-perception visible to readers from the periphery. The Latino migrant's peripheral theorizing in the heart of the modernizing world exemplifies Lisa Lowe's and Paul Gilroy's claims that "critical" or "counter-" modernities do not remain hermetically outside the European and North American center and are not belated results of European culture, because these other modernities in fact enable and resource the center's culture.[83] As these conceptual fields come into contact and struggle in a way that transforms the center itself, Martí's texts and acts—and the critical tradition they help to engender—remap literary and political histories of American modernities.

❧ "THE JUNGLE IN NEW YORK'S PIANO":
TRANSCULTURATION, POSTCOLONIALITY,
AND MODERNIST FORM

The belated acknowledgment in the U.S. academy that a migrant from Latin America generated some of the earliest experiments in modernist writing in the Americas bears witness to the center's dawning awareness that the periphery conditions the center's economic and cultural livelihood. This idea inverts the customary relationship of power between the marginalized, yet highly mobile and innovative, migrant cultures of Latin America in the North and the comparatively static—and proportionally shrinking—yet still hegemonic "white" or European-identified culture in the United States. This shift signifies a desirable restructuring for some and an alarming threat to others.[84] Linking aesthetic form and political decolonization, Martí's translations chart a course for later theories of transculturation, which insist on multidirectional interactions across the imperial divide in the space of an asymmetrical contact zone. As we have seen in his prison diary, Martí's writing remembers and attends to painful colonial wounds.[85] His modernist prose incorporates a critical recounting of the afterlives of colonial violence.

Much as late nineteenth-century Latino migrant writing resonates with Caribbean and African American theories of double consciousness, Martí's vaticinations of a U.S. empire and his call for alternatives serve as a springboard for Latin American theories of transculturation and, with them, for postcolonial approaches to the Americas that increasingly inform conversations in U.S. American studies. By citing "Our America" (1891) in one chapter of her book, *Other Asias*, a leading postcolonial critic, Gayatri Chakravorty Spivak, gives José Martí a prominent role in a planetary genealogy of contemporary postcolonial theory.[86] By insisting on heterogeneity while staking a claim to a definition, Spivak articulates an anti-imperialist continental formation that quite radically ranges across an immense Asian expanse, with nations from Afghanistan to Vietnam, that includes but is not modeled on the assemblage of Asian America (including, we suppose, Canada, Brazil, Peru, Cuba, and others). In an interview with Tani Barlow ("Not Really a Properly Intellectual Response"), Spivak describes reactions to a litany that she gave at the end of a lecture on "Our Asias." Reading the names aloud of the forty-nine-odd countries that make up this enormously powerful grouping, a perhaps never before articulated constellation, Spivak lends weight to the broad momentum of another version of Asia, in which women take the lead. In her altered citation of Martí in *Other Asias* Spivak both revises a key weakness in Martí's project—his sexism—and affirms his prescient critique and translation of imperial modernity. Elsewhere, Spivak draws on Martí to urge literary comparatists to "look for our definition in the eyes of the other, as figured in the text."[87] Paraphrasing W. E. B. Du Bois's famous definition of doubleconsciousness, Spivak uses Martí to define a strategy for reimagining the discipline of comparative literature in planetary terms and from the perspective of the subaltern migratory or diasporic writer.

Spivak's discussions extend and elaborate upon Roberto Fernández Retamar's claiming of Martí for his non-European "third" world decades

ago.[88] It also places the Cuban in an extended tradition of resident nonciti-
zen writers who launch their critique from within empire.[89] What Spivak
defines as "the impossible 'no' to a structure, which one critiques yet
inhabits intimately" evokes the deconstructive and decolonizing impulse
behind the transculturation and translation in which Martí and others
engaged during decades of residence in New York.[90] Angel Rama, who
similarly formulates this paradox of postcoloniality in his theorizing of
transculturation as a narrative practice, enables us to see how Martí might
be an uncanny ancestor for some of today's most influential contemporary
postcolonial and Latin American theory.[91]

The Uruguayan critic Angel Rama, in his 1971 essay "La dialéctica de la
modernidad en José Martí" (Martí and the Dialectic of Modernity), explored the process that he defined a decade later as "narrative transculturation."[92] This term, which Rama adapts from the Cuban sociologist and
ethnographer Fernando Ortiz, denotes the incorporation of imposed, foreign materials and techniques to create a distinctly decolonizing narrative.
Rama's essay portrays Martí straddling epochs, cultures of Europe and the
New World, and literatures of North and South America. Rama uses the
poetic figure of enjambment (*encabalgamiento*), a word that in both the
original French and the English borrowing only obliquely captures the
galloping power of the Spanish term. Rama's choice of *encabalgamiento*
salutes the subject of his essay by imitating Martí's strategy of using multivalent figures to express Latin America's conflicted relation to modernity.
The word suggests the mounting of a horse, the overlapping of crossbeams
to create an architectural support, and the military carriage of guns. In a
poetic register, Martí's translation of imperial modernity into modernist
prose spills like a poetic idea over the line break and pours into the next
line, thus linking the two verses, two time periods, or two cultural zones.
Martí enjambs imperial modernity with the alternative that his revolution
would help usher in. His modernist form creates a support with atypical
forms of grounding; it overlaps with prior forms as it manifests a call to
arms.

Rejecting the idea that transculturation derives from Latin America's
exportation of rich "raw material," Rama aligns this narrative strategy with
a postcolonial politics. Transculturation is an "effort to bring about a
decolonization of the spirit, through the recognition of the capacities acquired by a continent in an already long and fecund inventive tradition."[93]
In Rama's adaptation, "transculturation" refers to a Latin American lit-

erary form that absorbs and remakes the colonial and imperial culture through a valorizing and self-reflexive examination of the technologies of America's subaltern cultures.[94] Transculturators, including Martí, do not merely provide raw cultural material to insert into existing modes of literary production. That is the task of the hack.[95] Rather, transculturation demands the creation of an alternative worldview, a language and a technique with which to decolonize, study, and revalue long-standing submerged knowledges. In this sense, the Latin American theory of transculturation directly anticipates the contemporary remapping of modernity as a conflictive, relational concept that refers to diverse mutually transforming cultural locations. In challenging the notion of the empire's autonomy and diffusion of culture to the periphery, transculturation belongs to a history of postcolonial theory, as Roman de la Campa has argued.[96]

Translating from Fernando Ortíz, Mary Louise Pratt introduced transculturation to readers of English as the process by which "subordinated or marginal groups select and invent from materials transmitted to them by a dominant or metropolitan culture."[97] This definition of transculturation as filtering and appropriating metropolitan techniques emphasizes the agency of subject cultures undergoing colonization. Angel Rama creates a traveling figure for modernism in his posthumously published collection of essays, *Las máscaras democráticas del modernismo* (1985): the figure of the "word-suitcase" (palabra-maleta), a well-worn portmanteau of new and transformed terms and phrases, the contents of which the writer-traveler carefully selects and jumbles together while packing quickly en route.[98] Rama's suitcase of modernism revises and translates Nietzsche's metaphor of a large standing wardrobe for the costumes and masks of postmonarchical European nations.[99] The suitcase's portability facilitates the contact and translation that give rise to modernist form. It brings into contact peripheral perspectives of especially Latino American migrants in the urban metropolis, an encounter of nonnative speakers with other languages and forms to which Raymond Williams attributes the beginnings of modernism.[100] Following Pratt's exemplary use of Latin American theories of decolonization to make a pointed self-critique of an exclusionary imperial modernity, I propose, in this book, translation as a specific mode of transculturation. Translation—in the metaphorical sense I'm using it here to refer to the migrant's negotiation of language and cultural difference—sets modernist literary form flowing against the centralizing and homogenizing pressure of empire.

Martí's furious February 1889 review of a sort of "French Mark Twain"—
as one of Paul Blouët's reviewers refers to him—formally binds together
transculturation and decolonization and thus looks forward to Rama and
Pratt. In introducing a newly published English translation of Blouët's
book to readers of Mexico's *El Partido Liberal*, Martí translates back to his
America the French writer's spoof on U.S. culture, entitled *Jonathan and
His Continent* (1889). Blouët's flippant portrait of an Anglo-American continent reaffirms Martí's point that North American culture should not
serve as a model for the new nations of his America. European-identified
interpreters and audiences willfully and naively ignore the "natural reversal" (reverso natural) of decolonization in America. To Martí, the arrival
of the refined instrument of European civilization, the piano, to the supposedly barbarous homelands of the Dakotas dramatically transforms
European culture and its instruments. Even though the recently arrived
European traveler does not want to see this necessary "reversal," the wild
Dakotas shape the European-derived culture of the city, New York:

> It is not the *lynch* of the primitive town dwellers; nor the *pílori* [adapted
> from the English *pillory*, for whipping post or stocks], which still endures;
> not the revolver, which is the mode of speaking in the West; nor the belief in
> witches, which abounds today; nor the ease of divorce, less ugly than the
> interested reasons for the marriages, that we should rub in the face [echarse
> en cara] of this people, which it is not yet fitting to judge as a definitive
> nation. Rather this nation is a house of peoples where we see civilization
> being acted out [fungiendo] at the same time in all its states, being born
> here, half formed there, over there showing off the sciences and the arts like
> new-bought toys. From this [house of peoples] come railroads and policies
> that impose on one of its diverse members the piano of New York in the
> jungle of Dakota, which the novice admires, and as a natural reversal [re-
> verso natural], although the novice does not want to see it, the jungle of
> Dakota in the piano of New York. . . . We have yet to see if this people, a child
> of liberty, is standing up to augment liberty or to oppress it. (*Obras*, 12:154;
> the first two emphasized words are in English and French in the original.)

This long paragraph lists the various practices that demonstrate the uncivi-
lized comportment of European American arrivants. Mob killing, public
humiliation, the settling of arguments with shotguns, superstition, and
witch hunts all undermine U.S. claims to be civilizing the "jungle" at
its periphery, specifically in the former Indian territories of the Dakotas

(where the militant Ghost Dancers, which Martí also brings to his readers' attention in 1890, would eventually be crushed by the U.S. Army) (*Obras*, 13:513). "Fungir" (to act) in Cuban and Puerto Rican usage connotes performance, as in the poor person who puts on bourgeois airs. The notion that the United States represents "advancement" seems laughable in light of multiple, half-formed, or ostentatious enactments that perform their roles in disjointed fashion, and unconvincingly. The supposed signs of advancement—science and the arts—circulate merely for show, like store-bought toys with which the purchaser has only superficial and recent familiarity. The country's pretense to civilization raises the key question that Blouët's essay inspires Martí to ask: what will the reader's response be to the possibility that the United States, which has inherited so much and claims to be the legitimate defender of liberty in the New World, may in fact restrict rather than augment freedom? Although Martí's modernism remembers, mourns, and criticizes the effects of the violent imposition of New York's piano on the jungle, it also affirms the jungle's traces in the aesthetics of New York's piano. In the chiasmus of the piano in the jungle and the jungle in the piano, deprivations of liberty meet with rebellion in the crossroads of these opposing trajectories, even though the "novice" will not want to see it.

Martí's acknowledgment and critique of "intellectual dependency" (*Obras*, 5:189) on colonial and foreign forms, his indictment of national elites' disdain for indigenous and African cultures, and the memorable self-deprecation of his America masquerading in a hodgepodge of fashions from Europe and the United States uncannily anticipate characters and concepts of postcoloniality of distant regions and of more recent historical provenance. Martí's oft-cited passage from "Nuestra América" that begins, "We were a masquerade" (Eramos una máscara) underscores his America's tendency to import and adorn itself with distant, globally ascendant cultures, all while wearing the rope sandals of the classical, indigenous American civilizations.

In the 1950s, on the other side of the world in postcolonial India, the hit song was "Mera jotta hai Japani" (Oh, my Shoes Are Japanese); it catalogued the mixture of foreign and imported styles in postcolonial India and inspired Salman Rushdie to create Saleem Sinai, the narrator of his novel *Midnight's Children*.[101] We might include Martí in the postcolonial tradition of what Rushdie calls "translated men," though not in Rushdie's sense, that the displaced writer must imagine a homeland by writing in the

English language, as if the metropolitan language, or the migrant's natural-ization for that matter, were ineluctable. Rather, Martí's postcoloniality absorbs and transforms the center from a partial, double, and globally "southern" perspective, without severing or closing off the space in be-tween. Like Anzaldúa, Spivak defines the space in between with the graphic metaphor of an open wound: she calls for "keep[ing] the fracture or wound open."[102] This refusal of suture describes a tactic for resisting mod-ish, sweeping theories that efficiently mesh with the precepts of global capitalism and that move too quickly past and often forget the trauma of the colonial period. In keeping with this attention to the still unresolved trauma of colonization, we have seen various ways that Martí's "I" (*yo*) is wounded or fractured and actively responds to the effects of geographic, cultural, and linguistic alienation inside the Anglo-dominant urban center. Keeping the wound open, in Spivak's phrasing, prevents the forgetting or disavowal of material and epistemic violence. Keeping the wound open enables the postcolonial subject in the Americas to perceive continuities between colonial legacies and imperial modernity.

Martí conjures this striking image of the hastily bandaged colonial wound in his modernist manifesto of 1882 to portray imperial modernity's binding terms of progress. In his prologue to Pérez-Bonalde's "Poema del Niágara," the rolls of bandage (*venda*) apply the legacies of the colonizer's books, prescriptive religions, and foreign political systems to the open, broken, sensitive skin below it. With these bandages, imperial nations pe-dantically "complete" the postcolonial nation's development when it is on the verge of independence: "Pretending to complete the human being, they interrupt him. He is hardly born when the philosophers—or the religions, the parents' passions, the political systems—are already standing over his cradle with thick, durable, prepared bandages [vendas] in their hands. And they swaddle; and they bind. Then, for the whole of his life on the earth, this man is a blinkered and bridled horse. Thus is the earth now a vast abode of masqueraders" (*Obras*, 7:230; *Selected Writings*, 49, translation modified). If we read this passage in terms of the extended metaphor of the nation as a babe in the cradle, still wrapped in swaddling clothes, this scene of a child surrounded by adult family members evokes the powerful older siblings or colonial parent-nations that would set the emergent nation under tutelage. The bandage takes on the dual role of sealing off the wound, blinding and muffling the nation's critical self-study, and of delimiting the growth of the new nation by applying a cast or mold. This bandaged nation parades in the mask of an imported modernity. These entrenched colonial legacies and half-hearted reformers would "remake prisons for modern man," and set themselves up as "prison guards of the mind" (alcaides de la mente) (*Obras*, 7:237; not included in *Selected Writings*). Keeping the wound open and exposing the tormented breast to the difficult and never completed task of translation serves as an antidote. To keep the wound open is to raise fists to the sky and demand of life its secret rather than accept the sly tutelage of these envious "owls that keep vigil at the newborn's cradle and drink from its golden lamp the oil of life" (*Obras*, 7:237). To keep the wound open means peeling away the bandages and exposing to the air of critical inquiry the bleeding sores incurred during the fight for independence. An open wound refuses the inherited solutions of foreign religions, human sciences, political systems, and frustrated passions of imperial cultures that would take over, and thus curtail, the self-emancipation of the postcolonial nation.

Martí's passage concerning those who stand around the new nation's cradle looks in two directions, toward the past and into the future, toward Europe and America, as it prefigures twenty-first-century postcolonial theory of the Americas and critically translates Alexis de Tocqueville's *Democracy in America*. While Tocqueville rightly observes that American democracy originates with "the prejudices, the habits [and] the ruling passions" of the European empires that stood around the cradle at the nation's birth, he believed in the civilizing effects of these imperial role models for fledgling democracies in America.[103] Martí's critical adaptation of this European master text on democratic government—one that conceives of liberty in the restricted terms of safeguarding of individual private property—illustrates what I mean more generally in this book by "translating empire." Tocqueville, whose work Martí cites in his notebooks and in his journalism from the 1880s, compares a nation's development to a child in its cradle in a chapter in *Democracy in America* entitled "Origin of the Anglo-Americans, and Importance of This Origin in Relation to Their Future Condition." In it, he implants the myth of America's European, and specifically Anglo origin, which he attributes to an incorrect cause: that "all the emigrants [to the U.S.] spoke the same language; they were all children of the same people" (1:29).[104] Tocqueville embraces what he discerns as the new Anglo-American society's "surface covering of democracy, beneath which the old aristocratic colors sometimes peep out" (1:47).

The colonized Cuban distanced himself from Tocqueville's lingering investment in preserving Europe's aristocratic privileges and in affirming a restricted definition of liberty. He figures these imperial inheritances as a "bridle," by which the "parent" nations attempt to restrict the new nation's growth. Taking phrases and metaphors directly from Tocqueville's text, Martí transforms the European legacy through a critical translation. Unlike Tocqueville, Martí defines the liberty of the modern person as arising from reflexive self-critique and study of the migrant's own torrential "nature," in an attitude of reflection that forms the basis for another aesthetic and political modernity: "The roots of the old poetry are in decay, shaken by the wind and the critical spirit; personal life is full of doubt, unsettled, questioning, restless, Luciferian; and the feverish inner life, dynamic, clamorous, not fully anchored, has become the principal and, with nature itself, only legitimate subject of modern poetry" (*Obras*, 7:229; *Selected Writings*, 48). As Spivak's postcoloniality would keep open the wound, Martí's modern poem takes as its muse the southern migrant's feverish, unanchored, windshaken doubt and critique. Luciferian translations of holy scripture aerate the very notion of an originating word with a critical force. These translations by Martí provide a glimpse of how to define the modern poem without presuming a tabula rasa or a garden in which the poet claims possession by renaming everything. "Nature" here, as Spivak has argued in a reading of Martí's essay on rural pedagogy, evokes the labor of culture and its transformation of the human. From the peripheral perspective of rural-to-urban migrants of the nineteenth and twentieth centuries, "nature" refers to the specific give-and-take relation between people and a specific place on the earth that refuses to passively repeat didactic phrases from Europe.[105]

At the end of his life, Martí characterizes the rhetorical quality of his difficult textual corpus as a jungle, and demands repeatedly that the North American reader too wander into it, and be absorbed by this seemingly impenetrable, transforming, pulsating prose.[106] The magnificent contribution of "Nuestra América" is to make it possible to read "America" from the Latino migrant's distinct linguistic, cultural, historical, and political position. The Spanish title, "Nuestra América," transforms the politically dominant Anglo-American inflection of "Our America." Reading with a literary imagination, we can see how a shift of "America" to the prior, now nondominant Latin American Spanish in the hemisphere, makes "other" the term that once described the unmarked "us."[107] This decentering of the source text—as for example, Tocqueville's European and monolingual Puritan America—also redefines the original. Reading through the eyes of the other opens an internal rift, the implications of which still move the field. Although always directed first to Latin American readers, Martí's larger project, consciously or not, continues to transform the way the Anglo U.S. culture thinks of itself and of its Spanish-speaking neighbors. Martí's translated obituaries of North Americans, ranging from Thomas Alva Edison to Wendell Phillips—to which I now turn—teach us to read across languages and through the eyes and ears of the Latino migrant.

La América with an Accent:
North Americans,
Spanish-Language Print Culture,
and American Modernities

As proof of our sincerity, our accent responds.
—**José Martí**, "Los propósitos de '*La América*'"

◄❦ THE FIRST LINES of José Martí's mani-
festo on modern poetics, which appeared as the prologue to Juan
Antonio Pérez Bonalde's *El Poema del Niágara*, stages a diaglogue
about poetry on a train: "Wait a minute, traveler! (¡Pasajero, de-
tente!). The poet I'm carrying in my hand is not stitching together
rhymes, nor repeating old masters. . . ." Print culture in Spanish in
the United States provided a forum for quotidian interactions and
shaped the social relations in which Martí developed a modernist
aesthetic that began to diverge from the ideals of pure originality, innocence, and progress that prevailed in nineteenth-century
North American literary culture. Félix de los Ríos, a Gallego, who
later joined the cause of the Cuban Mambises or independence
fighters, attributes his decision to enlist to an encounter with Martí
in 1894 on a train from Ocala, Florida, to New York, which began
with an inquiry about a Spanish-language magazine. A skinny man
with a graying mustache, dressed in a well-worn black suit that had
a tiny homemade corsage of colorful ribbons on the label, struck up
a conversation that de los Ríos recounts in his memoirs of the war:

The traveler, looking at my magazines, asked:
—Are you coming from Cuba?
I answered, yes.
—May I borrow one of these magazines?
I handed him both of them and I felt pleased to know that he spoke Spanish.[1]

Pérez Bonalde's poem and de los Ríos's magazines, *Saeta* (Arrow) and *El Nuevo Mundo* (The New World), belong to a print culture of magazines, books, and newspapers in Spanish that circulated across national borders and along routes of migration and exile. Sharing the common ground of a minor language helped to forge cultural and political affinities. In the case of Félix de los Ríos, the intense conversation that began with the borrowing of two magazines led him to become a volunteer in Cuba's war of independence. A Spanish-language print culture with a history dating to the early nineteenth century in various urban centers in the United States became, in 1880s New York, a vehicle for the articulation of Martí's modernist form and a primary medium in which he developed critical translations of empire.

This chapter examines the formal strategies that someone in Martí's position, in New York and of the Americas, might deploy in order to navigate the Anglo-dominant milieu in which he landed in 1881 and where he found it necessary to remain for the next fourteen years, until his return to Cuba in 1895. Exemplifying a "surreptitious agility for survival" that Nancy Morejón attributes to Cuba's "deep Africanity," the maneuvers of a migrant in interpreting north to south and vice versa generate a modernism attuned to and expressive of the Latino migrant condition, while ostensibly discussing "North Americans."[2] As Arcadio Díaz Quiñones notes, Martí's translation of the North American culture, from a position "between empires" and between languages, sharpens the definition of his aesthetic and political projects.[3]

I draw on examples of Martí's navigation of the gap between languages in this bilingual, migrant print culture from the first half of the 1880s in New York to show how crossing languages denaturalizes a key medium of culture and makes it possible to see, in Giambattista Vico's words, "that the world of civil society has certainly been made by men, and that its principles are therefore to be found within the modifications of our own human mind."[4] Vico's secular and modern proposition that cultures and civilizations are human-made suggests that language provides access to the means to make change. Access to multiple languages facilitated Martí's subterfuge within an Anglo-dominant context. The three Martisian "texts" that will concern us here circulated in bilingual newspapers or in bound volumes published by small Spanish-language presses in New York. They exemplify how Martí transformed the limited visibility of Spanish into a space of clandestine rebellion. Writing in his unusual literary style in the monthly paper entitled *La América*, Martí helped forge an alternative to Enrique Piñeyro's *El Mundo Nuevo / La América Ilustrada* and to other hemispheric or continental magazines of the period. In particular, a series of newspaper chronicles intended for a bound volume to be entitled "Norteamericanos" (North Americans) and a prologue to a short-story chapbook by Rafael Castro-Palomino Jr., *Cuentos de hoy y mañana* (Stories of Today and Tomorrow) (1883) develop distinct criteria for another American modernity. The inadequacy of existing cultural and political forms stimulates Martí's commitment to education of the largest, nonelite sector as a social component of a broader revolutionary transformation. In contrast to Castro-Palomino, his editor and predecessor at *La América* and as a New Jersey-based spokesperson for the Cuban community in exile, Martí preserved a utopian commitment to collective transformation of the individualism, amnesia, and persistent colonial attachments he encountered in the mainstream United States. Martí's Latino modernism moves not only across languages but also across the gap between the existent and the possible to stress the role of the imagination as a force for creative political change.

By print culture I refer to the making and circulating of texts and to their contributions to an imagined community, as defined by the geographic scope, relations of exchange, and the mass production of printed text.[5] The nonimmigrant resident who carries meanings from one culture and language to another contributes to a print community that adheres to different assumptions from that of an assimilationist "immigrant press."[6] When migrant journalism critically translates U.S.-dominant texts, it generates an uncommon and prescient definition of Anglo America as incomplete and partial, even provincial, despite this sector's aspirations during these years to a hemispheric leadership role in the name of universal but never quite egalitarian values.

꧁   WHOSE CONTINENT? HOW CAME IT YOURS?
A BILINGUAL *LA AMÉRICA* AND OTHER
EARLY TRANSAMERICAN PRINT JOURNALISM

The first periodical that Martí edited in New York, *La América: Revista de Agricultura, Industria y Comercio* (America: A Review of Agriculture, Industry, and Business) reveals a strategic use of bilingualism and translation. Through traversing and exploiting the gap between languages and by selectively translating across it, Martí orchestrates a takeover of the U.S.-funded publication apparatus of this New York–based industrial advertiser and magazine of modern culture. Through articles and illustrations of technology and metropolitan industrial products, *La América* introduced readers of Spanish throughout the Americas to conflicting modernities, in two languages. Martí contributed essays, editorials, and advertising copy to this publication as a staff writer from March through November 1883, and as editor from December 1883 through at least July of 1884.[7] The magazine translated imperial modernity by explaining new machines and emerging technology on exhibition in urban centers of Paris and New York, in excerpts and analysis of writings by Charles Darwin and Herbert Spencer, in news selections from the U.S. press, and in detailed, literary accounts of engineering feats such as the Brooklyn Bridge.

During his association with *La América*, José Martí redirected it away from its U.S. funders' objectives and toward the needs and interests of a Hispanophone transamerican print community, which increasingly included a working-class and non-European perspective during these years. As a monthly showcase for U.S. technology and industry, *La América* functioned as a direct appendage to the market. Its wide focus meant that it mediated the increasing north-south economic, political, and cultural exchange in the hemisphere. In his early years of exile in the United States, while he was writing for *La América*, Martí initiated a polemical redefinition of America as América, with a Spanish accent. Through Martí's editorial intervention, the magazine and other migrant Latino writing from this period wrestled to form a judgment of U.S. modernity from a location in between languages and in figurative language that attends to the complexity of the social relations in distinct linguistic contexts. In one of his writings that survives as a fragment, Martí affirms this formal creativity in his America: "It is clear that la Am. [*La América*] can create and is creating a new language" (*Obras*, 22:143).

Through a comparison of *La América* under its first two editors and in relation to competing periodicals of the period, we shall see how Martí's innovations in literary form and cultural analysis began as a task of translation. While scholars have demonstrated how Martí's innovative writing in unconventional venues such as *La América* founded a hybrid Spanish American literary genre, *la crónica* (the chronicle), and helped to initiate Hispanic modernismo, in addition to launching a Latin American tradition of interdisciplinary cultural critique, the bilingual context of these new forms' emergence has not been explored.[8] By making science, politics, industry, technology, modernity, and mass culture topics for literary and cultural analysis, *La América* expanded the cultural critic's field. The crossing of disciplinary boundaries and the poetic treatment of technology mimic the work of translation insofar as both defamiliarize and redefine the object of literary-critical interpretation.[9]

Drawing on Walter Benjamin's theory of translation, we might say that only by "coming to terms with the foreignness of languages" can the reader fully appreciate how Martí turned *La América* from its original purpose.[10] The incomplete translatability and the divergence between the monolingual English sponsors' goals and the Spanish-language editors' content made this magazine an ideal place to foment Latino interpretation and clandestine revolutionary politics. According to its English-speaking readers, the magazine sought solely to assist sponsoring U.S. export companies to sell their products to Latin America's modernizing elites. By reimagining the term "América" (with accent) in his Spanish-language articles, Martí brings into relief the Anglo-dominant culture's not fully visible designs for the hemisphere. Putting into practice the philosophy of relation that we saw in his early notebooks, this translational process lays the cornerstone for the overtly revolutionary project that figures in Martí's late journalism and speeches nearly a decade later.

Before articulating a critique of imperial modernity, Martí embraced a New Worldist discourse that he inherited from an earlier generation of proindependence Cuban exiles in New York. Many of Martí's older proindependence colleagues and former classmates fled to New York after the outbreak of the 1868 war and contributed to the glossy monthly *El Mundo Nuevo: Revista Ilustrada de Ciencias, Artes, Literatura, Educación, Industria, Comercio, Etc., Etc.* (The New World: Illustrated Review of Sciences, Arts, Literature, Education, Industry, Commerce, Etc., Etc.) (1871–75), edited by the Cuban journalist Enrique Piñeyro.[11] Contributors to the magazine represented a broad spectrum of political views: they ranged from the Cuban annexationist and eventual U.S. State Department translator

José Ignacio Rodríguez to the militant separatists Francisco and Antonio Sellén.[12] Each of these writers had published translations, poetry, and essays in Havana's leading magazines.[13] Piñeyro's autonomism or toleration of alternatives to Cuba's national sovereignty resonated with *El Mundo Nuevo / La América Ilustrada*'s publication of traditional, European-influenced poetic forms and articles that privileged Euro-American origins of New World cultures.[14] Unlike Martí, who defined his America in terms of its cultural differences from the dominant Anglo culture of the United States, Piñeyro's magazine encouraged mimicry of the northern nation. As Kirsten Silva Gruesz has noted, *El Mundo Nuevo* anticipates Martí's distinct articulation of a supranational and oppositional print culture, with the crucial difference that Martí's transamericanism was to articulate a more trenchant critique of the Gilded Age's stratification along lines of color, class, and culture.[15]

   In contrast to a smooth map of the hemisphere organized according to language groups, Martí's literary journalism on the United States posits linguistic links across the rocky and multilingual terrain of inter-American conflict. Piñeyro's magazine characterizes itself as a textual link between the U.S.-based Latino migrant or exile community and the rest of the Spanish-speaking world: "we propose to serve as the link among the dispersed flowers of our literature."[16] *El Mundo Nuevo* cultivates readers who are sensitive, cosmopolitan purveyors of poetry and music, and who advocate charity as the best means to address social contradictions. This readership opposes slavery but endorses the North's civilizing mission in the U.S. South.[17] By contrast, *La América* initiates Martí's divergence from a stodgy, Europeanist, and counterrevolutionary Latin American elite that would segregate art and literature from history, economics, technology, and social politics. Ironically, this argument emerges in the compromised forum of a magazine ostensibly dedicated to promoting the sale of U.S. technology and products to Latin Americans.

   Piñeyro's New Worldism adopts a hemispheric perspective in the spirit of Alexis de Tocqueville's claim that class strife is an Old World problem that does not pertain to the New World. Published by the enormous New York house of Frank Leslie, *El Mundo Nuevo*'s first issue in May 1871 features scenes of the Paris Commune on its cover, including a bare-breasted woman waving the red banner of the workers' republic and singing atop a Montmartre café table with revolutionary bohemians cheering at her feet. This display of the events of 1871 in Paris reveals little sympathy for the Communards' revolutionary aspirations. In an unsigned paragraph about the cover art, the editor responds with common civilized disgust for the "vile multitudes":[18] the scene "symbolizes a political orgy."[19] Although Piñeyro's magazine is critical of the United States and of Europe for their lack of concern for the Cuban Creoles suffering from Spanish abuses, *El Mundo Nuevo* distances itself from the insurrection of Europe's impoverished masses and favors restoration of bourgeois stability and European culture. By contrast, Martí begins to question the prior generation's values.

Like Martí's Cuban predecessors at *El Mundo Nuevo*, Albion Tourgée's Philadelphia-based magazine *Our Continent* (1882–84) claims that western hemispheric values are "original" and argues that abundant "empty" space for individual realization of ambition make Communard-style class conflict unnecessary in America. Tourgée's English-language inter-American weekly overlooks the class implications of racial violence and growing worker unrest in the United States.[20] Coedited by the native Americanist Daniel G. Brinton and the Philadelphia news publisher Robert S. Davis, the first issue features a representative essay entitled "Americanism vs. Anglicism," which associates "a peculiar and distinctive American individuality —a life that is not English by imitation or inheritance," with freedom from "the rigorous rule of caste."[21]

In *Our Continent*, the United States takes the form of a biological organism, in which a "northern" mind controls a "southern" body and its resources. In an article entitled "Capital and Labor," the hard-working stomach looks to capital "for its support and reward and the [stomach and the rest of the body] must bow in acknowledgement to brains for a wise system and a careful provision of the interest of all three" (May 10, 1882). This corporeal figure of brains and stomach naturalizes an arbitrary arrangement in which body depends upon head and not vice versa. This common mind-over-body figure represents the sector of laborers as voracious, unthinking consumers, driven by appetites, and suggests that the brain may live independently of the stomach and body. The metaphor gives the illusion of harmonious hierarchy between the head of capital and body of labor, where capital safeguards and benefits labor. Rather than acknowledge the mutual dependency and distinct priorities of capital and labor, *Our Continent* forecloses the possibility of recognizing the structural differences between them.

Tourgée's image for the suppression of class contradiction echoes an influential ideological model set out by the Speaker of the U.S. House of Representatives and founder of the Whig Party, Henry Clay, in his arguments in favor of U.S. participation in Bolívar's congress on March 24, 1818. A Kentucky statesmen and orator known for his hawkish tendencies, Clay uses the head and body metaphor to describe a hemispheric system, in which a southern body awaits a northern, Anglo brain's wise and generous direction: "We [the United States] were the natural head of the American family."[22] Translating this hierarchy into a literary framework, Tourgée's *Our Continent* published literature almost exclusively by British and North American writers. Focusing on "American English" and the "Anglo-Saxon race," the magazine excluded other linguistic and cultural traditions in the hemisphere:[23] "'Our Continent' is for the New World that is the Old."[24] Even as it reproduced anthropological reports on cultural artifacts of "Indian Legends," Peruvian ceramics, and Mexican railroads, the magazine celebrated the supposedly Greco-Roman roots of Anglo-Saxon culture.[25] Tourgée, whom we remember in U.S. cultural history for his dissenting argument in the landmark segregation case *Plessy v. Ferguson*, reveals here his privileging of the Anglo cultural presence on the continent over Amerindian, African, Latino American, and Asian influences. Martí, who located American origins in ancient Incan and Mayan civilizations, which he later famously called "our Greece," challenged the common assumption of a singularly British cultural origin of America.[26]

༒ TRANSLATION AND BETRAYAL IN *LA AMÉRICA*

In contrast to both Piñeyro's New Worldism and Tourgée's Anglo-centered continentalism, Martí's print journalism represents a pivotal turning point in Americanist interpretation of Europe's legacy as benign and generous. Martí rejected the common assessment of Europe's cultural and political legacy within America's hybrid nations. Francisco Gonzálo Marín, eloquent Puerto Rican bohemian and Sotero Figueroa's adopted son, who was to die in a mangrove swamp while fighting for Cuban independence, defines Martí in dramatic opposition to Christopher Columbus in the last lines of his poem entitled simply "Martí":

> Colón es quien la esclaviza
> y Martí quien la liberta!
> (Columbus enslaves [the island]
> and Martí frees her).[27]

Transforming the conventionally celebratory interpretation of Columbus as discoverer, the poem evokes the destruction of original communities and importation of Africans as slaves to extract wealth for the primary benefit of Europeans and their descendants in the Americas. Insofar as the European colonial legacy persists in America's republics, it provokes a fissure *within* the hemisphere and within its diverse national groupings.

From a New Worldism that prizes the whole hemisphere and its pre-Columbian civilizations over Europe's "pale and puny" books (*Obras*, 7:198), Martí's understanding of the United States and of America enters into crisis shortly after he returns from Venezuela to reside in New York in 1881.[28] His contributions to *La América* reveal the increasing instability of the term "America" during these early years in Latino print culture. In some notes for a series of articles that he planned to include in *La América*, Martí sounds out a transamerican regionalism, but with the new concern that North America's influence was becoming as pernicious as European legacies. The irruption of multiple definitions of America parallels his growing suspicion of U.S.-led imperial modernity. The anaphoric structure of the following lines from a fragmentary and undated set of notes emphasizes North America's similarity to Spain and France and indicts their betrayal of Hispanic America:

> On Spanish influence in Hispanic America.
> On French influence in Hispanic America.
> On North American influence in H.A.
> Against this betrayal—on guard. Against this betrayal of America and of the American spirit, against this betrayal of our suffering, of our traditions, that some of these people still profess to love only so that their perfidy or their myopia might not reveal itself too clearly. For many err due to the short range of their intellectual vision and not from evil intentions. Against this betrayal of our spiritual constitution and of even our physical constitution, of our nature—on guard. (*Obras*, 23:43)

The insistent use of the vocable "America" (often without the modifier "Latino" or "Hispanic") in this passage reveals Martí's sense of the inadequacy of "H.A.," for the modifier "Hispanic" privileges a Spanish colonial legacy over America's pre-Columbian civilizations and, as we learn from other writings, ignores centuries of the African diasporic presence in the New World. Through myopia or malice, America's professed "lovers" threatened to erase centuries of indigenous rebellion and African maroonage. To fail to respect and recognize America's particular hybrid "nature"—as a result of the continent's long history of contact and violence—is to collaborate in the perfidy of the false or "feet-kissing ultra-Hispanics" (ultrahispanos besalospies") (*Obras*, 23:43). With this harsh neologism for Latin Americans who identified more with colonial Spain and a European legacy than with their own hybrid peoples, Martí imagines how Hispanism could become and ally of a new U.S. imperialism.

The shift toward a split within the Americas mirrors a tension between Spanish- and English-language interests in the bilingual magazine *La América* and in its affiliated clearinghouse for U.S. exporters, the American Agency of New York. Owned by the Cuban Enrique Valiente, the agency functioned as a "permanent exposition" and an intermediary between Latin American consumers and North American manufacturers. Founded in February of 1881, just as Washington was gearing up for the first Pan-American conference (which was derailed by the assassination of President Garfield), the magazine and agency together would overcome obstacles of time, distance, language, and lack of knowledge.[29] The agency sought to make accessible information about export products to "peoples of the Latin race" (*La América*, April 1882).[30] Its principal branch in Havana exhibited the newfangled machines, appliances, tools, utensils, and articles in extravagant salons, and it deluged Latin American readers with images of these objects in attractive catalogues.[31] The agency procured subscriptions and coordinated the distribution of the magazine to its representatives in sixty-two cities in Latin America, two cities in Spain, and to readers in the United States, in addition to fulfilling orders through U.S.-based commission houses.[32] The combined initiative helped U.S. manufacturers "to more effectively reach all Spanish American buyers" (*La América*, April 1882).[33]

The magazine's stated goals, in English and Spanish, in the template header that defined the magazine throughout its existence contradicted each other, even though they appeared next to each other as ostensible translations. The English-language statement defines *La América* as a "monthly review devoted exclusively to the development of the Export Trade of the United States with all Spanish-speaking countries. In furtherance of this object, it will contain articles about the products of American factories, compiled from standard authorities, with a supplement in English, when necessary, giving manufacturers and merchants of *this country* information which will materially aid them in the introduction of their goods" (emphasis added).[34] In this version, "America" and "this country" refer to the English-speaking United States. Although the magazine claims not to involve itself directly in selling U.S. technology in Spanish-speaking markets, the terms of address interpellate its readers as technologically minded potential buyers of North American products. The English editorial header does not indicate that the magazine also included material of a different kind: a review of Hubert Bancroft's history of California, essays on Julian Hawthorne, a study of *Buffalo Bill's Wild West Show*, and reports on the Latino community's cultural gatherings in New York.[35] In short, the English announcement unapologetically promotes diffusion of knowledge and products from the North southward, while the profits would remain in the North with the manufacturers. Martí's involvement in this magazine models a complex strategy, where language crossing provides the subterfuge through which he theorizes America differently.

During the course of Martí's involvement with and leadership of the magazine, *La América*'s official editorial goals changed in a way that made references to the United States as the referent for the sign "America" into a symptom of shortsightedness. In addition to lowering the cost of the magazine to make it more accessible to nonelites, the new editor announced the magazine's goal of interpreting with an eye to define his America's interests. *La América* asserted a divergence between the cultural identity and economic interest of each America.

The description of the magazine's purpose in Spanish under the first editor, Rafael Castro-Palomino, claims for the magazine the humanitarian goals of enlightening Latin America with U.S.-originated technological brilliance. Agricultural, trade, and industrial products from the United States appear to benefit Latin American peoples and U.S. exporters alike. The first edition of *La América* refers in Spanish to "a monthly publication dedicated to the fomentation of agriculture, industry and commerce in Hispanic American countries."[36] Whereas the English description promises exclusive profits to the U.S. export trade, the Spanish version dedicates the magazine to Hispanic American development. The unidirectional spread of U.S. products appears as a progressive force. The Spanish version promises aid to Hispanoamericans sitting in darkness through the miraculous introduction of foreign enlightenment. This northern-led model of progress appears as a powerful, unstoppable force of heat and light: "The flame of this progress that today illuminates the great North American nation can be communicated if we do not avoid contact with it: full of faith, we will alight our humble torch in this flame in order that it may be passed, hand to hand, to all the peoples of Latin America" (*La América*, April 1882). The fire imagery of the Spanish sentence effaces the Anglo investors' profit motive by suggesting a natural or random cause for the flame's hungry movement and by hiding the sponsors' direct interest in conquering markets and igniting consumer desires. The gap between the interests of North and South America shrinks as the fire spreads. If the numerous advertisements for North American electrical lights are any indication, U.S. companies planned to reap significant income through the dissemination of light.

A second metaphor in this first issue suggests that a key point of tension between Castro-Palomino and his successor, Martí, turned on their different conceptions of translation. In a feature that sounds like an editorial, entitled "Nuestro Programa" (Our Program), the magazine offered readers the instantaneous reproduction of "the latest words that Civilization . . . printed in the great book of Progress" (2). The editorial program conceived of *La América* as efficiently and uncritically translating a single, predetermined modern future, toward which all peoples trudge from savagery to civilization. Translation, in this instance, does not involve critical judgment and creative transformation so much as an objective, transparent reproduction. Like Tourgée, and in keeping with his Spencerian positivism, Castro-Palomino embraced a diffusionist modernity that would restructure the other America according to a hierarchy of functions within an expertly designed social body.

Rafael Castro-Palomino Jr. was the son of a Cuban proprietor of a stable in Manhattan and had lived for more than two decades in the New York metropolitan area, acting for many years as spokesperson for the migrant community that Martí joined in 1880. In addition to contributing to or directing various newspapers, including *El Avisador Cubano* and *El Avisador Hispano-Americano*, Castro-Palomino served as secretary of the Asociación Cubana de Socorro (Cuban Aid Society) and of the Sociedad Literaria Hispano-Americana de Nueva York (Hispanic American Literary Society of New York) during the same period when Martí was president of these organizations. Castro-Palomino was a painter, and his book of poetry, *Preludios* (Preludes) (1893), evokes the melancholy despair that also characterizes his short stories.[37]

Castro-Palomino's vision for redefining "Industry" authorizes a new elite made up of social scientific experts who divide, classify, and reorga-

Rafael Castro-Palomino Jr., Cuban migrant and spokesperson within the proindependence movement, editor of Spanish-language newspapers in New York, author of short stories and poetry, and resident for many years of Hoboken, New Jersey. Photograph from *Preludios* (1893), by permission of Harvard University.

nize the liberal professions according to rationalizing demands. Another article that reveals these priorities, "Industria" (Industry), features a Spencerian blueprint in which experts interpret society as a complex organism determined by natural laws, the definition of which mere social actors do not have the capacity to alter.[38] Castro-Palomino's social scientific model endorses the authority of the professional; Martí, on the other hand, observes and applauds a decentralized and democratizing practice of social theory and criticism.

Having already engaged in philosophical debates in Havana against positivist realism, Martí opposed the passive reception of imported, expertly administered laws that sought to update, rather than deconstruct, colonial legacies.[39] Whether Martí joined the publication apparatus of *La América* out of stealth, naiveté, or necessity, he subverted the original proprietor's promises to North American manufacturers while maintaining the English editorial template as a protective cover. In December 1883, *La América* announced the appointment of Martí as the new editor, and the imminent arrival of new owners: the *La América* Publishing Company and its proprietor, Ricardo Farrés, who would foster what Martí had previously carried out without explicit editorial sponsorship. Under Martí, *La América* delineated distinct Latin and North American interests as Martí discouraged purchases from "the greedy foreigner" and encouraged his readers to share information about quality and means to access Latin American products.[40] Identifying appropriate technology for Latin American contexts, translating technological information of use to Latin American industries, and blowing the whistle on illegal or dangerous products sold below legal health standards to Latin American consumers, the review abandoned its "pretense to being a publication of advertisements" (*Obras*, 28:214).[41] Ever gallant, Martí did not neglect to profusely thank the North American firms whose advertising funds provided the overhead to permit Martí to realize his long-cherished dream of defending his America's interests through print journalism. Acting as his America's interpreter, he achieves an assiduous deconstruction of the original enterprise from within.

With Martí at the helm and a slightly longer title in the masthead, *La América: Revista Mensual de Industria, Comercio, Agricultura e Intereses Generales Hispanoamericanos* (Monthly Review of Industry, Commerce, Agriculture and General Hispanoamerican Interests) departed from the former editor's Spencerian evolutionary realism and criticized the prior generation's segregation of art and technology. The January 1884 notice to *La América*'s readers clarifies its aim of cultural critique, by negatively referencing Piñeyro's purely artistic agenda: "The times demand something more than factories of the imagination and beautiful schemes. You can see in all the faces and all the countries, symbols of the epoch, hesitation and anguish—The entire world is today an immense question" (*La América*, January 1884; *Obras*, 8:266). To say that critical wonder before a new epoch must begin with a creative interpretation of the anguished and confused faces of migrants retains a literary quality, but its preoccupation is decidedly worldly. The new version of the magazine examined imperial modernity's effects for vulnerable migrants, working-class and racialized groups in the North, and for distant Latin American homelands. Martí continues here to subordinate an expository, informational function of his chronicles to interpretive reflection, in keeping with his 1875 travel writing about Paris.[42] Acknowledging the impossibility of an unbiased translation and the fruitlessness of exposition without interpretation, the magazine under Martí alerts its readers to the "times" that catalyzed distinct American modernities and calls them "not a jot less than critical."[43] The epochal changes under way demanded a critical translation of science, technology, history, culture, politics, and "Hispanoamerican interests," rather than a belletrist enchantment or a scientific copy of a U.S. product.[44]

La América, Revista Mensual
de Industria, Comercio,
Agricultura e Intereses
Generales Hispanoamericanos,
published in New York. Edited
by Rafael Castro-Palomino Jr.,
1882–83, and José Martí,
December 1883–July 1884.
By permission of the Centro de
Estudios Martianos, Havana.

In contrast to *El Mundo Nuevo*'s scant sympathy with revolutionary remedies for working-class miseries, *La América* under Martí anticipates Cuba's subsequent revolutionary project by defining a North-South grid of power in the hemisphere. His articles reveal a dark underside of the diffusionist modernity that Castro-Palomino sought to spread. And whereas Castro-Palomino propagated Latin America's voluntary incorporation into the "light" of North American models, Martí shows how the North's seeming monopoly on innovation could block Latin America's independence. The following passage clarifies Martí's sense of the disunited state of the Americas:

At the moment when both hemispheres are drawing together and asking mutual questions, *La América* arrives to act as an intermediary and explicator . . . for the anxious and embryonic greater America, to introduce the products that with the seasoning and sacred salts of liberty, have accelerated the maturation of Anglo-America to a marvelous degree. . . . To define, to warn, and to put on guard and to reveal the secrets of the seemingly—and

only seemingly—marvelous success of this country; to promote, with timely
and detailed explications and studies of applicable advances, the achievement of an equal—or perhaps greater, yes, greater and more lasting—success
in our own countries; to say to Latin America all that she longs for and needs
to know about this country that justly worries her, and to say it . . . for a
greater general benefit, . . . There are benefits, just as there are dangers that
come with the inevitable intimacy of the two sections of the American
Continent. The intimacy announces itself to be close at hand, and in some
points so sweeping, that there may be barely enough time to stand up, to see
and to describe its force. . . . As proof of our sincerity, our accent responds.[45]

The series of infinitives in this impassioned statement of purpose translate
the kernel of musings in Martí's notebook draft into a public proposal to
inscribe and affirm America's distinct accent against North America's implacable demand for intimacy. Here, the two hemispheres clearly do not
refer to Old and New Worlds. A fracture zigzags between North and South,
English and Spanish, and "Saxon" and Hispanic colonial legacies. To "define, to warn, and to put on guard" are acts that name an emerging relation
along a shifting multivalent North-South border.[46] The passage predicts
the mutual curiosity of northern and southern sections of the continent,
the North's desire, and the South's need for an interpreter. Martí makes
clear that the North's entreaty for intimacy poses a threat so worrisome and
so imminent that he fears that his curious readers may not be able to
recognize it in time. Martí attributes Anglo-America's accelerated growth
and astonishing technological development to the North's longer postcolonial experiment and capital accumulation. He observes the imminent impact, and calls for caution, as the rapid success of the United States might
be short-lived.

La América takes on the role of critically assessing the seeming marvels
of the North in order to emphasize the distinctive creative potential of the
South, which would eventually produce superior, more lasting results. This
translation advocates the equal or more stable success of a hospitable
"Latino nation" (nación latina"), which Martí refers to as "the United
States of South America" (Obras, 8:266).[47] This new federation would
extend from the Río Bravo to Patagonia (Obras, 8:319), but presum-
ably would not exclude Martí himself and other Latino migrants living in
the North. As intermediary and explicator, Martí's La América features
Spanish-language translations from North American magazines, including
The Century Illustrated, Harper's, North American Review, and the Popular

Science Monthly, so as to give readers insights into North American perspectives and prejudices.[48] Recognizing that translation cannot be objective, this statement of the magazine's aim asserts Martí's first obligation: to interpret the Anglo-American North for the benefit of the Latino South.

Written by someone who frequently walked through the city and who belonged to the influx of furious or yearning migrants to New York's Ellis Island, *La América*'s accounts of modernization shift the reader's location from the Latin American elite consumer of U.S. technology to Latino migrants who may suffer that technology's effects. Martí draws on a keen sense both of the power of technology and of its failures to address social needs. He uses a verb that becomes emblematic of his absorbing and resignifying of North American literature and culture so as "to glimpse" (entreverse) a distinct future:[49] "It is possible to make out [se entrevé] the Greater America; we sense the joyful voices of the workers; we feel a simultaneous movement, as if the shells of new drums were calling us to a magnificent battle" (*Obras*, 8:297). To the rhythm of beating drums, the new *La América* represents an alternative to either a Europe- or a U.S.-directed hemisphere.

Martí's contributions to *La América* make the divisions between the beneficiaries and nonbeneficiaries of modern technology starkly palpable. In his powerful study of the construction of the Brooklyn Bridge (*La América*, June 1883), Martí comments on the massive loss of workers' lives in the long and intense construction process.[50] Similarly, in a brief notice of an exhibition on hygiene in the areas of clothing, dwelling, school, and workplace, Martí depicts workers in scandalously dehumanizing conditions, which prompt an outburst of righteous anger: "They suffer so much! They expend so much energy! They are repaid so poorly!" (*Obras*, 8:437). Departing from *La América*'s original sales catalogue tone, Martí's report admonishes employers and champions workers' rights. Lowering the subscription price of the magazine to $1.50 per year put into practice the new editor's desire to reach a broader readership and to create a strong base for awakening "our Republics to the knowledge of their faculties and faith in themselves" ("La Suscripción a *La América* a $1.50," May 1884; *Obras*, 28:229). After elaborating a list of noxious dusts and fumes that workers inhale on the job, Martí offers a closing non sequitur that sounds desperately ironic: "The glory of our century is that since the times of Jesus, never has human love been so ardent or fruitful" (*Obras*, 8:438). Technology that fails to promote social justice, or that punishes workers in order to benfit employers represents a problem for Martí's *La América*. Technology ought rather to awaken the critical faculties of the mass of citizens, the group best poised to bring about revolutionary change and to constitute a representative government.

During the course of his association with *La América*, Martí shifted from an early New Worldist rhetoric to an articulation of and translation between distinct interests within the Americas, a commonplace that defines America today so pervasively that it is difficult to imagine the earlier time when it was possible to think of America as one. In the first five years of residence in New York, Martí was developing a critique of mistaken assumptions about the United States that had also been his. By 1889, Martí makes fun of the naive first-impression of a fresh migrant: "Neither the gossip column, nor grumbling envy, nor rickety antipathy, nor the admiration of the recently arrived is an appropriate measure of a nation such as this."[51] With a hint of self-reproach, Martí struggles to find an appropriate medium in which to express the stormy modes of his consciousness.

ᘓ "THE ENTIRE WORLD IS TODAY AN IMMENSE QUESTION": TECHNOLOGY, MODERNITY AND THE BEGINNINGS OF MODERNIST FORM IN AMERICA

Martí's critical comments on the effects of imperial modernity's diffusionist model leads him to define his "cartas enojosas" (angry letters) as part of an irreverent tradition that includes Edgar Allan Poe, Charles Baudelaire, and Gustave Flaubert. Turning from the magazine's predominantly technological and industrial focus, *La América* began to map a working-class, Latino cultural interrogation of its present. Martí's contributions to *La América* draw on intensely metaphoric and ironic language to represent marvelous technological inventions, modern ideas, and feats of engineering. But Martí's contributions to *La América* also prioritized cultural events in New York's Latino community alongside or in place of reports on technology. In his exuberant account of Simón Bolívar's centennial birthday party, when the luminaries of New York's late nineteenth-century Latino/a community took over the posh, midtown restaurant Delmonico's and transformed its staid décor with palm fronds, flowers, and Latin American flags, the reader sees cultural expression to be as valuable, if not more necessary, than mechanical efficiency and technological invention: "[*La América*] leaves in repose its usual business to make a brief note of the festivity with which Hispanic Americans [hispano-americanos] in New York celebrated . . . Bolívar" (*Obras*, 8:178). The address to the reader indicates an explicit transgression of the magazine's conventions in order to call attention to this gathering and its transformation of New York's cultural landscape.

Another unsigned but unmistakably Martisian contribution to the June 1884 issue of *La América* contrasts class-marked modes of consumption and leisure in poor and wealthy neighborhoods. With a title that makes a shared temporality the only link between divergent classes, an essay entitled "Verano" (Summer) reveals the desperation of the most populous sector in New York, which Martí describes as "a colossal city of workers" (*Obras*, 13:488). In this scene, the wealthy hide behind wide, luxurious fans in the doorways of their buildings, while the poor go to their building's sidewalk to air out a drunken family member, to balance a swollen-bellied infant on thin knees, or to lie down with intense thirst. From these scenes in the city's summer heat, the chronicle's setting rapidly shifts to a popular drugstore in Lower Manhattan that showcases the novelties of modern technology. The white-coated attendants, "like priests of soda pop," produce soothing tonics in a pleasant environment cooled by "moving crosses," which are powered by a steam engine (*Obras*, 13:489). Here, crystal, flower-shaped, colored bulbs glisten, and electronically powered systems for delivering cigarettes on demand display a modernity with marvelous effects. But its benefits are restricted to the small elite who can afford to pay for them. The cool, clean air of the drugstore magically contrasts with the inescapable, pestilent heat of the poor neighborhood. This drugstore's cult of an elitist, technological modernity—complete with priesthood and opiates—distracts the consumers' attention from the acute needs just blocks away.

Formally, the chronicle emphasizes the division between the two scenes despite their temporal and geographic coincidence. Each appears in a separate paragraph. The first reveals lower Manhattan in the heat of a summer night; the second depicts distracted crowds in the morning on their way to work. The marvelous technologies seemingly have the power to ignite the imagination of the same workers who would traverse both scenes. The chronicler who compares these two discrepant locations is moved to tears: "we say that it makes us weep to see what we see in a poor neighborhood in the summer, by night" (13:489). Class segregation breaks down and conditions in the compact urban space become glaring to the chronicler in the course of his narration.

Although the essays in *La América* acclaim the wonders of North American modernity—especially in reference to companies and firms that underwrote *La América* with advertising—they also employ satire to question the effects of diffusionist modernity for Latin American economies or for human flourishing in general.[52] Several articles reference contemporary dystopian fiction or the exoticizing translations of the Arabian nights in order to question the rush to put into practice new technologies.[53] Citing Edmond About's satire on surgical reconstruction, for example, Martí gives a gruesomely detailed account of a New York doctor's surgery on a German servant's face.[54] "Un rostro rehecho" (A Remade Face) (*Obras*, 23:29–30), begins with a litany of superlatives that seem ironic because of their excess: "Beauty takes all. Beauty is a natural right. Beauty is a sort of divine ministry" (29). These exorbitant claims echo the aestheticism that Oscar Wilde promoted during his U.S. speaking tour of 1882–83, and which ring hollow in light of the Frankensteinian scene described in the chronicle. Dr. Shrady of the Presbyterian Hospital removed pieces of skin from the arm of Bertha Tristler, a German immigrant and domestic servant. The chronicle gives a step-by-step account of how the doctor transplanted arm and finger skin onto her right cheek and encouraged them to adhere. Through these sutured pieces of skin, the doctor surgically remade Tristler's face. The operation filled a gaping hole in the maid's face, which another doctor had accidentally gouged out. The reader observes Dr. Shrady literally transforming Tristler's ability to speak, by surgically opening, lowering, and closing her lips. The tense, technical language of Martí's account mimics the surgical cuts whereby the domestic worker patiently submits to these experimental interventions. If Dr. Shrady reconstructs Tristler's face so that "today she parades her beauty," his heroic act is tainted by the previous doctor's impunity after having damaged a working-class woman's face.

Other articles in *La América* offer a sober assessment of the threatening instrumentalization of the human body in the process of advancing technology. As David Laraway's reading of Martí's poem "Amor de ciudad grande" (Love in the Big City) indicates, Martí's apparent enthusiasm for technological inventions in *La América* nonetheless leads him to criticize the potential of technology-driven modernity not only to make the voice massively iterable, but also to diminish the body to an empty shell, cup, or tool.[55] In his account of the recently invented "glossograph," Martí appreciates the magnitude of the inventor's aspiration to render immediate the abstract, fickle, mercurial signified in a technologically transcribed material signifier. But Martí takes issue with this fantasy of moving beyond the finitude of human perception and representation. He compares the glossograph's goal to the far-fetched task of inventing wings to supplant the human imagination: "Oh everything, everything may be invented—except for wings!" (*La América*, November 1883; *Obras*, 8:419). Even technology cannot replace the poetic image or figurative language's creative power, which makes it possible to traverse the gap separating past from present, living and dead. Similarly, in a February 1884 report on the introduction of an incubator in Paris's maternity hospital, Martí comments on the application of the technology of scientifically assisted human reproduction to the mass production of chickens: "Not for chickens, but for children" (*Obras*, 8:435) he declares at the start of this chronicle. The article, "La incubadora de niños," concludes: "The year 3000 of Emilie Souvestre [*sic*] is already becoming reality" (*Obras*, 4:436). By mentioning the futuristic account of the world in the year 3000 by the French dystopian fiction writer Émile Souvestre, the article questions the reduction of humans to animals through this application of modern technology to childbirth.[56]

In July 1889, a few years after the publication of his last surviving essay for *La América*, Martí wrote about the deadly applications of Thomas Alva Edison's ingenious electrical inventions, one that echoes his earlier writing against capital punishment in the years after his own experience of a forced-labor prison.[57] Martí reports to his Uruguayan readers a new use of electricity that was captivating New Yorkers' attention, "the execution chair" (la silla de ajusticiar): "In the papers, all the talk is of a new apparatus for execution, a horrible looking electric chair, which subjects the prisoner's feet in front, like stocks [un cepo] on high, and reclines the head as in a barbershop chair" (*Obras*, 12:272). Playing with the anagram *barbarie/barbería*, this chronicle depicts the condemned person relaxing as if awaiting a shave. Electricity revives and modernizes the inquisitorial punishment (*el cepo*, the stocks), now placed "on high." Electricity redefines execution as an act of state hygiene; or (to reverse the terms) the liberating power of Edison's invention reveals the barbarous implications of a barbershop chair. This everyday technology applied in state-administered violence derives from a society that distrusts humans' capacity for self-critical transformation. In the Gilded Age, the artificial form of illumination—electricity—makes state-sponsored killing more efficient, clean, and quotidian.

Unlike the glowing images emerging from the urban centers of the United States and dispersed throughout Latin America in the catalogues produced by the American Agency, *La América* describes modern life as trampling the spirit underfoot.[58] It prostrates its observer with incessant motion and noise. In the several chronicles Martí dedicated to Thomas Alva Edison, he reflects on the inventor's unceasing imagination as the means by which he created "a formidable and mathematical poetry" out of mechanical forms (*Otras crónicas*, 136). The chain-smoking former seller of newspapers and inventor of new modes of telegraphy and telephony fascinates Martí because of his lack of formal education and his impoverished origins. However, although Martí marvels at the fantastic magic of Edison's electrical light laboratory, he describes the rapid penetration of this technology throughout the world, like an "electric fever that has spontaneously invaded all the countries of the civilized world" (*Obras*, 28:181). The southward movement of northern technology does not flow gently, nor seek permission to enter. It invades, contaminates, and threatens to addict.

Edison's modern sensibility differs from Martí's in that the former uncouples the power of the imagination from the ethics of social transformation. His manipulation of the unknown generates individual change that reinforced existing social hierarchies of consumption and policing. In the midst of a chronicle on Edison, Martí cites a Euro-American modernist literary tradition that has come to epitomize a critical preoccupation with and desire to problematize the historical present, especially through the interpretations of Walter Benjamin and Michel Foucault. Characterizing the creative genius as seeing "the eternal in the accidental" (*Obras*, 13:43), Martí echoes Charles Baudelaire's definition of the modern artist as seeking "the transitory, fleeting beauty of our present life—the character of what the reader has permitted us to call *modernity*."[59] Martí's mention of Poe and Baudelaire cites a tradition of modernist interpretation into which he would intervene. Referencing this specific writer also gestures to the power of translation to transform literary history, insofar as Baudelaire's translation of Poe created a literary genre and challenged North Americans' lack of esteem for their own *poète maudit*.[60] The fantastic, imaginative elements of Poe and Baudelaire represent a limit to Edison's rational, modernizing genius. Although Edison asserts that he could transform a fistful of New Jersey dirt and some water into a bottle of Château d'Iquem (*Obras*, 11:165), Martí quips that beyond Edison's powerful eye, there exists an unknowable element that has the potential to shatter his transcendent vision of modern self-sufficiency and limitless technological power:

It is true that mystery flies like sparks from the eyes of Edison. . . . His pupil seems to be inscribed with a story by Edgar Poe or a stanza of Charles Beaudelaire [sic]. The green-winged sylph, beribboned with silver, dances inside a clear-eyed girl; it makes fun, it becomes bored, it shows off its cloven and luminous belly that glows like a Cuban firefly's abdomen. . . . They say that [Edison] sees everywhere bodies without form, that the silence contains for him magical voices, that the science of this world has brought him to the threshold of another more beautiful one, which he solicits and flirts with from this dark side. The world awakens a thirst that only death can quench. (*Obras*, 11:164).

The black hole at the center of the sovereign scientific mind is only visible to someone else, who stares into Edison's eyes. From that obscure place spring Edgar Allan Poe's complex psychic spaces and Baudelaire's flowers of evil, which mock the autonomy, authority, and self-presence of the intending, bourgeois subject. With this allusion to Baudelaire and Poe, Martí affirms these fantastic—more than realistic—texts that underscore the limits to European and North American dreams of order and control. The passage evokes the imagination that crosses the threshold of finitude in the form of the soulless fairy or winged girl who drives crazy the scientist who aims to hold her fast.

This "green-winged sylph" (silfo)—a fairy, a girl, a South American hummingbird—has characteristics similar to a Cuban firefly, the *cocuyo*, a large glowing insect. In the words of the Cuban poet Dulce María Loynaz's *Bestiarium*, the cocuyo is a "lamp without oil or shade, not ignited by anyone, nor extinguished by the wind."[61] Representing Martí's self-inscription into a modernist literary tradition, the "cloven and luminous belly" of this firefly figures the magical voices of another world that disturb any pretense to the bourgeois individual's autonomy and universality. The sylph flickers and glows on the dark bank of the present world, in evocation of another more beautiful order, which Edison sought to build. Although modern invention pretends to overcome human finitude and material conditions, "the heterogeneous in the singular" (*Obras*, 11:164) recalls the difference in the depths of the center, which make transformation possible.[62] Modernist self-critique and this quality of dehiscence—the splitting apart of the sovereign subject along structural lines—distinguish Martí's modernism from a dominant model of North American individual genius.[63]

⌒ "WINGED LAMENTS, LIKE WOUNDED CONDORS":
MARTÍ ON NORTH AMERICAN METROPOLITAN CULTURE

If one of the hallmarks of modernist writing is the representation of complex psychological states as a result of conditions of imperial modernity, the essays that Martí planned to collect in a volume to be entitled "Norteamericanos" examine the subjective qualities of metropolitan culture and plot his struggle to define the invisibility of Latino migrant writings within North American intellectual and cultural histories. Published posthumously, this series of literary critical and biographical studies includes interpretive essays on Ralph Waldo Emerson, Henry Ward Beecher, Peter Cooper, Wendell Phillips, Ulysses S. Grant, Philip Henry Sheridan, Walt Whitman, Bronson and Louisa May Alcott, Henry Wadsworth Longfellow, Thomas Alva Edison, and James G. Blaine, among others.[64] In addition to introducing to Spanish-language readers—often for the first time—a broad range of U.S. intellectual, political, and cultural figures, this volume inscribes an alternative Latino American intellectual tradition in the interstices of North America's representative figures.

The essays that were to make up the volume entitled "Norteamericanos" and related chronicles characterize modern U.S. culture as individualistic to the point of solipsism, forgetful to the point of amnesia, and corrupt to the point of undermining democratic self-government. The same individualism that stands for autonomous creativity sustains a model of competition and rivalry among migrant groups. In his chronicle on Christmas preparations of 1882, Martí notes how the "new rich" (neorricos) distance themselves from the "recently arrived" (recienllegados) or from their own disavowed and impoverished immigrant past (*Obras*, 9:333). Successful immigrants "take a villainous pleasure in humiliating others as they once were, and in making others drink the large cups of bitterness they themselves used to drink" (*Obras*, 9:333). The competitive mentality of those who savor success by lording it over more recently arrived immigrants undermines solidarity across cultures or national contexts. This assimilationist modernity leads New York's inhabitants to live isolated from one another. Gift giving and the visiting rituals of holidays strive yet fail to overcome this pervasive isolation: "each soul stays inside itself and this produces the great loneliness of each person" (*Obras*, 10:132). The loneliness that defines life "in this vast city, *where people live so alone*," fosters the migrant's forgetting of the culture of origin, as a condition of economic success (*Obras*, 9:334; emphasis added).

In the midst of cross-cultural global currents, the modernizing metropolis is poised to break down Old World provincialism and ethnic prejudice,
but instead exacerbates it. Although "[New York] is a city of cities, a sea of
peoples and a gulf, where the currents of modern life meet, break and boil"
(*Obras*, 9:334), U.S. culture proscribes the sense of self-critique and comparative reading that might foster support for other anticolonial struggles.
Martí observes that the United States had become "a nation preoccupied
with itself, and, in its own pleasure and contemplation, unable to compre-
hend the marvels and suffering of the rest of the human universe" (*Obras*,
10:107). Martí suggests that consumer culture and party sectarianism had
circumscribed political discussion to the extent that the voting process
barely engaged with issues beyond the frame of two-party conflict. Martí
was keenly aware that the United States failed to recognize and did not
assist Cuba's belligerents during the 1868–78 civil war, despite appeals from
abolitionists such as Wendell Phillips.[65] The unwillingness to recognize
Cuba's right to self-determination exemplifies this cultural solipsism, provincialism, and the United States' belief in its exceptional status.

   As *La América* plots Martí's political and cultural agenda in the space between languages, "Norteamericanos" reveals how the Latino migrant senses
his illegitimacy or invisibility as compared to well-established, widely published, admirable, or notorious U.S. contemporaries. For example, upon
the death of Peter Cooper (1791–1883), Martí declares his filial affection for
him and notes his own exclusion from North America's legacy: "I was not
born in this land, and [Cooper] knew nothing of me; and I loved him like a
father" (*Obras*, 13:48). This position of the bastard or *hijo natural* who has
no right to an inheritance plagues but also frees Martí, by problematizing
his claim to U.S. culture. Much as Du Bois would refer to himself as a
stepchild of America, Martí learns to resignify his "natural" and disinherited position as a route to defining an alternative American modernity.

   With admiration and respect, Martí celebrates North Americans such as
Peter Cooper and Wendell Phillips and thus reveals some of the values he
would adapt from the other America for his own. The son of a Revolutionary War officer, Cooper was a "modern wizard" whom Martí likens to the
powerful locomotive train that he invented (*Obras*, 13:47). Cooper gar-
nered Martí's admiration through his commitment to decentralizing cultural capital through education of the poorest, and because he avoided the
self-aggrandizing displays of new wealth that characterized the period after
Reconstruction. With only one year of formal schooling, Cooper moved
from making hats at age ten to brewing beer to making stagecoaches. A

master of several trades, an industrialist, a presidential candidate, and a philanthropist, he invented machines and tools to excavate the earth, to clear forests, to weave, to cut fabric, to steer a ship, to drain a swamp, and to produce colossal factories of iron. Above all, Martí lauded Cooper's Institute of Arts and Sciences, which he founded and built in 1859, to train students without economic means in the fundamental human task of "self-creation" (crearse por sí) (*Obras*, 13:53). A key concept in Martí's modernist vision of social transformation, this phrase may also be Martí's translation of Cooper's stated goal in creating the institute: to instruct the rising generation in "*the great mystery of their own being.*"[66]

Martí appreciates Cooper's curiosity and imagination, which drive him to demand answers of the world: Cooper "has spent his life inclining over abysses, asking of them their secrets" (*Obras*, 13:47). Asking questions plays an indispensable role in redistributing power and redressing the abuse of power, especially when ignorance makes justice itself into a seeming enemy: "[Cooper] preaches that sometimes ignorance reaches a stage where it makes justice itself hateful. He announces that there is no power that may resist cultivated human intelligence" (*Obras*, 13:52). Cooper's method shows students how to formulate a question, and does not offer them a prefabricated answer. This method of peering into the abyss taps curiosity's unrealized potential and confronts the mystery of an enigmatic and incomplete humanity.

Like Cooper, the abolitionist orator Wendell Phillips earned Martí's respect as a spokesperson for the economically and politically disenfranchised (*Obras*, 13:63). Phillips did not enjoy widespread popularity, because he peered into the foundation of modern American society and made tremble the centuries-old, seemingly immutable, institution of slavery.[67] According to Martí, Phillips's greatest skill was to prod the "monster" and to "keep it on its feet for the world to see" (*Obras*, 13:60). For readers of Argentina's *La Nación*, Martí describes Phillips's oratory as a volcanic eruption with sufficient force to awaken the dead: "Suddenly the whistles in the air become a maelstrom of flaming rocks. Tremendous ghosts populate the atmosphere. They emerge from their portraits with a vengeance, and go with closed fists, to the slaver, the fathers of the American nation" (*Obras*, 13:64). The scene links Wendell Phillips to the spectral founding fathers of the American republic. His words have the power to release their spirits from their picture frames, from where they fly to indict the slaver. These ghostly figures also represent the guilty traders amongst the founding patriarchs, including George Washington. Martí's respect for this radical abolitionist led him to display Phillips's portrait in his office.[68] Labeled by his critics "traitor to the nation" and "odious demagogue" (*Obras*, 13:61), Phillips appears in Martí's essay as "hanging on the borders of abysses," and attentive to the most dangerous, historical questions (*La América*, February 1884; *Obras*, 13:59).[69] The former journalist and illustrious orator, George W. Curtis, who was one of the original residents of the experimental communistic project of Brook Farm, lauded Martí's obituary of Phillips, and Martí published Curtis's note of appreciation in *La América*.[70]

In contrast to Phillips and Cooper, who were notable for their social commitments, a more complacent intellectual elite in the powerful new nation enjoyed relatively easy access to the means of knowledge production. Martí's essays in commemoration of this leading sector of North America betray frustration with his own marginality and with his limited ability to publish his writing in book form. Martí faced great difficulty in producing or even obtaining durable, beautifully crafted volumes from New York or Madrid, whereas a writer such as Henry Wadsworth Longfellow (1807–82) enjoyed—as Martí noted—delightful working conditions: "He works in a comfortable chair, at a large round desk full of books" (*Obras*, 13:226).[71] The hallowed halls of Harvard, where Longfellow, the grandson of a Revolutionary War general, served as professor, translator, and poet, were a world away from the intensely urban location and freelance writing Martí did in New York City. Similarly, multiple sojourns in Europe nourished Longfellow's multilingual mastery of the literature of Spain, France, Italy, Germany, and Nordic cultures, while the adult Martí had only traveled to Europe as a deportee.[72]

In Martí's sober estimation, Longfellow's poetry projects faith and sadness without capturing the frequencies of the variety of minor cultures in his midst. Written from inside Craigie House, which looked over the Charles River, Longfellow's verses gaze safely at the world with unruffled calm (*Obras*, 13:230). Longfellow's poetry, said Martí, stands erect and smoothly polished like well-wrought, European-inspired urns and Greek statues (*Obras*, 13:229), while his own emits "winged laments that fly like wounded condors, with a lugubrious look and a flaming red breast" (*Obras*, 13:229). These images contrast flight and stasis, fresh blood and the cold stone of the Greek statue, and the majestic but wounded South American condor with Europe's intact but inert works of art. Longfellow's tranquil position in Cambridge dulled his literary force, says Martí, who made his pain into a kind of muse: "and when the pain is enveloping you, you feel the shadows upon you, as when the twilight comes. Poets who have not suffered do not manage to lift their wings off the ground—Longfellow" (*Obras*, 22:324). This image, in one of his fragmentary writings, shows that Martí knew well the angst of approaching shadows. We may read between these lines his secret hope for literary longevity. In defining his Latino, southern difference—through his references to the wounded condor and to the image of a volcano smouldering—Martí uses the occasion of his writing on Longfellow to inscribe his colonial and migratory condition in the United States.

Martí's obituaries and salutes to North Americans also undermine U.S. claims to novelty and innocence and show how imperial modernity's conception of time works to marginalize the culturally different.[73] If U.S. poets and intellectuals claim for themselves an Adamic newness, Martí acknowledges his belated status. Under Longfellow's feet "the crush of virgin leaves can be heard," Martí writes, with a hint of sarcasm, for Longfellow's novelty is only relative, coming as it does in previously inhabited lands. Unlike the blue-eyed Longfellow, Martí acknowledges prior civilizations of Europe and of ancient Amerindian cultures: "we move deadened feet amidst the ruins."[74] Martí's texts bear the marks of what his German contemporary Nietzsche would call in 1888 "the twilight of the gods": "Those who are born today trip over the scattered rubble of crumbling altars, obscure altars which rise up in the distant shadows!" (*Obras*, 13:226).[75] In contrast to Martí's tragic sense of belatedness, "[Longfellow] speaks of faith, today when so many speak of desperation. From his verses emerges a beautiful sadness, the blue sadness of someone who has not suffered, not the biting, disquieting, savage sadness of the unfortunate. . . . Suffering ripens poetry. Longfellow's angels do not have bloodstains on their wings" (*Obras*, 13:227). Martí transforms his invisibility and "savage sadness" into elements that stain or mark and impassion his poetry.

Two other U.S. figures inspired a mixture of admiration and disappointment in Martí. One was George Bancroft (1800–91), a transcendentalist from New England who became an official of the Mexican War and a historian of the United States; the other was William Cullen Bryant (1794–1878). Bancroft's carefully disciplined life contributed to his longevity, his fame, and his productiveness; every day he wrote from eight in the morning until two in the afternoon. In Martí's view, however, Bancroft's seductive, amiable, but occasionally pompous writing style lacked an ethical dimension: "[His history] lacks the human warmth that connects a reader with the author of a book and makes the characters durable. But who does not envy this imposing work, and the assurance of health in old age that follows from a peaceful soul and pleasure in his work?" (*Obras*, 13: 312). Despite this envy, Martí is disturbed by Bancroft's serenity and prodigious writing because as a soldier Bancroft had used his intellectual talents to dispossess Mexico of California during the United States–Mexico War, a fact that Martí discreetly shares with his readers. While serving as the acting secretary of war under President Polk, Bancroft ordered the seizure of California posts upon the declaration of war on Mexico, and gave the order to General Zachary Taylor to invade Mexico. Martí notes that for Bancroft, "the liberty of others only exists to be violated" (*Obras*, 13: 312). Despite prolific historical research, Bancroft did not learn from his studies. Rather, he extended the long trajectory of British imperialism and undermined American principles of self-government.

Scarcely dissimulated envy and frustration also inform Martí's depiction of the celebrated, multilingual William Cullen Bryant, whom Martí describes as a "white poet" (*Obras*, 9:413). Unlike Bryant, who edited the *New York Evening Post* and was renowned as a cultural ambassador, translator, and critic for much of his life, Martí seemed at risk of never figuring in his country's still half-formed literary tradition, despite his voluminous and widely disseminated journalism. Unlike Bancroft, who in 1882 was bringing to a close his ten-volume *History of the United States*, Martí felt overwhelmed by unrealized projects and goals: "Miserable are those who sense this foreboding and who are fit to undertake [one's task], and yet who cannot give themselves over to the task! These die of a gnawing anguish. Genius without employment devours itself" (*Obras*, 9:306). Bryant's comfortable old age and privileged whiteness differentiate him from "those unfortunate and glorious ones, who eat from their own entrails" (*Obras*, 9:413). This internal conflict of the colonized or postcolonial subject repeatedly figures in Martí's self-representations. Weaving together commentary on Roscoe Conkling, George Bancroft, the Chinese Exclusion Act of 1882, and the music of Wagner, the chronicle in which Martí analyzes Bancroft's work reveals the internal splitting apart along structural lines (dehiscence) that registers Martí's experience of imperial modernity. Martí's "Norteamericanos" offers an image of the frustrated genius eating itself up, a problematic to which I turn in the next chapter.

Martí's self-inscription in between the lines of obituaries about North

Americans appears suddenly and without notice, rather than as progressive development. In the midst of a laudatory discussion of the life's work of John William Draper, the English-born New York chemist, historian, and first photographer of the moon, Martí veers from his apparent theme and launches into a strange, reproachful soliloquy. In this detour, the writer indicts himself and his Latin American audience for reproducing the hierarchy that values northern Anglo authors over Latino America's own un-recognized and not yet fulfilled literary potential. In this impassioned outburst, Martí berates himself and his readers for uncritically praising Anglo-American books. Having spent the first several columns of his essay applauding Oscar Wilde, Charles Darwin, and Draper, he concludes by denouncing the fact that his America's books have remained un-acknowledged and largely unwritten:

> How can we be ashamed before these Cyclopses, we who amply note the merits of this or that little beggarly book! How afflicting it is to live, as all of us Americans do, on the backs of warhorses! And, how good it would be to leave at once this battle gear and after returning from our labors, to write at home, upon a desk of pine, grave and certain things that we have learned in the beneficial space of restful hours! What marvels would we not take out of our minds, which tend to think of the marvelous! Our books would be rays of sunlight! And now, we go with our books unwritten and full of wounds to the grave! (*Obras*, 9:227–28)

This exclamation emphasizes the privileges that permit someone like Dra-per, who died after decades of teaching and research at New York University, to write so many books in addition to other accomplishments. Such writers have access to a desk, a home, the nation, a native fluency in the dominant language, and time in which to write. Perhaps thinking of his own slim volume of modernist poetry, *Ismaelillo* (1882), or the many other book manuscripts that he had conceived or begun, Martí rebukes his readers' and his own feeling of shame before one-eyed monsters, the authors of prolific "little" books, which it was his job as correspondent to puff. Like a slightly deranged, modern Quixote (and unlike the retired Bouvard and Pécuchet), Martí and many Latino intellectuals with anticolonial projects in the mak-ing were bound headlong toward battles for independence, and therefore had neither the time nor space to write their "wounded laments" into volumes that they would, perforce, leave unpublished.

Even this grave prediction flickers with guarded optimism, however.

Martí's multipurpose freelancer's office space and his small boarding-house room served as laboratories of marvelous invention. Martí anticipates Alejo Carpentier and Gabriel García Marquez in imagining the peculiar wonder of books that represent the marvelously real history of Latin America and its diaspora. In the humble forum of the newspaper column, the principal publication space to which Martí *did* have ready access, the chronicler inscribes himself as an American of a marginalized global South, whose books would eventually shine like a marvelous "ray of sunlight."

TO TAKE, TO ORIGINATE:
ON THE MAKING OF AMERICAN BOOKS

Martí conceived of a corpus of distinctly American books to which he probably would have made many more contributions had he lived at a different time, with different commitments or in different circumstances. As the Cuban intellectual historian Rafael Rojas has demonstrated, Martí proposed or made notes for, outlined, researched, and in a few cases had completely written (though never published) some fifty books in his short lifetime.[76] Already conceptualizing a distinct American tradition that would draw on non-European sources—"not from Rousseau nor from Washington comes our America, but only from itself" (*Obras*, 8:244)—Martí defines a specific kind of library as containing the very building blocks of a decolonizing American republic. An essay entitled "Biblioteca americana" (American Library), implies that the book's durability makes it an ideal material with which to craft cultural representation: "every book is a stone in the altar to our race" (*Obras*, 8:313). Lest this statement ring in our ears as an essentialist glorification of Cubanness, we should remember that in defining books as the very material out of which a nation or a people builds its monuments, Martí conceptualizes "raza" (race, nation, or people) as constituted by print culture. Prefiguring Benedict Anderson's influential thesis about nations as imagined communities, Martí's glorification of American books makes reading and writing, rather than the common nineteenth-century scientific concepts of race or blood, the basis of this eminently cultural concept that amounts to something greater than a nation—a "patria mayor" (larger country) (*Obras*, 8:313). This antiessentialist "raza" finds in the dimensions of print culture intimacy and familiarity in the absence of a nation-state: "in a foreign land, we sob with joy and fall weeping into the embrace of a stranger of our own lands, as if he were a brother" (*Obras*, 8:313). The "American" in the title of this article refers not to a single language or to fictively homogeneous ethnicity or nationality, but rather to a critical tradition, an anticolonial perspective, and an analysis. These American books build what Rojas has described as a "written republic."[77] Focused on literature, history, and culture of a tradition in formation, American books "gather up our memories, study our composition, give advice for the sane employment of our strength, [and] pledge faith in the definitive establishment of a formidable and brilliant nation" (*Obras*, 8:314). The intended readership, the focus, and the very method of production establish a historical foundation for an American republic of letters.

Martí's periodic commentary on the corpus he refers to as "Libros americanos" (American books), including his numerous projected volumes and an essay with this title on the material conditions of their making, reveal the process by which Martí went about appropriating and differentiating his America from mainstream North America. Among the outlines and titles—which are styled in italics, as if the books already existed, as Rojas notes—the writer planned a study of "Los poetas jovenes de América" (The Young Poets of America) to include modernist poets from throughout the Americas, including the Mexican Manuel Gutierrez Nájera, Nicaraguan Rubén Darío, Peruvians Amalia Puga and Ricardo Palma, and Cuban migrants Diego Vicente Tejera and Francisco Sellén (*Obras*, 18:287). He compiled ten pages of notes for a study of "Los milagros en América" (Miracles in America) (21:195–205), which focus on colonization and anticolonial resistance in the Americas.[78] Martí planned a long "Poema americano" (American Poem) on an indigenous and mestizo revolutionary tradition, which antedates and surpasses the insufficient revolutions of 1776 and of 1789. Historical revolutionary leaders to be featured in the poem included Tecúm Umam (Guatemala), José Antonio de Sucre (Bolivia), Túpac Amaru (Perú), and Beníto Juárez (México) (*Obras*, 18:286).

Although Martí embraces the dynamism, mobility, and democratic accessibility of the newspaper chronicle that became the dominant genre of his publications, he also expressed admiration for the book industry in New York and lauded its ability to make knowledge available in a lasting, widely available mass-produced form. Martí's reverence for books leads him to devour scholarly tomes, including Indian philosophy and Amerindian history and literature, along with the so-called classics of Greek, Roman,

Spanish, French, German, British, and Italian literature.[79] Martí's wide and frequent reading led him to feel vividly the communion that an inanimate object like a book may create between reader and writer across barriers of space, time, and language. The books become animate in his mind: "the lion-book, the squirrel-book, the scorpion-book and the snake-book are all familiar. And there are red-haired books with a lugubrious gaze" (*Obras*, 13:420). The "red" color and "lugubrious gaze" of this last image recall Martí's characterization of his poetic oeuvre as a sort of condor-book. In another chronicle about the books awaiting attention on his desk, the volumes take on human characteristics: Martí compares the reading of a Spanish edition of the Argentine García Marou's *Estudios literarios* to caressing "the white beard of a beautiful grandfather" (*Obras*, 8:320).

Martí carefully studied and dutifully reported to his Hispanophone readers the process of book production in the United States, which he resignifies to define a future tradition of his America's bookmaking. This practical information provides an occasion for reflection on the modern function of authorship and on the limits of bourgeois individuality on which it is based.[80] The piece entitled "Libros americanos" begins with exclamations about the enticing beauty of books printed in the United States. But U.S. books "tend to lack margins," he complains (*Obras*, 13:419). Overpacked with information, they seem to be weighed down with the load of ideas contained in them. Small margins have the effect of limiting the space in which the reader may elaborate a response. By contrast, Martí's "solid and beautiful American book" invites the reader to write by leaving a space around the text. Having worked as a printer during his residence in Mexico in the 1870s, Martí keenly appreciates the shaping role of form upon the content of any publication. The presence or absence of space on the page invites or precludes a writerly response. Marti's single-sentence paragraph performs this claim: "Marginous, surrounded by abundant margins" (*Obras*, 13:424). This uncharacteristically short sentence fragment begins with a neologism, "marginous" (marginosas), which suggests both a peripheral location and the quality of a wide margin on the text it surrounds. In offering a definition on the next line and in a separate paragraph, these few words formally leave an abundant margin around themselves, so the reader may register the invention of a new word that leaves space for another American literary tradition. This insistence on margins prefigures revolutionary Cuba's position on the margins of imperial modernity and in the World's crossroads.

The collaboration of numerous workers in this process of book publishing metaphorically represents the necessarily collective task of thinking. "Libros americanos" offers a detailed account of the various offices of the workers in the press who transform the manuscript into type. The compositor sets the type by filling a galley with lines of type, which are then wedged into cases; these cases are assembled into large type forms and leveled. The pressworkers perform the printing on a double-cylindered machine invented by the New York engraver Joseph A. Adams.[81] The huge machine dries and flattens the pages on rolls of hot steel. Male and female workers cut and sew the pages and then apply the binding. This collaborative American creation leads the chronicler to exclaim: "Seeing so many men [sic] working together on thought fills the heart with love!" (Obras, 13:420). While writing for La América, Martí begins to interrogate the validity of an individual author or leader who pretends to bring about change single-handedly, as, for example, by forging an American republic. Challenging the romantic, nineteenth-century ideal of autonomous authorship, Martí's study of U.S. culture offers insight into the troubled relationship between the representative individual and the multifarious masses of working people whom the author often seeks to represent.

Martí's "Norteamericanos" and his essays on American books bring into focus the interdependence of headwork and material labor and sharply criticize bourgeois individualism and capitalist modernity's devaluation of manual labor. Everyone is needed to achieve the republic's goals. As he notes in "Nuestra América," "liberty, in order to be viable, must be sincere and full. . . . [I]f the republic does not open its arms to all and include all in its progress, it dies" (Obras, 6:21; Selected Writings, 294). Martí's translations emphasize a collective and inclusive liberty, with a special focus on the active contributions of people and groups who have historically been excluded from access to the means of representation. In developing this concept of intertwined theory and practice, Martí's "Libros americanos" includes himself among the "little authors" (autorcillos) of newspaper articles like the one in the reader's hands, whom he mocks in the chronicle for their unfounded sense of self-importance as lamplighters or pathfinders for the masses. "Libros americanos" ridicules the author or leader who declares his leadership irreplaceable, or who demands unquestioning obedience.

Considering themselves "mistreated divinities, [or] statues of themselves," such authoritarian figures regularly demand hours of work from the typesetters and other workers in order to carry out their whims, without considering the ramifications for the multiple workers whose labor makes the book possible (*La América*, November 1883; *Obras*, 13:421). The author becomes an object of comment among the typesetters. One of the many errors of such diminutive and dictatorial Joves is to presume their expert knowledge of the path to progress:

> Authors and little authors should know that in order to insert one word in something already composed, or to remove one without substituting another, requires that all of the lines of the paragraph—if not the page or several pages—be reset and changed. This occurs when the author is the pompous type . . . one of those who ends up in the joyful and newfangled arms of Progress, writers like this one, of whom the typesetters say strange things.[82]

In this playfully ironic and self-deprecating comment, Martí describes the material effects of an author changing his mind and editing a passage during the process of publication. This description evokes the ramifications of Martí's larger project: to revise *La América*'s original goal of immediate replication of the North's book of Progress.

The passage just quoted parodies narratives of authority, progress, and originality by acknowledging the extent to which Martí—one of the "autorcillos"—has participated in the construction of these myths and has been constructed by them. The word "original" erroneously attributes such powers of creation to the author when, in fact, it takes four or five hundred workers to make a book. The typesetters who do the bulk of the labor in the printing process are as indispensable to the book's success, just as an army is to a political or military leader, who is impotent without the soldiers' consent and cooperation: "A printing press is an army," says Martí (*Obras*, 13:421). Underscoring the massive power of the press, and privileging the model of persuasive argument over a hierarchical chain of command for shaping ideology, "Libros americanos" prefigures the public critique that Martí would register with the main military leader of Cuba's ten-year civil war, General Máximo Gómez.

In a letter dated October 1884, Martí admonished the celebrated general for his antidemocratic suppression of the dynamic, participatory political process that Martí fervently advocated.[83] In this sort of "Divinity School address" to Gómez, Martí challenges the top-down, militaristic decision-making process that Gómez applied in his interactions with civilian leaders. Martí was only thirty-one, but he fearlessly questioned the single most important military hero of the decade-long war: "A nation cannot be established, General, in the same way that one gives orders in a military encampment."[84] From 1884 to 1887, Martí maintained his distance from the revolutionary movement, which had enormous psychic and political implications for him. As a result of his stance, Martí faced a barrage of ad hominem attacks from the émigré community.[85] His article on American books reads like a preliminary study for the momentous letter to the general. An alternative American modernity would no longer tolerate authoritarian tyranny: "The idea of giving orders is obsolete!" (*Obras*, 13:421). Martí proposes that a leader or author must work together with and persuade a majority of the nation, must enjoin their participation, in order for any revolutionary change to be effective and lasting.

Recognizing that consent and participation of the represented masses are necessary for the communication of an idea, Martí criticizes authoritarianism for reproducing the outdated approaches of Old World colonial regimes. A consensus on a progressive alternative to the colonial structures must be elaborated collectively. It needs to be invented from the unique resources of the self-governing society. For example, Martí here distinguishes between United States, Mexican, and more general Spanish-language definitions of an "original." Just as each American culture views the world differently, each produces its own government and leadership. No single "origin" or model is applicable to all the distinct American cultures. Above all, the claim to exceptional originality becomes suspect. The moment the "original" hits the page, the cultural and historical context in which it materializes situates and constrains what it may say. A passage from "Libros americanos" alerts the reader to a vast gap between any two languages, and among regional vernaculars in the Americas: "In the United States, they call the quantity of material that they give to each typesetter to be converted into pages *takes*, or *tomas*. With excessive goodness they call it an *original* in Spanish-language presses. And in Mexico, they call it a *hueso* [bone]. Having to gnaw on it, they have given it this name" (*Obras*, 13:421). The term that appears in English in the original "takes," and that is translated as "tomas," carries the connotation of usurpation, capture, or seizure. Here, Martí suggests that the language of typesetting echoes national dispositions, as in the case of the United States, which misrepresents itself and its government as native, autochthonous, and original, when in fact it violently "takes" previously occupied land or ideas. Multiple "takes" do not tend to produce a more inclusive version. By contrast, the "quantity of material" or rough draft to be printed in a Spanish-speaking editorial is referred to as an "original": the source, cause, or motive that springs forth into being without outside influences. Martí notes the "excessive goodness" of the Hispanic press (421), as if to suggest his nostalgic distance from this romantic, sanguine conception of origination.

Martí's enigmatic comment about the Mexican term "hueso" plays on multiple forms of anguish associated with his own labor of writing and publishing for a living. Martí calls to mind the scraps of income upon which Latino writers must survive, especially when trying to live by the pen in Mexico, as he himself had.[86] The figure of the bone also implies non-originality, in that it suggests the physical remainders of prior writers and traditions. The leftover "bone"—like Yorick's skull—precludes illusions of ex nihilo creation and individual autonomy. With the rattling of bones, we hear the melancholy that plagues the writer who attempts to write Mexico into a universal modernity, and then realizes that the Enlightenment promise of universality is false. In the wake of 1848, and in light of the continued, less overt designs of the United States, the narratives of modernization, democracy, and progress cause anguish to those who live between modernization's promises and its uneven or detrimental effects.

∾ VIOLENT FICTION AND REVOLUTIONARY PEDAGOGY: MARTÍ'S PROLOGUE TO RAFAEL CASTRO-PALOMINO'S *CUENTOS DE HOY Y MAÑANA*

Whereas Martí's best-known prologue, to Juan Antonio Pérez Bonalde's *El Poema del Niágara* (1882), specifically addresses the qualities and preoccupations of the modern poem, his neglected prologue to the short story collection by the first editor of *La América* assumes an intimate connection between social transformation and modernist form. Martí's prologue to Rafael Castro-Palomino Jr.'s *Cuentos de hoy y mañana* (Stories of Today and Tomorrow) (1883) theorizes the role of education in utopian social movements and affirms the possibility of revolutionary cultural and political self-criticism as a necessary foundation for lasting change. At stake in Martí's framing of Rafael Castro-Palomino's short stories is nothing less than the viability of creating an alternative to persistent colonial structures in the Americas.[87] In the 1880s Martí and *La América*'s first editor led a movement to introduce a Cuban society more conducive to the flourishing of equal and lasting justice for all Cubans through the derogation of the Spanish colonial bureaucracy. Would it succeed? By what means should it proceed? What modes of representation—aesthetic or political—would make it possible to imagine and bring about an alternative to the social hierarchies of the colony and of North American society in the 1880s?

In the two stories that make up Castro-Palomino's *Cuentos*, the plots turn on the conversion of European communists, anarchists, and socialists into pragmatic liberal capitalists, a shift that in these stories represents the only rational and viable alternative to failed revolutionary or utopian movements of the nineteenth century. Fundamentally conservative in impulse, each story reproduces debates concerning the problems of the inequitable distribution of wealth and the effects of panoptic or secret state-sponsored surveillance, where citizens spy on each other at the behest of their government (*Cuentos*, 31). Both stories introduce a deus ex machina character, an older New Englander who preaches the "truth" of British social science and North American pragmatism to pensive, yet naive, revolutionaries. These recent immigrants, who pull at their unkempt black hair in concern for the frustrated masses they have been charged to represent, come to accept the New Englander's assumption that the human being's fallen constitution mandates a liberal capitalist investment in private property as the essential prerequisite of civil society. The migrants with revolutionary demands slowly acquiesce to the idea that the oppressed must conform to a gradual, "natural evolution" beyond their control.[88]

Martí credits Castro-Palomino's short fiction with illustrating the importance of critical analysis of society and culture: the stories show, according to Martí, "the need to know the elements of a problem in order to resolve it" (v). These interpretive activities build from the most basic action of reading, which engages social making and unmaking within sign systems. As Castro-Palomino's staff writer at *La América* at the time of the short stories' publication, Martí reads against the grain of the elder Cuban's pessimistic conclusion that revolutionary restructuring amounts to naive utopianism. Martí's prologue to Castro-Palomino's fiction interrogates the romantic idea, promoted by these stories, that a corrupt human nature requires the intervention of a superior being to prevent human self-destruction. As Martí redirects the agenda of *La América* he does so without making his long-standing senior colleague and collaborator in the Cuban independence movement into a political enemy. He achieves this by reframing Castro-Palomino's own introduction to the volume, in which his colleague presents the *Cuentos* as the first in a series of didactic "Cua-dros políticos y sociales" (Political and Social Scenes). Because the series appears to have ended with the first volume, we might read Martí's pro-logue as an effective intervention to limit this sort of antiutopianism within the proindependence movement.[89]

Castro-Palomino's literary art poses a question about the relationship and commitment of migrants to their homeland after living over a decade in the United States. In writing his *Cuentos* and in reciting and publishing his volume of unadorned, lugubrious poems, entitled *Preludios* (1893), Castro-Palomino did not make a name for himself in Cuban or U.S. liter-ary history.[90] Against that oblivion, Martí published a literary-critical study of *Preludios* in *Patria* in which he refers to this "truthful book" (*Obras*, 5:213) as a conduit of unexpectedly intense feeling that he associates with the migrant condition.[91] Castro-Palomino crafts poems from the existen-tial despair of exilic displacement. With a soul "like a cemetery" and a heart stripped of faith, the poet had become the migratory bird of his verses. Martí wonders fatefully: "Will he fall prostrate in the end against the 'mysterious barrier,' or 'will he fly beyond'? he asks in vain of the sepulchers and the stars" (*Patria*, April 22, 1893; *Obras*, 5:212).

Castro-Palomino was not the only Latino migrant to question whether revolutionary change was possible. Martí's definition of modern Ameri-can literary art as provoking "an unexpected and intense feeling, which at the precise hour culminates in resonating emotions" (*Obras*, 5:213) sug-gests that Martí concurs with this evocation of the Latino migrant's condi-tion. Moreover, Castro-Palomino rightly recognizes that nonelite working classes have justice "on their side" (iii). In opposing European-style impe-rialism and in challenging the applicability of radical doctrines imported from Europe—including anarchism and existing forms of Marxism—both Cubans agree upon the need for cultural study and widespread education in order to protect against imposed doctrines and the use of "blind force" (fuerza ciega) (*Cuentos*, 19).

Martí's prologue diverges from Castro-Palomino's stories in that it em-braces the general spirit of European radical movements, which envisioned a rapid implosion of the existing social forms rather than a gradual evolu-tion to a new, reformed state. The younger activist does not share the elder's view that the oppressed masses of the Americas, which have always been made up primarily of people of color, are inevitably and naturally anarchic, and therefore incapable of organizing a systematic response to the "times of ire and madness" (iii) that the stories depict. For example, the title of Castro-Palomino's story "Del caos no saldrá la luz" (Chaos Will Not Give Rise to Light) casts judgment on two unnatural propositions: that love might exist outside the order of patriarchal marriage, and that work and creativity might exist without competition or private property. The story portrays a failed utopian experiment by two ex-Communards and asserts the inexorably chaotic, competitive tendencies that inhere in the Caribbean's working-class masses.[92]

By contrast, Martí envisions a popular education that will ensure the active self-emancipation of the most disenfranchised, including African descended workers. He challenges the scientific axioms of British sociology and North American–derived "truths" about the working or immigrant masses as inherently unfit for self-government or prone to internecine violence, a version depicted by Castro-Palomino's stories. In one of those tales, a North American character, Mr. Wisdom, quotes Herbert Spencer's dictum that societies "are born as any organism is born" (*Cuentos*, 14), and thus betrays these stories' investment in social evolution and the British sociologist's suspicion of attempts to change social structures from the bottom up.[93] Castro-Palomino's authorial introduction sets his work in the tradition of French popular writers Jules Verne, Edouard Laboulaye, and Louis Jacolliot, who widely disseminated knowledge of science and celebrated U.S.-style liberal democracy.[94] Seeking to induct a popular working-class audience into Spencer's positivist sociology and U.S.-style liberal capitalism, Castro-Palomino's stories summarize utopian social theory and experiments ranging from the cooperative communities (phalanxes or phalanges) that Fourier envisioned to Brook Farm and the Paris Commune of 1871—but only in order to show the inevitable failure of each. Martí, by contrast, proposes that education teaches each person to develop criteria for judgment and action based on cultural critique.

Martí's proto-Gramscian position advocates the cultivation of critical working-class subjects who wield the only democratic power with which to transform society. The emphasis on education in his prologue challenges Castro-Palomino's portrayal of intellectual leadership deriving from an expert and North American elite. Instead, the prologue celebrates radical pedagogy and popular education as the only means to ensure a durable decolonization of American culture and politics.

The surprising alliance of capital and labor at the end of Castro-Palomino's story "Un hombre por amor de Dios" (A Man for the Love of God) does not address the problematic classist assumptions that inform

Herbert Spencer's evolutionism. Spencerian positivism demonizes socialist or communist popular organization as chaotic and socially destructive and preaches conformity and obedience to the status quo.[95] Adhering to what Martí calls a "closed logic" (*Obras*, 15:387), Spencer characterizes as a form of slavery the society that assumes it has collective responsibility to transform conditions that create poverty. In his review of Spencer's pamphlet on socialism, *The Coming Slavery*, Martí indicts Spencer for strutting about with aristocratic disdain in a society where exhausted workers surround and serve him (*Obras*, 15:388–91). Like one of the crumbling, dust-covered statues among which the new generation must find its way, Spencer's ideas, in Martí's estimation, resemble a "crust of bread" gnawed by rats.[96]

In contrast to both Spencer and his uncritical follower, Castro-Palomino, Martí offers a strongly antiaristocratic appreciation of the values and possibilities within utopian social experiments. His reading of Spencer asserts the legitimacy of a socialist desire to go to the root causes of economic inequality and to provoke radical change. Socialism represents, according to Martí, a "very noble tendency, . . . born of all the generous thinkers who see that the just discontent of the popular classes leads them to desire radical and violent improvements, because they find no other natural remedy for this rooted damage than to remove the causes of the discontent" (*Obras*, 15:389). Although Martí does not endorse an imported European socialist doctrine, he believes in the possibility of radical social equality through cultural, economic, and political transformation, grounded in popular education.

With respect to the possibility of social change in the Cuban context, the specter of radical antislavery and a multiracial nation has profoundly marked social theory about the possibility and character of a revolutionary strike for independence. As discussed earlier, a key debate between the old guard of Cuban leaders in New York, many whom also happened to be on the staff of Enrique Trujillo's newspaper *El Avisador Cubano* (The Cuban Adviser) and Martí's generation turned on the hotly debated issue of the role of recently emancipated Afro-Cubans in the new nation. The older generation of separatists, autonomists, or annexationists associated darker, formerly enslaved, and African-descended people with a heterogeneous and anarchic, and therefore threatening presence within the future nation. For example, the wealthy annexationist merchant, Fidel S. Pierra, and his colleague Juan Bellido de Luna opposed the nationalist movement and defended annexation to the United States because it would avoid the lawlessness and ungovernability that the white Creole elite attributed to black insurgency in response to Haiti's "disavowed modernity."[97] Castro-Palomino extends and updates these fantasies about Afro-Cubans in his characterization of the revolution as a scientific reaction of an "inferior social form," in which "imperfect organisms"—such as Cuba's—move inevitably toward a "period of true liberty and equality, such as those the great North American Republic has enjoyed and continues to enjoy."[98] Castro-Palomino assumes that the goal of both evolution and revolution is to reach the superior condition of the United States.

In contrast to this analysis, Martí's prologue preserves the possibility of revolutionary social change, so long as its members temper it with careful study of their island society's historical and cultural complexity. In place of Spencerian sociology, Martí proposes the "pleasures of creation, the embrace of foreign spirits, research into the unknown, and the permanent and proud exercise of the self" (ejercicio de sí) ("Prologue," vi) as strategies for creating knowledge and making change. Martí reiterates his commitment to human, imaginative invention informed by a critical interpretation of the past. Martí's subtle reframing of the triumphant position of the New England characters in Castro-Palomino's two stories—Mr. Truth and Mr. Wisdom—undermines North America's claim to have established the only practical alternative to Old World social ills.

Castro-Palomino's stories associate chaos with the absence of authoritarian institutions such as the factory owner-boss, the monogamous patriarchal family, and a Hobbesian liberal government designed to protect property; chaos inheres in the unprecedented and unknowable possibilities outside the contemporary social structure: "The emptiness surrounding everything that exists would leave chaos. And as humanity, in its immense majority, is not prepared today to live without some checks, all the morbid elements of the current society, the fruit of ignorance and of misery, will overflow" (Cuentos, 52). The story from which this quotation is taken, "Del caos no saldrá la luz" (Chaos Will Not Give Rise to Light), blames the poor and excluded masses for their lack of preparation, but the fundamental problem seems to lie in the chaotic possibility of revolutionary change itself.

Martí's prologue, by contrast, insists on the value of antiteleological thinking: "What [the future] may be, it is good to discuss. To predict it is vain. . . . To give it a premade form would be to deform it" (vii). Martí was not a socialist and never endorsed Marx's philosophy, even though he likely had access to Marx either in German or in the translations that began to circulate in the 1850s. The essay he wrote on the commemoration of

Marx's death at Cooper Union Hall nevertheless honors Marx's study of such themes as radical social change, which are at the center of Castro-Palomino's *Cuentos*. Subtitled "Honores a Karl Marx, que ha muerto" (Honors to Marx, Who Has Died) it portrays Marx as a "seer" with profound insight into the causes of human misery: "Karl Marx studied the means of establishing the world on new bases; he awoke the sleepers and showed them how to cast down the cracked pillars" (*Obras*, 9:388: *Selected Writings*, 131). Martí's prologue to Castro-Palomino was written within a decade of the Parisian Communards' toppling of the Vendôme monument to Napoleon I. It also begins by defining its historical moment as one of radical structural transformation: "These are times of ire and madness, in which we see something like an immense social edifice reeling in the air as it is taking shape and wanders in search of a place to seat itself" (iii). He finds the image to define this moment in the engineering challenge of securing the support towers on either side of Brooklyn Bridge, but the language reaches beyond this local, contemporary analogy to Marx's search for a means to awaken cadaverous sleepwalkers and to transform societies in crisis.

The workers' commemoration of Marx during his funeral inspires Martí's sympathy with this German philosopher who placed himself "on the side of the less powerful [debil]" (*Obras*, 9:388; *Selected Writings*, 131, translation modified). He understood that Marx's violent European remedy was inappropriate to the less angry and poorly organized workers of America in 1883; nevertheless, the chronicle in which he discusses Marx's funeral conveys to the reader the explosive social contradictions of the Gilded Age in the United States. Martí juxtaposes the scenes of workers with calloused hands and in work clothes at the Cooper Hall commemoration with a description of the very wealthiest of North Americans attending a ball at the Vanderbilt mansion. Stepping out of the internationally diverse gathering of male and female workers in lower Manhattan, the chronicle transports the reader abruptly to the crossroads of the "imperial highway" of New York (*Obras*, 9: 399; *Selected Writings*, 136). At Fifth Avenue and 52nd Street, a sumptuous evening of excessive consumption is in full swing. The chronicler spares no details of the spectacle of accumulated wealth:

> The clock struck ten, and all in that house of wonders was alight. A thousand carriages pulled up at its doorway. Monarchs, gentlemen, dukes and colonists of former days stepped out. . . . All that they behold is sculpted, gilded, chiseled. . . . And others dressed in dazzling white moiré, and suits of snow-white silk, with powdered wigs and a white narcissus in the buttonhole, like

gentlemen of the old German court, resemble the Dresden porcelain figurines whose famous brand name is embroidered on their clothes! . . . The
procession moves on: now, behind the quadrilles, comes the opulent reti-
nue. Hardly a word is spoken: the eyes do not look but count. Everyone is a
Duke of Buckingham, a trainload of rich jewelry. (*Obras*, 9:394; *Selected
Writings*, 136–38)

Without explicitly mentioning the gross class differences within New
York's Gilded Age, the figurative language evokes a precarious toy-like and
top-heavy social structure. These guests not only unabashedly imitate various members of the European courts; they have become the brand-named
porcelain figurines of European companies. Martí's description of the
mansion and garments of the arriving guests conveys the weight of these
luxurious objects as they bear down on the rickety platforms of borrowed
forms of European nobility.

The postrealist literary form of this passage is also found in the prologue
to Castro-Palomino's short fiction and clashes with the conventional realism found in those stories. Calling for new forms of both political and
aesthetic representation, Martí's resistance to positivism wrenches open
the association of justice with an established order, and refuses to ascribe
moral turpitude to chaos. This change sets the stage whereby modernist
and vanguard aesthetics might recognize the value of chaos and the abyss
of the unknowable as catalysts for innovative representation and unexpected literary form. These new aesthetic principles and their related radical politics continue to have valence into the period of the avant-garde.
This aesthetic and philosophical shift responds to European and North
American imperialism, which furnished the wealthy elite with capital, generated the impetus for war, and circumscribed the liberty of postcolonial
nations.[99]

Whereas Castro-Palomino's investment in science blinds him to the
power of words, Martí's prologue celebrates the imagination's winged cre-
ations that unmake the existing social forms and generate indignant responses to social inequality: "with one single beat of the wings, [these ideas
in flight] wish to laugh at the implacable, unbridgeable gap" between the
existent and the possible ("Prologue," vi). This inexorable abyss and distance between the idea and its material representation defies closure. At the
same time, the imagination and the vehicles through which it moves cannot cease to traverse the aporia between them. Figures of change arrive
suddenly, like an insurrection. Martí describes the successful search for a

new form to define and redirect modernity as the "rude triumph of the men who have on their side the largest portion of justice" (vii). In thinking through the problems that pertain to them, the less powerful yet numerically greater group, or what Martí calls "the minor mass" (vii), may act out their will to cross over from imperial modernity to an alternative.

As in the elaboration of a tradition of American books, here Martí defines reading and writing as a form of revolutionary action: "to read is to work" (v). Like writing, interpretation is necessary to defining a revolutionary project. Martí closes his essay by cursing the power of signification when it does not serve an honorable cause or act in the name of love. Like the mystery that defies the mastery of the inventor Thomas Edison, words themselves have the bedeviling power of "an abominable coquette" (vii), because they cannot ever be fully harnessed. Nevertheless, without words, revolutions could not proceed.

Revolutions depend upon the power of rhetoric to awaken the imagination of the colonized so that a people will together risk their lives in the fight for independence. The first step toward that kind of revolutionary self-consciousness is for those who will fight the revolution to understand themselves. In Martí's critique of colonial education in a remarkable series of letters that he addressed to *La República* of Honduras in 1886, he notes that schools designed in accordance with the colonizer's need for a dependent, easily exploited population tend to brand the learner's mind as if she or he were capable of functioning only as part of a herd. Educational systems based on foreign models produce a university-educated minority, ill equipped to interpret the local cultures in their midst. The following excerpt suggests that pedagogy within postcolonial Latin American contexts has done little but reproduce students bound to and identified with the colonizing project (*Obras*, 8:20):

> The flowery and ornamental education that sufficed during centuries of well-defined aristocracies for men whose existence was provided for by the unjust and imperfect organization of the nations; the literary and metaphysical education, the last bulkhead of those who believe in the need to raise a barrier—made up of an impenetrable and ultraillustrated class— against the new impetuous currents of humanity that overcome and triumph on all sides; . . . they [the students] need to know what makes up the world, what moves it and what causes change on this earth that they will have to perfect and from which they have to extract with their own hands the means for universal well-being and survival. (*Obras*, 8:429)

In the postcolony, professors raised barriers to protect their elite status and prevent change, and education was for an elite whose focus was to represent in translation the colonizer's interest to the masses.[100] To address this predicament, instead of fostering only a small, ultraeducated, and colonial-minded elite, Martí proposes schools to prepare those who would transform the world so that all can survive in it.

Largely neglected by critics, Martí's prologue to Castro-Palomino extends the discussions of popular education that he first broached in *La América*. Martí's proposal in this unlikely publication venue emphasizes material relations over spiritual ones: physics over theology, mechanics over rhetoric, and agriculture over logic ("Escuela de mecánica," *La América*, September 1883; *Obras*, 8:279, 281). This commitment to practical methods for exploring local environments does not preclude literary study, nor does it suggest an accommodationist model of postcolonial vocational-technological education along the lines proposed by Booker T. Washington. Rather, this model orients literary and cultural study to the peculiar time, place, and material conditions of the postcolonial world (*Obras*, 8:282). Unlike Macaulay's British imperialist policy of forming an elite class of local interpreters, the function of which is to reproduce amongst the governed the opinions, morals, and intellect of the imperial metropolis, this education seeks to eradicate patronage and revalue the local, submerged knowledges of the oppressed.[101]

In a related unpublished treatise entitled "Educación popular" (Popular Education) (*Obras*, 19:375–76), Martí contrasts the enduring usefulness of education to the changing value of money. Conveying something like the idea of universal, free, public education that challenges rather than preserves social stratification, his adjective "popular" refers to a curriculum not for the poor, but for the entire postcolonial nation. As in his praise for Cooper's institute for students without economic resources, Martí indicates that national well-being depends upon the education of all in order to create a basis for informed self-government. Popular education creates a national culture that refuses to abide enslavement of some citizens by others. This education also radically opposes the colonization of one nation by another.

Rather than centralize education in the Europeanized urban metropolis or lettered city, Martí envisions its distribution throughout the country by "ambulatory teachers" in his essay "Maestros ambulantes" (Wandering Teachers). Appearing in this essay on rural education, the adage that "to be cultivated is the only mode of being free" (ser culto es el único modo de ser libre) addresses the etymological roots of the word "culto" (cultured). As Raymond Williams notes, "culture" derives from the Latin verb *colere*, to inhabit, to cultivate, to protect, and to honor.[102] In Western civilization, culture has become associated with bourgeois exclusions. Like Herder who criticized the notion of a European monopoly on civilization, Martí associates the definition of intellectual, aesthetic, and spiritual development with dispersed, "savage" literatures such as his own.[103] The definition of culture as a condition for liberty extracts the word *culto* from a disembodied, Eurocentric notion and relates it to the popular, usually collective activities of cultivating the land.

Wandering teachers involve the most marginal peasants and workers in the exercise of judgment and self-study. Thus, if colonial pedagogy historically devalues in the mind of the colonized "his own nature" (*Obras*, 8:289), this model calls for self-study of peripheral modernities and redirects the European legacy that privileges the urban over the rural and the head over the heart and body: "The cities are the minds of nations. But the city's heart, where it beats and where it distributes the blood, is in the countryside. Men are still eating machines, and they are sacred chests, full of preoccupations. It is necessary to make of each man a torch" (*Obras*, 8:290; 48, translation modified). This passage compares blood circulation to radical transculturation and redistribution of cultural capital. Human beings in the center and the periphery need material sustenance, and they protect and preserve collective memories. They eat like machines and keep their worries inside their hearts, like holy relics. Thinking, Martí suggests, must be understood as circulating outside the privileged center or isolated periphery in order to survive because the mind-city absolutely depends upon the rural heart, stomach, and body for its functioning. Against Tourgée and Clay's mind-body hierarchy, Martí figures the heart as vivifying the urban center and igniting a fire in the minds of exploited bodies in the rural periphery. Thus, the marginalized learner, sector, or region may move by the light of its own torch.[104]

In engaging discourses of technological innovation, utopian social movements, and pedagogy in the context of a Latino American print community, Martí aligns his modernist form with an ethical commitment to redistribution of wealth and culture. In discussions of North Americans and in the pages of the new *La América* we find his articulation of an alternative pedagogy and a program of reading and writing that might literally provide the blocks with which to build a self-governing postcolonial nation.

The "Evening of Emerson": Martí's Postcolonial Double Consciousness

> . . . like a sequel to a larger idea, the height of which hid the smaller ideas, upon the larger ideas being drawn aside, those that came afterward became discoverable.
> —**José Martí,** "Emerson"

> Por todo el continente anda mi nombre;
> No he vivido. Quisiera ser otro hombre.
> (Throughout the continent my name is uttered.
> I haven't lived; I'd prefer to be another.)
> —**Jorge Luis Borges,** "Emerson"

ᔕ ALTHOUGH JOSÉ MARTÍ perceived Ralph Waldo Emerson to be a cornerstone of the U.S. literary canon in 1882, he did not totally identify with Emerson. Martí's essay "Emerson" (1882) and other related manuscripts on the margins of his corpus critically resignify, rather than passively transmit Emerson's ideas. Although Martí criticizes the kind of retrospective writing that merely builds sepulchers for Old World fathers, his writings after Emerson's death in 1882 reveal increasing skepticism of Emerson's brand of self-generation through thinking and writing: Emerson's writing simply provided insufficient explanatory power to sustain Martí's radical project.[1]

ᔕ MARTÍ'S "HYPERINFLATED" IDENTIFICATION WITH EMERSON

The interpretation of Martí's relationship to Emerson as one of near total identification has recently entered the mainstream of American literary history along with a transnational turn in American studies. Echoing Cuban literary historian Félix Lizaso—who defined Martí's affinity with Emerson as "one of the most significant cases of spiritual approximation between two minds"—Oscar Montero claims that the parallel between the two writers is so complete that "it becomes difficult to establish [in Martí's texts] where Emerson ends and Martí begins."[2] This long-standing interpretation also informs Lawrence Buell's conclusion that Martí's response to Emerson was "fervent" (146) and "hyperinflated" (327). In the notes of his argument for Emerson's lasting critical value for transnational American studies, Buell suggests, and I agree, that perhaps Martí scholar José C. Ballón Aguirre "may exaggerate in claiming that Emerson was the single greatest influence on Martí's style of writing and thought."[3] The conclusion that Martí totally identified with Emerson occludes the subtle and shifting reactions of a less powerful, Spanish-speaking migrant translator (Martí) toward one of the United States' most prominent writers.

Buell draws on several influential studies by Ballón—who offers perhaps the most meticulous reading of the Martí-Emerson relationship to date—in which Ballón provides evidence of and applauds Martí's identification with Emerson.[4] Although Ballón does not make the claim in such hyperbolic terms, his studies of Martí and Emerson draw on celebratory cold war–era interpretations of Emerson to establish some of the qualities to which Martí may in fact have been initially attracted: originality, political and cultural autonomy, and the fantasy of exclusively male, metaphysical regeneration.[5] Anne Fountain's study of Martí and U.S. writers concurs with Ballón, in that both describe Emerson and Martí as "kindred" authors, locating textual citations of Emerson in Martí's poetry and prose in order to demonstrate the North American's "enormous influence" upon the Cuban.[6]

As we saw in chapter 1, traditional inquiry into sources and influences tends to obscure the "space in between," in which a peripheral or postcolonial reading cannibalizes and thus aggressively remakes the center's literary tradition.[7] To ignore this in-between space risks construing the formerly or still colonized as incapable of or uninterested in defining an alternative cultural trajectory in the hemisphere. By contrast, I propose to read for the reactions of the dominated in order to confound a moral narrative of progress from backwardness to a singular modernity, from imitation to originality, from dependence to autonomy. In this chapter and those that follow, I argue that Martí's necessarily camouflaged reactions interrogate the moral narrative that shores up the imperial dominant's innocence and that blames the peripheral postcolonial culture for its oppressed condition.

To read Martí as extending Emerson's legacy grafts Latin American letters onto a "universal" or "classical" North American, Emersonian trunk. Latin American literature merely "continues and brings up to date, through Emerson, a classical literary tradition."[8] Martí does indicate, in an 1881 notebook fragment, that the American who can put into writing "the multiple, confused conditions of this epoch" would join a pantheon of European thinkers of the caliber of Dante, Luther, Cervantes, and Shakespeare.[9] But while Emerson may have belonged to that pantheon in Martí's mind between his first visit to New York in 1875 up until 1882, after 1883 Martí begins to see conflict between the imperial modernity of the United States and another modernity arising from American nations affiliated with autochthonous civilizations anterior to Greece and Rome. To Martí, the emerging canon of North American writing lacked the perspective that would permit understanding of postcolonial conditions in his America. Martí rejects a view that might shrink the possibilities of Latino, Cuban, or another American anticolonial writing to the model of a far from universal, Euro-American tradition. Martí's returns to Emerson's texts up until the time of his death serve to remind him of the different sort of writing he sought to create to represent a different American modernity.

❧ EMERSON'S NEW ANGLOCENTRISM

Recent scholarship critically examines Emerson's investment in the racial system that afforded a youthful Anglo culture a privileged status in the United States and in the New World, notwithstanding his courageous support for John Brown and his outspoken abolitionism.[10] Whereas a previous generation of critics celebrated a self-revising, Nietzschean, deconstructive Emerson, recent scholarship interrogates the inward movement of Emerson's thinking insofar as it may hide contradictions between imperial expansionism and the principles of liberty and self-government. This critical development invites us also to reconsider the assumption that the Cuban revolutionary Martí identified totally with the philosopher of Concord.

Emerson, according to some critics, reproduced the biases associated with his position, a fact that undermines his role as the principal spokesperson of America's cultural independence from Europe. For example, Jenine Abboushi Dallal argues that Emerson's writing reveals a key difference between U.S. and European imperialist rhetoric. Whereas British and French empires invested in, studied, and constructed discourses on colo-

nial difference, she argues that the United States abolished the difference
between itself and the nations that it occupied; rather than conquest, the
process becomes a naturalized, inevitable, and self-contained "inquest."
Abboushi Dallal finds an example of U.S. imperial rhetoric in Emerson's
condemnation of the removal of the Cherokee nation from its ancestral
lands in the East. Emerson does not take issue so much with the Cherokees'
loss of their land by force, as with the U.S. foreclosure of the Cherokees'
ability to "redeem their own race from the doom of eternal inferiority, and
to borrow and domesticate in the tribe the arts and customs of the Cauca-
sian race."[11] Emerson, in other words, laments the fact that because of their
removal, the Cherokees will no longer be able to learn from Caucasians in
the East. In keeping with Emerson's privileging of Anglo-Saxon arts and
leadership over that of other groups, Emerson's Anglo-centered ideas became useful to annexationist groups that did not recognize Cuba's right to
exist as a culturally and politically separate nation.

The current reinterpretation of Emerson takes issue with his endorsement of the nineteenth-century notion of the "arrested development" of
allegedly inferior races, and with his use of this racial idea to displace
responsibility for acts of colonial occupation onto the colonized. As Doris
Sommer has observed, Emerson believed "an imperial Saxon race" would
be "given" hundreds of Mexicos, and would absorb Mexican, Irish, and
German immigrants, as well as free and formerly enslaved African Americans, all of whom, after a life of drudgery, were destined to become so
much fertilizer for Anglo pastures.[12] Susan Castillo suggests that racial
assumptions buttress Emerson's understanding of English cultural power:
"It is race—is it not—that puts the hundred millions of India under the
domination of a remote island in the north of Europe?"[13] Brady Harrison's
Agent of Empire locates in Emerson's essays a self-reliant subject that imagines the world like a "ball" or a "bauble" in his hands.[14] In his 1844 speech,
entitled "The Young American," to the Mercantile Library Association in
Boston, Emerson nominates youthful New Englanders to act as leaders of a
nation destined to accumulate "cheap land" in order to balance the new
and old worlds: "Which [states] should lead that movement, if not New
England? Who should lead the leaders but the Young American?"[15] Despite
Emerson's association of empire with "egotism" (*Complete Works*, 1:355),
the Young America movements inspired by Emerson's talk by and the
written version he published in the same year, provided popular support to
the Pierce administration's bid for Cuba.

In its individualism, the Emersonian subject considers adherence to a collective a compromising circumstance, whereas for Martí unity through coalition helps ensure the anticolonial nation's futurity.[16] Emerson's subject is sovereign, autonomous, and entirely self-engendering. It achieves self-reliance by heeding and acting on a solitary will. To the poet in particular, Emerson attributes an "invulnerable essence" and eternal oneness: "The poet is a sovereign, and stands on the center."[17] The poet's mind or soul, not his body, "is the only reality": "I—this thought which is called I— is the mold into which the world is poured like melted wax."[18] This thought defines a world according to the hard shape of an individual will. To Emerson, those who merely perform an imposed cultural script and who bear "the gentlest, asinine expressions" on their faces are like minors, invalids, cowards, charity cases, bastards, interlopers, or members of a mass or herd, against which the North American individual should distinguish himself.[19] By contrast, for the Latino migrant Martí, this imposed condition must permit less direct forms of transgressive mimicry and requires creative evasion of constraints and pressures from his editors and from the host culture.[20] The effects of imposed receptivity, colonial economics, or racial stereotype do not seem to touch Emerson, whereas they indelibly mark Martí.

If Emerson imagines himself as homogeneous and invulnerable—a standing house and not a storm-tossed ship—Martí defines subjectivity through figures so internally heterogeneous and transitory that they threaten to split open. Such figures in Martí's published essay on "Emerson," in Martí's journals, and in other New York chronicles reveal an effort to write a distinct American tradition through a translation to which, as Borges has it, the original is unfaithful.[21] Take, for example, Emerson's metaphor for human consciousness: "we are not built like a ship to be tossed, but like a house to stand" (Emerson, *Centenary Edition*, 1:48). Martí translates this phrase twice. First, in his "Emerson" essay, a minor discrepancy distinguishes between the active infinitive "to stand" and the transitory spatial or temporal state of being expressed by the uniquely Spanish verb "estar": "No estamos hechos como buques, para ser sacudidos, sino como edificios para estar en firme" (We are not made, as ships are, to be shaken, but as buildings to be on firm land) (*Obras*, 13:30). If this translation casts a little doubt as to the solidity of the building's foundation, the second translation amongst his less visible work in his notebooks does so even more strongly: "There is something of the ship in every home in a strange land. The sensation of indefinable disgust endures. It is possible to feel the earth move under the feet that totter upon it. Sometimes, one stands by holding onto [se sujeta uno] the walls—and where others go firmly, one staggers" (Notebook 8 (1880–82); *Obras*, 21:242). The nineteenth-century migrant's fresh memory of seasickness and of Anglo disdain, the difficulty of feeling at home in an American country that sought to swallow up his own, and the sense of an unbalanced, uncertain footing all contaminate and ultimately reject Emerson's distinction of the solid, standing house from the ship at sea. Martí's notebook translation reveals the semiclandestine criticism of Emerson that his published work would assume in subsequent years.

◌ MARTÍ'S POSTCOLONIAL DOUBLE CONSCIOUSNESS

During his first four or five years in New York, Martí inhabits a space in between U.S. imperialism and European colonialism, while formulating and reformulating his assessment of the northern republic as a possible model and collaborator in Cuba's pursuit of self-government in the Americas. While preparing to publish the little book of poetry that launched modernist poetics in the Americas, *Ismaelillo* (April 1882), Martí is also defining the relationship between his two careers as poet and anticolonial activist while reading and reflecting on Emerson. Although Martí's journals indicate that as early as 1871 he sees unbreachable cultural differences between the United States and Cuba, the potential imperial relationship between the United States and Cuba takes a monstrous shape in his mind only during the 1880s. Martí's writings about Emerson bring these two positions of colonizer and colonized into relief.

To read Martí's "Emerson" in light of this emerging neocolonial relationship helps us rethink the convulsions and contortions that set Martí's pen trembling in the very opening line of the essay, which appeared just weeks after Emerson's death. The Tunisian theorist Albert Memmi associates anguish and trembling with the long and conflicted process of the colonized person's self-estrangement as he attempts to "dissolve himself in the midst of the colonizer."[22] Although it is difficult to imagine the father of Cuban independence and of Latin American anti-imperialism in the grip of coloniality, let us for a moment consider possible psychic parallels to the scars on his back that the teenaged Martí sometimes presented to other exiled Antilleans by way of self-introduction.[23]

According to Memmi, the colonized subject is indelibly marked by colonization and desires to change his or her status. The first and most readily available model for liberty from colonization is that of the colonizer, and this model implies a telos that eventually provokes a dramatic crisis: "The candidate for assimilation almost always comes to tire of the exorbitant price which he must pay and which he never finishes owing. He discovers with alarm the full meaning of his attempt. It is a dramatic moment when he realizes that he has assumed all the accusations and condemnations of the colonizer, that he is becoming accustomed to looking at his own people through the eyes of their procurer" (*Colonizer and the Colonized*, 123). The colonized subject contracts enormous financial and figurative debts in the pursuit of liberation. The colonizer's capacity to make the loans structures a hierarchy in which the position of the free, self-governing master—in Hegelian fashion—defines itself against and also depends upon the position of the unfree, the colonized, or the enslaved for sustenance and self-definition, although the master can never fully acknowledge that dependence.[24] As the colonized becomes aware of the colonial power's dependence and debts—as, for example, when Frantz Fanon declares that Europe is a product of the Third World, and not vice versa— the dialectic of modernity entails an inevitable revolutionary upheaval. Even as Martí praises Emerson's intellectual creativity and breadth of knowledge, his portrayal of himself reading Emerson distinguishes his position in a fashion that points toward W. E. B. Du Bois's later field-defining adaptation of Emerson's phrase "double consciousness." Du Bois uses this phrase to define modern black subjectivity in terms very similar to Martí's definition of a modern Latino subjectivity.

Emerson uses the term "double consciousness" to portray a free back-and-forth movement between publicly and privately defined modes of perception and intellection, and between two unreconciled viewpoints that "show very little relation to each other."[25] Du Bois's adaptation of Emerson emphasizes the constitutive relationship between black and white subjectivities. In the passage from Memmi quoted above, the condition of the colonized echoes Du Bois's description of what it feels like to see himself through others' eyes. In terms that hauntingly evoke the cultural dependence that Emerson condemns, Du Bois describes the experience of the African-descended person in the United States in this way: "It is a peculiar sensation, this double-consciousness, this sense of always looking at one's self through the eyes of others, of measuring one's soul by the tape of a world that looks on in amused contempt and pity" (*Souls of Black Folk*, 2). The sense of "twoness," of nearly being "torn asunder," that Memmi describes is rendered by Du Bois with notable understatement as a "peculiar sensation." Memmi refers to a "dramatic moment" when colonized subjects realize they have become used to gazing at themselves and their racialized group from the perspective of someone who would own them. The measure of value, in Memmi's thought, as in Martí's, derives from an outsider's perspective. As Martí writes in his manuscript fragments: "What an embarrassing enslavement! . . . It's as if we took the measure for our wings from foreign wings" (*Obras*, 21:227).

About a decade earlier than Du Bois, Martí imagines the Yankee Emerson gazing with contempt at still colonized Latinos who have not achieved national self-government. This group includes, of course, Martí himself. Martí acts out this divided consciousness and double vision by directing the following series of self-deprecating rhetorical questions to his readers: "What must the vain little minds that go about perched on conventions, as if on stilts, have seemed to him? Or the unworthy men who have eyes and do not wish to see? Or the shirkers, the men of the herd, who do not use their own eyes but see through the eyes of others?" (*Obras*, 13:19–20; *Selected Writings*, 119). Martí does not celebrate here the peculiar insight afforded by double consciousness, what Du Bois calls the gift of second sight. In reading through Emerson's eyes, Martí's own group appears vain, lazy, and dependent. Nevertheless, the passage evokes a deep longing to study and express the strivings of his soul—to achieve self-consciousness, recognition, and self-respect—in a world where Anglo-America defines modernity. This Cuban reader of Emerson performs the very act that to Du Bois defines racialized subjectivity: he sees himself and his group through the eyes of another who looks on in pity and contempt.

As we have seen, Martí's early writing on North Americans provides evidence of unreconciled strivings and contradictory double aims between at least two Americas. Martí experienced the peculiar sensation of which Du Bois and Memmi speak while seeing himself darkly through the veil of Emerson's eyes—though with "some faint revelation of his power, of his mission" (*Souls of Black Folk*, 5). Martí foregrounds the effects of networks of imperial power upon the colonized or postcolonial Latino consciousness in the Americas, in much the same way that Paul Gilroy challenges the U.S.-centeredness of African American identity, though his redefinition of Du Bois's consciousness in terms of a transnational black Atlantic geography.[26]

To live under the gaze of the other is a perspective largely unavailable to Emerson after 1848. The assumptions of Anglo-Saxon expansionism project onto Martí and his America the burden of being a "Latino" problem.

What happens to the migrant Latino subject when the anticolonial revolution of 1776, or the 1810 to 1824 revolutions in South America, or even the 1868–78 Ten Years War in Cuba threaten not to make good on the promise of offering an alternative to antidemocratic models of government?[27] In Martí's self-representations and personal writings during the first years as a resident in New York, the hemispheric tensions appear to lodge themselves within him. It is as if the fear that his dream of liberation, if unrealized, would eat him up. In writing this consuming anguish—quite unlike the romantics who give birth to themselves—Martí becomes an unknown half-brother to W. E. B. Du Bois, appropriating and remaking the legacy of Emersonian double consciousness.

Migratory Latino subjectivity engenders metaphors for consciousness that suggest division and dehiscence. Martí describes the experience of reading and thinking with images of violent destruction by fire and lightning, which set siege to the serene self-presence that Emerson idealizes. In the essay "Emerson," for example, the chronicler longs to physically dissolve his own skull: "Ah, to read when you are feeling the pressure of flames buffeting within your brain—it is like holding down a live eagle! If only our hands were bolts of lightning and could vaporize our skulls without committing murder!" (*Obras*, 13:24; *Selected Writings*, 124).[28] Reflection here figures as a violent struggle to pin down a powerful eagle, as the removal of barriers to the fire of thought, or as angry eyes staring into the blinding light of the sun. In his notebooks, this eagle takes on the characteristics of a demanding muse: "it takes a lot of work to receive an eagle: many are terrified by the visit [a muchos aterra la visita]" (*Obras*, 22:324). The act of interpretation depends upon the opening of the mind as much as it requires the mind's tenuous constellation. This figure of a mind on fire or evaporating suggests the way historical, material, linguistic, and political circumstances condition the thinkable and stoke the fire of invention. This burning skull seeks to circumvent determinations seemingly beyond its control. Receiving the eagle's visit demands a daunting combination of theory and practice. However, to miss the opportunity to be thus visited causes an even greater terror.

The striking metaphor of a mind in the process of opening recurs in Martí's work and references the peculiar difficulty of Latino alterity inside the space of New York's mass culture of entertainment and consumption.

This condition anticipates W. E. B. Du Bois's description of two contradictory strivings that torment black souls in a land of dollars. While writing about New York City's seaside resort, Coney Island, Martí conjures the struggle of the eagle to evoke an definition of liberty as an active fight:

> Other peoples—ourselves among them—live in prey to a sublime inner demon that drives us to relentless pursuit of an ideal of love or glory. And when, with the joy of grasping an eagle, we seize the magnitude of the ideal we were pursuing, a new zeal inflames us, a new ambition spurs us on, a new aspiration catapults us into a new and vehement longing, and from the eagle goes a free, rebellious butterfly, as if defying us to follow it and chaining us to its restless flight [revuelto vuelo]. (*Obras*, 9:126; *Selected Writings*, 92, translation modified)

The "we" in this passage exists as part of a broad set of "other peoples" marginalized by the frenetic, almost freakish consumption at Coney Island. Martí notes, for example, the role of exoticized and abused ethnics, including the African American at Coney Island who makes a living as a human punching bag or as a minstrel singer (*Obras*, 9:127, 125), and whose performances in sideshows reinforced a privileged white norm.[29] As in his essay "Emerson," here "other" peoples' simultaneous attempt and failure to grasp the eagle releases a remainder, a rebellious butterfly. Cross-pollinating as it moves, the butterfly zigzags in the wake of the escaping eagle, in a figure that evokes a phrase in one of Martí's manuscript fragments, also entitled "Emerson," in which previously hidden "smaller ideas" arrive in the wake of a large idea. The mobile, migratory, and racialized subject may envy the ease and stability of Emerson's erect sovereignty and centricity, but it ultimately values more its own agon of a "sublime inner demon."

If "the world is mind precipitated"—a phrase that appears repeatedly in English in Martí's notebooks—then no condition is fixed, immutable, or natural.[30] The premises of historical mutability and of human construction of social forms are necessary and useful to a revolutionary seeking to turn the tables on colonization. However, while Emerson drifted inward in his later decades, Martí increasingly observed the limitations of Emerson's vision of Man Thinking. My reading of Martí and Emerson is in line with Paul Giles's impression of Martí's spectral difference from the U.S. literary culture in which the Cuban puts into practice his revolutionary commitment, though I see Martí's distinct position as marked by the historical context of a new and aggressive phase of U.S. imperialism.[31] Whereas Giles suggests that Martí's position reflects a cosmopolitan response to "globalization and displacement," I believe that to privilege such universalizing terminology over imperialism places Martí in limbo with respect to the United States.[32] In the process of interpreting Emerson, Martí sculpts an anticolonial grassroots movement and confronts U.S. anti-immigrant violence and racism with an untimely vision of a multiracial postcolonial nation. The coincidence of these historical threads convinces Martí of the ultimate insufficiency of aspects of Emerson's thinking, as I shall show in the remaining sections of this chapter. On balance, Martí's writings suggest that it is not so much Martí's—as Giles implies—as Emerson's life and work that prove to be "hopeless" and "impossible."[33]

～ "THE EVENING OF EMERSON"

The dramatic turning point in Martí's responses to Emerson's texts is an event that he called "the evening of Emerson" (la tarde de Emerson), an evening in which he reached an epiphany and to which he refers repeatedly in his journals.[34] I read Martí's anticolonial project as torn asunder and horrified at what it might become if it were to adhere to an Emersonian model. The "evening of Emerson" occurred on a night on or around Martí's thirtieth birthday in January 1883, and it marks an awakening of consciousness after long hours of laboring over Emerson's texts. Others have read this event as the " 'hour' of the Cuban's identification with his mentor," a confirmation of Emerson's role as "an inspiration for Martí's own life," or as Martí's self-portrait of the artist.[35] To me, this epiphany records a rupture and redefinition of Martí's sense of himself as a critic, artist, and revolutionary. The discrepancies between his position and Emerson's became more acute as Martí grew intimately acquainted with the culture that Emerson's writing helped to engender. His divergence from the now spectral Emerson transformed the inextricably interrelated spheres of Martí's aesthetics and politics.

Martí's interpretation of Emerson leads him to question both the peripheral status of Caribbean culture and of Cuba and Puerto Rico, in particular, in relation to the United States. The ethical and literary culture of the northeastern cities of the United States becomes in this reinterpretation heterogeneous and, finally, secondary. Upon realizing the exorbitant price of looking at himself and his people through the eyes of the imperial subject, Martí reflects on the baneful predicament of dying as if he had not lived—which was Borges's assessment of Emerson's life years later, as my epigraph suggests. His epiphany is infused with an oxymoronic sense of "absolute luck" (dicha absoluta) (*Obras*, 21:387) upon realizing that he will not simply carry forward Emerson's legacy: "I have walked through life enough, and I have tasted its various delicacies. Well then, the greatest fortune [dicha], the only absolutely pure pleasure that I have enjoyed up to now was that evening when from my room, half naked, I saw the prostrate city, and I glimpsed [entreví] the future, as I was thinking of Emerson."[36] In giving this event the name "evening of Emerson," Martí underscores the evanescence of Emerson's explanatory power. Martí defines a post-Emersonian pivot from which he sees the city lying before him and senses what the future may bring. The verb he uses, *entrever*, signifies a vague suspicion, a guess, or a conjecture: literally, it means "to see between." The verb points to the notion, to be defined in the future, of the "in between"; in using it, Martí distinguishes himself from Adamic Americanism or Columbian New Worldism, which take possession by renaming and domesticating the continent without acknowledging historic and continuing prior civilizations in the Americas. Whereas Longfellow expresses neither anticipation nor anxiety about the future as he safely awaits the empty evolving of day into evening and evening into day, Martí leans over his windowsill and makes out a future of unexpected interruptions.

Evoking a chaotic, built environment, the urban setting of Martí's "evening" memory differs markedly from the context and content of Emerson's fantasy of exerting the power of the gaze while becoming imperceptible to others. On the bare grounds of Boston commons, Emerson's "I" assumes panoptical, invisible force as he becomes a "transparent eyeball": "I am nothing; I see all" ("Nature," *Selections*, 24). In contrast to Emerson's "I" in New England's groomed, harmonious, semirural park, the shirtless, thirty-year-old deportée in his apartment presents a physical body for view and perceives others as prostrate before forces outside their control. He sees and hears migrants and workers, doubled over before the forces of the north's capitalist industrialization, party machines, and the threat of expansion. The noise of the hawker's market cries and the sight of belching factories assault Martí's ears and eyes in his room. This encounter with "the tumultuous and resplendent city" (*Obras*, 13:17; *Selected Writings*, 116) contrasts sharply with Emerson's bodiless floating and thinking upon a silent mountain summit, as Martí presents him in the opening scenes of the "Emerson" essay. Elsewhere Martí states that Emerson "walks above the living" (9:335), whereas Martí in his boarding house dwells amongst marginalized migrants and workers and senses the naked force of imperial modernity.

Martí's interpretive labor in the aftermath of the "evening of Emerson"
also appears as a point of departure for his self-definition insofar as it
heads up a list of key "moments" that Martí planned to narrate in an
autobiographical book entitled "Los momentos supremos" (The Supreme
Moments). This proposed, intensely personal account of the formation of
his consciousness aims to reconstruct "the Life of One Man" from "the
little that anyone remembers" (*Obras*, 18:288). The narrative would construct a persona in autobiographical mode in open acknowledgment that it
is based on partial, limited memory. The book, as outlined, disobeys the
rules of progressive chronology, patriarchal succession, or evolution over
time and parallels his theory of American invention as a crafting out of
ruins. In "Los momentos supremos," meaning would accumulate achrono-
logically and against reigning notions of progress, sovereign control, or
fatherly engendering.

Martí's "The evening of Emerson" resembles other, deeply personal
memories on a list of incidents in his life that he planned to include in this
book, all of which appear solitary and private (*Obras*, 18:288). Yet the
incidents he outlines (translated, paraphrased, and annotated below) also
point to situations in which political movements or institutions bind the
individual to the social:

> The evening of Emerson [around the time of his thirtieth birthday in Janu-
> ary 1883]
>
> Feeling ingratitude [between April and December 1870, while he was in
> prison and learned of the departure of "the family of M"]
>
> The time when María, Martí's goddaughter or illegitimate daughter, was
> stung by a bee [sometime after November 1882, when María Mantilla was a
> toddler]
>
> The view from a mountaintop in Guatemala [sometime beween March
> 1877–July 1878]
>
> Being kissed by his father, (in the house of Borell) [after his return to
> Mexico and before his departure by steamer for Guatemala in March 1877]
>
> An afternoon at an amphitheater in the Catskills; Martí notes that he had
> his hands on the clubhouse balcony [probably August 1888 or 1890]
>
> [The influence of] Sybilla [*sic*] [a figure for a complex of attributes dis-
> cussed below]
>
> Being shown his newborn son, Pepe [November 22, 1878]
>
> A letter from Adriano Páez [sometime between 1880 and 1882][37]

Relating to intimate vulnerabilities within public institutions, such as prison, to encounters among the family, the club, on the dock, at the theater, or in the printed letter, each of these "supreme moments" publicizes a turning point in Martí's personal narrative. They represent spaces of mystery, of possible illegitimacy and of illegibility.[38] Here we see Martí's tense relationships as a rebellious son of Spanish and Canary Islander immigrants, as a prisoner, as a traveler, as an absent or unacknowledged father, as a reader, and as an aspiring writer. These moments gesture to the vital significance of Martí's other country, as he calls it in his poetry, "the night," which unfolds without heeding enlightened narratives of mastery and progress. At the same time, they represent the threshold between the private night and the public nation, between youth and maturity, and between the personal and the political.

Two literary exchanges frame this list. In the first, Martí figures as a reader of Emerson, and in the last, Martí has become a widely circulated text that has struck a chord with Latin American readers. Because of its mention in this list of supreme moments, scholars have long wondered about Martí's relationship to the Colombian newspaper editor and poet Adriano Páez (1844–90). Luis García Pascal notes that out of admiration for Martí, Páez's son sold the three thousand volumes of his father's library and donated the proceeds to the Cuban Revolution in 1897.[39] Although scholars have not identified with certainty the specific letter to which Martí refers, a letter from Páez that appeared in *La Pluma* of Bogotá ascribes to Martí's writing, in Spanish and in English, a quality that will rank him among the greatest writers of his time and of all times from either America or Spain. The distinguished Colombian specifically compares Martí to Emerson, stating that "Emerson would not speak of [then U.S. president] Garfield in English with greater originality and feeling than Martí."[40] If this resembles the letter that Martí counts among the determining moments in his life, we observe a Martí who is deeply gratified that his America recognizes him and favorably evaluates him in relation to Emerson. More generously, we might view the supremacy of this moment as Martí's realization of his ability to connect with and generate Latino and Latin American readerships, even while living in New York and publishing texts that had been translated across French, English, and finally Spanish, and even when his readers were initially led to believe the essay on Garfield was by a leftist Spaniard in exile.

These references to key events in Martí's life also catalogue the forma-

tion of a fundamentally politicized consciousness in which cultural and
historical forces enmesh and condition each other. In listing the most significant events of his life, Martí includes a mysteriously coded reference to
"Sybilla"—a name that derives from a Greek word referring to a prophetess
—that connects this narrative of Martí's life-defining moments to a female
oracular interpreter, who makes intelligible a pre-European, chthonic female deity. This emblematic figure of female mediation of knowledge
prefigures Martí's evocation of "Madre América" in 1889. Marti's translations flowing below the visible European cultural systems link the poet,
cultural theorist, and revolutionary to definitions that precede, exceed, or
remain invisible within the nation form because of its often homogenizing
and masculinist discursive structures.

The "supreme moments" in Martí's list represent, too, extremes of
bodily vulnerability, such as when Martí was serving a forced labor prison
sentence, or when, as the poet of the *Versos sencillos*, he remembers how he
trembled at the sight of a bee stinging a child with whom he seems to have
had a parental relationship: "cuando la bárbara abeja / picó en la frente a
mi niña" (when a savage bee stung / the forehead of my little girl) (*Selected
Writings*, 274–75). Martí constructs a memory of himself as a father also of
a son, from whom he was estranged between October 1880 and December
of 1882, and again after three years of cohabitation, between 1885 and 1891,
which was the last time Martí saw his son. The moment encapsulates a
paternal perplexity at a child who seemingly appears out of nowhere and
would later disappear just as arbitrarily. The son's creation depends on an
inscrutable and infuriating maternal intervention, not reducible to thinking, as Martí had supposed in his essay on Emerson.[41] These "moments
that count" oddly evoke the utterly incalculable, interdependent elements
that escape the normative sovereign subject's rationalization and control.
Starting with the "evening of Emerson," these conjunctures also serve as
the matrix for Martí's coming to a consciousness of his divergence from
Emerson's ideal of man thinking.

ᔆ MARTÍ'S DIVERGENCE FROM EMERSON

The "evening of Emerson," as I noted above, marks the beginning of Martí's postcolonial double consciousness, which is to say, it catalyzes self-
definition through self-criticism. By February 1889, Martí's textual references to Emerson have taken on a dramatically different tone from his

earlier writings. Emerson appears in the midst of a vehement critique of superficial misconceptions of the United States by its own writers and by others. Couched as a review of a French Mark Twain—Max O'Rell, pseudonym of Paul Blouët—and of his light burlesque travel essay that pokes fun at the prudish and materialistic Gilded Age, *Jonathan and His Continent* (1889), Martí's critique amounts to a rejection of Emersonian transcendentalism. Although often cited in Martí scholarship as evidence of Martí's identification with Emerson, this passage in fact claims that Emerson's ideas, dating back some fifty years, have become obsolete, not only because they belong to a different historical and cultural moment and have proved inadequate to the political and cultural complexities of the late nineteenth century but also because one or two great authors neither should nor could speak on behalf of several hundred years of literary culture:

> As [Max O'Rell] does not know Emerson, and thus omits the name of the first American poet from his list of poets, he asserts that the United States has not yet produced a transcendental genius. As if any epoch could give of itself more or less than it carries within itself! As if today, as before, sufficient ignorance and passion had accumulated in the minds of the highest men of that time when, in fact, their height was due to the valley's failure to rise up! The mountains had not yet been brought low! Today there is no space for this. Transcendence is today in the laboratories: not in the laboratory of one, but in the laboratories of all. It is the epoch of development and of lowering the head to recognize, not of raising it up to prophesy. Today the prophecies come from below! (*El Partido Liberal*, February 7, 1889; *Obras*, 12:163)

The passage asserts the New Englander's obsolescence, linking it to the Latino migrant's own era, in which revolutionary restructuring of cultural value was becoming both possible and necessary; the passage thus moves from the past to a much larger claim about the present. Referencing Martí's own manifesto on modern poetry in the prologue to Pérez Bonalde's *El Poema del Niágara*, which he wrote the same year as his essay on Emerson (1882), Martí describes here a process akin to the "decentralization of intelligence." This description dissents from Thomas Carlyle's idea that all history is made by a few great men, and does so even more radically than Emerson, with his idea that "representative men" embody the potential of each individual.[42] Martí's omnivorous reading and translating of little known popular performances, forms of speech, and urban scenes shape his distinct understanding of text and culture as popular phenomena belonging especially to the working masses, as they are the society's primary producers. When Martí claims in this passage that "today, there is no space for this," the pronoun "this" refers to the accumulation of a wealth of knowledge in a single mind through years and years of isolated study and privileged conditions, the glorification of which depends, significantly, upon a sufficient level of "ignorance and passion" among the largest class. The intellectual "mountains" no longer appear great if the valleys rise up.

While this passage reproaches an account of the poetry of the United States that focuses on Whitman to the exclusion of Emerson and thus reveals Martí's own preferences with regard to these two poets, it more pointedly faults the Europeanist assumption that no genius had emerged, *or could emerge*, from America. Martí's comment also defines the limits of what the United States could produce, given its situation as a republic that tolerated postslavery racism and wars of aggression. The quiet mountaintop genius of Emerson, out of touch with the valleys, exemplifies these limits. By 1889, genius does not exist only in the silence of solitude on high, but in the bustling laboratories of chaos below. Detranscendentalizing Emerson's vision, Martí's conception of American genius begins with a bowing of the head toward study of the material creativity in the immediate, quotidian space of the largest number of people. This reversal of Martí's own reading of Emerson coincides with a historical process that Martí associates with an emergent phase of U.S. imperialism.

⟑ REPLACING THE PURITAN FROCK COAT WITH THE ROMAN CLOAK: THE WAR OF THE PACIFIC AND THE CHINESE EXCLUSION ACT

Two related hemispheric and U.S. domestic policies in the early 1880s exposed the limit of American renaissance ideals of transcendence, individualism, and originality: Chinese exclusion and a new phase of economic intervention in Latin America. Martí figures the transition between Peter Cooper's generation of North Americans and his Gilded Age contemporaries as the replacement of "the Puritan frock coat" with the "Roman cloak" (*Obras*, 9:306). His image describes the proposed replacement of the principled New England man of letters, James Russell Lowell, as ambassador to England, with Roscoe Conkling, the preening, resentful, Republican career politician. Although Martí eventually observes the slowing of

Lowell's creativity as a result of his extreme prosperity, he praises Lowell's *The Biglow Papers* (1848) for its daring experiment in Yankee dialect and fierce opposition to the annexation of Texas and Mexico (*Obras*, 9:305). The proposed change in garb represents a shift in the United States' self-representation and politics, from the humble and courageous protesters of religious persecution and of colonial control to the self-seeking consolidation of a pseudo-imperial nobility. The replacement of the austere black Levitic coat with the generous dimensions of an aristocratic cloak, ample enough to cover up profitable international schemes, links the new aggressive foreign policy of the United States with the construction of certain immigrants as "barbarians" who were beyond the pale of citizenship protections. Both of these developments irrupted in Martí's chronicles within months or weeks of the writing of "Emerson" in early 1882.

In stark contrast to Lowell's diplomacy and poetic experiment, the New York Republican Party boss Conkling represents to Martí newly vapid and dangerously myopic political practices. The Republican Party historian Lewis L. Gould explains the emergence of Conkling as part of a move away from a historical opposition to slavery toward an embrace of careerism: "the earlier generation [of Republicans] that had opposed slavery and fought the Civil War was giving way to professional politicians who approached their calling with less concern for ideology and more for their continued electoral survival."[43] The vengeful Conkling harbored a lingering grudge against Republican powerhouse James G. Blaine for deriding his "grandiloquent swell" and "over-powering turkey-gobbler strut."[44] To Martí, who anxiously monitored the dire effects of party squabbles for Cuba, for Mexico, and for other parts of his America, the professional politician's focus on personal gain signifies the transformation of the revolutionary lava of the emergent democratic nation into the cold, craggy rocks in the breasts of the later generation.[45]

Martí's U.S. contemporaries in the Gilded Age extended long-standing efforts to annex strategic islands and territories in Asia and Latin America, including Mexico, Samoa, Hawaii, Cuba, and Puerto Rico. Domestically, they redefined U.S. citizenship through race-based immigration exclusion and the widespread official tolerance or unofficial promotion of extrajudicial racial terror after the ratification of the Fourteenth Amendment. There are several different points of emergence for what Martí perceives as the corruption of North America's revolutionary legacy. His 1884 essay "Filiación Politica: El Origen del Partido Republicano de los Estados Unidos"

(Political Filiation: The Origin of the Republican Party of the United States), underscores the historical roots of the Republican Party in Wendell Phillips's radical abolitionism, which denounced any national authority that protected slavery.[46] But beginning in 1848, and more aggressively after the U.S. Civil War, a trend emerges that promises to bring about, in Martí's words, a "grave historical change of transcendental importance for the peoples of America."[47] With the closing of the Western frontier, economic expansion in contravention of rights to self-government introduced a system of inter-American commercial treaties and concessions for transportation and the mining industries in Central and South America that signified to Martí nothing less than "the pacific and decisive occupation of Central America and of the adjacent islands by the United States" (*Obras*, 10:87). Creating relationships of common interests between wealthy planters (many of whom were descendants of missionaries from the United States) and the agricultural barons of sugar and coffee plantations, these trading agreements sought and in many cases successfully created a virtual protectorate of Central and South America, and of several islands in the Caribbean and in Asia, notably Hawaii, the Philippines, and Samoa.[48]

With the invasion of Mexico, the United States began to betray its own principles of revolutionary self-government by invading and annexing territories. Martí would later describe this expansionist practice as a retrograde shift in the mode of North American government: "Under the old names of Republicans and Democrats, with no more novelty than the elements of place and character, the republic was becoming Caesarian and invasive, and its methods of government were taking monarchical forms, with the spirit of classes within monarchies" (*Obras*, 13:135). Democrats and Republicans were both complicit with this monarchical or imperial tendency. But during the decades after the Civil War, the Republican Party largely controlled the government and played a key role in shaping this transformation. Since its founding, the party had become, in Martí's assessment in 1884, "restless, powerful and conquering"; the party put to use "its arrogant display of its power and the disdain for all other races that today characterizes the North American people."[49] This racial "disdain" and arrogance characterizes both foreign and domestic policies created largely by Republicans in the Gilded Age. Unfortunately Emerson's intellectual legacy provided Martí's era inadequate guidance in addressing this trend, as I will show through a discussion of the anti-Asian discourse that became law in this period.

As Emerson aged in Concord, Massachusetts, James G. Blaine of Maine —a masterful orator and perhaps the most powerful Republican politician of the latter half of the nineteenth century—threw his hefty weight behind inter-American regionalization and advocated the legal exclusion of Asians from the United States. Serving first as an influential congressional representative and then as senator for eighteen years (1863–81), and having completed two terms in the office of secretary of state under the Garfield and Harrison administrations, Blaine used diplomatic posts in order to pursue what his biographers have called an "American imperial system." The Monroe Doctrine (1823), designed to resist European efforts to extend their power in the hemisphere, informed Blaine's "dearest ambition," which, according to one sympathetic biographer, David Saville Muzzey, "was to draw the republics of Latin-America into a voluntary recognition of a sort of benevolent protectorate on the part of the great republic of the North. . . . That was to be but the entering wedge for the penetration of American influence in those countries, to wean them from their traditional orientation toward Europe."[50] This political objective led him to advocate an innocuous-sounding "Peace Conference" in 1881, at which all the American republics might establish intimate friendship and reciprocity treaties.[51] As Edward P. Crapol notes, although Blaine "disavowed any intention on the part of his government to annex Hawaii or Cuba, . . . in his imperial blueprints they were integral insular parts of his 'American commercial system.'"[52]

Although the assassination of President James Garfield led to Blaine's replacement by Frederick Frelinghuysen in December 1881 and thus temporarily curtailed plans for the first Pan-American conference, Blaine's incipient version of "dollar diplomacy" reveals a keen awareness of the resources of South American countries and informs plans to harness these countries' raw materials and industries for U.S. manufacturing and investment. This strategy for achieving annexation or de facto economic control involved reciprocity treaties, which in contradiction to his voting record and outspoken defense of protectionism, proposed to admit at a reduced rate specific nations' materials in exchange for reduced tariffs on U.S. exports. During the years that Blaine advocated for the conference to further peace and friendship in the Americas, he sought to make Peru a protectorate of the United States and he made arguments in the U.S. Senate on behalf of Asian exclusion based on the racial threat that Asians posed to the survival of white Anglo-Saxon Protestant civilization.[53]

Thomas Nast's lampoon of Blaine in *Harper's Weekly* interweaves the

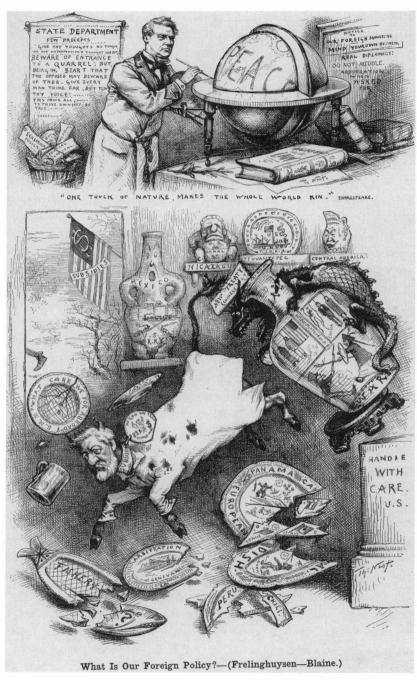

Thomas Nast, "What Is Our Foreign Policy?" *Harper's Weekly*, March 18, 1882.
By permission of MacCullough Hall Historical Museum.

domestic and foreign ramifications of Blaine's "spirited" policies by juxta-
posing ceramic artifacts of Central and South America and a giant, reeling,
orientalist jar that represents the collapsed 1868 Burlingame Treaty with
China concerning immigration (see facing page). The largest piece in this
display of exotic jars and jugs, the Chinese urn, depicts the "strange fruit"
of mass lynching and potential war, figured as a duel between Uncle Sam
and the Chinese emperor. The lynched bodies also recall attacks by whites
against the Chinese, which Blaine predicted as a natural and inevitable result of the presence of unassimilable Asian migrants in the United States.[54]
Blaine is the bull in this china shop, being chased by a dragon, and in
the process trampling a dish inscribed with the enlightened, modernizing
idea prized in his rhetoric—"arbitration." Above the bull's horns teeters a
cracked plate that advertises his isolationist views: "What Care We for
Abroad?" The American flag hanging by the door features a single dollar
sign instead of multiple stars, and Blaine wears a collar engraved with the
word "subsidies."[55]

Drawing on accusations in *The Nation* and testimony from minority
Democrats such as Perry Belmont in the Senate, José Ballón Aguirre persuasively argues in *Martí y Blaine en la dialéctica de la Guerra del Pacífico*
that Blaine's attempt to arbitrate between Chile and Peru during the War of
the Pacific (1879–83) undermined the negotiations. Ballón concludes that
Blaine in fact "speculated" upon Peru's divided and powerless situation
during the period prior to the war (99). Rather than support General
Nicolás de Piérola's guerrilla force—the group that enjoyed majority popular support in Peru and that was leading the fight against Chile from the
mountains—Blaine groomed and helped install the Lima-based lawyer
Francisco García Calderón. In return, the U.S firm Morton, Bliss and
Company, owned by Blaine's close political allies, gained rights to exploit
Peru's guano and nitrate resources.

Although racial attitudes toward Latin America did not produce a similarly exclusionary immigration policy in the nineteenth century, assumptions of Anglo-Saxon superiority inform foreign policy in the period. In
his biography, Muzzey perceives in the secretary of state's dealings with the
Peruvians and Chileans during the War of the Pacific a response to what
Blaine saw as an inherently irksome quality of the "Latin mind." Muzzey
notes that Blaine lacked "patience in dealing with peoples with whose
peculiar temperament he had little sympathy. The pride and punctilio of
the Latin mind irked him. His nervous vigor would have swept away the
web of obstruction woven by the factious and dilatory diplomacy of the

belligerents. He could not see why Chileans and Peruvians should not hasten to accept as beneficial to them what he assured them was beneficial" (212). Imposing his will, Blaine negotiated between the parties with the view that he could interpret the South American nations' interest better than they could. Blaine proposed to act as an arbitrator because he saw his culture as possessing greater vigor and efficiency. The means to Blaine's goal of controlling Peru's resources included keeping the Peruvians for months "under a delusion that the United States were going to help them out of the trouble" (248), or that the U.S. would back them in their claims against the Chileans.[56] Blaine portrayed as obstructionist and dilatory Peru's resistance to the building of U.S. naval bases on its territory or to the handing over of Peruvian nitrate, guano, coal, and railways to the U.S. government or to New York-based capitalists and diplomats.

Catching wind of these developments in the winter of 1881–82 and sensing their enormity but feeling uncertain as to how to translate them to his readers, Martí alludes to the terrifying implications of Blaine's policies in his chronicles. References to U.S. dealings in Peru appear in the midst of descriptions of New York's Christmas decorations:

> In the midst of the bustling streets, the weaving of wreaths and the green boughs of Christmas trees, monstrous conceptions appear of a Peruvian company that maintains that people of North America have a right to all the gold and riches of South America, and that Peru is becoming what Mexico has begun to become. In order to repay a loan to a venture capitalist, this process must begin by opening all of Peru's mines, its beds of gold, its seams of silver, its guano fields, and the crowning jewel of the contract, its ports and railroads, to the truly avaricious. (*La Opinión Nacional*, June 6, 1882; *Obras* 9:205)

This excerpt from Martí's description of the rituals of Christmas and Hanukkah (La Chanucka) appeared in *La Opinión Nacional* (a newspaper based in Caracas, Venezuela), just months before he published his essay there on Emerson. It offers a concrete example of the dehiscence that manifests itself in Martí's consciousness on the "evening of Emerson." Internally conflicted about frenetic consumerism and empty rituals as the multitudinous city gives itself over to the "unlimited pleasure of shopping" (*Obras*, 9:201), the narrative geographically straddles the richly decorated metropolis and the South American spaces that were increasingly being subject to North American economic exploitation. Martí uses the awkward phrase "monstrous conceptions" to allude to the antithetical idea of a so-called Peruvian company making claims on behalf of North American concessions. These inter-American business proposals appear distant and unrelated to the joys of the holidays. But the repeated figures of accumulation—as for example, shoppers bowing down before jewelry display cases in Tiffany's and the "jewel of the contract" with South America—forge connections between these spaces and economies.

In the hustle and bustle of "people crazed with greed [locos ávidos]" (*Obras*, 9:204), the chronicler feels doubly exiled. He uses the word "deterritorialized" (desterrado) twice in this holiday account, once in the opening lines and once to emphasize the hollow religiosity of the descendants of those pilgrims who had arrived 271 years before in pursuit of liberty, but who now wear military boots rather than work boots. In his description of Hanukkah that follows, Martí contrasts the trappings of the Christian religion to the Jewish commitment to preserving a language and a religion as an alternative *patria*, in celebration of which they recount Judas Maccabeus's blows to the heads of tyrants (*Obras*, 9:205). Building on this minoritarian Jewish claim to cultural self-preservation in a Christian dominant culture, Martí inscribes his place amongst the others: "Others make [their home] by falling in love, or if [love] has died, they go through the land as if in exile! Others make their patria out of a dream!" (*Obras*, 9:205). His alternative patria takes form in the interstices of the dominant binary of the Christian and Jewish religious holidays. So monstrous are the conceptions of South American expropriation and proposed protectorate status that Martí cannot name them as such, except through figurative depictions of the inter-American circuits of extraction and exchange that feature New York holiday shoppers and U.S. foreign policy makers.

The development of Republican machine politics in the hands of leaders such as Blaine and the phenomenally wealthy Levy Morton (who left Morton and Bliss to became William Henry Harrison's vice president during Blaine's second tenure as secretary of state in 1889) made real what Martí had tentatively defined as monstrous, unnatural, and unmentionable on that troubled Christmas Eve. In a chronicle dated January 19, 1883, weeks before Martí's thirtieth birthday and thus around the time of the "evening of Emerson," Martí speaks cynically about the Republican Party's political practices, its handing out of political offices, its collusion in voter fraud, and the antidemocratic nature of its convention, which Martí characterized as "closed and autocratic" (*Obras*, 9:344).[57] This 1883 chronicle reports

in a deadpan tone how a section of the Republican Party judged the Constitution to be overly restrictive and outdated: "The 'stalwarts' maintained
that the Constitution is a threadbare rag, and something of another time,
and that a powerful nation needs steel tracks on which to charge forward
and not a low-ranking constable that ties its hands" (*Obras*, 9:345). To
override the Constitution's protection of civil rights would facilitate the
Republican attempt to realize party leaders' political ambitions for influence well beyond U.S. borders. Martí paraphrases with sarcasm the
ideals driving this assessment: "a continental power, in sum, must accumulate capital and back-up funds, and win the will of the people with large
amounts of money, in order to spread itself over the continent when the
time comes" (*Obras*, 9:342). Martí reserves special vehemence for "the
people with large amounts of money," who stand to benefit financially
from the policies constrained by the Constitution's provisions. Anticipating the phrasing of his last letter to Manuel Mercado, written days before
his death in Dos Ríos, Cuba, this description of southward expansion
emphasizes the role of bribery in manufacturing electoral consent. It also
shows Martí's realization that only revolutionary violence could prevent
the United States from spreading itself through the Antilles and into the
rest of his America, precisely during the months when he had Emerson on
his mind.

When Blaine's presidential nomination in 1884 breathed new life into
the decades-old idea of buying Cuba, Martí held not only the United States
responsible, but also Latin American leaders whose complicity was necessary in order for Blaine to "force, under the pretext of a conference, the
countries of Hispanic America to become protectorates of the North"
(someter, so pretexto de conferencia, a un protectorado del Norte, los
países de Hispánoamerica) (*Obras*, 8:87). The Latin American elite's necessary collaboration in the Republican strategy of economic imperialism
contributes to Martí's anger at Latin American leaders who accepted bribes
at the expense of the interests of their citizenry and the democratic process.[58] With the Republicans' return to power in 1888, Martí argues that the
republic had "fallen into the hands of a conquistador party, which has
terminated in founding an aristocratic caste" (*Obras*, 11:435). This sharp
definition of the Republicans as "conquistadors" defines this leading force
within imperial modernity in terms of a European colonial tradition.

Just months after "Emerson," Martí informs his readers of the May 1882
ratification of the amendment to U.S. immigration law that prohibited any

state in the Union from granting citizenship to any person of Chinese origin (*Obras*, 9:312). A month earlier, writing on the topic of "social warfare," Martí described the assassinations of African American leaders, the strikes of white miners and railway workers, and demonstrations of armed Anglos against the Chinese in San Francisco. The following gripping passage employs the cinematographic, minimalist style of a screenplay in order to place the Latin American reader on the scene. It depicts aggressive, "native" vigilantes and creates readerly sympathy for vulnerable and unjustly demonized migrant workers. The "loyal citizens" of the United States appear here as armed perpetrators of violence and not as the vanquished victims of a foreign invasion, as the demonstrators in favor of Chinese exclusion claimed:

> In the immense city, immense silence. It was a holiday, but it looked like a day of combat. The calm provoked fear. In their houses, the women. In the streets, the men, unsociable, red-faced and armored [rojos y espaldados]. In the alleys and corners, the trembling Chinese. But at the hour of the gathering, the city was clamoring. They looked like crusaders, once they began to march with their muskets on their shoulders, and to point their lances. Tribunes arose in the plazas. The Chinese must leave the city of San Francisco for good! The city must defend its civilization and its homes! . . . As a single man, as one people, as loyal citizens of the Republic, the people of San Francisco, meeting together, beg the Congress to liberate them from the damages of this engulfing, servile, corrupting, insurmountable Chinese invasion. . . . And no, it is not the threatened European civilization that builds a wall of foam on its shores against the Chinese: it is the ire of the city's needy, who need higher salaries, acting against a group of workers that is conquering them because they work for low salaries. It is the rancor of the strong man against the capable [hábil] man. It is the fear of a population vanquished by hunger. (*La Opinión Nacional*, March 31, 1882; *Obras*, 9:283)

Backed into alleys, the trembling Chinese occupy the space left to them by the Anglos, who shout demands and decrees from spontaneous tribunals in the city's centers. The unusually short sentences formally echo the tension created by the threat of the Anglos' bullets. Martí repeats almost verbatim the rhetoric of then senator James G. Blaine's racially motivated argument for Chinese exclusion before the U.S. Congress, and thus exposes the circulation of stereotypes of disenfranchised workers."[59] By repre-

senting the Anglo domination of Chinese migrant workers, Martí reveals
to his reader the rhetorical and physical excesses of panicked white supremacy. The heterogeneity his perspective represents within the North
American scene calls into question the Anglo claims that migrants threatened to imperil North American civilization in general. The account
shows that in the chronicler's view, the United States engaged in exclusionary wall-building by defending the use of anti-immigrant force
with demonizing racial rhetoric. Similarly, Secretary of State Blaine's meddling in the War of the Pacific and his avid pursuit of Cuba's annexation
depended upon a white, nativist, anti-immigrant discourse at home. By
studying these historical events in relation to each other, Martí discovers
the role of racial discourse in constructing a domestic imperial subject
that, in keeping with Emerson's rhetoric, considers North America's youth
to be destined to transform the New World into the United States' private
garden.

ᑫᔆ EATING EMERSON

As Martí grappled with the monstrosity of North American expansionism
and made final revisions to his essay "Emerson," he received explicit editorial pressure not to publicly criticize the United States. In a letter dated
May 3, 1882, the editor of *La Opinión Nacional*, Fausto Teodoro de Aldrey,
stipulated that his New York–based correspondent should "arrange in
[his] critical judgments not to touch acerbically upon the vices and customs of this [U.S.] nation, because it pleases no one here and it would be
damaging for me."[60] Although the editor had praised the correspondent's
critical acuity in December 1881, when he compared Martí's incisive brilliance to a sharply cut diamond, a second undated letter echoed the first by
abruptly informing Martí of the public's complaints about the length and
literariness of the article on Emerson. His editor demanded lighter fare and
shorter paragraphs. Aldrey's repeated reprimands indicate the need for
subterfuge and clandestinity if Martí were to respond critically to the
United States' preeminent poet and philosopher, for whom the nation was
in mourning.[61]

Martí identified neither with the European colonial ideals, nor with a
Yankee definition of American originality. Both recognized incompletely
the rights of those who were not Anglo-Saxons to self-government and
citizenship in the hemisphere.[62] A space in between the opposition to and

identification with Emerson became necessary, especially because of Emerson's powerful legacy, which continues to apply a censoring pressure in contemporary critical rewritings of American literary history, an example of which I examine here.

A recent essay by Jeffrey F. L. Partridge on the award-winning contemporary poet Li-Young Lee reveals the structural blind spots that block scholarly perception of Anglo-American racism, anti-immigrant violence, and U.S. expansionism. Partridge shows a tendency to blunt the critical edge of the migrant response to Emerson in his interpretation of Lee's work. Lee's poem "The Cleaving" (1990) creates a poetic persona who eats Emerson as if he were a steamed fish. This eating makes Lee, who was born in Jakarta, a participant in a history of "savage" cultural rituals to which I argue Martí's essay makes an early contribution—his voracious consuming of Emerson configures an alternative to the progress narrative of assimilative U.S. multiculturalism.

Lee's eater not only consumes Emerson and his depiction of the Chinese, but he also swallows all the Chinese deaths due to anti-Asian violence, some of which Martí took pains to document. The act of eating reduces the transcendental eyeball to a tiny blind morsel. At the same time, this cannibalistic feast in Lee's poem sheds light on Emerson's complicity with the predominant Anglo sentiments toward Asians, which Blaine and other lawmakers converted into law in subsequent decades:

the walking deaths in the streets,
the death-far-from-home, the death-
in-a-strange-land, these Chinatown
deaths, these American deaths.
I would devour this race to sing it,
this race that according to Emerson
managed to preserve to a hair
for three or four thousand years
the ugliest features in the world.
I would eat these features, eat
the last three or four thousand years, every hair.
And I would eat Emerson, his transparent soul, his
soporific transcendence,
I would eat this head,
glazed in pepper-speckled sauce,
the cooked eyes opaque in their sockets [63]

Lee's quotation of a passage from Emerson's *Journals*—the three lines in italics in the middle of the above excerpt—formally mimes Lee's ingestion of Emerson.[64] This performative gesture demonstrates how undocumented citation need not signify harmonious melding between two texts. It also suggests that scholars may have too quickly compared Martí's allusions and quotations of Emerson's texts to the interpenetrating flows of a "bilingual ocean" or web.[65] I read the "eating" and quoting of Emerson as neutralizing Emerson's Anglo-Saxonist poison, while at the same time preserving a collective memory of the "walking deaths," of "deaths far-from-home," of the dead whose ghosts have not settled because the root causes of this racial violence have not been remedied.

Together with three or four thousand years of Asian culture, together with the stereotyped hair and features, Emerson becomes something to chew in the poet's mouth. The poem reduces Emerson and his texts to their materiality and commingles them with the millennial Asian civilization that his naive journal entry reduces to "a single hair." Cooked, and on a plate in front of the eater, the small eyeball loses both transparency and transcendence. It is part of a large and diverse banquet—in the Chinese tradition—where Emerson's famous eye constitites a minor, sleep-inducing ingredient. Lee's humorous comment about the "soporific" quality of Emerson's transcendental writings levels Emerson's position with respect to other long-standing cultural traditions.

In Partridge's reading of this eating, the poem belies a deep-seated "indebtedness to Emerson" (114). Partridge reads the fish as standing for the supposedly mute community of victims, rather than for Emerson and subsequent political movements such as the nativist Young Americans in an interpretation that allows Emerson to escape the poet's powerful jaws. Explaining that "this kind of racialized discourse was common to nineteenth-century thinkers" (115), Partridge excuses Emerson and chastises Lee's poem for "misconstru[ing]" Emerson's thought as "causing lethargy or leading to inaction" (117). This reading glosses over Lee's dangerous desire to eat Emerson and assimilates the poem to Emerson's influence: " 'The Cleaving' is Emersonian," concludes Partridge (120). Reading for Lee's debt, Partridge reverses the poet's irreverent belch by flatly claiming that Emerson's intellection "was by no means a soporific transcendentalism" (117).

Whereas Partridge portrays Lee as an implicitly "ethnic author" of the United States who seeks and gains membership in the nation in Emerson's tradition, we might rather read these migrant texts as provincializing Emerson and the small New England minority he nominates as the world's future leaders. Martí's juxtaposed essays on Emerson and anti-Asian violence dramatically highlight the powerlessness of Emerson's philosophy to challenge anti-Chinese violence. Notwithstanding Emerson's public opposition to the extension of slavery into new territory and to the invasion of Mexico, his thought fails to raise an effective obstacle to the notion of an Anglo-Saxon manifest destiny. In the remainder of this chapter, rather than minimize the migrant texts' difference, I will tease out how Emerson's sense of Anglo-Saxon superiority and imperial destiny become sticking points for his Latino migrant reader, José Martí.

ᖶ MARTÍ'S POSTCOLONIALITY AND DECONSTRUCTION IN AMERICA

In his 1997 book *At Emerson's Tomb*, John Carlos Rowe respectfully dissents from an Emersonian interpretation and structuring of modern American literature, which, in his view, "has effectively depoliticized that tradition" (25). He arrives at a similar conclusion to Martí: that Emerson's thinking proves inappropriate for addressing the contradictions at the heart of nineteenth-century U.S. society. Rowe's book identifies the limitations in Emerson's legacy in order to begin to reconstruct American literature "without inevitably subscribing to the values of Emersonianism" (25). Although Rowe does not mention Martí, we might consider how such a critical turn owes a debt to Martí for helping, over a century ago, to make visible the political and discursive shift in the definition of the United States.

Rowe's reinterpretation of a more diverse canon of U.S. writers challenges the way Emersonianism has "effectively minimiz[ed] the differences between abolitionist rhetorical practices and the 'aesthetic dissent' of Emerson" (10–11). His book, like postnationalist American studies more generally, echoes Silviano Santiago's critique in *The Space In-Between* of the search for influences. Rather than use Emerson as a measuring tape by which to gauge recovered texts by women and African Americans, Rowe proposes to read these marginal texts in a way that emphasizes their distinct, overtly confrontational activist tradition. In her comments on Rowe's work, Priscilla Wald notes Rowe's parallel commemoration of the "death" of a certain legacy of poststructuralist reading (in his book's dedication to Joseph Riddel).[66] But the proposed vision of an American literary history beyond Emerson does not necessarily dispel poststructuralism's lingering afterlife. Rowe rightly attributes the deconstruction of Emerson to feminist and antiracist social movements in the 1960s and 1970s rather than to some contradiction intrinsic to the aesthetic realm; similarly, solipsistic metropolitan theories of postmodernism have too long ignored their debts to a generative push from "decolonizing knowledges" in the periphery.[67] The problem is not merely Emerson's slowness to move from thought to action, as if these realms were separable by an abyss of space or time, but his lack of attention to strategies for altering material and rhetorical form.

Martí's essay on Emerson poses an alternative to the persistent logic of forward-moving progress at work in the national focus of many multiculturalist arguments. A common U.S. multicultural view erroneously assumes that the greatest compliment that the critic may pay to Li-Young Lee or to Martí is to find room to accommodate their savage or humorous insights in a Procrustean bed of U.S. literary modernity. Following Robert Young's argument that deconstruction most urgently allies itself to more-than-national relations of coloniality and postcoloniality, let us consider how Martí's redefinition of Emerson's America anticipates the tactics and methods of a revised "deconstruction in America" that Rowe defines in his work.[68]

This rereading of Martí's relationship to a North American tradition raises the question of the contestatory potential of defining another American modernity rather than preserving a now heterogeneous European modernity in opposition to a non-European nonmodernity. Martí's eulogies for dead North American representative men might be read through the lens of early deconstruction, as intratextual relationships in which the latecomer relates to the precursor along the lines of the "paradigmatic encounter between reader and text."[69] In this formulation, the difference in cultural locations between the earlier Yankee authors and the belated Latino migrant reader become equivalent to a misreading of essentially linguistic events. While this version of deconstruction challenges naturalized conceptions of patriarchal causality—of fathers begetting sons to make history—it empties out the political content of the transnational force field of empire. In the contemporary struggle over the legacy of deconstruction, postcolonial critics continue to challenge a dehistoricized and depoliticized version of American deconstruction that held sway in the 1980s. By reading the long history of U.S. empire in the Americas as a key subtext for understanding nineteenth-century literary history, we can plot and make visible the tensions between precursor and successor, originality and secondariness, high and low, "native" and alien, inside and outside, as structured within this imperial grid.

Breaking a path for a postcolonial deconstructive and Marxist tradition recently extended by Pheng Cheah in his definition of a "spectral nationality" of Africa and Asia, Martí depicts culture as a medium that encodes and shapes political relations.[70] Rather than a "newer" or emergent twentieth-century U.S. empire, then, postcoloniality appears in the late nineteenth century in the Americas, alongside high British and French imperialism, and alongside nationalist movements elsewhere. Figured repeatedly in terms of a living organism, a human body, a plant, a flower, the anticolonial nation in Martí's rhetoric feeds on and transfigures a German idealist tradition as limned by Cheah. This national organism is caught between life and death in the face of the neocolonial power of the United States. Taking shape in relation to imperial modernity, Martí's nation is haunted by and haunts the United States even before it actually invades Cuba and sets it under its tutelage in 1902. The insistent theme of death in Martí's essays on "Norteamericanos" and other writings underscores the spectral quality of the postcolonial Americanist project. Specters crowd into Martí's texts to demand an epigenetic—as opposed to an evolutionary —relationship to the betrayed North American revolutionary tradition.

Whose specters, we may ask? Specters of whom? What or who does Martí see as haunting imperial modernity's sumptuous banquet? Writing an essay entitled "Emerson" in 1882 at the edge of a freshly dug grave certainly seems an invocation of the Yankee eulogized therein. In *Lecturas norteamericanas*, Ballón identifies the ghost in Martí's modernist prologue to Pérez Bonalde's poem as Emerson:

> An immense pale man, dressed in black, with gaunt face, weeping eyes and dry lips, is walking gravely across the earth without rest or sleep—and he has taken a seat in every home and has put his trembling hand on every bedstead! Such a pounding in the brain! Such fear in the breast! Such demanding of things that do not come! Such unawareness of what one wants! And in the spirit, such a sense of mingled nausea and delight: nausea for the day that is dying, delight for the dawn! (*Obras*, 7:225; *Selected Writings*, 44).

To read this gaunt specter's grave steps as a heroic "Emerson penetrating towards the south of the continent" grants the North American the conventional role of model, catalyst, and triumphant bearer of the key to a perplexing modernity.[71] But Martí already in 1882 begins to see that the U.S. book cannot explain the Latin American enigma: the demands articulated here explicitly do not meet with answers; the object of desire itself is unknown; how to achieve the object remains vague. In the absence of a key to the enigma of Latino America, the lowering of the heights and the uprising of plains (llanos) facilitate lateral exchange and migratory movement. If his conclusion after reading Emerson is that the colonized need to cultivate critical self-study as an alternative to the partial memory of the imperial culture, Martí might be foreseeing his own weeping specter clamoring for the distinct modernity to which his America gives shape. The ghost catalyzes another modernity as it reaches from the past into the future to disorder a progressive, evolutionary logic.

Martí's 1882 manifesto-prologue to Pérez-Bonalde makes it difficult to believe that this specter could be the Emerson of self-reliance. While apparently rejecting a well-marked route set out by parental passions, or by existing political or religious systems, Emerson nevertheless belongs to the era of the "single labor that is taken to be marvelous and supreme" (*Selected Writings*, 47, 49). His audience represents a small North American elite that enjoyed the equivalent of "the repose of the monk's cell," in which the beneficiaries patiently composed volume after volume while others cooked their meals (*Selected Writings*, 45). Just as Martí perceived the monstrous shape of empire decades before the United States declared war on Spain, this text projects a ghost with a deconstructive agenda: it goes from household to household to announce the "dismantling of the human mind" and the parallel restructuring of literary and other institutions (*Selected Writings*, 45, 44). Emerson's ideal of sovereignty in life clashes with this ghost's trembling touch of death.

In the era of the modern poem, as Martí calls it, the beauty of political and aesthetic representation becomes the province of the many instead of the few. In the chronicler's adduction of the qualities of modern poetry, he takes delight in the evanescence of "individual geniuses," which are beginning to lack "the smallness of the periphery that previously heightened their stature" (*Obras*, 7:228; *Selected Writings*, 47, translation modified). As in "Emerson," here the center loses its definition without the periphery's fixed and subordinate status. The emergence of another American modernity witnesses a period of broken fences, of peoples in transit, and of multiple languages: "Now men are beginning to walk across the whole of earth without stumbling. . . . Cities have more tongues now than there are leaves on the trees of the forest" (*Selected Writings*, 45, 46). Like Martí's "Norteamericanos," post-Emersonian American literary history brings into focus the aesthetic and political insufficiency of a singular, autonomous modernity.

Repeated apparitions of a post-Emersonian specter appear in Martí's chronicles. An American Banquo shows up in the midst of a feast to rebuke the intellectual and political leadership of the Gilded Age.[72] Reminiscent of a pair of bedraggled beggars in the foreground of the cartoon that helped to dismantle James G. Blaine's 1884 bid for the presidency, Shakespeare's character in the North American scene calls attention to the social contradictions between the extreme wealth of an aristocratic elite and the growing poverty of an increasingly outraged workers' movement: "The good life and light thinking are agreeable and comforting things; but they are insufficient to chase away the problem of the times, which has taken its seat, against our will, at the banquet like Banquo's ghost" (*La Nación*, June 4, 1886; *Obras*, 10:411). Surprisingly, Martí uses the possessive second-person pronoun to describe a collective will to resist this ghost's presence. Against whose will does the ghost take its seat?

This disavowal of the ghost at the table pertains also to Martí's America. Martí's unsettling and unsettled ghost prefigures his untimely death. A spectral American modernity, made up of Martí's postcolonial nations of the future, traverses the space between past and present, between center and periphery. It crosses the borders between the living and the dead. As Jacques Derrida says of Marx and Marxists, this ghost causes an inescapable fear, for "it is as if they had been frightened by *someone* within themselves."[73] Martí speaks in "Nuestra América" of tigers that pose a threat from within, and when entering through a crack, also from without (*Obras*, 6:21; *Selected Writings*, 294). These openings also let in light and air. They speak the impossibility of an airtight sovereignty of the nation or of the subject. For without the productive circulation of self-critique, we ignore the mysterious revolutionary agent, "the problems of the times," which will eventually reveal the writing on the wall. This ghostly premonition of a spectral Martí points to Cuba's revised American revolution.

౭ "AS EMERSON THINKS": PROBLEMS AND PLEASURES OF THE GILDED AGE UNITED STATES

Martí's divergence from Emerson becomes explicit as early as 1885. Let us consider, for example, a chronicle entitled "Placeres y problemas de septiembre" (Pleasures and Problems of September) (*La Nación*, October 22,

1885), which juxtaposes the conditions of workers with the extravagant consumption of a spectacular America's Cup sailboat race and armaments display. By figuratively hanging a portrait of Emerson in the background of the scenes depicting "anglómanos" (Anglomaniacs)—a neologism that appears among Martí's subtitles—the chronicle conveys the celebration of Emerson by an increasingly imperial system that thrives off competition between Europe and the United States for control of Latin America's material resources: "à la London, they paint and write, they dress and strut, they eat and drink, as Emerson thinks, as Lincoln dies and as the blue-uniformed and blue-eyed captains of war look toward the sea and triumph" (*Obras*, 10:298). This post mortem reference to the victorious Union army and to Emerson's faint echo in the midst of a militarily aggressive Gilded Age that recalls some of the excesses of imperial Rome calls attention to persistent Anglophilia in the United States, especially among the wealthy and upwardly mobile classes. While Martí's expectations for the life work of the preeminent U.S. philosopher and declarer of cultural independence may be perhaps too high, this short passage rues the inefficacy of repeated exhortations to cast off the Old World mantle. The gesture toward a second declaration of independence in the North sadly did not transform the elite citizenry's exploitation of a class of disenfranchised workers, nor did it end this influential group's imitation of a British imperial prerogative over other nations. Britain and North American competitors vie for the trophy of Latin American resources, as anti-Asian racism and the exploitation of workers makes possible this sumptuous pageantry at home.[74]

The chronicle about a boat race in September 1885 culminates with a rich passage that exposes the exclusion of certain migrant communities from the benefits of transcendental individualism and imperial modernity. The verbs in a series of rhetorical questions shift in mood from the present subjunctive to the past subjunctive. This mood shift emphasizes the startling effect that these contradictory scenes might have had upon the Latino reader. However, the scenes do not appear to ruffle the city's consumers:

> Whoever may see this luxury, these privileged hippodromes, these mercantile palaces as large as a Roman circus; whoever may see these New York streets, exhausted by brownstones and by monotonous architecture, sustaining these places of business that are taller than church steeples, with sculpted moldings, bronze and marble roofs and atriums of granite; whosoever, upon seeing pass before their eyes during working hours an enormous procession of chariots

laden with ammunition, percherons for shooting it, and carts themselves decorated like works of art; whosoever, having seen this justice at the head of the city, and guiding this entire hymn, would believe that at the edges of rivers, along the Monongahela River, where they dig up coal, live thousands of starving and anguished miners like insects, without even a crust of bread in their cupboard, nor clothing for their children, nor more furniture than a wooden bench, nor more shelter than houses made of shipping crates? Living in New York and witnessing what he takes to be the blessing of human saintliness, a perennial ceremonial coronation of personal freedom, of the pacific life of a flock of kings, who would believe that where miners prepare and create, where the hot sand and black wind accumulate, where the miners dig up from the earth the coal that moves and sustains it, there are men without fear of the law or of a judge who might oppose them, who incite each other to battle, congregate with arms and pounce upon a town [*pueblo*] full of life, and kill its inhabitants and then set fire to it?

In its sins, in its errors, in its stumbling, it behooves us to study this nation, so as not to stumble as it has. (*La Nación*, October 22, 1885; *Obras*, 10:298–99)

These densely ornate sentences mimic the hurly-burly of the Roman circus in a series of questions that introduce an alterity from which to judge the "justice" governing this coronation of the "free person." Martí's passage constructs an alliance with the racialized migrants under attack and criticizes the festive consumption and military display of the regatta. The indefinite pronoun "whoever" at the head of these sentences constitutes an anonymity neither fully within nor fully outside the scene. The unnamed observer translates and conjoins disparate venues of the trembling immigrants and workers outside the city and the oblivious "flocks of kings" for a distant Latino reader. This "whoever" laments the aestheticizing of war by "Anglomaniacs" or imitators of crowned kings and self-absorbed individuals who benefit from the labor of exploited, impoverished, and marginalized workers. Martí's chronicle introduces a racialized migrant workers' critique of such displays of "personal freedom."

Collapsing the distance between center and periphery upon which any illusions of singular modernity depend, the chronicle plays out the shift from the beautiful-sounding turns of phrase of Emerson's declaration of cultural independence only to become a hollow clanging in brassy tones. Personal freedom, justice, and blessings to humanity captivate a sheepish "nobility" that fails to perceive, much less criticize, the exploitative conditions that make possible their coronation and parade. A hyperwealthy New

York elite, angry workers, and the victims of racial violence—the pleasures and problems of the title—sit side by side in the chronicle. Making visible the margins of the New York metropolis, the text skips nimbly from this military parade to the edges of the Monongahela, where masses of workers live in box shacks and breathe billowing coal dust. But rather than confront the complacent consumers in the opulent city, the white miners displace their rage in September 2, 1885, and massacre Chinese miners in Rock Springs, Wyoming. The massacre is the subject of the second installment of Martí's chronicle—dated, like the first one, September 19, 1885—and entitled "El problema industrial en los Estados Unidos" (The Industrial Problem in the United States).

Emphasizing the connections between the foreign war, exploitation, and domestic racial xenophobia, the second part of Martí's chronicle documents how coal miners who were recent immigrants from Europe attacked their Chinese coworkers, killing twenty-eight and wounding fifteen. Several were burned alive in their homes, shot in the mines where they worked, or attacked and eaten by wolves as they fled into the hills. Angry strikers looted and then burned to the ground seventy-nine dwellings in a Chinatown of some five hundred people on the site of the largest mining operation in the Union Pacific system.[75] Martí's chronicle notes that the mob returned to set fire to homes and to cadavers and forced the remaining Chinese to flee. The phrase "where one appears, the whites hunt him down" (*Obras*, 10:307) suggests the terror that such anti-Chinese violence conveyed to other racialized communities. Those who administered justice did not reprimand any of the sixteen "natives" who stood trial. The chronicle shows us how men "without fear of the law" may pounce upon a town or a nation, kill the inhabitants, and burn the evidence.

These grotesque scenes pertain more to the culture that embraced Emerson than to the ideals Emerson embraced. The target of Martí's chronicle-critique is the failure of social movements that claim Emerson as an ancestor to address the imperial elitism and white working-class racism that surfaced during the Gilded Age. Martí's chronicle theorizes the transgressive difference that a heterogeneous, anticolonial protest movement seeking to address the complexity of "its own problems" and pursuing another American modernity would signify in the 1880s United States: "This is not a European socialism that is being transplanted. It is not even the birth of an American socialism" (*Obras*, 10:308). No existing word or literary form could name the task facing Martí and other Latinos and

Latinas seeking social justice. In Martí's notebooks, political praxis propels this shift: "Not the resistance of the word, but the resistance of organization" (notebook entry dated 1890; *Obras*, 21:425).

∽ "WRITING IS A PAIN": ON MIMICRY, TRANSLATION, AND THE SEQUEL

Given the conscious and unconscious constraints on expressions of his divergence from Emerson, how did Martí translate Emerson? While he was thinking about the twilight of Emerson's explanatory power, Martí composed a set of partly typed, partly handwritten paragraphs entitled (like his better known essay) "Emerson," which examine the loaded question: how did Emerson create original poetic images?[76] This literary fragment illuminates the relationship between Emerson's central position in what we have long understood to be American literature and the semiclandestine condition of Martí, the non-Anglophone Latino migrant writing in the United States. Martí's attempt to study Emerson's method may suggest that he wanted to reproduce the self-assured capacity to create as Emerson did before him.[77] Yet, a close examination of these drafts of an essay reveals the New Englander's creative power as it encounters the limits of its ideals of autonomy and originality.

Any interrogation of Emerson's major status occasions the definition of another kind of writing: the minor. By this term I refer to the relationship of power between languages at the site where the border blurs. Gilles Deleuze and Félix Guattari define a minor language as existing "only in relation to a major language."[78] The problem is that the heightened location and hyperopia of the "I" of Emerson's essays make it next to impossible to appreciate or even perceive the small or the minor. Martí's draft paragraphs describe Emerson's thought: "Other times, the ideas came to him together in a mad rush. But like a sequel to a larger idea, the height of which hid the smaller ideas, upon the larger ideas being drawn aside, those that came afterward became discoverable. And since there were so many, he did not stop to reap the minor ones" (*Obras*, 19:353). The voluminous accumulation of ideas and lofty position prevent the Emerson of this passage from noticing multiple, smaller, and subsequent ideas. The minor, which Emerson did not think to look for, much less glean, remains hidden from his transcendental view, even as its minoritarian position defines his relative height. According to this description, a person who adopts this all-seeing mode of perception cannot conceive that others see what he or she cannot, or that they see differently: it is difficult for those in positions such as Emerson's to accept that "the rest do not see what they see" (*Obras*, 19:353). The minor is given to see something more, and to see it distinctly because of its view from below and from a multitude of angles. At the moment when Martí analyzes the structural limitations of the vision limned in Emerson's texts, he carves out another space that is paradoxically imperceptible to the "all-seeing" eye. He recognizes a space of invisibility in which minor variations flourish. Instead of pretending to conquer or extirpate the English language, Martí's essay and draft on Emerson introduce this principle of variation, of multilinguality, and of translation to America and to its modernity.

A recurring image in Martí's poetry, essays, notebooks, and correspondence refers to the experience of teaching or learning as an act of bodily penetration.[79] This submission can be pleasurable—a penetrating iron that "damages not" in *Ismaelillo*, also from 1882: "¿que hierro es el tuyo / que no hace daño?" (What iron have you that damages not?) ("Valle Lozano," *Poesía completa*, 46). The "Ismael" of Martí's first volume of poetry, a "labriego" (farm laborer), who is the young and banished son of Hagar, remakes his poet-father and the "lush valley" of the poem's title with a kind of iron or branding that does not wound. But an iron can, in other contexts, leave a deep wound. In one of Martí's fragments, the writing subject undergoes a "branding" at the hands of two imposing human figures (who suggest Emerson and Whitman as described in Martí's essays about them):

> What I see: a man goes up a mountain with an unsheathed sword: a figure strewn with clouds, another comes who brands my forehead with a red-hot iron; he brandishes it and impresses it, and as if satisfied at having wounded me, he goes.
>
> My gaze wanders over the book, like the wind of a hurricane over plains. Thoughts cross my forehead, like mounted steeds upon a battlefield.
>
> Work, this sweet consolation, this source of sources, this source of origins, this chisel, this paintbrush, creator, evoker, this friend which brings together, adds, smiles, invigorates, cures . . .
>
> Yes, because the statues of our ideas are broken and covered with dust. (*Obras*, 22:321)

The first figure remains aloof in the clouds, as the second brands Martí as if he were a piece of property. Although he wounds him, the branding figure fails to take possession. These two figures, one dressed in clouds, the other brandishing the iron, suggest defining elements of a U.S. literary tradition. Two poles—New England and New York, Emerson and Whitman—delimit the U.S. literary tradition during Martí's first years in the United States. The experience of a person reading these pillars of U.S. culture takes the form of a warrior climbing a mountain. The writer's persona goes armed with a sword. Transfixed by these two figures, who seem to collaborate in holding and branding him, the armed climber observes the satisfaction one of them feels at having wounded him. But this wound does not prove sufficient to cow the minor writer, because the scene of the fragment shifts abruptly to a desk space. In this reduced space of the book and its reader or the page and its writer, thoughts continue to move with the indomitable force of a hurricane, with the stampede of horses prepared for battle. Thus, in this reading, rather than Martí and Emerson exchanging glances through their texts as if in a mirror, Martí's texts on Emerson impress upon the reader the insurmountable temporal and political distance between the Cuban migrant and his Anglo predecessor. The space of the material text and of Martí's translation mediates this distance.

Increasingly conscious of the divergence between himself and the great North American author, Martí the "daily writer" translated Emerson much as the squirrel reprimands a mountain in Martí's version of Emerson's poem "Fable." In this poem, which Martí included in the first edition of *La Edad de Oro*, published in July 1889, Emerson's original fourth line, "Bun replied," expands to show the reader how the squirrel's presumption enraged the mountain: "la astuta ardilla" (the astute squirrel), says Martí, treads on the mountain's skirt (*Obras*, 18:325). In Martí's version, the loud-mouthed mountain does not merely call the squirrel a "little prig," but orders the squirrel to move: "¡Váyase usted allá, presumidilla!" (Move off me, little prig!)" The mountain, in Martí's translation, seems defensive, and perhaps lacks access to the squirrel's rapid skills of decipherment.

The most radical transformation occurs in the squirrel's response to the mountain's epithet. Emerson's "Bun" defends with pride the right to stay in his place: "And I think it no disgrace / To occupy my place" (Emerson, *Complete Works*, 9:71). By contrast, in Martí, the squirrel faults the mountain for ridiculing him because of his position of relative weakness:

Yo no sé que me ponga nadie tilde
Por ocupar un puesto tan humilde. (*Obras*, 18:325)
(I don't know why anyone would call me names
For occupying a less powerful position.)

The squirrel here indicts the mountain for attacking an obviously smaller opponent, and at the same time, transgressively moves outside his position to tread on the mountain's large "skirt" (falda). In Emerson, by contrast, the squirrel defines this space a "track," as if to suggest the squirrel must follow the mountain in order to move forward. Martí's translation of "Fable" thus uses Emerson's poetic device of a struggle in an obviously hierarchical power relation to reflect—for the youthful readers of his America—on their mutable, but not powerless, position.

As David with his slingshot to Emerson's Goliath, Martí used his on-going translations and interpretations to reflect on and clarify distinct locations in the Americas. In them, Martí defines tactics employed by the minor writer who is composing the not-yet-visible sequel to a larger idea. Not only the published essay "Emerson" and translations of Emerson's poetry but also unpublished and less visible works inscribe Martí's differ-ence in an attempt to make it difficult for Emerson's America to continue to ignore Martí's. More than descriptions of Emerson's writing on the occasion of the author's burial, the published and unpublished writings entitled "Emerson" stage the Cuban chronicler's difference.

In the published essay "Emerson," the protagonist of the first sentence is the trembling pen itself, an object that draws out similarities and differ-ences between the Emerson and the revolutionary poet: "Sometimes the pen trembles, just as a minister who is capable of sin may believe himself incapable of carrying out his ministry. The agitated spirit flies high above. It wants wings that exalt, not a pen [pluma] that cuts and sculpts like a chisel. To write is a pain, it is a lowering; it is like yoking a condor to a cart" (*Obras*, 13:15; *Selected Writings*, 116, translation modified).[80] The trem-bling pen recalls Emerson's rebellious rejection of his ministry in order to pursue a career as a writer, lecturer, and philosopher; the image affirms the Cuban writer's inevitable and impending rebellion against a colonial con-dition, revising Emerson's original act, and introducing the writer's South American difference. Writing in a specific place and time holds Martí down in the way that a slow-moving wagon hitch might pull on a condor.[81] The idea of hitching a condor to a cart alludes to and revises a romantic image that Emerson uses in his essay "Civilization," that of a star-drawn wagon.[82] Here, a South American, pre-Columbian deity replaces the star in the firmament, making Martí's source of inspiration a powerful bird of prey from an Andean culture that symbolizes centuries of resistance to European colonization.

Although the writer's agitated spirit desires the agency of whole wings that might carry its ideas or the meaning of the text upward, his clipped colonial wings force him to use a feather-pen (the word in Spanish, "pluma," means both) to nervously scratch out a migrant Latino subjectivity within an emerging imperial sphere. The remnant of the flapping wing, the feather-pen, works like a chisel. It is bound to a stony medium. Writing and writers figure here, as they do in Martí's notebooks, as the "*tilling of words—caretakers of bones—cultivators of language*" (*Obras*, 21:159, emphasis in the original). This curious series of phrases appears in violet ink script among the first pages of a notebook with yellow sheets dated 1881. The images locate the origin of writing and of the writing subject in an artisan's labor. Writing requires the work of plowing through words, of carefully burying the remnants of prior writers, of cultivating new words and literary forms. If Emerson would ask in his essay "Nature," "why should we grope around among the dry bones of the past" (21), Martí's oblique response is that these burial rites, the cultivation and tilling of the ground, acknowledge writing to be an action bound and determined dialectically by its cultural forebears and historical medium. Writing causes "pain" because the process of representation and communication inevitably circumscribes and colors the powerful, winged idea. The struggle to wield the chisel in a trembling fist represents the writer's effort to do more than merely extend or replace Emerson. The opening sentence of "Emerson" enacts this struggle. The trembling hand calls attention to the essayist's distinct historical and political position and to his refusal merely to retrace the great writer's line.

Emerson connotes for Martí the initially attractive but ultimately false promise of a fully sovereign individual standing above a rapidly changing world. Emerson claims to occupy a stable subject position from which to organize the flow of history, the space of the nation, and his own literary texts. This solid, mountainous quality of Emerson's, although mutable by nature, connotes stability. Let us look at a sentence from Emerson and see how Martí paraphrases or loosely translates it, without citing the original. Leaving aside the question of plagiarism, we can see how Martí's version sifts through and reworks the original.

[Emerson] Hence arises a pleasure mixed with awe; I may say a low degree of the sublime is felt, from the fact, probably, that man is hereby apprized that whilst the world is a spectacle, something in himself is stable. ("Nature," *Selections*, 44)

[Martí] El Hombre, frente a la naturaleza que cambia y pasa, siente en sí algo
estable. (Face to face with nature that changes and passes, the Man feels
something in himself which is stable.) (*Obras*, 13:26)

Martí's translation eliminates the tentative and attenuated phrasing through
which Emerson arrives at his conclusion that "something is stable": in
Martí's version, the stability of self-consciousness derives from a seeming
contrast between a fixed self and a changing and historical nature. Visible
mutability and the marks of time, thus, would erode the credibility of this
"something" stable that holds itself apart from nature. Martí's translation
contrasts sharply with his later characterization of Emerson's universe as an
edifice surrounded by scaffolding that he promptly demolishes: "But he
immediately tears down the scaffolding, ashamed of the meanness of his
edifice and the poverty of the mind that, when it sets itself to building
worlds, seems like an ant dragging a mountain range behind it" (*Selected
Writings*, 127). The "something stable" of the universe has become a tiny ant,
and the spectacle of the world or of the seemingly immutable mountain
have become the cargo that the ant pulls behind it. In other words, Martí's
interpretation of Emerson undercuts the great poet's claims to float un-
changing and all-seeing, above time. The smaller idea trudging down below
has the ability to make mountains quake. Each of these translated phrases
comments on and offers oblique answers to Emerson's question, "Why
should not we also enjoy an original relation to the universe?" ("Nature,"
Complete Works, 21). Why not indeed, the islander threatened with annexation might reply. The impossibility of a direct reproduction across languages mimics the fantasy of transparent equal access to universal promises
and goods. What mediate the postcolonial subject's relation to the universe
are the conditioning histories that produce multiple modernities.[83]

The fiction writer and contemporary of Martí, Henry James, concurs
with Martí's final skepticism of Emerson's individualism. James compares
his experience of the fragmented quality of subjectivity to Emerson's pretense to a fully conscious self-governing unity. James acknowledges envy of
Emerson's luxurious self-certainty, but ultimately attributes this ideal to
the blindness of Emerson's privileged location:

As most of us are made up of ill-assorted pieces, [Emerson's] reader . . .
envies him this transmitted unity, in which there was no mutual hustling or
crowding of elements. It must have been a kind of luxury to be—that is to
feel—so homogeneous, and it helps to account for his serenity, his power of

acceptance, and that absence of personal passion which makes his private correspondence read like a series of beautiful circulars or expanded cards *pour prendre congé*. He had the equanimity of a result; nature had taken care of him and he had only to speak.[84]

James claims that Emerson did not recognize his passionate connections to and dependence upon others. Even his correspondence—an intimate and necessarily relational mode of writing—dismisses as it takes leave in the manner of impersonal circulars or preprinted cards with the French phrase "pour prendre congé" (for leave-taking), inscribed in the corner. The distance from intimate connections perhaps enables him to retain the illusion of unmitigated autonomy. The luxury of time, of Emersonian America's geopolitical position and Emerson's social position in it make the semblance of detachment possible.

Emerson trumpeted sublimeness unavailable to most, and especially not to those minor, piecemeal, or daily freelance writers who came after him and who remained invisible to him. Martí describes his different circumstances in his diary: "The daily writer cannot pretend to be sublime. Such grunts end up sounding extravagant. . . . It is as if someone wanted to walk in normal steps from mountaintop to mountaintop. That person would fall into the abyss" (*Obras*, 21:254). Made up of ill-assorted pieces, skeptical of the fabled "true" self-consciousness, and suspicious of those who move from summit to summit, Martí "eats" Emerson while grunting about his belatedness, secondariness, and nonoriginality. But with the sagaciousness and mercurial insight of the squirrel, Martí's text articulates a detranscendentalizing alternative to the hierarchical, progress narrative of the young writer, who is condemned to merely reproduce the dead father.

The ceremonious closing toast to the "marvelous old man" in the published essay "Emerson" affirms this difference by leaving behind two emblematic remainders: a sheaf of green palm fronds and a sword of silver (*Obras*, 13:30; *Selected Writings*, 129). Martí's divergence from what I shall call a "United Statesian" way of seeing belongs to a process whereby Martí accepts that as part of his creative chiseling of another America, he will die with seemingly impossible hopes to free Cuba from Spain and to safeguard the island from annexation. At Emerson's gravesite Martí bestows a silver sword, evoking the clashing weapons on the colossal battlefield in the city far below Emerson's protected and silent remove, where his giant genius floats ponderously from summit to summit. The palm fronds represent tokens that carpet the ground in honor of dead warriors; they also recall the tree branches that in the Cuban poetic tradition symbolize the island's tropical location and cultural difference.[85] In addition to rendering a tribute, the essay's closing gesture confronts Emerson's idealism with the Cuban's militant strategy for fighting against North America's monopoly on the definition of modernity and liberty. For not only the process of reading, consuming, and burying Emerson, but most especially the labor of writing make possible the creation of other literary forms. This form revises a definition of America by projecting nonmimetically a survival with and beyond the scars of colonization.

ᴄ᷇ᴏ CONCLUSION: EMERSON, EAT YOUR HEART OUT

> Not I,—I will subject my word in exile, and I will allow myself to be eaten by her.—**José Martí,** Notebook 18 (1894)

> Human activity is a monster that when it does not create, it devours.
> —**José Martí,** "Carta de Nueva York" (1881)

In the last few weeks before Martí and others would depart for Cuba to launch the long-awaited revolution, Bernardo Figueredo, the fifteen-year-old son of one of the veterans and historians of the Ten Years War accompanied the delegate Martí during a return voyage by train from the Cuban migrant community in south Florida to New York. According to Bernardo Figueredo's oral account of this trip, Martí carried with him a book of Emerson's early essays and had bookmarked a page with a colored ribbon. He copied down a verse, which Figueredo paraphrases as saying: "the hero his heart every day devours."[86] What does it mean to devour one's heart, or—as the first of this section's epigraphs puts it—to allow oneself to be eaten by one's own words? Martí gave Figueredo the book as a gift, and made this comment when he did so: "This book I'm going to leave with you so that you may take care of it, and if by chance we do not see each other again, you will stay with it/him forever [te quedas con él para siempre]. But don't read it now because you are still too young and you need to learn more about what life is in order to benefit from it and take pleasure in it, as you ought" ("Recuerdos de Martí," 151). Martí's thoughts on parting with Emerson's essays informs us that he is wary of a naive misreading of Emerson, to which the green reader might fall prey.

Figueredo's version of Martí's advice, retold to two of Cuba's leading writers and Martí scholars, Cintio Vitier and Fina García Marruz, may be interpreted as a reconfirmation of Martí's role as the father and martyr of the nation, who prepares for his death by reading Emerson's advice about the cultivation of self-trust while facing the terrifying demands of heroism. This anecdote—from an avowed disciple of Emerson, for Figueredo claims Emerson as "one of [his] guides" ("Recuerdos de Martí," 151)—nevertheless also accounts for Martí's final separation from Emerson. With knowledge of "what life is," his careful perusal of Emerson prepared him to define an alternative to imperial modernity. And the modernism that Martí defined began when he allowed himself to be devoured by his own words in exile.

The passage to which Figueredo alludes in his oral history is probably the motto to the essay "Heroism," which defines the hero as an eater of his own heart. Rather than receiving food, especially the sugary products of slave labor, the hero opts for what Emerson calls "the counsel of his own bosom":

Drooping oft in wreaths of dread
Lightning-knotted round his head;
The hero is not fed on sweets,
Daily his own heart he eats.

This self-eating proves better than feeding on others. In one of his literary fragments, Martí wrote: "Poets should not be among the voracious ones, but among those who are eaten" (*Obras*, 22:42). My argument in this chapter for recognition of the divergence between Martí and Emerson enables us to gloss what Oscar Montero has termed "autocannibalism" or "a gutting of the self for the sake of a poetic vision" (*José Martí*, 111). This daily eating of one's own heart has political as well as aesthetic implications. It transforms the monster of unrealized or truncated creativity from a self-destructive colonial silence into an outspoken critical edge, sharpened in acts of reading in between the lines of prior, much more visible, texts. The critical self-relation replaces a passive reception of sweets "fed" to the hero. More than a portrait of the artist, Martí's "evening of Emerson" results in the shadows of dread and bolts of lightning that accompanied his realization that he would—having faced Emerson's insufficiency —write his America differently.

Philosophical texts from Plutarch to Cicero to Dante to Bacon mention Pythagoras's dictum "Cor ne edito" (Eat not the heart), to which Emerson's motto alludes. Francis Bacon defines the condition of someone who does not follow that advice: "those that want friends, to open themselves unto, are cannibals of their own hearts."[87] This definition of "eating one's heart out" has come to refer to silent grief, vexation, worry, isolation, and above all a friendliness so extreme that one is "eaten up" by anguish. To tell someone to "eat his/her heart out" also rings like a vindictive riposte after an underdog's victory. Indeed, Martí's Colombian friend Román Vélez remembers Martí lamenting in 1891, concerning the Cubans in the independence movement: "They take [Generals Máximo Gómez and Antonio Maceo] to be visionaries and they consider me crazy."[88] The doubt that many of the veteran Cuban leaders harbored about the feasibility and sanity of Martí's radical vision for Cuba left him isolated and alone. In Martí's journals and essays, the image of the colonized subject of "unequal and new nations" (*Epistolario*, 1:364) who acts in the world as an artist and as part of a self-governing nation yet to be, lives this aspiration as an overwhelming, unfulfilled desire. This desire infuses his writings.

Martí in his notebooks and essays cultivates language, tills words, and takes care of bones as an antidote to his postcolonial condition of non-recognition or misrepresentation. His translation of Emerson's phrase "our America" from the late essay "Fate," generates the key concept that has become Martí's legacy: "Our America has a bad name for superficialness. Great men, great nations, have not been boasters and buffoons, but perceivers of the terror of life, and have manned themselves to face it."[89] The phrase "our America" does not celebrate the newborn innocence, Adamic perception or autonomous creativity we usually associate with Emerson. Martí adopts this self-critical mode and insists on the phrase's distinct significance and tone when uttered in another language and from another perspective.

The "evening of Emerson" represents the end of the day in which New England could imagine itself as the transcendent center of American modernity. Martí's translations of Emerson invite the reader to see the small, minor, or subsequent ideas, which are the very ideas that have become a necessary supplement to Emerson's own. The next chapter examines how Martí's early ambivalence toward Emerson takes the form of a fierce parody of Walt Whitman's embrace of the United States' sense of its "manifest destiny" in the hemisphere.

Martí's "Mock-Congratulatory Signs": Walt Whitman's Occult Artistry

> FALSTAFF: I will not lend thee a penny.
> PISTOL: Why then the world's mine oyster
> which I will with sword open.
> —**Shakespeare,** *Merry Wives of Windsor* (1.1.1–3)

> We have lofty views of the scope and destiny of our American Republic. It is for the interest of mankind that its power and territory should be extended—the farther the better.
> —**Walt Whitman,** "Mr. Gallantin's Plan of Settling Our Dispute with Mexico"

> First teach [the Spanish American Republics] to respect us, and when they are so far civilized and educated as to have learned what the first principles of a republican form of government are, it will be time enough to think of annexation. —**Walt Whitman,** "The Spanish American Republics"

❧ A MINOR AND SHORT-LIVED BEING WHO SUFFERS IN THIS WORLD

On April 14, 1887, literati from the northeastern United States convened in New York to humor and honor Walt Whitman as he presented his annual commemoration of the anniversary of the assassination of Abraham Lincoln to a distinguished audience. They filled only a fourth of the Madison Square Theater, but it was an illustrious group, including professional authors such as James Russell Lowell, William Dean Howells, and Mark Twain. Academics such as Harvard's Charles Eliot Norton and the president of Johns Hopkins, Daniel Coit Gilman; power brokers such as Andrew Carnegie, the future secretary of state John Hay; and writers such as Mary Mapes Dodge and Frances Hodgson Burnett attended, along with some of Whitman's youthful admirers and several unknown foreigners.[1]

José Martí's ironic account of beatifying newspaper reports uses the tactics of camouflage to convey the semiclandestine reactions of the Latino migrant to Walt Whitman's imposing poetic and prosaic propositions. Martí's interpretation and incorporation—or cannibalistic ingestion, to use Silviano Santiago's metaphor—of the now celebrated poet of democracy provide further evidence of Martí's divergence from the imperial modernity that an emerging canon of U.S. literature rhetorically articulated in verse and prose. As in the shift in Emerson studies that we considered in the previous chapter, Martí's interpretation of Whitman's poetry anticipates a contemporary turn toward a more critical reading of Whitman. Positioning himself inside a widening fissure between American modernities, Martí reveals an artfully concealed, sometimes antiegalitarian, dilating, and contradictory politics that tended to present itself in the rhetoric of camaraderie and *libertad*.

In a now well-known essay entitled "El poeta Walt Whitman" (The Poet Walt Whitman) that appeared shortly after this event in Mexican and Argentine newspapers, Martí introduced readers of Spanish to what Whitman termed his "barbaric yawp" sounding "over the roofs of the world" in an "untranslatable" language.[2] Martí's transposition of this image to the bragging and swanking of "bárbara fanfarria" (*Obras*, 13:341) changes the register of Whitman's words.[3] Whereas Whitman's "yawp" conveys untamed, rebellious speech, Martí's "fanfarria" gives the impression that the North American swaggers as he moves. Anticipating the image of a giant with enormous boots that appears later in "Nuestra América" (1891), Martí's reference to Whitman's boastful way of moving emphasizes Whitman's physical, rather than merely verbal, imposition. Whitman's literary art, "que oculta por entero" (which he entirely conceals), exemplifies the tactics of imperial modernity hidden within the rhetorical flourishes of democracy.[4] Most twentieth-century interpretations of the Martí-Whitman encounter miss the mock-congratulatory aspects of Martí's chronicle and emphasize the North American's real or supposed seduction of the Cuban. But as I will argue, Martí's essay recasts Whitman's paean to liberty and democracy in *Leaves of Grass* in metaphors that draw out Whitman's investment in a national political project that has betrayed American principles of equality and self-government.

By calling attention to Whitman's assumption of divine status in his poetry's figurative language and in his performance onstage the night that Martí reviews, Martí lodges a secular critique of the northern nation's sense of its "manifest destiny" to expand the American Union west and south. Although the poet needed help to hobble onto the stage with his cane, the opening sentence of Martí's chronicle depicts him as a powerful, hieratic figure: Whitman "looked like a god" (*Obras*, 13:131; *Selected Writings*, 183).[5] Martí's paraphrase of news reports about Whitman and his disciples that evening respond to the poet's belated beatification by the brokers of culture at the end of his life: he seats the poet on a plush velvet red armchair, his white hair flowing, and a crook or crosier in his hand. This description of Whitman in a red throne-like chair does not quite concur with *The Sun*'s evocation of the "gorgeous blue plush and gilt boudoir scene" on stage in the Madison Square Theater, but it is congruent with the lavish reception that Whitman's wealthy friends John Johnston and Robert Pearsall Smith sponsored in the luxurious Westminster Hotel that evening.[6] In all likelihood, Martí could not have afforded the price of the ticket that William Dean Howells was collecting at the door of the Madison Square Theater, which netted Whitman some $600 in one night (over half of the proceeds came from Andrew Carnegie). But Martí—with another American poetry on his mind—may well have been among the visitors who stepped close to shake Whitman's hand at the evening reception.[7]

The second sentence of "El poeta Walt Whitman" assumes a hyperbolic tone that evokes Whitman's preference for "the fiery whirlwind of prophecy" and "the fervor of certainty" over reasoned argument (*Obras*, 13:142; *Selected Writings*, 194). In describing Whitman's over-the-top performance, Martí positions himself as a silent dissenter in a crowd of acolytes. Whitman himself recollects the affair in mixed terms, as a drunken jamboree that he opposed from the beginning, but also as "the culminating hour of his life."[8] I quote the first paragraph of Martí's essay in full, so that the reader may grapple with the excess of meaning that Martí sets loose in this inter-American introduction:

> "He looked like a God last night, seated in a red velvet chair, with his shock of white hair, his beard spread out on his chest, his eyebrows as thick as forests, his hand resting on his crosier [cayado]." This is what one of today's newspapers says of the poet Walt Whitman, now seventy years old, to whom profound critics—who are always the least critical, or who are the least in number [que siempre son los menos]—assign an extraordinary position in the literature of his country and of his time. Only the sacred books of antiquity offer a doctrine comparable in prophetic language and robust poetry to the doctrine this old poet emits, in grandiose and priestly maxims,

like mouthfuls of light, and whose flabbergasting book is banned. (*Obras*, 13:131; *Selected Writings*, 183, translation modified)

This passage attributes observations of the poet's divine status to "profound critics" in the newspapers. Although Martí's essay in no way offers a candid critique of the celebrated poet, his translation counterpoints the reportage with the multivalent phrase that could mean "who are always the least in number," but also, "who are always the least critical." This qualifier suggests that in addition to being in the minority, these critics may lack criteria for judgment in their "profound" treatment of Whitman's self-presentation. The unspoken question of Martí's opening paragraph lingers: how profound can these critics be, who write articles that merely reprint or summarize Whitman's discourse without critically examining its form and significance?

In this sacral and regal *mise-en-scène*, Martí places Whitman on a red throne, authorized by his long staff and emitting "priestly maxims" (*Obras*, 13:131; *Selected Writings*, 183). Martí's Whitman includes within himself "the priest who defends a part of the truth as if it were the whole" (*Obras*, 13:136; *Selected Writings*, 188). Whitman's contradictions provoke at first a disconcerting feeling or even a temporary sense of "prodigious aberration" (portentoso extravío), but his art quickly resolves this disorderliness or errancy into a superhuman natural order: "Whitman's apparent irregularity, initially disconcerting, soon turns out to be—but for brief moments of prodigious aberration—the same sublime order and composition as that of the mountain peaks outlined against the sky" (*Obras*, 13:132; *Selected Writings*, 184). Whitman's iconoclastic carriage on the national literary stage models the role of the United States in relation to the rest of the Americas: immutable like a mountain, designed in accordance with nature, and prophesied in Scripture. Whitman is the poet of "the arrogant peace of a redeemed mankind," the poet who declares himself divine and who, in Martí's translation, "*believes* that he sanctifies everything that he touches."[9] Whitman represents in poetic form the birth of the era of U.S. imperial modernity; but in Martí's careful selection and translation, he also prefigures its death.

From his earliest notebook musings to his mature essays on North American culture, Martí adopted something similar to what Edward Said calls "secular criticism," despite addressing a strongly Catholic readership in Latin America.[10] According to Said, "secular criticism" is characterized by an "absence of divine originality" and challenges universals or hermetic systems by paying attention to the "complexities of many-stranded history."[11] By planting a doubt as to the validity of Whitman's passionate celebration of United States after the annexation of half of Mexico, Martí's fame—and notoriety—as a cultural critic grew. The former president of Argentina, Domingo Faustino Sarmiento, recommended that his friend Paul Groussac undertake a French translation of Martí, but also called upon Martí to disseminate the United States' exemplary modernity rather than his own Latino criticism.[12]

Years later, in an 1893 speech to the migrant Latino community in Tampa, Florida, Martí warns the migrant community not to base its conception of the United States on its books and sermons.[13] This thoroughly bitter statement calls upon Latin Americans and migrants to read the United States with skepticism:

> And if we look outside, and at what is outside of this North where, because of a phantasmagoria and our imprudence we came to live, and because of the foolishness of taking peoples at their word, and of basing the realities of a nation on what they say in their Sunday sermons and in their books; if we, anxious with goose bumps, look at our life in this country, where upon the first dispute of its interests . . . it shows its profound cracks shamelessly [enseña sin verguenza, sus grietas profundas] we will see that in more than a few of the homes of the sons without a country, . . . domestic virtue struggles in shame against the sordid animality around them [sordidez y animalidad ambientes], against the greatest of all the threats to humankind, which is the total devotion of life to the blind and exclusive cult of the self [culto ciego y exclusivo de sí mismo].[14]

If Martí acknowledges the daring strangeness of "Song of Myself" in 1887, his early concern has become a pointed critique of a characteristic "cult of the self" by 1893. "El poeta Walt Whitman" (1887) sought to expose the pretense of liberty that increasingly posed a threat to Martí's America. In 1893 Martí more directly denounces a U.S. "phantasmagoria," and turns away from what many had perceived as a captivating evangelism.

By the end of his life, Walt Whitman had become a spokesperson for democracy, for the postbellum American Union, and above all, for the self-satisfied singing of oneself. Whitman's stature would only increase over time and throughout the Western hemisphere, but Martí's essay raises questions about the "I" that emerges in Whitman's poetry and prose, which occasionally expresses longing to be master to others' bodies and territories. In defining his interpretive task, Martí acknowledges the aggressive force and attractive pull of the economy and politics of the United States, which was actively pursuing greater influence in Latin America during the 1880s. It reacts to Whitman's poetry from a position of impoverished invisibility in American letters, by indicting the way Whitman seems to view the other Americas, as a "pensamiento pordiosero" (beggarly thought) (*Obras*, 13:141; *Selected Writings*, 193, translation modified) or as a "useless excrescence" that the majestic braggart pushes to one side "with a swift kick" (de un solo bote) (*Obras*, 13:139; *Selected Writings*, 191, translation modified). Martí inscribes himself in the margins of Whitman's North American world, whose celebrated poets "look upon a minor and short-lived being who suffers in it" (mira un ser menor y acabadizo al que en él sufre).[15] The referent for the pronoun *él* in "que en él sufre" may be "the world" rather than Whitman. The sentence preceding clarifies: "What haste can drive him [Whitman] on, when he believes that all is where it should be, and that the will of a man must not turn *the world* from its path?" Rather than a drama internal to Whitman, this suffering of a short-lived being pertains to a writer like Martí, who is in Whitman's world but not in Whitman's skin.

Martí shared Whitman's disapproval of European-oriented, elitist academicism, and appreciated the power of Whitman's embrace of the erotic, physical body (although Martí wrote about him with a certain self-repressive homophobic blush).[16] For example, Martí adopted the title "Versos libres" (Free Verses) for one of his collections of poetry, which is reminiscent of Whitman's defiant refusal of poetic and cultural conventions. Although Martí's poems make use of internal rhyme, this collection and Martí's poetics generally emphasize rhythm over rhyme, which suggests Whitman's influence. Martí, like Whitman, worked as a newspaper editor and freelance writer. Like Whitman, Martí rejected the cloistered, Eurocentric orientation of nineteenth-century men of letters, or *letrados*. Martí's *Versos sencillos* (1891) and other essays declare Martí's preference, like Whitman's, for association with workers over pompous academic writers. Nonetheless, I argue that Martí's critique of this giant's searing rhetoric outweighs his admiration. In adopting Martí's reference to Whitman's "occult artistry" for my title to this chapter, I refer to a paradoxical combination of world-swallowing force and of seductive affirmations of equality, liberty, and respect, which tends to make the articulation of American exceptionalism an enormously durable and—at least for Martí's America—a pernicious ideology. As an apology for empire, Whitman's occult artistry naturalizes the giant's southward march. Martí conveys Whitman's textual "I" to Latin American readers through a strange tangle of bloody metaphors that describe their effects for a "minor" writer of another America.

∾ OCCULT ARTISTRY AND NATURALIZING VIOLENCE

> Los romanos, al entrar con César en Roma:
> Urbani, servate uxores, moechum calvum adducimus.
> (The Romans, as they entered with Caesar in Rome:
> Gentle citizens, take care of your wives; we are carrying a
> death's head.)
>
> —**José Martí**, Notebook 7, *Obras*, 21:224

After several pages about the event in Madison Square, about the purpose of poetry and on Whitman's reputation, "El poeta Walt Whitman" turns to a description of Martí's experience of reading Whitman's poetry. Martí gives "Whitman's poetry" the character of a Roman emperor. Figured as riding atop a Roman chariot, whip in hand, and implicitly accompanied by conquered slaves, Whitman's poetry leaps out of the page with "a dominator's fist" (puño de domador) (*Obras*, 13:141; *Selected Writings*, 193, translation modified).[17] The violent imagery that erupts in Martí's essay on Whitman amplifies his early concern and anticipates contemporary observations of Whitman's participation in the dynamics of enslavement and mastery or his endorsement of the invasion of Mexico. Martí prefigures Ali Behdad's claim that "[Whitman's] poetic project aestheticizes the nation's geography by way of disavowing its expansionist history."[18] In anticipation of the twentieth-century Dominican poet, Pedro Mir, who opposes a Latino American "nosotros" (we) to the antique "yo" (I) of Whitman, Martí sings a "contracanto" (countersong) in the late nineteenth century.[19]

To Martí, poetic language's protean quality has a unique power and responsibility to catalyze critical reflection. According to this passage from Martí's essay on Whitman, poetry, even more than industry, stimulates a will to transform the course of events in the pursuit of liberty: "Poetry that congregates or separates, that fortifies or brings anguish, that shores up or demolishes souls, that gives or robs men of faith and vigor is more necessary to a nation than industry itself. For industry provides the nation with a means of subsistence, while literature gives it the desire and the strength for life. Where will a people go when they have lost the habit of thinking with faith about the scope and meaning of their actions?" (*Obras*, 13:135;

Selected Writings, 187, translation modified). With the capacity to give or to take away desire and strength or the faith and vigor of a people, poetry enjoys enormous significance in Martí's ideology. This philosophical reflection on the role of a national poet indicts a literary failure to stimulate critical reflection on a nation's history and on its present actions.

Even Whitman himself in a period of unemployment and insecurity after leaving his editorial post at the *Brooklyn Times* characterizes his celebratory singing of the self as "blab whose echoes recoil upon me" in his self-critical poem "As I Ebb'd with the Ocean of Life" (1860). Here a "Me" that "[has] not once had the least idea who or what I am" introduces the mockery of Whitman that seems to characterize Martí's reactions:

> Withdrawn far, mocking me with mock-congratulatory signs and bows,
> With peals of distant ironical laughter at every word I have written,
> Pointing in silence to these songs, and then to the sand beneath.[20]

The self-mocking stance of these remarkable lines presents an attitude that aptly describes Martí's semiclandestine, muted reactions from an American space in between. In fact, Martí ends the essay on Whitman with a paraphrase of an image from this poem. Returning the reader to the jubilant scenes of uncorked champagne with which the essay begins, Martí's last sentence anticipates Whitman at the happy hour of his death, when he "becomes blossom and fragrance on its swells" (*Obras*, 13:143; *Selected Writings*, 194), which echoes Whitman's poetic self-description as "a limp blossom or two, torn, just as much over waves floating, drifted at random" (*Leaves of Grass*, 214).

To Martí, literature provides a forum where it is possible to represent, to reflect on, and to imagine alternatives to the suffering and shock triggered by an imposed, imperial modernity. Martí's depiction of Whitman's "disjointed, lacerating, fragmented, drifting sentences" focuses on the intellectual rebellion of the Latino migrant reader to the condition assigned him within Whitman's American modernity (*Obras*, 13:141; *Selected Writings*, 193). It elucidates Whitman's occult artistry, which skillfully renders socially constructed hierarchies natural, immutable, and exempt from secular critique or historical inquiry:

> Assured in his mastery of the impression of unity he sets out to create, [Whitman] employs his artistry, which he entirely conceals [emplea su arte, que oculta por entero], to reproduce the elements of his picture in the same disorder he observed in Nature. Though he raves, he never strikes a wrong

note, because the mind does wander thus, without slavish order [sin orden ni esclavitud], from one matter to its analogies; but then, as if he had only let the reins go slack for a moment without letting go of them, he suddenly gathers them in and steadies the team of bucking horses with the fist of a dominator [con puño de domador], and his lines go at a gallop as if they were swallowing up the Earth with every movement. (*Obras*, 13:141; *Selected Writings*, 193, translation modified)

This comparison of the effect of Whitman's figurative language to a conquering charioteer or a horse driver exposes the special technique of achieving and maintaining a position of power without acknowledging the historical use of force in its achievement. The passage uses the metaphor of a horse driver and his manipulation of the reins to figure the relation between Whitman's rhetoric and the reader who diverges from the North American's celebrated definition of America. The horses, feeling the constraints slack about their necks, live with the illusion of freedom. But when they are about to get out of control, they sense the driver's power to whip them and an occult artistry moves efficiently and forcefully to quiet them, just as Whitman's occult artistry silences the critical thought. Apart from crucial exceptions when Whitman manages ironical laughter, his rhetoric proclaims beautiful ideas that distract the horses with the carrot of future equality, sovereignty, and liberty. The celebrated poet of democracy shores up a semblance of freedom, but only partially veils its threat to crush potential resistance with a dominating fist.

In referencing the mind's wandering from one matter to analogous situations, Martí observes in Whitman's poetry the problematic imperial tactic of generalizing by analogy. Mary Louise Pratt describes this generalization as the "monopolistic use of categories."[21] Granting that such generalizations reflect a human tendency, Martí underscores the will to monopoly on definition in Whitman's *Leaves of Grass*, which enables him to draw boundaries and assign meanings that redefine the United States' growing imperial power as a natural result of free choice, as exemplified in his depiction of immigration from Asia. Whitman's poem "A Broadway Pageant" portrays the United States, personified as "Libertad" as the site of pilgrimage for a pageant of peoples who appear "sultry," "florid," and "sunburnt," and seek to be "renew'd as it must be."[22] Chanting "the greater supremacy," the imperial power recasts itself in its national poetry as capable of renewing and refreshing the decadent "Asiatic" or "Oriental races." This definition of the United States as a destination for migrants from across the globe positions the United States as a choiceworthy regime, at the very center of the world.

Martí, with his provincializing agenda, translates and analyzes this poem so as to expose the occult artistry that redefines imperial modernity as a guise of liberty. He directs his readers to the poem by translating the first line of section 2, but his translation brings to the foreground the latent assumption of superiority in the poem. "Superb-faced Manhattan!" becomes "Manhattan de rostro soberbio" (Manhattan of the haughty face).[23] In response to Whitman's use of Spanish in this poem to congratulate his audience on their position in the globe, Martí simply notes Whitman's debts to the Spanish-speakers whose territory and resources have bolstered the nation to global prominence: "Walt Whitman, the patriarchal poet of the North never says [liberty] in English, but as he learned to say it from Mexicans."[24] In arrogating to himself the power to give the sign of democracy, however contradictory it may be in its northern acception, Whitman "never strikes a wrong note." Whitman's lines of poetry charge forward by subduing resistance or difference, trampling minor worlds, ostensibly in a charge for liberty and democracy.

What Martí in "Nuestra América" (1891) defines as a fundamental battle to be fought with ideological weapons appears first in "El poeta Walt Whitman" as a terrifying potential future and an intimate physical betrayal. Whitman's sacred verses foment a militant response: "After listening for a while to this poetry, one can make out that it sounds like the earth's surface when triumphant armies are coming across it (or after him), barefoot and glorious" (*Obras*, 13:141; *Selected Writings*, 193, translation modified). Is this ill-equipped army following or charging on Whitman's poetic persona? Is the chronicler who hears the thunderous pounding of the cavalry's hooves among the glorious barefoot army's ranks? These images suggest an army's resistance to the world-swallowing mouth and imposing strides of this towering figure of North American letters. To hear this army of stamping feet, the chronicler would have to be among or near to them. Given Martí's long history as a militant for Cuba's independence, we can imagine Martí armed in opposition to a poetic celebration of expansion.

ᕼ SUPPLEMENTING WHITMAN SCHOLARSHIP

To the Chilean critic and novelist Fernando Alegría, who has written an influential book-length study on Whitman's reception in Latin America, José Martí is the translator who opened Latin America's door to Whitman's ideals and poetics. Alegría's study portrays the Cuban as laying the cornerstone for a Latin American monument in Whitman's honor.[25] Alegría's depiction of Martí as longing for the "freedom to work and [for] liberty to develop spiritually" in the United States renders the Cuban a would-be immigrant who not only seeks assimilation, but also would proselytize these values throughout Latin America.[26] Yet Martí's increasingly acute criticism of the Whitmanian cult of the self raises questions about the assumption of Martí's faith in Whitman and in the United States. The mainstream of Latin American criticism follows Alegría's assertion of a spiritualized brotherhood between Whitman and Martí, and sublimates the corporeal violence that Whitman's writing signifies for Martí as a Latino migrant from an island threatened by annexation.[27]

Alegría's interpretation of Martí's honoring of Whitman adheres to a dominant reading in the United States in the first half of the twentieth century, which defends Whitman against the previous century's puritanical rejection of his unconventional sexualizing of the body.[28] Alegría's Martí cherishes a heterodominant Whitman who defended marriage and family, even though neither he nor Whitman lived a conventional married life or raised the children they claimed or did not claim.[29] At odds with the goal of monumentalizing Whitman as founding father, Martí enthusiastically directs the reader to Whitman's most passionate same-sex poetry amongst the Calamus poems.[30] Martí's riveting description of a Whitmanesque figure placing a searing hot brand on his reader's mind (the figure we examined in chapter 3), as if the Good Grey Poet were marking an animal or a slave, introduces charged corporeal figures of domination and submission. To reduce Martí's complicated signifying on Whitman's text to either an Arnoldian "simplicity" and "beauty" or a sublimation of bodily impulses to a spiritual calling neglects Martí's complicated response to Whitman's text.

North American readings have recuperated a queer, sexually liberated Whitman—whom Martí problematically tries to "straighten out," even as he reveals his fascination with Whitman's bodily freedom. However, even this generative and sexually liberated version of Whitman has continued to sidestep Whitman's expansionist politics.[31] In mounting a defense of Whitman's challenges to a repressive heterosexual dominant, the scholar Michael Moon aligns Whitman's sexual transgressiveness with an inclusionary American pragmatism but avoids a sustained analysis of Whitman's expansionism.[32] Moon propounds the still urgent argument that the United States needs to recognize and end violent exclusion of nondomi-

nant sexualities in order to democratize its culture, and in the course of
that argument affirms Whitman's undecidable gendering of the American
landscape. Its conclusion, however, reduces differences between imperialism and anti-imperialism by attributing both to a heterosexual imperative.
Differentiating a queer reading from celebrants of territorial expansion
and from adversaries of imperialism alike, Moon argues persuasively that
both Henry Nash Smith and Quentin Anderson invest in the idea of America as a female body to be heterosexually possessed and occupied.[33] Quentin Anderson's attack on Whitman's psychological imperialism problematically renders Whitman a "deficient or inadequate person" (*The Imperial
Self*, 114), while it challenges the principle of expansionism that Henry
Nash Smith trumpets. Moon is right that Whitman's "Preface" to the 1855
edition of *Leaves of Grass* offers a transgressive alternative to oedipalized,
heterosexist structures of identification. While Whitman liberated sexuality from the straitjacket of the heterosexuality that dominated his era
and ours, his poetic figures nevertheless celebrate an expansiveness that
resonates with the expansionism of his era: "When the long Atlantic coast
stretches longer and the Pacific coast stretches longer he easily stretches
with them north or south."[34] The indeterminacy of the sexual object does
not contravene the poem's celebration of a Yankee's desire to expand and
penetrate the continent from end to end, in its widest and longest dimensions. Indeed, up to the end of the twentieth century, U.S. critics embraced
Whitman's sexually transgressive poetics while leaving unchallenged Whitman's role in giving "final imaginative expression to the theme of manifest
destiny."[35]

Around the turn of the new millennium, Whitman criticism began to
take its distance from the historic disavowal within U.S. American literary
studies of both Whitman's racism and imperialism.[36] Ed Folsom's sobering
reading of Whitman's antiblack and anti–Native American racism acknowledges a "compromise" of the poet and the nation's ideals, which Folsom
rightly attributes to long-standing tendencies in the society.[37] David Reynolds also acknowledges "deeply unsettling" passages where Whitman depicts African American intellect as on par with that of "baboons," and where
he describes "the nigger," and "the Injun" as "minor rats" to be cleared out
by a superior grade of rats.[38] Kirsten Silva Gruesz connects Whitman's
racism to an imperial ambivalence toward black and brown bodies that the
mid-nineteenth-century wars incorporated into the body politic. Yet these
revelations have not fully revised the firm scholarly embrace of Whitman as

"indisputably American," "radically egalitarian," and "the democratic poet to an extent never matched" (Reynolds, *Walt Whitman*, 138). These claims depend, I suppose, on what "democracy" or "American" mean, which is precisely why Martí aimed to redefine these terms. These critical appraisals of the racial attitudes in Whitman's prose and in his published conversations with Horace Traubel face this embarrassing aspect of the United States' democratic past and raise interesting questions about the debts of U.S. criticism to its precursors in Latin America.

If Ralph Waldo Emerson occasionally balked at the U.S. annexation of Mexico and other places, Whitman's editorial journalism from the late 1850s energetically advocated expansion. Both the journalism and poetry adamantly promoted the Free Soil Party's proexpansion position. Quoting his friend and editor John L. O'Sullivan, the coiner of the phrase "manifest destiny," who published some of his prose, Whitman specifically desired Cuba as jewel for his America's crown: " 'Manifest destiny' certainly points to the speedy annexation of Cuba by the United States."[39] Beyond a sexual interpretation of this inter-American frolic, we might also read Whitman's figures of enlargement as provoking Martí's mock-congratulatory responses to the poet of democracy in "El poeta Walt Whitman." The Mexican critic Mauricio González de la Garza builds on Martí's criticism of Walt Whitman's duplicitous position by setting in motion a contemporary reappraisal of the poet with his book-length study *Walt Whitman: racista, imperialista antimexicano* (1971). By recovering and reprinting in Spanish and English the now widely cited examples of Whitman's attitudes toward Native Americans, people of African descent, Mexicans, and immigrants generally, González de la Garza's research reveals Whitman to be "the poet *par excellance* of manifest destiny" (*Walt Whitman*, 10). This research trajectory informs Silva Gruesz's evocative reference to Whitman as the "mouth of a new empire."[40]

González de la Garza exposes Whitman's editorial leadership in articulating the popular mainstream view of African Americans and Mexicans as somehow beyond the pale of civilization and as having benefited from their enslavement or annexation. Whitman's appraisals of the United States–Mexican war also help elaborate an ideology that clashes with Martí's vision of cross-racial equality and solidarity. In one of many statements in favor of the U.S. invasion and appropriation of Mexican territory, Whitman makes a cultural-racial argument about Mexicans being unfit for self-government: "What has miserable, inefficient Mexico—with her superstition, her burlesque upon freedom, her actual tyranny by the few over the many—what has she to do with the great mission of governing and peopling the New World with a noble race? Be it ours to achieve that mission!"[41] This eugenicist rhetoric extends the assumption about Mexican ineligibility for self-determination by questioning Mexicans' rights to reproduce themselves and their culture in the New World.[42]

As editor of the *Brooklyn Daily Eagle*, Whitman's editorials chastised criticism and debate concerning the war in the years leading up to the invasion of Mexico.[43] Such critical inquiry might illuminate the ethically dubious impetus behind the war and thus cast doubt on its rhetorical justification. Whitman challenges the legitimacy of open, historical, and secular reflection on the causes of the war by propagating the common argument that war hastens peace: "*Will not the future effect of even this war extend the area of Peace Principles—and hasten the advent of that holy era when all swords shall be beat into plough shares and spears into pruning-hooks?*"[44] This logic seems strained given the aggressive nature of the war. Rehearsing similarly hackneyed arguments in favor of slavery, Whitman's editorials argue that through enslavement, modern New World Africans attained the opportunity to become civilized.[45] Whitman endorses racial segregation in accordance with a popular conception of white America's manifest destiny: "Who believes that the Whites and Blacks can ever amalgamate in America? Or who wishes it to happen? Nature has set an impassable seal against it. Besides, is not America for the Whites? And is it not better so?"[46] Even as Whitman asserts the exclusive rights of whites to America (both North and South), his rhetoric minimizes whites' role in enslavement or territorial invasion by portraying the conditions and effects of modern slavery and colonization as divinely or naturally fated.

In González de la Garza's assessment, the poet's "ambition was to see the countries of the earth in submission to the United States."[47] Although González's sweeping judgment did not find a receptive audience in the United States for several decades, scholarly consensus has inched toward a more critical view of Whitman's politics by reading his prose from before and after the Civil War with greater care. Both Doris Sommer's and Kirsten Silva Gruesz's comparative American literary projects cite González's recontextualization of Walt Whitman, but neither reach González's more radical conclusion about Whitman's twisting of the rhetoric of democracy to such an extent that it might become an instrument in effecting domination of the world.[48]

Neither did Martí ever reach this level of pessimism concerning the possibilities for liberty through democratic government. But González's sense that Whitman rhetorically undermined secular criticism in the propagation of a new American religion of democracy echoes the figures in Martí's 1887 essay. González ascribes to Whitman the role of high priest in a new American religion (*Walt Whitman*, 169). Expecting to die while fighting for another American modernity, Martí wrote essays on the mainstream U.S. culture that embraced Whitman as its poet in the 1880s, several decades after Whitman published these now obviously problematic editorials. Martí's essay questions restrictive definitions of citizenship and of humanity that continued to inform daily social practices, Supreme Court law, and foreign policy throughout the Gilded Age. Martí challenges the northern poet's generalization from his individual subjectivity to define a universal American identity to which the other Americas ought to assimilate, in keeping with the progress of a singular modernity.[49] As the Whitman fêted by Carnegie chanted a new phase of incorporation and expansion, Martí dissented in his translation of Whitman's texts. If "Song of Myself" declares that a "Yankee" had "the limberest joints on earth and the sternest joints on earth," Martí alludes to and revises this phrase: "already he feels his joints [or his situation or circumstances] are beginning to move" (ya siente mover sus coyunturas).[50]

Ꭿ LATE NINETEENTH-CENTURY VIEWS OF WHITMAN'S ABSORPTIVE SUBJECT

Readers of Whitman in the 1880s often did not have the same investment as twentieth-century readers in the view of Whitman as the American poet of democracy. Some late nineteenth-century readers of North and South America shared Martí's critical suspicion of Whitman's politics. E. Clarence Stedman published an even-handed reading in 1880 that establishes a precedent for Martí's questioning of Whitman's celebrated stance.[51] Like Martí's, Stedman's essay values Whitman's unconventional poetics and his public performances as a Broadway rough, strolling the streets, crossing on Brooklyn ferry, and riding the omnibus with fare collectors.[52] Describing Whitman's literary contribution as the "hideous progeny" of Emerson's and Carlyle's intensely individualistic philosophies, Stedman attributes to Whitman's overwhelming subjectivity a threatening expansiveness: "To one so watchful of his own individuality, any creed that involves a merger of it is monstrous and impossible. . . . His subjectivity is so great that he not only absorbs all others into himself, but also insists upon being absorbed by whomsoever he addresses. . . . Whitman's personality is too strong and individual to be universal, and even to him, it is not given to be all things to all men."[53] Stedman is here reacting to an absorptive will and forced universalism. And Martí's reading echoes Stedman's mixed reactions.

Similarly, the renowned modernist Rubén Darío, who was one of the earliest readers to perceive the profuse "plasticity," vivid color, and formal experimentation going on in Martí's writing, corroborates this less-than-hagiographic reading of Whitman.[54] Martí's 1887 essay so deeply impressed Darío—Martí's adopted "son"—that in 1890 the precocious twenty-year-old published a revised edition of his modernist volume *Azul* (1888), with the addition of a "Medallion" entitled "Walt Whitman."[55] In this sonnet, the North American poet announces himself as the prophet of progress, but nestled in the "Olympic wrinkle" between his serene and saintly eyebrows lies a sinuous viper that both "inspires and conquers" (inspira y vence).[56] Written in postwar Chile, in the wake of the half-hearted attempt of the United States to arbitrate in the bloody War of the Pacific, Darío's sonnet underscores Martí's unmasking of Whitman's "face of an emperor" (*Azul*, 175).

Although the sonnet renders Whitman the emblem of a seemingly magnificent modernity, it also unflatteringly shows Whitman ordering around his underlings. As Manuel Pedro González demonstrates, by counting the number of Martí's words (thirty-five) that Darío uses in his fifty-seven-word sonnet, Martí's description of the Yankee who holds himself superior, the "man who strides, loves, fights [and] rows" (*Obras*, 13:131; *Selected Writings*, 183) reappears in Darío's sonnet:[57] "[Whitman] Dice al águila: '¡Vuela!'; '¡Boga!,' al marino, / y '¡Trabaja!,' al robusto trabajador / ¡Así va ese poeta por su camino / con su soberbio rostro de emperador!" (He says to the eagle: "Fly!" to the sailor "Row!," and to the robust worker, "Work!" / This is how this poet makes his way / with the haughty face of an emperor!) (*Azul*, 175). Darío borrows the images in Martí's essay to warn his readers of the impetuous giant steps, domineering orders, and poetic voicing of a new world power.

Similarly, Darío's eulogy to Martí in *Los raros* (1895) recalls Whitman's memorable figure among Martí's chronicles of the United States. To Darío, Martí's modernist prose introduces an ironic twist to his depiction of Whitman:

My memory gets lost in that mountain of images, but of course I remember . . . a patriarchal, prestigious, lyrically august Walt Whitman. . . . In those letters he spoke of the dangers of the Yankee, of the careful vigilance that Latin America should maintain with respect to its older sister, and of the deep substance of that phrase that an Argentine speaker opposed to the sentence of Monroe. . . . [D]ue to his constant contact with all that is modern and his universal and polyglot knowledge, [Martí, the prose stylist] created his special and extremely particular style, . . . making continual use of the English hyperbaton, setting loose his chariots of metaphors, twisting the spirals of figures.[58]

This obituary offers one of the earliest appraisals of Martí the writer in the year of his death. In it, Darío remembers Whitman as august, patriarchal, and lyrical, but for Martí he chooses the verb "twisting" (retorciendo), thus highlighting the role of figurative language in potentially expressing a clandestine warning concerning Whitman's incomplete conception of democracy, which he camouflages in the form of an encomium. The verb also emphasizes that Martí's elaborate modernist form responds to and remakes the imperial modernity of the United States.

Darío first uses the word "modernismo" in 1888 to refer to "a style composed of new jewels and old silver."[59] As a literary revolution that originated in exchanges between Martí, Darío, and other Latin American contemporaries, modernism in Spanish reworks European, and especially French, symbolist, pre-Raphaelite poetics from a peripheral perspective, in order to generate a new literary aesthetic.[60] In an 1892 assessment of contemporary Cuban poetry, the eminent Spanish literary critic Marcelino Menéndez y Pelayo describes the contemporary literary experiment under way on and off the island (by authors who go unnamed, for neither Casal nor Martí appears in his account) as producing a "Frenchified mestizo slang" and of harboring an ungrateful "aversion to the *madre patria* [Spain]."[61] With the term "modernismo," Darío describes the Latin American transformation and remaking of predominant literary forms. This inventive appropriation creates a literary form able to accommodate new modes of psychological and political consciousness of Latin America, which radically challenged Europe's concept of itself as an originary cultural center.

Following Gerard Aching's study of Darío and other modernists as presenting a politically conscious challenge to Europe's presumed cultural superiority, I propose that Darío's "Walt Whitman" alerts the reader to the mesmerizing effect of Whitman's enchanting poetic performance and maintains the mock-congratulatory tone of the essay by Martí that inspired it.[62]

Martí's approach to Whitman gains clarity when we contrast it with another nineteenth-century contemporary, the fellow poet, literary critic, and diplomat who headed the Nicaraguan legation in Washington, D.C., Román Mayorga Rivas. Rivas's admiring essay bears a title identical to Martí's, "El poeta Walt Whitman" and appeared in the preeminent Spanish-language literary magazine of the late nineteenth century, *La Revista Ilustrada de Nueva York*, of which Mayorga Rivas served as coeditor between 1889 and 1890.[63] Unlike Martí, Mayorga Rivas fully endorses Whitman's poetic celebration of the United States. Rivas lauds Whitman for "forging a literature for Liberty and for the twentieth century" ("El poeta Walt Whitman," 8). Based on a firsthand report of several reporter friends who visited Whitman's Mickle Street home in Camden, New Jersey, in 1890, Rivas's essay censors anyone who would dare to mock the United States, its people, and its poets:

> Those who make fun of the North American people as materialistic or prosaic only observe its astonishing mercantile movements; but he who studies the sphere of its thought and its soul must recognize its artistic qualities, and its idealistic spirit, which in its generosity and daring, runs parallel to its love of progress and of humanity. . . . These Yankees have set off enough light in these skies with their inventions to surround themselves with an inextinguishable splendor that will illuminate their greatness throughout the centuries. (8)

Rivas's condemnation of humorous attacks on the materialistic tendencies of the United States bears witness to an acrid debate transpiring in the Latino intellectual community in New York city during these years. Although a fragment of correspondence from Martí to Rivas indicates the two were acquaintances, this passage suggests his sensitivity to Martí's criticism.[64] Martí enjoyed a certain notoriety for his critique of Latin American leaders' overidentification with the United States, ever since his December 1889 speech "Madre América," delivered to the Sociedad Literaria Hispano-Americana de Nueva York, which was attended by many Latin American diplomats residing or visiting New York or Washington, D.C. In that speech, Martí challenged Latin America's elites to reject the United States as a model and embrace the diverse subaltern masses of people who made up the vast majority of their countries' populations.[65] Whereas

Darío's sonnet affiliates with Martí's critical stance, Rivas embraces Whitman's celebration of the United States as an irreproachable example of progress and humanity. I now return to Martí's complex poetic prose on Whitman, by way of the heated critical debates that have emerged over how to read it.

ᴄᴡ "MY WORDS ITCH AT YOUR EARS TILL YOU UNDERSTAND THEM": WHITMAN'S WORLD-SWALLOWING RHETORIC

Although Martí's essay on Whitman does not cite the journalism that González de la Garza cites, it attributes assumptions of mastery and superiority to the organizing poetic persona of *Leaves of Grass*. As several critics have noted, Whitman began to pen his free verse in notebooks around the same time that he was writing many of his editorials, and continuities extend across the prose and poetry.[66] Whitman's poetry deploys a much more nuanced and inclusive version of a U.S.-centered ideology, while the journalism makes no attempt to hide sometimes unsavory—if mainstream—views.

I wish to stress that Whitman's prose interests us not as a measure of Whitman's *personal* malevolence or aberrant arrogance. The ideas that appeared in his journalism and in his poetry pertained to the vast majority of liberal white northerners who opposed slavery but did not endorse social equality. Whitman's journalism and poetry function in Martí's critique as an icon for the fairly widespread vision of racially coded U.S. dominance of the hemisphere. These passages exemplify the occult artistry that Martí found so alarming about U.S. imperial modernity, even as he acknowledged Whitman's daring, poetic experiment.

To read the tone of "El poeta Walt Whitman" as a mock-congratulatory response to the celestial, white-bearded Whitman resonates with González's disinterred evidence, but does not hinge upon it. The journalism from between the United States–Mexico War and the U.S. Civil War revealed North American attitudes that Martí encountered in the United States and in which he desperately did not want to believe. Moreover, Martí's and González's interpretations push U.S. American literary criticism to imagine empire, language, race, and nation as fundamental and intersecting categories that have become indispensable to research in American literature and culture.

Whitman's poetry and prose cheers the North American subject's removal of limits or challenges to its mastery by sheer force of will. For example, freedom from so-called degrading contact with people of color or subject peoples required unencumbered and privileged movement by whites into new territory. Not only did Whitman's editorial "Prohibition of Colored Persons" endorse the constitutional exclusion of African-descended peoples, enslaved or free, from the state of Oregon as a means to protect white labor from the "interference and competition of Black Labor," but the "settling" of the West forms part of the backdrop to Whitman's "Song of the Open Road," in which an uncompromising will achieves the goal of unrestrained movement:[67]

> From this hour I ordain myself loos'd of limits and imaginary lines,
> Going where I list, my own master total and absolute, Listening to others,
>   considering well what they say,
> Pausing, searching, receiving, contemplating,
> Gently, but with undeniable will, divesting myself of the holds
> that would hold me. . . .
> The east and west are mine, and the north and the south
> are mine.
>   ("Song of the Open Road," sec. 5, *Leaves of Grass*, 128)

While this evocation of the independent traveler setting forth into and claiming ownership of new terrain has become an icon of freedom in the United States, it implies a problematic fantasy of total self-mastery that denies settlers' dependence upon indigenous knowledge and techniques of cultivation for survival. As "master total and absolute," the persona of *Leaves of Grass* exemplifies the Emersonian fantasy of seeing all while being invisible. Whitman's catalogues take stock of long inventories. As Martí notes of Whitman's poetic form, "Accumulation strikes him as the best sort of description" (*Obras*, 13:142; *Selected Writings*, 194). Whitman's long chants accomplish world-swallowing where the eye cannot: "My voice goes after what my eyes cannot reach, / With the twirl of my tongue I encompass worlds and volumes of worlds."[68]

The poetic use of oxymoron celebrates rather than interrogates contradictions between imperial expansion and democracy in the poetry and in the prose. Whitman acknowledges and even relishes the seemingly impossible contradictions between the practice of racially restrictive citizenship and his indiscriminate kisses for "the cotton-field drudge or cleaner of privies."[69] Martí's translation of this line transforms this worker-cleaner from an object of the poet's familiar affection to the more intimate position of a family member: "That one who cleans the filth from your house, he is my brother" (*Obras*, 13:132; *Selected Writings*, 184). Martí prods Whitman to see that in postslavery cultures, distinctions between "pure" white and black groupings break down. In New York and New Orleans, argues Martí, "they do not have a fixed color in their eyes, just as they do not have a single race in their veins: in their eyes are painted all shades, as in their city, all races."[70] Whitman's poetry disavows the presence and subordination of African, Mexican, and other oppressed groups when it joyfully announces liberty through conquest: "Americanos! Conquerors! Marches humanitarian! Foremost! Century marches! Libertad! Masses!"[71] With this triumphant appropriation of Spanish, Whitman's poet chants "the copious islands beyond" and a "new empire, grander than any before," all the while singing "Libertad! for themselves and for you."[72]

The contradictory twirls of Whitman's rhetoric apologize for U.S. empire by denying that the United States imitates Europe. For while he asserts an essential U.S. difference from Europe, he promotes the nation's conquest of the hemisphere: "We claim those lands, thus, by a law superior to parchments and dry diplomatic rules . . . for we have not vassal provinces, like the monarchies of old Europe. We do not take them to be our inferiors in any respect, but to be our equals."[73] The divine or natural impetus for manifest destiny fabricates a distinction between the "rightful" claiming of lands by the United States and European monarchy's "bad" imperialism. This rhetorical contradiction exploits the promise of democracy in order to justify the contravention of other American nations' self-government. The chanting of "democracy" propitiates the nagging suspicion that the United States was becoming a pale, blood-stained copy of European empires.

The history of decisions and acts by which the United States arrogates territorial control becomes a homogeneous and empty progression of time.[74] If Whitman prophesies in "Democratic Vistas," "Long ere the second centennial arrives, there will be some forty to fifty great States, among them Canada and Cuba," Martí parodies this confident prediction in his essay on Whitman, through a translation and commentary on the original:[75] "The world, for Walt Whitman, was always as it is today. If a thing is, then it needs to have been thus, when it no longer must be, it will not be. . . . He laughs at what they call disillusionment and knows the amplitude of time; he accepts time absolutely."[76] Despite his piercing insight about his own death in "As I Ebb'd," Whitman's nation tends to fancy itself to be in full control of the vagaries of history and as the living fulfillment of divine destiny.

By contrast, as a colonial subject, Martí literally runs everywhere, for he cannot accept that the world will remain the same. Sprinting from his office on Front Street in Lower Manhattan to meetings with co-revolutionaries, then back to the office, where he would often write furiously until dawn, Martí worked incessantly in order to establish Cuba's equal claim to independence and mutual respect from the other American republics. Whitman need not hurry, says Martí: "Walt Whitman is satisfied: . . . Why shouldn't he observe human suffering calmly, since he knows that beyond it is an endless being for whom a joyous immersion in Nature awaits?" (*Obras*, 13:139; *Selected Writings*, 191). Martí translates Whitman's poetic claim in "Song of Myself" to "know the amplitude of time" (*Leaves of Grass*, 42). This knowledge sets Whitman at ease, in the comfort of a secure sovereignty. Expansion, emancipation, and enslavement all happen only in accordance with time's progress and divine mandate; human actions and the social relations of force that bring about and maintain slavery and colonialism, for example, become irrelevant.[77] To achieve mutual recognition among independent and emancipated states and persons, Martí's task demands that he interrupt the continuum of progress and articulate "a revolutionary chance in the fight for the oppressed past."[78]

Martí's most poignant dissent from Whitman concerns the natural growth of Whitman's engulfing body and its excrescences. Although the words apparently agree with Whitman's engulfing and endless growth, the bathos and exaggeration of the anticlimactic closing phrases raise questions about the common U.S. celebration of the melting pot: "[Whitman] must melt everything in the oven of his heart; over everything, the white beard should be allowed to fall" (debe dejar caer la barba blanca) (*Obras*, 13:136; *Selected Writings*, 188, translation modified). The poet's white locks and "the stuff of far more arrogant republics" should be allowed to descend over all, to engulf worlds in their flow.[79] Even if we read "dejar caer" ([be] allowed to fall) with Martí's eloquent translator Esther Allen, as saying that "above all, he must let his beard grow" (*Selected Writings*, 188) the excessive, imperative tone raises these questions: Why? Why must Whitman's beard be allowed to grow and engulf all?[80] Why should everything melt down in the cauldron of his heart? In light of these views that Martí conveys to his readers, it is not surprising that Martí characterizes Whitman's poetic invitation to celebrate North America's enfolding of Cuba, Mexico, and the other Americas into itself as "flabbergasting" (pasmoso) (*Obras*, 13:131; *Selected Writings*, 183, translation modified).

DID WHITMAN SEDUCE MARTÍ?

Beginning in 1986, Doris Sommer published a series of essays that constitute the most prolonged engagement with the inter-American literary relations of Martí and Whitman.[81] Calling attention to the ambivalent dynamics of sexual attraction and violation in Martí's essay, Sommer interprets the North and South American writerly positions as mirror images of each other. Her essays explore a range of metaphors for the relationship between Martí and Whitman that connote interchangeability and seeming reflexivity. These metaphors tend to minimize political and economic hierarchy between Whitman and Martí. How do we interpret, then, the strange images of physical and sexual violence in Martí's depiction of the experience of reading Whitman? Erupting almost out of nowhere, such images do not follow the heterosexual ordering of most colonial discourse, but they help us to think through literary relations in the imperial framework of the Americas.

Transfixed in Whitman's "loving" gaze and as a clone of Whitman's "liberal self," Sommer's Martí has the role of a sales representative, who tries to get his America to buy into Whitman. His employer, Whitman the "monopolizer" and "archcapitalist," presents his product "cheaply" in a supposedly free market.[82] However, the market proves less than free, as the vastness of Whitman's North American equity has the capacity to "flood" the Latin American markets. Sommer's "we" in 1986 affirms the North American's "feat" of giving birth to a silent Latin American copy of Whitman's absorbing identity. This Martí parrots Whitman's ideals of self-liberation, and thus, expedites Latin America's fateful seduction and sedation. Moreover, in this view, Whitman's reader supposedly perceives the poet's threat—linguistic or otherwise—as "an incitation to heightened passion."[83] Sommer suggests that, as late as 1891, Martí wanted to "shore up differences" between North and South America.[84] While Martí created transnational alliances between some Spanish speakers located in the North and in the South, his disdain for U.S.-led Pan-Americanism (see discussion in chapter 5) casts doubt on the idea of his minimizing differences between the two halves of the hemisphere. Could Whitman's absorptive American union of North and South be admissible, much less a source of attraction, to Martí?

Martí's 1893 speech to the migrant community in Florida (discussed above) states that assimilation to a nation cracking under the pressure of its social and political contradictions suggests neither a utopian promise nor a remote goal for Martí. Sommer assesses the hemispheric relations of power as such that a group of Hispanophone readers finds Whitman "impossible" to refuse ("José Martí, Author of Walt Whitman," 88). Román Mayorga Rivas's defense of Whitman corroborates the applicability of this claim to some Latino readers. In both cases, the first-person plural pronoun "we" is spacious enough that the bilingual reader, a poet who borrows words like "libertad," and especially mobile elites like Mayorga have no trouble crossing the imperial/national divide. Although Sommer's recreation of Martí and Whitman's interaction records Martí's ambivalence, passion, and efforts to break free from Whitman's seductive spell, it shows the two in a mesmerizing dance in which the asymmetry of the relation between them too easily dissolves into mere rhetorical flourish.[85] For example, in "Proceed with Caution," she writes that Whitman successfully seduces Martí: "[Whitman] takes the words, and his partners, so passionately to heart that they [his partners] are overcome" (99). Sommer's tropes of Whitman as Narcissus gazing into the pool at his own reflection, as monopoly capitalist distributing to and controlling markets, and as a sexual partner who hears "no" as the "moan of irresistible seduction" ("José Martí, Author of Walt Whitman," 87) all begin from pretended parity, but result in the secondary partner's violation, loss, misinterpretation, or disintegration. The victim's violation appears to be the result of an engagement based on mesmerized consent. In an act of submission that Sommer curiously claims "the reader cannot help but enjoy" ("Supplying Demand," 78), Martí's dissent and difference become imperceptible, even inconsequential, as the dominant partner inevitably mishears the nondominant, Latino American's "no" to mean the opposite. This projection of the reader's pleasure upon witnessing Martí's seduction provides one clue as to why it has taken so long for U.S. critics to perceive and grapple with the Whitman we observe in González de la Garza, and in Martí.[86]

By subsuming Martí's position into Whitman's Free Soiler imperialism, the conclusion that Whitman seduced Martí elides the southernness of Martí's text and ignores the Cuban's identification with the multiracial postslavery cultures of the greater South.[87] Martí explicitly denounces a northern Republican capitalist plan to dominate the U.S. South and Latin America. Although Martí's efforts to build cross-class and cross-racial co-alitions led him to underestimate the persistent historical effects of racism in the postslavery Creole-dominated societies of Latin America, there can be little question that Martí's views differed from Whitman's. Unlike Mar-tí's multiracial anticolonialism, Whitman's rhetorical celebration of New World democracy and of its masses reinforces a vision of an empire so colossal that it outstrips those of the Old World.[88] Moreover, Martí chal-lenges the depiction of the U.S. South as merely a collection of slave owners and annexationists. His reading reveals a nuanced understanding of the purposes to which the North put racial discourse in its management of Southern cultures. Sympathetic to a southern spokesperson like Henry Grady, for example, Martí sees how the North's focus on the South's tropic empire abets the antislavery *and* antiabolitionist northern majority's ploy to deflect attention away from its own lucrative and largely unacknowl-edged history of investment in the slave trade, whiteness, and imperialism.

In keeping with his distance from Whitman's Free Soil annexationism, the subtitle that Martí gives to an 1890 chronicle defines "The Problem of the South" not as the so-called "Negro" problem of which George Wash-ington Cable and others would write, but as the greater South's vulnerabil-ity to the depredations of a northern, Anglo, political and economic elite: "Neighboring nations, whether islands or frontiers, are not more free to-day from the threat of aggression, because before the North excused itself by blaming the South for seeking to conquer more slave states and more votes in Congress; and now, is it not the West's *Belford Magazine* that says . . . 'We want the continent, and the politics of our statesmen should be to seek the extension of our land by all legal means until our flag flies from the North Pole to the Isthmus'?" (*Obras*, 13:393). Martí observes the North's and West's strategies of blaming the racially diverse U.S. South as a means to avoid acknowledging a far-reaching white supremacist ideology. Martí stresses cultural and political continuities between Latino America and the U.S. South's economic and political vulnerability to the North.[89] He re-serves his criticisms for a white privileged sector in both multiracial U.S. and Latin American contexts, including many U.S. citizens who owned land and slaves in Cuba.[90] These U.S.-descended residents of Cuba did not tend to support Martí's program of a postslavery antiracism and anti-imperialism.

Martí did not endorse the evolutionary whitening and disappearance of

America's postslavery African-descended cultures, as Whitman and many other whites did. The largest network of Cuban emancipationists lived in southern Florida in the U.S. South, of whom the vast majority were working-class, African-descended, Caribbean people with whom Martí ate, shared lodging, and worked in a multiracial, anticolonial struggle. Moreover, Martí explicitly articulated an antiracist vision at the center of the Cuban Revolutionary Party's and his own personal politics.[91] Although his antiracism problematically "foreclosed the invocation of race," as Louis A. Pérez argues, and imagined that national liberation would wash away the effects of centuries-old racist institutions overnight, his minimizing of race as a factor determining moral character challenged white-supremacist thinking and practice among the Creole elite in the movement.[92] In a letter to one of his co-revolutionaries, Serafin Bello, Martí uses the first-person plural in order not to exempt himself from this self-critique:

> The man of color has the right to treatment based on his qualities as a man, without any reference to his color: and if there is to be a criterion, it should be that of excusing the errors that we have prepared for him, to which we invite him with our unjust disdain. The worker is not an inferior being, nor should there be a tendency to corral him, and govern him with a prod, but rather to open to him, brother to brother, the considerations and rights which assure peace and happiness to a nation. (*Epistolario*, 2:159)

This passage criticizes a white-dominant "we" that prejudges the person of color. It envisions the urgent goal of equality before the law *and* in social situations as foundations for a multiracial and postcolonial nation in the Americas. Martí criticizes the white supremacist thinking that governed U.S., Caribbean, and Latin American societies, and affirms mestizo cultural resistance to Euro-American cultural "whiteness." This embrace of a mestizo America may be why Edouard Glissant adopts several of Martí's concepts in his Caribbean discourse and includes Martí among the forgers of a Pan-Caribbean history.[93]

In sum, to conclude that Whitman seduced Martí hastily reproduces the assimilative logic that subordinates and submerges Martí's crucial differences from Whitman.[94] The multiracial character of the grassroots movement that Martí helped to organize informs his calling upon the leaders of his America to place the mestiza, hybrid quality of their American republics at the center of their governing; in Martí's view, the cultures of his America defy U.S. racial categories. By reading Martí as *either* exotic

European-identified Creole *or* Whitmanesque liberal, we miss Martí's articulation of another American modernity from a space in between colony and empire. Martí sketches this critique of Whitman's racism and expansionism in his close reading of Whitman's poetic form.

ᘯ METAPHORS OF BLOOD

> Does liberty produce the same results as despotism?
> —**José Martí**, *El Partido Liberal*, January 11, 1887

The most hermetic imagery of Martí's essay on Whitman associates the experience of reading Whitman's poetry with acts of branding, rape, whipping, imprisonment, and rescue. As Karen Sánchez-Eppler has argued, Whitman's persona in *Leaves of Grass* studies the pure corporeality of the enslaved body through the eyes of a slave auctioneer, who describes in detail a back man for sale on the auction block in section 7 of "I Sing the Body Electric." The lines of the poem read like an advertisement for the specific body parts in a catalogue and describe these part-objects as desirable for the potential purchaser:

> Examine these limbs, red black or white, they are cunning in
>   tendon and nerve,
> They shall be stript that you may see them.
>
> Exquisite sense, life-lit eyes, pluck, volition,
> Flakes of breast-muscle, pliant backbone and neck, flesh not
>   flabby, good-sized arms and legs,
> And wonders within there yet.[95]

The description of "wonders" between the man's legs suggests an erotic desire, but its object is enchained, subordinate, and commodified. The reference to "common passions and desires" subsumes the relations of power that structure enslavement under universalizing, Enlightenment rhetoric. Karen Sánchez-Eppler notes that in the very gesture toward the enslaved person's priceless humanity and heroic heart, the poet "strips away the slave's skin, dismembering the body in the act of celebrating it, until all that is left is eternal and ubiquitous blood."[96] She observes the coexistence in Whitman's poetry of rhetorical equality, fascinated voyeurism, and the poet's privileged position in institutions of American racial domination. As he appeals to equality, Whitman's text rhetorically engages

poet and reader in forbidden—and disturbing—acts of looking and longing that depend on racial and imperial hierarchies.[97]

If this scene of an auction block implicitly sets in relation the white poet
in the position of auctioneer and the black man as property about to be
sold, Martí's essay also features a scene of implicit comparison between two
male bodies, in which the established, patriarchal poet, brands the youthful poet, who belongs to another species:

> Like the pudding in its mold, man is formed by the book or forceful teacher
> that happened to come his way, or by the fashions of his time; schools, be
> they philosophical, religious or literary, only straitjacket men as the livery
> does the lackey; men allow themselves *to be branded*, like horses and bulls,
> and go about proudly displaying their brands so that when they find them-
> selves before a man who is naked, virginal, amorous, sincere, and powerful—
> a man who strides, loves, fights, rows, a man who does not let his mis-
> fortunes blind him but reads the promise of a final joy in the grace and
> equilibrium of the world—when they find themselves before so sinewy and
> angelical a father as Walt Whitman, they flee as if from their own con-
> sciences and balk at recognizing the true nature of their dimmed, house-
> bound, gimcrack species in his fragrant and superior humanity. (*Obras*,
> 13:131; *Selected Writings*, 183, emphasis added)

Martí compares this group of branded men to the angelical and superior
father species whose innocence and autonomy are expressed in the poet's
naked, virginal, and amorous qualities. The two species do not exist independently: each defines itself in relation to the other. The chronicler self-
deprecatingly depicts the former as if he knows it well, in explicit rejection
of Whitman's command: "We have had ducking and deprecating about
enough."[98] Martí translates this phrase in his essay to emphasize a North
American lack of interest in this sort of self-criticism: "ya se ha denunciado
y tonteado bastante" (already there has been enough denunciation and
foolishness) (*Obras*, 13:136–37). Whitman belongs to the superior category, whose condition represents the true and universal condition to which
all aspire.

In setting into play this hierarchy of master and slave in his discussion of
Whitman, Martí locates himself amongst those who flee their conscience,
who balk at recognizing their condition, and who are branded. Whitman,
by contrast, occupies the position of an influential, authoritative master.
Whitman, of course, entertains fleeting sympathy or fascination with the
enslaved body and even claims to "be" a slave or to see the slave's priceless-

ness. But his imperious will demands that the other, branded man, Martí included, see his own group as a "gimcrack species," which is Allen's translation of Martí's self-deprecating words: "descolorida, encasacada, amuñecada" (discolored, coated, doll-like) (*Obras*, 13:131; *Selected Writings*, 183). For all his poetic flourish concerning camaraderie and humanitarian marches, Whitman defines a hierarchical relationship between superior and inferior *species*, and Martí senses the weight of this classification. These naturalized categories stand in for historical relations of power that are shaped by the threat of force.

Against its own positive description of the angelic Whitman, this sinewy paragraph articulates a critique not merely of postcolonial intellectual dependency on imported foreign models, but of the seeming innocence of the colonial and imperial fathers who promote and perpetuate the colonials' dependence. For the branded, whether they sport their scar with pride or rage, are marked by a history of colonial institutions that do all in their power to prevent their subjects from developing distinct, self-generated criteria for judgment. Whereas a colonizer openly ridicules and attacks, the "angelic father" with his "fragrant and superior humanity" invisibly causes the colonized to cringe in consciousness of their supposedly inferior position. Whitman's proclamations of liberty and equality would seem to absolve him from responsibility for the relations of power in the hemisphere that shape the consciousness of the scarred, straitjacketed, or colonized subject. Unlike the angelical father who fancies himself as acting without imitating, the subject marked by a colonial history adopts mimicry as means to indicate that he resists the position of the impressionable lackey. Combative parody proves a powerful weapon in confronting the effects of the colony's afterlife in American republics.

The Spanish literary historian and philosopher Marcelino Menéndez y Pelayo, at the height of his powers and just a few years before Cuba would declare war on Spain, draws on images identical to the passage from Martí's "El poeta Walt Whitman," which appeared five years earlier. The passage in question is Menéndez y Pelayo's disdainful review of work by Plácido (pseudonym of Gabriel de la Concepción Valdés), the mulatto poet who died by firing squad, having been accused of organizing a revolt of slaves and free blacks. The relation of this prestigious European literary critic to the insurgent Cuban poet Plácido parallels Whitman's relationship to Martí. Menéndez y Pelayo occupies the position of cultural authority and superiority from which he judges the sample of a "gimcrack species": the self-educated, upstart, improvising, and supposedly plagiarizing mulatto poet, Plácido. Whereas Martí refers to Plácido as the Cuban poet whom he planned to commemorate with other members of La Liga, Menéndez y Pelayo argues that Plácido "was a half-cultured man with a good memory and a lively wit, in whose mind everything he heard or read impressed itself as in soft wax. He aspired to mimic the beauty of the great masters, like a lackey who dresses himself up in the clothes of his master."[99] The Spanish critic's attack on Plácido starkly contrasts with Martí's celebration of Plácido's creation of the golden chalices in which Cubans might drink their own wine, made of plantains (*Obras*, 7:287). Intentionally or not, Menéndez y Pelayo assumes the position that Martí's essay gives to Whitman. Menéndez y Pelayo's characterization of Plácido corroborates the idea that a colonial relation exists between Whitman and the representatives of the "gimcrack species" who gaze up at him as if he were superior.

Like Martí, characterizing the colonized here as branded, other Cuban separatists often drew on the rhetoric of enslavement to describe the condition of the colonized island. Martí followed several Afro-Cuban leaders, including Juan Gualberto Gómez, Rafael Serra, and Antonio Maceo, in making emancipation and Afro-Cuban and national liberation inextricable. So when Martí refers to these images of the branded, gimcrack species in Whitman, he introduces the subtexts of his persistent preoccupation with the intertwined goals of anticolonial struggle and abolition.

Martin Robison Delany, the black abolitionist and strident critic of the annexation of Cuba, made the Afro-Cuban poet Plácido a conspirator in a transnational black uprising in his novel *Blake, or the Huts of Cuba* (1857–62), and ridiculed José Antonio Saco's 1833 warning that the growth of the slave population should be feared. Saco's argument represented white Creole anxiety that Cuba might follow in the footsteps of Haiti, a possibility that Delany looked forward to. Comparing the United States to the great prostitute of Revelation, Delany criticizes the seductive wielding of "the enchanting words of Justice, Freedom, Liberty, Equality, Democracy and Republicanism" by the United States in its attempt to teach the immigrants of the world to love the name of America.[100] Similarly, Whitman's occult artistry cloaks an expansionist agenda of a white America in meretricious images of freedom and democracy.

Martí's description of the experience of looking up at Whitman revisits the political rhetoric of the Free Soil Party inspired by U.S. representative David Wilmot. Wilmot's "proviso" passed in the House in 1846, when the United States was about to acquire massive tracts of land through the invasion of Mexico. The bill never became law, but it articulates the emergence of a new white, working or middling, imperial subjectivity. Wilmot's Proviso, which became known in the U.S. as the "White Man's Proviso," sought both to stand up to the powers aligned with slavery and to preserve for the white working man a space free from contact with African-descended peoples, free or slave. David Reynolds notes that Wilmot and most Free Soilers, including Whitman, endorsed racial segregation and saw the proviso as a means to "preserve for free white labor a fair country, a rich inheritance, where the sons of toil, of my own race and color, can live without the disgrace which association with Negro slavery brings upon free labor."[101] As we have seen, Whitman shared Wilmot's concern about the need to preserve a privileged place for a postbellum, white, imperial subject by prohibiting a potentially revolutionary, multiracial alliance among the "sons of toil."

In providing arguments for preventing the spread of slavery through this legislation, Wilmot outlines the troubling conditions that would follow from either annexation of territories without the abrogation of local self-government or from the extension of the southern empire of slavery into the West. In other words, the curtailing of self-government in annexed territories became a corollary to a northern antislavery position. In a speech to the House in August of 1848, Wilmot indicated the complicity of Free Soil rhetoric with both expansionism and with its goals of protecting whites from contaminating contact with the formerly enslaved or the formerly colonized of Latin America. The speech was part of Wilmot's reiteration of the bid to prohibit slavery from entering the West, and it was reprinted in an African American abolitionist newspaper in which leading figures such as Delany called upon the community of three million African Americans to join in a revolt with Cubans against annexation and against slavery. In this excerpt, Wilmot alludes to two masculine pairs that closely resemble the male figures in "El poeta Walt Whitman":

[The extension of slavery] brings degradation upon the poor white man, who is brought into close contact with the servile labor of the black. It mars his manhood. It destroys his self-respect and dignity of character. He feels a sense of humiliation, when he looks up to the vast distance between himself and the lordly planter, in the shadow of whose aristocratic possessions he lives an inferior, if not a dependent. He lives in the midst of a system of lords and vassals; and if he cannot rise to the condition of the former, he must sink to a level with the latter.[102]

Subordination of the white worker in relation to the white master threatens
to cast white and nonwhite into a threatening relationship of equality and
solidarity. Just as Wilmot played upon the widespread sentiment of white
workers as "marred" by seeing themselves on the same plane as the formerly enslaved, Whitman's poetry imagines a striding, loving, fighting
man whose condition of possibility depends upon, but does not acknowledge, the subordination of others. Wilmot's rhetoric denounces the hierarchy between lord and vassal, but fosters in its place a new white imperial
subject through the jettisoning of multiracial and transamerican social
equality. Without facing this relation of power, the members of the weaker
species learn to accept blame for being branded or for being unable to
think outside the position of subjection established by a powerful father.

Wilmot's appeal to prevent slavery from entering the new territory coincided with arguments for annexation without the extension of local, state
sovereignty. In addition to appealing to the whites-only practices of U.S.
citizenship, the arguments against the spread of slavery required as a corollary a legal means to abrogate local self-government. For without the power
"to dispose of, and make all needful rules and regulations respecting the
territory, and other property of the United States," the annexed territory
would become "as independent as the Republic of France," notes Wilmot in
his speech (32). Taking as examples Cuba and the remaining parts of Mexico, Wilmot proposes that the United States acquire these possessions without granting sovereignty. This denial of local self-government would prevent the possessions from becoming part of the "Slave Power," under whose
control Wilmot predicts that "[Cuba and Mexico's] effeminate and unre-
sisting population will be exterminated and enslaved" (32). Opposing slave
power by abrogating self-government of Mexico and Cuba, Free Soil antislavery reiterated the ideals of imperial manifest destiny.

Martí's chronicle repeats Whitman's deprecation of an uncivilizable,
effeminate, lackey species that allows itself to be branded by foreign ideas,
but Martí believes that this "species" is dominated through historical acts
of conquest. The branding is neither natural nor divine; a self-critical
resistance to persistent coloniality can remake the categories. While in a
subordinate location, the pale, cloaked, doll-like figure may hide in shame
before the optimist who promises a future of equilibrium and grace. Gazing up at the superior humanity of Whitman, the flabbergasted freedman
and the still colonized Latino subject witness the white imperialist emerging as a new, efficient version of the aristocratic slaveholder. The humilia-

tion of the worker that Wilmot denounces will apply equally to the colonized, the slave, and the worker who depends upon an employer. Martí's
chronicle implicitly calls upon the self-deprecating black or Latino/a laborer, himself included, to move from this position to one of fundamental
equality.

I have suggested that Whitman's rhetoric of a future of equilibrium and
grace might itself represent an ideology that encases the postcolonial subject in the Americas "as the livery does the lackey" (como al lacayo la librea)
(*Obras*, 13:131; *Selected Writings*, 183).[103] Whereas wearing livery (librea)
signifies a dependent condition, the word "livery" etymologically and ana-
grammatically (at least, in Spanish) alludes to the Latin verb *liberare*, to
liberate.[104] Thus, wearing the master's livery paradoxically signifies the
opposite of what its etymology suggests: a servile condition in which you
are dressed in a uniform that marks your servitude, in a guise of seeming
freedom.[105] In the chronicle to which Sarmiento responded with a wish for
Martí to give Latin American readers "less Latino" and more modern
United States, Martí also foreshadows the fundamental struggle between
the branded lackey and the angelic father that surfaces in the opening
paragraphs of "El poeta Walt Whitman." Facing the Statue of Liberty and
Walt Whitman, Martí becomes an insect wallowing in the mud and looking up at eagles, a crawling "slapped lackey" (lacayo abofeteado), who
senses "his body's flesh falling in pieces to the ground" among an army of
gleaming soldiers.[106] In this despairing description, Martí's persona in the
chronicle resembles the oppressed lackey rather than the duped acolyte.

While some scholars have read the branding scene in "El poeta Walt
Whitman" as Martí's ardent longing to embrace Whitman and American
exceptionalism, I think the passage emerges from a bleaker, if not tragic,
postcolonial perplexity before the impossibility of full self-government
and sovereignty within the United States' emergent sphere of imperial
influence.[107] The dream of American originality, as phantasmatically exempt from the markings of the past, becomes hard to swallow in Martí's
reading of Whitman. As a colonial subject with an anticolonial consciousness, he is aware of the lack of a firm ground for the hierarchy. The
revolutionary trembles at the implications.

As in the scene where Whitman the master brands the foreheads of doll-
like, easily molded inferiors, references to whipping and rape directly
modify the effect of Whitman's poetry upon the chronicler's ear. Whitman's words strike Martí harshly: "it sounds like a rough kiss, like a rape,

like the snap of dry leather cracking in the sun" (*Obras*, 13:141; *Selected Writings*, 193). This series of images links images of corporeal sexual advances and the North American poet's overwhelming desire to possess the other's body, even by the lash. In contrast to Whitman's sacred books of the new humanity that apparently just "fell" from the Old World into a new continent, these images smack of brutality, and of profitable blood: "At times Whitman's poetic language resembles the entrance to a butcher shop [carnicería], hung with sides of beef" (*Obras*, 13:141; *Selected Writings*, 193). Not at all a straightforward, romantic, or realistic image, this figure of poetry as a carnicería deserves our consideration. The word connotes "massacre," as much as it does the cutting up and sale of domestic animals.

By comparing Martí's chronicle on Whitman to Martí's political correspondence from the period, we may begin to make sense of Martí's attribution of "Satanic force" to Whitman's poetry, which he likens to a "ravenous hero licking his bloody lips" (*Obras*, 13:138; *Selected Writings*, 190, translation modified). The figure of bloody violence recurs in Martí's correspondence with Ricardo Rodríguez Otero, in response to the latter's publication of his little-known travel writing, *Impresiones y recuerdos de mi viaje a los Estados de Nueva York, Nueva Jersey y Pennsylvania* (Impressions and Memories of my Travels to the States of New York, New Jersey and Pennsylvania) (1887). The annexationist Rodríguez Otero was a planter from Sagua la Grande, Cuba, and in his reading of the economically and politically marginal migrant Latino community in the United States, which deserves more scholarly attention than I have space for here, he describes his participation in a meeting of North Americans and Cubans in favor of annexation. He also mentions a separate encounter with "Pepe Martí, as he is affectionately called," in New York.[108] Rodríguez Otero characterizes the meeting as one of warmth and respect, but he took the liberty of libelously attributing to Martí a statement in support Spain's sale of Cuba to the United States:

> When I had the pleasure of visiting Pepe [Martí] in New York, I heard from him a statement that advantageously sums up all the comments that he made: "Whatever may be my past, I will respectfully submit without reserve to the solution that Spain proposes to Cuba's problems, if it proves satisfactory to the majority of my compatriots." May the meritorious and illustrious Cuban excuse me for my reporter's indiscretion in citing without his authorization, given the intention that guides me. (114–15)

Implying the intimacy that accompanies the use of a nickname, Rodríguez Otero puts words of happy submission to Spain into Martí's mouth. Like Pierre Menard, Rodríguez Otero's Martí seems to have a penchant for saying or representing the direct opposite of what he in fact means. Making Martí into a mouthpiece for his colonialist views, Rodríguez Otero uses the questionable tactics of a *reporter* (in English in the Spanish original) to encourage Cuban migrants to adhere to either autonomy under Spanish rule or annexation to the United States. Right after "quoting" Martí, but before apologizing for citing him without authorization, he takes advantage of Martí's clout in the migrant community to reinforce the travel essay's celebratory account of the United States: "Noble and generous words, which in coming from Martí, well deserve the endorsement and sympathy of the emigrant community" (114). This appropriation of Martí's voice belongs to a long tradition of attempting to attribute to the influential Cuban migrant leader views diametrically opposed to his own.[109]

Referring perhaps to Martí's forced labor as a political prisoner of Spain, Rodríguez Otero insinuates that historical oppression under Spanish colonial rule no longer drives Martí to pursue Cuban independence.[110] It is as if, for Rodríguez Otero, the scars from a whipping Martí received for insubordination during six months of forced labor ceased to be legible as a public sign.[111] Rodríguez Otero's assertion wills the erasure of history's scars on Martí's body through an amnesia that to Martí was anathema.

Rodríguez Otero's misrepresentation of Martí's position prompts Martí's recourse to an atypically irate metaphorics of blood. In his response, which appeared in the emigrant newspaper *El Avisador Cubano* in May 1888, Martí clarifies his position with respect to the United States and Spain in some of the strongest language that appears in his *Obras*.[112] This letter attacks Otero's proannexation position and especially his misrepresentation of him as a supporter of Spain's sale of Cuba to the United States in order to avoid a military conflict. Study and daily life in the United States during a long residence convinced Martí that no amount of professed goodwill toward Cuba would alter the United States' ultimate desire to acquire Cuba and all its resources, with or without its inhabitants' consent. Martí rebukes Rodríguez Otero and predicts that the United States would invade, a prediction that came true in 1898:

> But someone who has lived in them [the United States], exalting their legitimate glories, studying their characteristics, examining the roots of their problems, seeing how politics follows the interests of money, confirming

with this study the antecedents and the real nature of their involuntary or
confessed tendencies; he who sees that never, except in the hiding spots of a
few generous souls, has Cuba been for the United States more than a desirable possession, with nothing inconvenient about it, except its inhabitants—
whom they consider to be rebellious, weak and despicable; someone who
reads without a blindfold what they think and write in the United States, beginning with the odious letter with instructions from Henry Clay in 1828 . . . ;
someone who loves his country . . . does not think about the possibility of
annexation with complacence, but with mortal affliction. And it may be our
fate that a successful neighbor will leave us to bleed on its doorstep, so that
afterward, the blood might serve as fertilizer for when they lay their hostile,
egoistic and disrespectful hands on us. (*Epistolario* 2:31–32)

Contrary to Rodríguez Otero's portrait of happy annexation to the United
States, Martí asserts that migrant Latinos wrestled constantly with stereotypes of themselves and of their nations. In his estimation, the United
States valued Cubans more as a kind of fertilizer than as human beings,
subjects and citizens of a neighboring nation. The simile of slaughter
surfaces in Martí's profoundly ironic image of the carnicería in the neighborhood of the United States, just months before Martí had read about and
perhaps witnessed Whitman's commemoration of Lincoln and the American Union in April 1887. The 1888 letter of response to Rodríguez Otero
helps us to decipher the metaphors of butchery, slavery, and blood in the
chronicle as references to the brewing, still pertinent conflict that Martí
foresaw between the neighboring nations.

The unfolding of this historical subtext during the period of Martí's
composition of the essay on Whitman elucidates Martí's understanding of
the complex challenge he faced in trying to convince the colonized, imprisoned, or enslaved to refuse the normalcy or naturalness of a subordinate
condition. When hundreds of thousands marched for an eight-hour day
and came under attack during the United States' first red scare in 1886–87,
Martí sees the yeast of the Paris Commune fermenting in the United States.
This uprising in turn gives rise to the desperate rhetorical question that
Martí posed in October 1886: "Does liberty produce the same results as
despotism?" (*Otras crónicas*, 74). The events of the later 1880s pushed Martí
to a far more pessimistic view of the ability of the United States to make
good on its commitment to liberty, an equitable justice system, and democratic self-government.

A natural or scientific explanation of oppressive conditions and racism secures the thickest prison walls around the potential rebel. Martí's essay on Whitman alludes to just such a prison. In one striking figure, the oyster in its shell comes to stand in for an imperceptibly imposed autocracy: "He who lives under an autocratic creed is like an oyster in its shell, seeing only the prison that traps him and believing, in the darkness, that it is the world. Liberty gives wings to the oyster" (*Obras*, 13:136; *Selected Writings*, 187). "Autocracy," like "livery," etymologically refers to its opposite. Its roots— *auto* (self) and *cracy* (power, authority)—suggest a now obsolete meaning of the word: "possessing the right of self-government, or political independence," according to the *Oxford English Dictionary*. But "autocracy" comes to mean the opposite of self-government in the mid-nineteenth century: it begins to signify the absolute, controlling authority of one person in government. Martí in his war diaries defines an authoritarian society as "one based on the concept, feigned or sincere, of human inequality, in which persons to whom all rights are denied are forced to carry out social duties to serve the power and pleasure of those who deny them those rights" (*Obras*, 19:204; *Selected Writings*, 370–71). Such a society functions by convincing its members of the divine, natural, or scientific fact of inequality. Martí asserts that autocracy develops when freedom becomes defined as the hidden enforcement of inequality.

To contest the autocrat's will, Martí offers the notion of "the practice of the self," or critical self-relation in the essay on Whitman and elsewhere (*Obras*, 13:136; *Selected Writings*, 187). This fundamental concept in Martí's lexicon surfaces here to define a technology of the postcolonial self. Cloaked in the guise of liberty, the autocrat rises to power with the fealty of those whom he has convinced of their fundamental species difference. Commenting on the global expansionism and the naturalizing of manifest destiny, Martí's essay "Nuestra América" (1891) features a passage that is very probably drawn from Whitman, but with an exemplary resignification. In "Song of Myself," Whitman proposes a rescue that features his signature insistence on the other's inferiority:

> I seize the descending man and raise him *with resistless will,*
> O despairer, here is my neck,
> By God, you shall not go down! hang your whole weight upon me.
>
> (*Leaves of Grass*, 65, emphasis added)

In this passage, Whitman directs the "descending man" to depend upon him as if he were incapable of standing up on his own.

By contrast, in Martí's recreation of the scenario of aid to a less powerful neighbor, Whitman is revised so as to replace dependency with a transformed self-relation: "Nations must continually live with self-criticism [han de vivir criticándose], for criticism is health; but with a single heart and a single mind. To lower oneself [bajarse] to the unfortunate and to raise them up in our arms!" (*Obras*, 6:21; *Selected Writings*, 294). Martí's passage calls for neighborly aid, so that the unfortunate may rise—aid that the United States in fact declined to supply during Cuba's ten-year strike for independence from Spain and to end slavery. While these politicized practices of mutual respect became watchwords for Martí's vision of liberty, Whitman's politics of incorporation obliterates this recognition.

This reading of Martí's "Whitman" goes against the grain of much previous commentary, but it draws on the insight of the Cuba-based Martí scholar Mary Cruz, who deciphers in the essay a practice of "camouflage" (enmascaramiento).[113] This protective covering, she argues, enables Martí's critique to reach its mark more effectively. Cruz suggests that the essay demands a careful deciphering of the hieroglyphic form of the essay in order to involve the reader in "the exercise of judgment, from the Greek *kriterion*" ("Una de las más sorprendentes creaciones martianas," 130). In the Spanish original, Martí's opening sentence takes the form of a septenary: it reads like a poem with seven stanzas of seven lines, with seven syllables each. The septenary echoes the seven days of creation, the Seven Seals guarding the entrance to the temple, the seven chords of Orpheus's lyre. This form mimics—and mocks—Whitman's divine status. Whitman becomes Martin R. Delany's Babylonian enchanter, who casts his spell with rhythmically mesmerizing promises of equality, democracy, republicanism, and freedom, which do not translate into political practice in the Gilded Age.

"El poeta Walt Whitman" encrypts Martí's judgment of U.S. literature's complicity in betraying an American revolutionary tradition. He picks up these themes again in a more direct statement on the verge of his departure for home, in the final weeks of 1894. In an article in *Patria*, entitled "Honduras y los extranjeros" (Honduras and the Foreigners), Martí differentiates between his America and the treacherous "America that is not ours" by showing how this other America had implemented "a false and criminal concept of Americanism" (*Obras*, 8:35). This sense of two Americas appeared much earlier in the essay on Whitman, where Martí subtly criticizes the United States' turn away from its founding principles. His exercise in judgment suggests that self-critique gives the oyster "wings." The oyster is not your world, Martí's essay warns a domineering figure who, like Shakespeare's Pistol in the *Merry Wives of Windsor*, declares the world to be his oyster. For with wings to take flight, the island will not be available for him to open by force.

This image in the Whitman essay also directs itself to the prisoner enclosed in the oyster shell of (post-)coloniality. Looking only at the shell, the prisoner may mistake the surrounding enclosure for the world, and thus fail to see that it may not be what it appears. In an article that asks rhetorically in its title "¿A los Estados Unidos?" (To the United States?) Martí warns potential young male immigrants to the United States that "a serpent may live hidden in the shell that appears to be the dwelling place of the pearl."[114] Despite misogyny of the article that only addresses males and genders the United States reductively as femme fatale, the article promotes the exercise of migrant critical practice. The United States, Martí adds in this same article, is not the place of marvels that it appears to be "for those who know how to see." An exercise of judgment reveals the false dilemma between the deceptively marvelous United States or a Latin America seen as a preponderantly Spanish place. Insisting on neither the myth of the American dream nor the perpetuity of a colonial legacy, Martí advises the migrant in search of options to learn how to read critically. The "ejercicio del criterio" that he explores in the essay on Whitman suggests a strategy by which to safeguard the island's future.

The next chapter examines texts by Martí from the five years following the essay on Whitman and leading up to the founding of the Cuban Revolutionary Party. In these years, the divergence that began as a lonely epiphany in a boarding house in Manhattan becomes a public project that is visible in his work as an interpreter of Helen Hunt Jackson, Buffalo Bill, and Lucy Parsons, and as a diplomatic representative who forces the United States to see that it is not the only America.

Martí's Border Writing:
Infiltrative Translation,
Late Nineteenth-Century "Latinness,"
and the Perils of Pan-Americanism

> With the preoccupation of a son, I have been following the events that have at last expressed the accumulated passions of the peoples [pueblos] on either edge of the Rio Grande: the urgency and imminence of these developments demand their unvarnished and precise narration: oh, that it might be possible to purchase the peace of the nation one loves with the blood of one's veins!
> —**José Martí,** unpublished submission to *El Partido Liberal*, August 2, 1886

> This country guilty of downright highway robbery, of going to the rewards, Monroe doctrine in hand, and casting against the wall the feebler peoples, while with the other hand they take from their pockets the coveted concessions of supremacy, the decree signed by these peoples of their perpetual and irredeemable servitude? This villainous conception cannot have entered a true American mind.
> —**José Martí,** fragment 14, originally written in English

❧ WITH THE SAME concern over a possible second U.S. invasion of Mexico that a son feels for a beloved parent, José Martí's writing about the U.S.-Mexico borderlands imagines diverse communities uniting to oppose Anglo-dominance and imperialism and prefigures subsequent theories of border subjectivity. The long history of anti-Mexican and anti-Native American violence in the Americas highlights parallels between the annexed portion of Mexico, Native American territories, and the Latin American nations or still colonized islands that Martí saw as vul-

nerable to an emergent U.S. imperial power. Because the passions of ongoing border conflict often found expression in popular culture, Martí's
writing about the United States' dilating borders in the South, Midwest,
and West criticizes English-language representations of "Latin" peoples
from his perspective within the Latino migrant community. A racial discourse on Latinness proliferated in the Gilded Age in conjunction with
growing economic investments south of the Rio Grande, and this discourse
permeated daily life in New York, too. For example, Martí encountered a
Murray Hill Hotel staff member who responded with such a disdainful
gaze and imperial tone to an inquiry after Latin Americans who were
stopping there that he compared living in the United States to being physically beaten.[1] In addition to analyzing and responding to the United States'
greed for the raw materials that it needed to compete with Europe, Martí's
border writing probes colonization's psychic effects and illustrates the
power of translation to undermine narratives of settlement and civilization
that attributed expansion to a "natural" racial hierarchy (*Obras*, 6:115).[2]

In keeping with the long-standing tendency to read Martí as embracing
North American culture, a tendency that we have examined in previous
chapters, the scholarship on Martí's chronicles about *Buffalo Bill's Wild
West Show* and on his translation of Helen Hunt Jackson's *Ramona* concludes that Martí celebrates and reiterates these immensely popular narratives of "the drama of civilization."[3] Jackson's novel of California's
post-1848 mission culture launched a caravan of Anglo tourists to southern
California. And Cody's show recruited and contracted the U.S.'s "former
foes" such as Sitting Bull and Rain-in-the-Face to reenact repeatedly the
scenes of combat that led up to their communities' present imprisonment
on reservations; it also commemorated the entrance of Roosevelt's celebrated Rough Riders into Cuba.[4] Richard Slotkin and Shelley Streeby have
observed that Buffalo Bill's 1899 replacement of "Custer's Last Fight" with a
reenacted battle of San Juan Hill marked "the Wild West's evolution from a
memorialization of the past to a celebration of the imperial future" in
popular border narratives.[5] Despite all this, Martí's work on William "Buffalo Bill" Cody and Helen Hunt Jackson have been read as uncritical applause for them. To read Martí as emphatically identified with the North
American narratives of Buffalo Bill's show in the decades before 1899 supposes that the Cuban migrant could not see structural parallels between
"Indians" and "Latins" in the North American imaginary and on the hemispheric map.[6] It also underestimates Martí's ability to foresee the apolo-

getic function of Buffalo Bill's show after the "closing of the frontier," in the midst of racial violence and during the official birth of Pan-Americanism in 1889–90.

I define Pan-Americanism broadly as a discourse that sought to bring about U.S. "economic expansionism" into Latin American markets in the name of order, progress, neighborly friendship, and peaceful arbitration of conflicts.[7] Pan-Americanism assumed and propagated the model of U.S. culture and government as appropriate for all nations in the hemisphere. From political scientist Gordon K. Lewis's intellectual history of the Caribbean to Latin Americanist Debra Castillo's envisioning of a bilingual American culture, the term "Pan-American" has slipped into the vocabulary of English-language scholarship on the Americas with a progressive connotation. Such usage ignores Martí's late nineteenth-century assessments of the term in reaction to the inauguration of an officially U.S.-led Pan-Americanism. Ironically, Lewis attributes to Martí a "defense of Pan-Americanism," by which the historian refers to some of the principles that Martí did in fact endorse, such as opposition to the emerging imperialism of the United States and promotion of the Latin American and Caribbean cultures of the Americas.[8] Lewis grasps Martí's values but applies to Martí terminology that the Cuban explicitly rejected. Similarly, Castillo's readings of Latino/a and Latin American literature demonstrate the benefits of abandoning national language paradigms for literary histories, in "favor of a larger pan-American context for scholarly inquiry" (*Redreaming America*, 194). While it is true that Martí straddled U.S. Latino/a and Latin American positions—an in-betweenness that Castillo's book carefully brings to light—Pan-Americanism as an idea and as a movement practiced bilingualism only as an afterthought, and only in response to the explicit pressure of Latin Americans who challenged the United States' vision for the hemisphere.

References to Martí as an advocate of Pan-Americanism reproduce an inherent problem with this term, the prefix of which suggests a totalizing perspective—of, comprising, embracing, or common to all. Martí became skeptical of totalizing views of America, especially those formulated from within a white, Anglo perspective among elite northeasterners. Against such totalizing perspectives, he claims the viewpoint of a worm or a parasite, burrowed deep within the guts of the system he criticized. In Martí's own usage, the adjective "Pan-American" carries connotations of deceit and fabrication: he denounced, for example, the "unlawful end—barely averted in time—of that stilted fabric, the Pan-American Congress" (*Obras*, 3:49, 56; *Selected Writings*, 323, translation modified). Sarcastic references to "los panamericanos"—or the U.S. and Latin American delegates to the 1889 conference who toured the major industries in the United States—reveal Martí's animosity toward this term and the concept (*Obras*, 6:57). These Pan-Americans include the leaders who engaged in loud conviviality while the U.S. Congress passed prohibitive tariffs on Mexican silver, precisely as the Pan-American conference was ostensibly discussing reduced tariffs in the Americas. No longer representing a Bolivarian coalition of American republics that would commit to mutually guaranteeing one another's independence and sovereignty against the threat of imperial invasion, Pan-Americanism was from its inception in English usage always freighted with the expansionist and duplicitous economic designs of the United States.

In the years leading up to and immediately after the first Pan-American conferences of 1889–91, Martí increasingly saw Latino/a and Latin Americans—himself included—being "read" through the racializing lens of the U.S. racial system, the force of which he measured by observing and reporting on the experiences of various racial groups and nations within the United States. Martí defined a theory and method for his work as a translator of U.S. culture during an 1886 diplomatic crisis that almost resulted in a second United States–Mexico War. Discussing his current and future task, he defines translation as a weapon against the racial stereotypes that gained currency through and helped to subtend Pan-Americanism. Martí's translations of texts and dramatic performances from the period between 1886, the year of the Haymarket bombing, and 1892, when he began to contribute almost exclusively to the revolutionary proindependence newspaper *Patria*, imaginatively convene a broad popular coalition of Latino migrants, politicized working-class immigrants, Mexicans who became subject to U.S. administration after 1848, and others excluded from citizenship and human rights on "racial" grounds. Accounts of the displaced American Indians who continued to sustain the blows of the U.S. military up to and beyond the 1890–91 massacre at Wounded Knee and the African American, Asian, and Italian victims of many public lynchings were among the reports that Martí translated to warn Latino/a and Latin American readers what might await them in the United States upon migrating or if they underwent annexation. Martí imagines and writes about a multiracial movement that might resist the abuse of power among nations and among racial groups. The key that enables us to unlock the connecting corridors among these

disparate border spaces and distinct ethnic histories (which prefigure contemporary cross-border, cross-racial, and class conscious organizing) derives from Martí's translation of Helen Hunt Jackson's Indian Reform novel
Ramona, to which I return at the end of this chapter.

Martí shared Frederick Jackson Turner's view that the end of westward
expansion in 1890 would create a demand for imperial expansion in the
Americas (and Asia), but he did not consider this future possibility to be
either inexorable or progressive, as Turner did.[9] Whereas Turner provided
historical explanations for Pan-American expansion, and his successor
Herbert Bolton proposed the "Spanish borderlands" and "Greater America" as a region that might provide resources from throughout the hemisphere for the United States to draw on during the Second World War,
Martí's border writing digs up dispersed and forgotten histories of resistance to U.S. expansion in the hemisphere. Westward expansion's effects
on Chicano/a and indigenous communities became an emblematic warning.[10] Martí, in fact, as I show in this chapter, uses his canny insight into
U.S. popular culture and into journalism's influence over public opinion to
elaborate critical interpretations of an Anglo-American imperial subjectivity in formation.

During the years that mark Martí's radicalization after his internal criticism of the military leaders of Cuba's ten-year-long civil war, and in conjunction with the 1891 publication of his most influential and widely read
essay, "Nuestra América," in New York and Mexico City Martí locates
himself within a vilified, explicitly "Latin" perspective within the United
States, which corresponds to Latin America's weaker geopolitical position
within the hemisphere. This position refers rhetorically to cultural groupings doing battle on unequal terms, and ridicules concepts of natural hierarchies based on ethnicity, nationality, skin color, language, and culture. In
an 1887 chronicle that appeared in Mexico's *El Partido Liberal* entitled
"México en los Estados Unidos," Martí parodies such conceptions by referring to girth and sheer force to connote his America's structural disadvan-
tages: "There is no need to hide the fact that corpulent and vigorous races
look with anger and annoyance upon the races with smaller bodies and
with difficult lives resulting from the obstacles that history has placed in
their pathway" (*Otras crónicas*, 101). While it is not irrelevant that Martí
personally knew the experience of having a small stature—he was an
"hombre-ardilla" (squirrel-man), as Enrique Collazo described him, for his
small frame and quick movements—these descriptive terms "corpulent"

and "vigorous" refer to massive accumulation of national wealth, a glut of production and growing geopolitical force as a result of long histories of colonialism and slavery.[11] Martí begins this chronicle on representations of Mexico in the United States by placing the relationship of power in the foreground. To hide such a determining relation of power is to miss a difference tantamount to that between the giant Goliath and a small David. Martí's strategy for addressing this difference is to defeat brute force with ingenuity. He proposes in his theory of translation to infiltrate the giant's massive body: "One must be perennially inside the corpulent race, and convince it little by little" (*Otras crónicas*, 101). Such a strategy authorizes the perspective of the dissenting minority deep within the monster's gut, precisely the position that Martí claims he occupied while living in New York.

In his 1891 review for *El Partido Liberal* of David Lloyd Demarest and Sydney Rosenfeld's wildly successful musical comedy *The Senator*, Martí employs a similar figure, placing two Latin Americans in the midst of the anti-Latin xenophobia of the years leading up to the military intervention in Cuba in 1898. With a 227-night run extending from January 18, 1890, to early 1891, *The Senator* enacted intertwined personal and political struggles on Capitol Hill. In it, the senator of the title, Hannibal Rivers, wins a $73,000 claim for a war veteran, marries the veteran's daughter, and defeats an insincere Austrian diplomat, Count Ernst von Strahl, whom he bankrupts through his political influence with an Austrian firm. The secretary of the Chinese legation, Ling Ching, offers comic relief in his attempts to persuade the wealthy senator to invest in China. The villain in the play is a former congressman who ruthlessly pursues a consular appointment to a foreign mission. The play's anti-Asian and antiforeign stereotypes generate sympathy for the titular character, the eligible young senator, and dramatize the odious and strange quality of the foreign. Martí sums up the play's hyperbolic message thus: "virtue is entirely national and everything foreign is Satanic."[12] In addition to calling his readers' attention to the play's portrayal of Bolivia as "that land with a funny name," Martí in the last two sentences of the review records the silent terror of two Spanish-speaking foreign ministers who watched the play among a crowd of Washington's elite: " 'It is the most perfect piece of American theater,' says the *Washington Post*. At the door, amidst the crowd near the exit, two silent and pallid foreign ministers left the theater arm in arm."[13]

Martí's review of *The Senator* demonstrates an acute consciousness of occupying a minor position in a crowd that applauds the stigmatization of

foreigners and that assumes annexation of Cuba to be inevitable. Quite
possibly referencing himself and another Latin American diplomat (Martí
took up his function as Uruguay's delegate in Washington, D.C., for the
first session of the International Monetary Commission in early 1891), the
haunting image of these two foreigners holding on to each other for protection and scuttling away from the theater illustrates Martí's sense of
vulnerability and difference in the United States of the Gilded Age. This
lonely perspective from within a hostile mass resembles that of Martí,
writing as a chronicler of *Buffalo Bill's Wild West Show*, of the Oklahoma
land rush, and of conflict on the U.S.-Mexico border in 1886. In the array of
works leading up to and including his most incisive criticism of the United
States—for augmenting and elaborating upon the tactics of European
empires—we find a perspective that predicts and alerts potential immigrants to white supremacist, anti-immigrant, and expansionist tendencies
of the United States in this era.

☙ THE SIGNIFICANCE OF *LA FRONTERA* IN AMERICAN LITERARY AND CULTURAL HISTORY

At the embattled edges of modern U.S. empire, borders have long been and
remain sites of violent struggle, surveillance, and transgressive insight.
Martí's texts about the borderlands and border subjectivity contribute to
the defining of this influential concept-metaphor of late twentieth-century
Chicana/o, Latina/o, American, and postcolonial studies.[14] In talking
about Martí's "border writing," I mean texts describing U.S. expansion
from the perspective of those whom the border cut across and violently
incorporated. For Martí, *la frontera* (border or borderlands) refers to the
material and historical effect of a rush for lands previously inhabited and
cultivated. Alerting readers of Spanish throughout the Americas to less
widely publicized attacks on Asian, European, and Italian immigrants, and
on Amerindians and African Americans in the United States, Martí's border writing puts a different spin on the usually triumphant story of Theodore Roosevelt's "winning of the West." The translation of "frontier" rhetoric into Spanish undermines such characterizations as Frederick Turner's,
of the borderlands as civilization's vanguard at the edge of "empty" lands,
and discredits both Turner's and Herbert Bolton's adaptation of Hegelian
Pan-Americanism.[15] By noting how the United States' empire simultaneously threatened various regions and racialized groups, this field of Martí's

late writing articulates a long history of diverse border subjects whose backs bridge the geographical spaces of urban and rural migrant communities in the South, the West, and the northeastern United States, and their Latin American, Antillean, and diasporic places of origin. Like other nineteenth-century Latin American writings, these texts posit alliances with what Rodolfo Acuña has called "occupied America" and across what Kirsten Silva Gruesz refers to as the "Gulf of Mexico System."[16] Martí's America takes on the qualities of a palimpsest in which traces of subaltern cultures and dispersed locations are very much visible and interconnected. Sedimented histories of the border coalesce in Martí's dream of a diverse coalition allied against U.S. expansion.

As the "guiding metaphor of Latino studies" and as "one of the most significant contributions of Latino studies to cultural studies," the border defines not just historical, geographical, cultural, and transnational points of violence and exchange, but also the intranational divisions of class, language, race, and sex.[17] According to José David Saldívar, Chicana/o theory laid the groundwork for a comparative American studies, and Martí occupies a prominent role in this field's genealogy.[18] A founding mother of this field, Gloria Anzaldúa, theorized the "borderlands" or "la frontera" as the specific site where the Third World "grates against the first and bleeds," and this conflict permeates the psychic life of the border subject.[19] Martí records and circulates in his translations and in his criticism of westward expansion some specific nineteenth-century instances of border violence. By inviting his readers to imagine through the eyes of Amerindians and northern Mexicans their colonized islands or their nations' potential absorption and violation, Martí's writing about the borderlands adds to the alternative archives that will enable us to remap American studies. Like Anzaldúa's, Martí's border writing specifically valorizes the work of translation as a strategic response to an imposed imperial language.[20]

Feeling out of place or imprisoned in the United States and longing to make and maintain contact with those on the other side of the North-South hemispheric fissure, Martí seeks to bridge the expanse separating the migrant and exile community from their Latin American homelands. Martí's 1889 lecture "Madre América" (Mother America) articulates a dream of another America in which Cuba and Puerto Rico might take their places among the continent's independent, self-governing nations. In his speech to a meeting of the Hispanic American Literary Society of New York that many Latin American delegates to the first Pan-American conference attended, Martí allies himself with Benito Juárez's ouster of Maximilian and laments the distance between Latin America's migrants or exiles and their now distant homelands: as if in a golden cage, he peers out with pleading eyes at his mother's representatives: "What can the imprisoned son say, when he sees again his mother through the bars of his cell?" He begs the Latin Americans in the audience to report to her that in New York "we found brothers! Mother America, there you have sons!" (*Obras*, 6:133, 140). This angst-filled encounter and longing for reunion with the motherland posits a common and unifying origin for Latino/as and Latin Americans, but also notes the thick metal bars and the watery abyss that divide them. Requiring them to stay in the United States even while they remain passionately invested in and connected to their places of birth, an intangible and infrangible border separates them from the motherland because they can never go back to being the person they were when they left.

Much as Martí makes the ancient civilizations of the continent the common "mother" of estranged children, Gloria Anzaldúa draws on a Nahuatl term, "nepantla," to interpret the effects of expansion upon land, bodies, and subjects in the borderlands.[21] Referring to a location between two bodies of water, "nepantla" suggests a postconquest contact zone in which translation becomes a weapon against linguistic and cultural violence. In his theorizing of the borderlands, Carl Gutiérrez-Jones endorses "the productive betrayal implied by La Malinche as a Chicana feminist cultural force."[22] This feminist reappraisal of Chicano nationalism embraces La Malinche, Cortez's mistress, as a strategic translator who enabled survival in the face of overwhelming force. The reappraisal also transforms common misunderstandings of this maligned woman as treacherous because she knew many languages. Unlike Turner's long-standing definition of the American frontier as a place of opportunity and escape from the past for a monolingualizing crew of Europeans and their descendants, Martí's and Anzaldúa's border writing recuperates historical memory of indigenous resistance to both Spanish and Anglo-American invasions.[23]

Although neither Anzaldúa nor Martí cites Turner, their discussions of la frontera critically diverge from his take on the popular Hegelian notion of the frontier as a safety valve that relieves the pressures of sectional or class conflict that would otherwise result from U.S. American culture's supposedly intrinsic tendency to grow.[24] In Martí the border refers to an effect of violent expansion that generates, reproduces, or exacerbates, rather than dissipates, internal conflict. Similarly, Anzaldúa's essay on the borderlands proposes that border subjects carry within themselves the grating, bleeding abrasions resulting from these conflicts and tend to re-open cleanly sealed dualisms of culture. In her critique of the term "His-panic" and of the nostalgic myth of the Spanish Southwest, Anzaldúa observes how the emphasis on Spanish origins and suppression of indige-nous legacies implicates the vanquished (Chicanos/as) in the dominant culture's abhorrence of Indians (and of this part of themselves), and thus "alleviate[s] [Anglos'] guilt for dispossessing the Chicano."[25] The term "Hispanic," in Anzaldúa's analysis, assimilates Chicanos to the civilizing goals of the Spanish empire, which in turn minimizes resistance to the Anglo-Americans' new imperial role. Anzaldúa's and Martí's border writ-ing throws a wrench into this logic. It prevents the colonized Chicano/a, Latino/a of Latin American cultures from delivering into the imperial power's hands the "concessions of supremacy," through which Martí's America is expected to sign itself over into unredeemable slavery, as Martí furiously exclaims in the passage I quote in my second epigraph to this chapter.

As noted above in a prescient lecture of 1893, Frederick Jackson Turner highlighted and affirmed "expansion" as one of the distinguishing charac-teristics of U.S. imperialism, along with the struggle against and domina-tion of "savagery" and the demand of "a wider field for exercise." He aligned that imperialism with four hundred years of colonization since the arrival of Columbus in the Western hemisphere.[26] The backdrop to Turner's lecture was the 1893 World's Columbian Exposition, also known as the Chicago World's Fair, which presented itself as the culmination of Europe's presence in the New World (the site of the exposition was called the White City). Just as Turner's close reading of history and U.S. culture is the basis of his thesis, so the detailed observations of historical develop-ments in the Americas that Martí made while working as a journalist led him not to a naive "naturalistic organicism" in his definition of America, but to a militant anticolonialism and sympathetic endorsements of re-bellious indigenous immigrant workers, and African American move-ments of resistance and self-defense.[27] One of Martí's late chronicles criti-cizes the people of New Orleans who lynched eleven Italian immigrants who were in jail awaiting trial in 1891; another reveals the inquisitorial tendencies of a town in Texarkana, where a white woman set fire to an African American tied to a stake, while thousands watched as he burned to death.[28] Turner offers an influential narrative to enable white imperial civilization to forget its role in a long history of violent conflicts, whereas Martí studies these conflicts to demonstrate that the United States was, effectively, taking over Europe's imperial role in the Americas.

Heeding Robert McKee Irwin's admonition to American studies to think about the border in Spanish-language as well as in English-language texts, this chapter compares a selection of border narratives in Spanish and in English, with reference to historical conflicts between Mexican, Native American, and U.S. cultures. I seek to complicate Irwin's claim that Martí "was not really concerned with Mexico, and even less with the U.S. Southwest."[29] Excavating strategies for rewriting the popular narratives through which imperial subjects were learning to recognize themselves in the Gilded Age, I argue that Martí's writing on the border uncannily prefigures reading strategies at the forefront of today's increasingly comparative, transnational, cross-cultural, and multilingual Americanist research.

Martí's border writing resonates with Eliana S. Rivero's suggestion that Cubans on and off the island are "border people."[30] Because borders mark sites of contact and struggle, border dwellers perceive commonalities and differences among diverse yet structurally aligned groups that struggle for survival in the colonial and imperial borderlands, first of Spain and then of the United States. Complicating the "hurtful stereotypes of the islander as a brainwashed cog of a Marxist state and the immigrant as a soulless worm lacking any concern for social justice," Ruth Behar's anthology of contemporary Cuban writing on and off the island (*Bridges to Cuba*) adapts the metaphor of a body-bridge that bears the weight of Cuba's history of anguished separations.[31] Behar's volume focuses on the post-1959 period and cites Martí's reference to books as a healing balm for wounds opened by weapons.[32] Martí likens his position and function to that of a textual bridge, which mediates between North and South American readers in the 1880s. His 1883 paean to Brooklyn Bridge refers to the elaborate metal structure that linked cities and words as a "steel hyphen" (guión de hierro) and a "clasp" (broche); the bridge of translation spells an alternative to war and associates the imposing, powerful metal structure of Brooklyn Bridge with a hyphen connecting two words on a page, or with a paper clip that holds together two pieces of paper (*Obras*, 9:424). Especially in Martí's early period, writing is a form of staging conflicts that might offer an alternative to military violence, so this chronicle pleads hopefully: "Better to bring cities together than to cleave human chests" (*Obras*, 9:432).

However, by late 1886, Martí depicts the bridges that enabled constant traffic across the thin, dark ribbon of the Rio Grande as claws digging violently into Mexican territory, where Mexicans lived in constant and justifiable fear of a second U.S. invasion: "on the other side is the U.S. with its vanguard of new cities, its hotels and arrogant houses, with its bridges that cross the river as if its claws were grasping the Mexican earth, and with its soulless populace staring at Mexico as if the country were theirs, and anxiously desiring to pounce upon her pastures and mines."[33] As a kind of fighting, this 1886 chronicle recognizes the necessity of self-defense against even bridge structures, because they impinged and invaded, rather than facilitating two-way crossings and mutual understanding.

Although they are sites of ongoing violence and risk, border spaces continue to represent in Latino studies a laboratory in which to develop or imagine alternatives, precisely because they represent a space of clandestine transgression and ingenuity in the face of asymmetries of power: "The border houses the outrageous, [and stimulates] the imagination needed to turn the historical and cultural tables."[34] The tendency to read within monumentalizing national, monolingual paradigms has long restricted ways in which people have thought about Martí and thus marginalized Martí's role as a translator-bridge in the large field of Martí scholarship, as Leonel de la Cuesta has noted.[35]

Martí's distance from his homeland and estrangement from the comfort of a mother-tongue cultural context explains his tendency to depict himself straddling an abyss or struggling to hold together fragmented parts of himself. He was a Spanish colonial and racialized Latino subject, a deported migrant, and an organizer of a clandestine revolution based in New York. In 1894, Enrique Collazo, a coconspirator but also a political detractor, recalls that in the final years of preparing the revolution of 1895, while subject to surveillance by the Pinkerton Agency (which had confiscated the Cubans' three shiploads of weapons), Martí nearly fell apart: "he sometimes looked a crazy victim of delirious feelings of persecution, which led him to see spies and detectives everywhere."[36] For the Cuban Rafael Merchán, exiled in Colombia and writing to José Ignacio Rodríguez, Martí figures in his memory as "so noble, partially unbalanced [medio desequilibrado], so worthy of admiration and of compassion at the same time."[37] Like W. E. B. Du Bois's exploration of life behind the veil, Martí's writings describe a Latino migrant double consciousness whose "I" housed unreconciled ideals that threatened to tear him asunder, leaving him with a "life in pieces" (vida de retazos) (*Obras*, 20:90–91).

Not only does Martí explore his own fragmented consciousness, but he also observes this border subjectivity in the poetry of Francisco Sellén, a veteran of Cuba's Ten Years War, a professional translator, and author of a volume entitled *Poesías* (1890). This book features two distinct sections with poetry from and about the two distinct political, cultural, and social periods on either side of the "Grito de Yara" (1868), the first action that launched the decade-long struggle for Cuban independence and that sent Francisco Sellén and his brother Antonio into exile in New York.[38] In Martí's review of Sellén's poetry, he characterizes migrant Latino consciousness outside the nation in terms of a tree damaged by the fires of war: the nation and the postwar Cuban subject is "like a trunk that lightning has split in two" (*Obras*, 5:184). Martí takes this resonant image of a postcolonial split or double consciousness from Sellén's poem "La palmera solitaria" (The Solitary Palm Tree) in which the poet describes a charred trunk, "Por el rayo calcinada" (burned by a bolt of lightning).[39]

Not only migrant Cubans go about their lives in this condition of dehiscence—of splitting open—that prevents the nation, or the subject, from developing a solid, unified foundation. In his obituary for the Cuban modernist poet Julian del Casal, Martí generalizes this fragmentary, split subjectivity to a general condition of uprooted, postcolonial subjects estranged from themselves: "And so we all wander this poor earth of ours, split in two, with our energies spilled throughout the world, living without personhood in strange nations, and with a strange person sitting in the chairs of our own!" (*Patria*, October 31, 1893; *Obras*, 5:222). As a comment on the Latino migrations to the United States that date at least to the displacement of Cubans and Puerto Ricans in the late nineteenth century, this description of wanderers "living without personhood" and excluded from citizenship aptly conveys the persistent effects of imperial modernity on Latino subjectivity inside the transnational framework of empire. The figure of the divided tree for the human person, the book of poetry, and the nation captures well the condition and aesthetics of the border subject.

Although Martí differs from Anzaldúa because of his near silence on the oppressive role of traditional sex and gender prescriptions in both imperialist and anti-imperialist discourses, Martí shares her acute understanding of the psychic effects of colonial difference. Like Anzaldúa, he sees parallels between his contemporary colonial condition and the long history of

Amerindians in the Americas. For example, while describing the invasion of forty thousand Anglo settlers into the Indian Territory during the Oklahoma land rush of April 1889, Martí invokes the ghost of the Seminole Indian leader Osceola. In keeping with his chronicle's title, "Como se crea un pueblo nuevo en los Estados Unidos" (How to Create a New Nation [or State, or Town] in the United States," Martí gives a step-by-step account of how the United States adds states to its Union through theft, internecine struggle, subjugation, and erasure of memory. This chronicle makes the loss of certain memories and the construction of others a condition of nation-state formation, during the same period that Ernest Renan publishes his claim that the essence of the nation is that its citizens "have many things in common and also that they have forgotten many things."[40]

Mimicking Renan's claim—with which Martí was familiar because he'd translated excerpts of "What Is a Nation?" when it first appeared in 1882—Martí's chronicle begins with a sentence that announces New York's amnesia: "New York forgot everything in an instant." This chilling indictment prefaces Martí's description of a conflagration in Manhattan. In the second paragraph's repetition of the phrase, the tense of the verb "to forget" (olvidar) shifts from past to present.[41] Not only did New York forget the indigenous origins of the state of Oklahoma almost as the land rush was happening, but it continues to forget in the chronicle's present this aspect of each U.S. state's foundation. Martí observes how rapidly the combination of amnesia and annexation transforms the cultural landscape: "Oklahoma, Indian until yesterday, is already a white country" (*Obras*, 12:365).

Rather than freely translating the headline of the chronicle in Spanish into the familiar phrase that celebrates the "boomers and sooners" (pioneers and settlers) of the Oklahoma land rush, as does Juan de Onís in his 1954 translation, I've opted to preserve, for the purposes of this discussion, Martí's ironic characterization of his chronicle as a sort of "how-to" manual: "How to Create a New Nation/People/Town in the United States." Together, the title and the first sentence associate Oklahoma's beginnings with the forgetting of the forcible relocation of the Choctaw, Creek (Muskogee), Cherokee, Chickasaw, and Seminole Indians from the Southeast into the Midwest of the United States between 1830 and 1842. Rather than a celebrated and courageous "settler," the "invading white" (el blanco invasor) is portrayed by Martí as occupying land that the Seminole leader Osceola sold to Washington in order to guarantee a territorial refuge for self-emancipated Africans and Indians (*Obras*, 13:206). Osceola's ghostly presence in Martí's story of Oklahoma's origins reminds the reader of the treachery employed by the U.S. government in its response to the Seminoles' indefatigable resistance. The past of indigenous displacement in the borderlands of Florida and Oklahoma illustrates for Martí's readers a possible future of invading Anglos, against which he hopes his readers will join him in plotting.

Recent reinterpretations of Turner's thesis about the frontier in American history celebrate the diversity of a multicultural U.S. West, in which non-English-speaking Europeans, Asians, Mexicans, Amerindians, and African Americans created a "composite" non-English nationality through their struggle with a savage natural environment.[42] The challenge remains for those who celebrate multiculturalism to respond fully to the forcible dispossession of Indian lands. Martí's Oklahoma chronicle shows how European arrivants create a new U.S. pueblo by forgetting the fratricide and genocide that shaped the future inhabitants' relations among themselves:

> They disappear behind the hills, reappear, they fall out of sight again and three step foot on the same acre at the same time. They face each other, with blood in their eyes. Another stops suddenly on his horse, leaps to the ground, and drives his knife into the soil. The wagons begin to stop and unload onto the prairie where the father drives the stakes, and unloads the hidden cargo—the woman, the children. They don't step down; they drop. They roll their children onto the grass, the horses whinnying and flicking their tails, the mother shouting to one side with her arms up high. One who arrived afterward does not want to leave the land. The rival unloads his rifle in his face, continues driving stakes, and kicks the dead body as it falls on the borderline. (*Obras*, 13:210)

Here the border is literally a place of death. Unlike Turner's definition of expansionism in the West as a struggle with a vague form of savagery, Martí's story of the Oklahoma land rush calls attention to the desperate competition among settlers who waited for weeks along the borders of the Indian Territory with thousands of others in order to stake a claim by invading and, if necessary, by killing. This violence echoes the earlier displacement and dishonesty in dealing with the indigenous inhabitants.

The Oklahoma land rush proved so alarming to Martí in part because it coincided with the Harrison administration's projected acquisition of Cuba, which he believed could result in a similar torrent of settlers unleashed on the island. Martí's chronicles define the invaders' loss of memory and solipsism as facilitating policies of cultural and physical violence. In numerous newspaper articles on the subject, Secretary of State James G. Blaine constructed Cuba as an ideal field for applying U.S. technology, discipline, and entrepreneurship in order to properly exploit and order the "diseased" island. For example, an article in the *New York Herald* of February 1889 expresses Blaine's arguments in favor of the convenience and timeliness of purchasing Cuba: "The Next Secretary of State Casts Longing Eyes on Cuba: Shall We Buy the Island? Mr. Blaine on the Advisability of Making the Purchase: For Health and Prosperity."[43] In March 1889, Martí responded to arguments for and against the "taking" of Cuba with his letter to the editor of the New York *Evening Post* entitled "A Vindication of Cuba" (published in both English and Spanish simultaneously).[44] These discussions form the backdrop for his analysis of the seemingly unrelated situation in the borderlands of Oklahoma. Martí's border writing makes visible the connections between the islands and the Midwest in what Martí calls a strategy of infiltrative translation. The contemporary turn of American studies to translation, borders, and cultural bridges is indebted to this strategy. Infiltrative translation was for Martí a means to prevent preemptive invasions and to ensure his America's survival. Translation proved an indispensable resource for calling into question the legitimacy of a proliferating discourse on Latinness.

∾ "DE LAS COSAS LATINAS": TRAVEL WRITING
AND THE PRODUCTION OF A RACIAL DISCOURSE
ON LATINNESS

Although the adjective "Latino/a" did not denote in the late nineteenth-century what it does today (Latinos make up the largest subculture in the United States at the start of the twenty-first century), it did point to an incipient form of this major cultural formation in the Americas. Even then, the term served as a figurative umbrella under which multiple nationalities, ethnicities, racial groupings, and speakers of different languages began to gather, in common refusal of Anglo-American misconceptions, distorted portraits, and imposing political and economic projects. Like Puerto Rican and Chicana/o movements for empowerment and civil rights that rejected the Europeanizing, government-assigned term "Hispanic" in the 1960s and 1970s, Martí's late nineteenth-century terminology repels the suggestion that Anglo imperial expansion might be natural, beneficent, or what most Latino American people in the hemisphere wanted.

In the late 1880s and early 1890s, a discourse proliferated on "Latinness" as the exotically different, decadent, chaotic, and desired object of a U.S. hemispheric policy of Pan-Americanism. Commonly attributing to Latin America effeminacy and "racial" underdevelopment, this discourse made the indeterminacy and supposed impurity of Latinness the determining cause of a natural inability to achieve self-government: "And what a kaleidoscopic scene it was of shifting oddity and color—every complexion invented by man, from black to cream—black hybrids, yellow hybrids, Spanish types, Indian types—all a jumble of miscegenation in bright serapes, graceful ribosas, big hats, wonderfully decorated tresses; and most notable of all, the dandies of the city, slender-legged, effeminate young milksops, the fag-end of a decayed civilization, without virility or purpose."[45] Charles Dudley Warner, coauthor with Mark Twain of *The Gilded Age* and friend of Helen Hunt Jackson, offers this depiction of a street scene in Morelia, Mexico in *Harper's Monthly*. Martí translated Warner's phrase "slender-legged" with ire and exclamation marks, as "¡Piernas pobres!" (Weak legs!) to refute Warner's depiction of Mexican civilization as decaying because miscegenated, or purposeless, and doomed because of its culturally and racially mixed intellectuals or "dandies."

Like Martí's later "Vindication of Cuba," his translation of Warner's description and response to it defends the contributions of literary men like himself to the struggle for self-government. "Grabbing the beards" of the North American travel writers who were slowly creating this distorted U.S. "national judgment" (juicio nacional) of Mexico, Martí's analysis of this and other travel essays admonishes readers to counter such representations immediately and "at home" (en su propia casa) (*Obras*, 5:57). Whether this home be in Mexico or in the United States, Martí warns that the "fine threads" of these very simplistic arguments could be the instrument to deliver Mexico (or Cuba) into the hungry mouth of the northern empire (*Obras*, 7:50).

Numerous U.S. travel writers sculpted exotic portraits by gazing out the windows of luxurious inter-American railroad carriages in the Gilded Age; others ventured into the communities themselves. During a brief sojourn in the United States after a twenty-year residence in Europe, Henry James encountered in the New Hampshire hills one of the "aliens" who threatened to alter American character in an alarming way. James portrays the young man's strangeness as a function of physical and linguistic difference in relation to his New England surroundings. When the young man does not promptly respond to James's request for orientation, James infers a racial identification and a language and peremptorily fills in the silence: "But his stare was blank, in answer to my inquiry, and, seeing that he failed to understand me and that he had a dark-eyed 'Latin' look, I jumped to the inference of his being a French Canadian." When James exhausts his knowledge of European languages and decides that he cannot pinpoint the origin of this "Latin," he tries a starkly Anglo question to prod the stranger to speech: " 'What *are* you then?' I wonderingly asked—on which my accent loosened in him the faculty of speech."[46] The man turns out to be Armenian. James's account of his encounter with foreignness with a "Latin" look, and with linguistic difference in the heart of Anglo-America, belongs to a racial discourse that begins to proliferate in the 1880s, especially in U.S. travel writing about Mexico.

A discourse "on all things Latin" (de las cosas latinas) (*Obras*, 6:114; quotation marks in Martí's original) burgeoned with special reference to Mexico in the years after the 1885 launching of the three-thousand-mile Mexican Central and Mexican National railroad lines.[47] Unlike James's multilingual response to the Armenian with a Latin look, often these writers did not have the language skills to converse with Mexicans if they actually got off the train. This discourse fabricated and disseminated stereotypes of Latins in Anglophone contexts, in a language to which the stereotyped group often had no access.

For example, the widely published economist David Wells based his *Study of Mexico* on a train journey that he completed in 1887; his study exoticizes Mexico by likening it to geographically distant places such as China, another planet, Timbuktu, or the Holy Land.[48] Wells not only admitted that he did not speak Spanish; he characterized the Spanish language as "not well fitted for the uses and progress of a commercial nation," and hence claims that it would "constitute a very serious obstacle in the way of indoctrinating the Mexican people with the ideas and methods of overcoming obstacles and doing things which characterize their great Anglo-Saxon neighbors" (94). Wells's racializing gloss on the Spanish language not only reveals the presumption and arrogance of many of these travel writers from the United States; it also hints at his awareness that this other language might constitute a bulwark of cultural resistance to assimilation. Although Wells laments Mexico's cultural differences from the

United States—especially the millennial agricultural technology that enabled Mexicans to live without having to work all the time—he characterizes Mexico "as one of the very poorest and most wretched of all countries, . . . not speedily or even ultimately likely, under any circumstances, to develop into a great (in the sense of highly civilized), rich, and powerful nation" (39). He proclaims U.S. economic control to be inevitable and defines ways for the United States to make this future economic intercourse profitable (213). Drawing parallels between Mexico and British India, Wells comments on the fact that Mexican wages are one-half to one-third of what they are in the United States. Such a discrepancy lends support to his proposal that by speculating on real estate, or by privatizing Mexico's land tenure system, North American owners might collect rents and turn a profit on the inevitable future intercourse between the two nations.

Reviewing Wells's book in *El Partido Liberal*, Martí alerts his readers to how the essay fortifies a racial stereotype of Mexico. Wells depicts the "unjust and fearful concept of Mexico as a weak and incapable people, a view held by many North Americans" (*Otras crónicas*, 102). In contesting Wells's views, Martí attacks North American ignorance of Mexico's capacities, historical beauty, and natural riches. He faults Wells's unwillingness or inability to consider the "historical causes" (razones históricas) of Mexico's conditions, more than his ignorance (102). Fundamentally opposed to the popular theories of scientific racism common in U.S. print journalism, Martí recalls for his readers the historical factors of Spanish colonialism and of U.S. imperialism in Mexico: both denied the indigenous masses the ability to flourish, and both tended to inculcate a small minority with an alienating, Eurocentric point-of-view.

Wells's study was first published by the privately owned *Popular Science Monthly*. By contrast, William Eleroy Curtis's travel and writing of *The Capitals of Spanish America* (1888) was commissioned and funded by the U.S. government. In over seven hundred illustrated pages on Latin America's urban centers, the monolingual Curtis repeatedly betrays assumptions of Yankee superiority in relation to the premodern backwardness of Latin America that are similar to those of Wells. Curtis's volume so incensed Latin American delegates to the Pan-American conference in 1889–90 that they vigorously protested his appointment by Secretary of State James G. Blaine to the position of conference secretary, and demanded, in his stead, two bilingual secretaries who would produce bilingual conference minutes. In his report Curtis racializes Mexico's leaders, noting their "tawny skins and straight black hair," and laments the slow progress of Latin America toward a U.S. model: "the historic halls of the Montezumas are only spattered with the modern ideas we [the United States] exemplify."[49] Representations of Latin American cultures, as in the case of the people of Tierra del Fuego, whom Curtis refers to as "the ugliest mortals that ever breathed" (518), provided a cognitive map on which an emerging Anglo-American imperial subject was plotted. Popular culture—including novels, exhibitions, extrajudicial violence such as lynching or military expansionism—reinforced a predetermined end of imperial modernity. Whether blood-based or cultural, this concept of racial hierarchy helped rationalize the need for a U.S. invasion, occupation, or "protection" of less powerful nations.

In the same period that these travel narratives were being published, expositions, romance novels, theater, newspapers, travel writing, and social movements educated the mostly immigrant masses of the United States into the racial system of imperial modernity, in which white, Anglo, imperial subjects appeared naturally advanced and Latin cultures appeared decadent, obsolete, or unfit for survival. Despite this tendency of fictive and nonfictive representations of the Mexican "race" from an Anglo viewpoint to demonstrate what Martí called a "fatídico desdén hacia la raza de color trigueño" (ominous contempt for the brown-skinned race), Martí held open the question of which nation would emerge as the victor in this encounter: "It remains to be seen who invaded more, or who was invaded when the rapacious nomads of the North entered the beautiful, warm, joyful and weak Latino cities: it may be that the South entered into the North, and refined it, in larger degree than the North entered in the South and oppressed it" (*Obras*, 8:395). Even though this interpretation recognizes the violent, "rapacious," and oppressive tendencies of the North, Martí understands that the final outcome of the encounter remains undecided. The question of who will have succeeded in this struggle belongs to the future.

Martí deprives the disdainful, powerful North of certain victory also in his review of a popular romance novel, *Niñita* (Little Girl) (1883), in which a beautiful Indian girl's love for a blond American man supposedly represents the relationship between Martí's America and the imperial modernity of the United States. The novel's title character, Niñita, is in the course of the story crushed by a powerful locomotive train in which the blond northerner is traveling. Martí notes that the author laments the death of the Indian maid, but having done so, turns from this patronizing conclusion to indict both author and reader, for as each pities the dead Indian they also continue along the same tracks as "the Texans [who] crush her."[50] The novel's representation of Anglo expansion in terms of North American technology's penetration of the "beautiful, broken body of the vulnerable, loving mestiza virgin, 'Niñita' " portrays Mexico as desiring this violent entry (Obras, 8:394), but Martí implicitly rejects this inference with his indictment. In this review, as in his other writings of the time, Martí locates in the various popular genres of his day the common will to violence of the Texan Anglo toward the Mexican, but he does not grant certain victory to such shows of force. The caricature of Mexico as a woman in love with her conqueror, which might have inspired the rank and file of annexationist leader A. K. Cutting's more than ten thousand supporters, vigorously endorses assimilation to Anglo-America.[51] By contrast, Martí's translations posit a dissenting, divergent reading of these popular narratives.

∾ "TO INFILTRATE THE BORDERLANDS": INTERPRETING THE "CASES" OF CUTTING AND SEDGWICK

Preparing his readers to protect themselves against the effects of U.S. delusion about its "natural dominion" over Latin America, the infiltrative translator discreetly enters Anglo-American cultural settings, studies the rhetoric of imperialism, and then translates it for readers in the lands that would be most affected by it. Infiltrative translation unmasks the imperial ambitions that the rhetoric of democracy and equality sometimes obscures from view.[52] In reflecting on the case of A. K. Cutting, a Canadian-born British subject and editor of a Mexican newspaper, who nearly sparked a second U.S. invasion of Mexico, Martí describes his "duty" (deber) as a correspondent in the United States for Mexican readers in a letter to his editor, Manuel Mercado, who received the bulk of Martí's most intimate correspondence: "[There is] the need on the border for a numerous element of cautious people of good counsel to infiltrate and to launch among the masses of this country an indefatigable campaign that might be called 'an explanation of Mexico.' By knowing and respecting Mexico more, the [United States] masses might esteem Mexico as do those who already know and respect her."[53] The infiltration of the border that Martí proposes would counter such misinformation by educating a Mexican readership, but also

by "explaining Mexico" to North Americans. The infinitive verb, "to infiltrate," connotes an undercover military operation, as it portrays the translator slipping past checkpoints or inserting himself into Anglo culture
where he gathers material for his journalism with the express goal of
fomenting informed critical opposition to pervasive misrepresentation of
Mexico and Latinness. Infiltrative translation seeks to prevent an invasion
from the North on false pretexts, a grave injustice that according to Martí
nearly became a reality in 1886 primarily because of the news media, travel
narratives, and popular culture's construction of Mexico.

It is hard to overstate the passionate concern with which Martí assumed
this task of infiltration and translation as weapons of self-defense. After
Mexico and the United States reached the brink of a second war over the
Cutting affair, Martí exhorts his readers to study carefully "all the currents
of opinion in the United States toward Mexico":

> It is not only useful, but indispensable, even vital, and of such importance
> that we must not allow [this knowledge] out of our sight for one mo-
> ment. . . . Here, there exists constant preparation for [a war with Mexico],
> which is favored by a crude and traditional confidence, by the memories of
> the victory of force and treachery over justice and heroism in 1848, by the
> unemployment of former military professionals who do not know how to be
> peaceful having had a taste of war; by the penetrating and invasive character
> of men in the United States, and perhaps above all, by the U.S. masses'
> generalized lack of knowledge of the virtues, originality, resistance, intel-
> ligence, difficulties, and human resources for which Mexico demands re-
> spect. ("El Caso 'Cutting,'" *El Partido Liberal*, August 6, 1886; reprinted in
> *Otras crónicas*, 57)

Smuggling information to Mexicans concerning the bellicose aspirations of
the U.S. masses, infiltrative translation disseminates a counterdiscourse on
Mexico and cultivates potential allies. Martí's reinterpretation of a dominant discourse on Mexican culture thus sought to dismantle the assumptions that had developed into caricatures of Mexicans in the wake of the
United States–Mexico War. Enlisting Mexicans, Chicano/as, and migrant
Latino/as in the reeducation of the masses of the United States, he proposes,
via infiltrative translation, that Mexico send out scouts who might study the
terrain and then, if necessary, help block expansion by force.

Infiltrative translation presents an honorable alternative to the activities
of the unscrupulous newspaperman A. K. Cutting, who in Martí's view,

sought to create a pretext for a second U.S. military invasion in June 1886. Cutting was the editor of *El Centinela* (The Sentinel), then the principle newspaper of El Paso del Norte (which became known as Ciudad Juárez in 1888), when he was found guilty in a Mexican court of defaming the Mexican editor, Emigdio Medina. Cutting became incensed when he learned that Medina, a Mexican citizen, planned to launch a rival newspaper to be named *La Revista Internacional*.[54] He published libelous comments accusing Medina of being an untrustworthy "fraud" who proposed to "swindle advertisers."[55] Although Cutting agreed to publish an apology and desist from attacking his competitor, he immediately went to El Paso, Texas, and published not a retraction but a reiteration of his attack on Medina's character. Mexican police apprehended Cutting in the act of personally distributing copies of this second instance of libel in El Paso del Norte.

Jailed a second time, Cutting and his supporters claimed that the Mexican court was improperly asserting extraterritorial jurisdiction over what Cutting had published in Texas. Although Cutting was allowed to go free on bail, he contemptuously refused to leave the jail, stating: "I am now in the hands of my Government and ignore your court altogether" (*New York Times*, July 25, 1886). Declaring himself an exception to Mexican laws, Cutting reportedly contacted the Texas governor, John Ireland, who offered to liberate Cutting with or without support from the federal government (*New York Times*, July 22, 1886).[56] Militias began to gather for "inflammatory mass meetings throughout the Lone Star State" (*New York Times*, August 4, 1886). As Martí wrote in *La República* of Honduras: "Everything in those moments announced war" ("Carta de Nueva York," *La República*, September 11, 1886; rpt. *En los Estados Unidos*, 683). Volunteer militias marched on the Texas side to "take the country for the Americans, with the goal of raising it up to the standards of modern civilization," and Mexican troops began to dig trenches to hold the border along the Rio Grande ("Crónica no publicada"; *José Martí y el Caso Cutting*, 131). In Martí's analysis, Cutting sought to use his incarceration to stir up popular support for a second invasion, in fulfillment of persistent longing and unofficial plans among U.S. southerners and northerners alike, to annex the four mineral- and metal-rich Mexican states along the border.

After the United States consul in El Paso del Norte, J. Harvey Brigham, and the United States ambassador to Mexico, Henry Rootes Jackson, charged Mexico with holding Cutting without bail in a dank, dirty dungeon for an act he committed outside Mexico, Secretary of State Bayard demanded Cutting's unconditional release. Mexico's minister of foreign relations, Ignacio Mariscal, declared that his constitution prohibited the U.S. federal government from interfering in the state of Chihuahua's judicial process. Only when Illinois congressman Robert R. Hitt disclosed that Cutting had "scornfully" refused to post bail, did the prospect of an invasion dissipate.[57]

As a Cuban refugee whose family lived for many years in Mexico, where he met his dear friend Manuel Mercado, Martí followed the Cutting case with such keen interest that he wrote six articles about it for Mexican, Honduran, and Argentine readers. Martí's letters on the incident reveal his keen awareness of the power of public opinion in the United States and of the urgent need to study and contribute vigilantly to its shaping in the press. For example, largely because of newspaper reports, the "appetite for war" to which Martí alerts his readers did not die with the resolution of the Cutting case (*Cutting Case*, 156). The close of the case augmented Martí's sense that education alone would not have the power to disarm a proliferating racial discourse and lucrative economic policy. In a chronicle that reports on a meeting of the American Annexation League at a New York hotel in June 1887, Martí infiltrates and translates snippets of whispered conversations as if he were overhearing them at the meeting: " '[Cutting] is coming,' they said in whispers, to unite the forces of the Annexation League with the Occupation and Development Company of Northern Mexico" (*Obras*, 7:52). Founded in 1878, and enjoying the support of ten thousand members from various states of the American Union and from several proannexation states in Canada and Mexico, the American Annexation League pursued a dual strategy. On the one hand, the league planned to take advantage of civil strife in Mexico, Honduras, or Cuba; on the other, it worked under the auspices of private companies to achieve its objective of acquiring control over territory and resources (*Obras*, 7:51–53). Martí's chronicles on the Cutting case reveal a long history of public and private cooperation in order to achieve U.S. imperial objectives.

In addition to providing another example of the abuse of state power that contributed to Martí's radicalization, the Cutting case reveals the imbrication of sexual and racial discourses. In silent divergence from the major newspaper reports on the case, Martí did not report on the most prominent story related to Cutting's antics in Mexico: the widespread defamation and "queering" of Secretary of State Thomas Bayard's special envoy, Arthur George Sedgwick.[58] A liberal legal scholar who had served as an editor for *The Nation* and the *New York Evening Post*, Sedgwick became the target of merciless vilification by the mainstream U.S. press.[59] As Cutting's imprisonment in Mexico was on the verge of catalyzing a second United States–Mexico War, Bayard secretly commissioned Sedgwick to investigate the facts surrounding Cutting's imprisonment. As a utopian anti-imperialist and opponent of political party machine politics, Sedgwick became a target of the proannexation popular culture that helped cast suspicion upon his person and that made his relations with Mexicans into an object of lewd fascination and controversy. Sedgwick and Bayard who were both Democratic appointees at a time when Republicans were eager to return to the presidency, faced opponents in the press and in positions of power. Such people wanted to see President Grover Cleveland, a Democrat, blunder into the Republicans' established policy of aggressive financial and political expansion, but did not want him to win political credit as a result. From the time of his appointment, the press accused Sedgwick of not being quite what he presented himself to be. Initially, Bayard flatly denied that he had appointed Sedgwick, but under pressure from reporters, the State Department acknowledged that Sedgwick was on his way to Mexico to investigate the case (*New York Times*, August 15, 1886).

Ascribing to Sedgwick words that were not his and insinuating Sedgwick's illegitimate sexual liaisons with "savage" Mexicans, press reports clouded Sedgwick's mission with suspicion and fantasy about licentious Mexican cultural practices. In an article entitled, "Lying about Mr. Sedgwick" (a title that suggests both falsehoods and sleeping around), a reporter was described as "father[ing] upon that gentleman [Sedgwick] a statement of conditions in which war is nearly, if not quite, inevitable" (*New York Times*, August 20, 1886). A newspaper from Emporia, Kansas, reported that Sedgwick was arrogating to himself the right to declare war.[60] The undermining of Sedgwick's legitimacy only increased as he penetrated into Mexican territory, where he presented a challenge to the authority of the proannexationist United States ambassador and former Confederate brigadier general, Henry Rootes Jackson.[61]

Martí launches a critique of A. K. Cutting and of U.S. expansionism at a time when such a critical position ran counter to (or, in the early sense of the word, would have seemed "queer," unusual) to the mainstream view reported in the press. Unlike the popular Theodore Roosevelt, who in 1899 fondly remembered organizing a brigade to support the imminent invasion of Mexico in 1886, Martí, like Sedgwick, held the view that the United

States ought to maintain peace through fair and respectful relations with the neighboring republic.[62] However, instead of focusing on diplomacy between the U.S. and Mexico, the New York press reported on allegations and insinuations about the escapades of Sedgwick, with such headlines as "Mr. Sedgwick Hilarious: He Beams Upon the Gilded Youth of Mexico" (*New York Times*, August 28, 1886). In a familiar maneuver, whereby stories of politicians' illicit sexual behavior distract national attention from transnational ramifications of U.S. policies, Sedgwick is presented in such news reports as having come under the influence of Mexican sexuality. He was reported carousing until 6:15 a.m. with the gilded youth of Mexico's Jockey Club. Detailed descriptions of Sedgwick gaining the attention of "young bloods," "in the hands of Mexican dudes," sporting flowers in his hat, and "full" upon "painting the Greaser Soil a bright red," complicated and delayed Sedgwick's verdict on the legitimacy of Cutting's imprisonment, while distracting press and public attention from Cutting's own libelous acts. These sensationalized stories about Sedgwick protected Cutting from public reprisals more successfully than any report could have done. Within weeks of the war scare's dissolution, Cutting's possible prevarication and provocation of war became invisible. In *Life* magazine's opinion, "the American mind has ceased to take heed at all of Cutting in its keen anxiety to know the truth about Sedgwick" (September 23, 1886, 2).

In citing these news stories of questionable factual content, I wish to draw attention to the association of a critique of imperialism with queer sexual behavior. The sexualized racial discourse on Latinness that we find in travel writing of the period is mirrored in sexualized, racial reporting about Mexico and its allies in contemporary newspapers. Martí studiously avoids any mention of the insinuations against Sedgwick's comportment, but he notes the "distressing disorder" (penoso trastorno) (164) in the State Department's handling of the press's representation of Sedgwick's identity. To counteract the effects of intraparty intrigue upon U.S. foreign policy toward his America, Martí turns his newspaper columns toward the dual purpose of translating for Mexicans the expansionist racism and sexual fantasy that circulated in the United States and of defending Mexico's right and ability to maintain control of its threatened border states.

Simply by entering Mexican cultural space and refusing to endorse the plot to invade Mexico, Sedgwick became a character in a U.S. fiction about properly virile or "failed" Latin masculinities that informed Gilded Age inter-American politics. While we may fault Martí for maintaining an enigmatic—or perhaps panicked—silence about the smears on the character of the anti-imperialist jurist Sedgwick, we should also recognize his refusal to endorse or reproduce such bigotry. By joining in the widespread attack on Sedgwick, Martí might have easily diverted negative attention away from attacks on his own person by performing an aggressive heterosexism. Only a few years earlier, his "effeminate" (in some militant's eyes) interest in poetry and art, his work as a writer (rather than as a soldier), and his willingness to criticize the political movement to which he belonged became the subject of other party members' comments, as I discuss below. Avoiding such mudslinging, Martí interpreted the ad hominem press campaign against Sedgwick as an attempt by the Republicans to capitalize on the Democrats' prevarication with respect to Sedgwick's identity. With the possibility of war palpable on the border, Martí quickly brought into focus the transnational implications of stereotypes of Mexican culture and U.S. politics and sought to generate critical discussion about them in the United States and in his America.

ᥫ "EXAGERACIONES MUJERILES": MARTÍ ON EDGE, LATINO/A WRITING, AND THE NEW WOMAN

Martí's dissemination of news about the Cutting case and about the widespread support for annexation of Cuba that was gathering momentum in the United States nearly coincided with an effort within the proindependence movement to discredit Martí by insinuating that his criticism of the movement's leadership reflected his own treacherous effeminacy. This coincidence reveals similar anxieties around nonnormative gender and sexual practices among both proimperialist and anticolonialist movements. As a poet and writer of newspaper columns rather than an experienced military veteran of the Ten Years War, Martí lost political status when he took his transgressive public stand in October 1884 against the authoritarian tendencies of General Máximo Gómez. His criticism of the party leaders resulted in an anguished separation from the nationalist movement up until 1887. Having stepped down from consular posts in expectation of active involvement in a strike for independence from Spain, Martí suddenly found himself without employment and ridiculed by former comrades and anticolonial separatists (in addition to being estranged from his wife, Carmen Zayas Bazán, who returned to Cuba with their son, Pepe, in 1885).

Adherents in the movement associated Martí's lack of combat experience and his insistence on civilian, democratic leadership with effeminate cowardice, and he responded with a hyperbolic reproduction of the same association of masculine virility and leadership. According to one anecdote from this period of Martí's distance from the independence movement, a Civil War veteran and leader in the pro-independence movement, Antonio Zambrana, took the podium when Generals Gómez and Maceo were fundraising in New York for the reinitiation of the war in 1885, and accused anyone who did not support this initiative of "wearing a skirt." In this construction, to criticize the military leadership, as Martí had, becomes a cowardly, effeminate—or perhaps a feminist—act. In assuming that only those in the audience or in the nation who wore pants were capable of bravery and leadership, this anecdote reveals the misogynist tone of the revolutionary movement.

Quesada de Miranda's version of this story portrays Martí responding to these insinuations by asserting his own virile masculinity with such excess that it is possible to perceive ironic bitterness in his response: "And you should understand that not only am I unable to wear a skirt, but I am such a man that I don't fit into underwear."[63] Despite his public defiance of these charges in the aftermath of these incidents, Martí's correspondence reveals his awareness that his challenge to Goméz's authoritarian leadership and his subsequent silence appeared to others in the movement as "womanish exaggerations" (exageraciones mujeriles) (*Epistolario*, 1:311). So as not to fracture or weaken the movement, Martí settled into several years of self-imposed silence, during which time he refrained from speaking or writing on behalf of Cuban independence.

Nearly fifty years after the incident, but fifteen years before Quesada de Miranda published the "I don't fit into underwear" anecdote, Martí's contemporary Alberto Plochet adds further tantalizing details to this charged confrontation between Martí, the civilian leader and poet, and the veteran military leader General Gómez. Giving further stereotypically feminine characteristics to Martí, Plochet describes Martí's eyes at the moment of his confrontation of Zambrana as "veiled by long black lashes, half-closed," gazing on his opponent with compassion. At the close of the meeting, reports Plochet, tears welled up in Martí's eyes, so copiously that his lashes stuck together. The spurned Martí demonstrated his self-sacrificing commitment to Cuba and to the generals by performing the same evocative gesture that Gómez and Maceo had, of ripping off their copper buttons in order to donate them to the cause of Cuban independence. As Martí handed over his contribution, he murmured: "I cannot leave here buttoned up, when Gómez and Maceo are leaving unbuttoned."[64]

This period of estrangement and silence also internally unbuttoned Martí. He confessed to Manuel Mercado in Mexico the psychic fragmentation that resulted from his new condition as an isolated economic migrant, expelled from national and familial roles. To Mercado, the Cuban migrant figures himself as "a doe [cierva], torn to pieces by hounds" (*Epistolario*, 1:330), an image that he later uses to describe his poetry:

> Mi verso es un ciervo herido
> Que busca en el monte amparo
> (My verse a deer wounded
> Seeking forest cover unseen)[65]

The fact that Martí was in an unstable, wounded condition motivated his appeal for Mercado's help in a new economic and creative venture. Putting into practice the strategies of infiltrative translation, Martí proposed to establish an editorial house to produce books, translations, and articles about the United States for Spanish-language readers. The two-pronged initiative would place translation and interpretation of U.S. public opinion in Mexican newspapers and would produce books in Spanish that might be both educational and entertaining for readers of Spanish in Latin America and in the United States. By 1889, Martí began to conceive of and actually proposed to Mercado a related phase of the project, which would include an English-language magazine with Latino analysis for distribution in the United States.[66] The chronicles he proposed would explore political incidents, social studies, news of literature and theater, and other aspects of North American life and culture, all with a view to inform and to organize the growing Spanish-speaking communities in urban centers along the East Coast, and in the south and southwestern states that had previously been part of Mexico. These proposals, which Martí ambitiously pursued during his final years of working as a full-time correspondent in New York, sketch a vision of bilingual publication by and for Latino/a peoples and cultures from inside the United States. These projects navigate borders and translate cultural hierarchies with the goal of distinguishing his America's future from European-identified imperial modernity. Martí's infiltrative translation thus sought to rupture a paradigm of merging of borders within a single hemispheric, Pan-American union.

Martí's chronicles, as a minor literature of interest to Latino/as in New York (in addition to his long-standing Latin American audience), coincide with a period of stateless impoverishment in his life, of psychic vulnerability, disaffection from the movement, and separation from his family. In a letter to Mercado, Martí asserts a Latino/a print community both positively and negatively, that is, widely available in print, but directed to a subculture. He mentions a newspaper that is "of this city, but for [and of] Latino/as" (de esta ciudad, pero de gente latina) (*Epistolario*, 1:299). The adjectival phrase "of Latino/as" describes a New York newspaper—possibly *El Latino Americano*—where seven of his pieces had already appeared.[67] In making his appeal to Mercado, Martí promised to analyze U.S. culture and events for Mexican readers, but "without compromising comments" (*Epistolario*, 1:286). As he explained, the critical essays that he proposed to publish would simply turn U.S. society inside out, so that his readers might see its usually hidden, "ugly and wrinkled interior" (*Epistolario*, 1:331). Such work would enable him to avoid having to push papers for a commercial firm such as Herbst Brothers, on whose letterhead he composed, in a poem for his Uruguayan friend Enrique Estrázulas, "the shoots of his tortured thoughts" (esos retoños / Del pensamiento en tortura!) (*Epistolario*, 1:293). Alluding to the angst-provoking falling out with General Gómez, the poem obliquely expresses his desire to return to his post as interim consul, from the position of a Latino/a writer with limited options inside U.S. borders.

While formulating these U.S.-based translation projects, Martí depicts himself in terms that echo the protean, unstable, nontraditional, rebellious, and wounded characteristics of Anzaldúa's border subject. Anzaldúa defines such subjects as the "squint-eyed, the perverse, the queer, the troublesome, the mongrel, the mulatto, the half-breed, the half dead."[68] In Anzaldúa, as in Martí, the border subject is the target of derogatory epithets and of accusations from within her or his own community. Given that Anzaldúa's border theory radically challenges "male-derived" Indo-Hispanic and Anglo assumptions, we should ask: to what extent does Martí participate in the common confusing and fusing of "manhood and nationhood, in the figure of the revolutionary hero" and to what extent does that fusion derive from others in the movement?[69] Martí's discourse on gender and sexuality proves so contradictory that he simultaneously reproduces and unravels this bond between nationalism and masculinism. On one hand, Martí tended to reproduce traditional narratives favoring conservative, private femininity and heroic, heterosexual masculinity, even when this repressive discourse forced him into years of anguished silence. On the other hand, Martí did not confuse nationality and conventional masculinity all the time, because he acknowledged with wonder, curiosity, and perhaps anxious fear, new practices of gender and sexuality that were already altering the course of American modernities.

Martí could not and did not ignore the impact of changing practices of gender and sexuality. His chronicles record personal encounters with key figures and events of what came to be called the Mauve Decade. He describes meeting the first woman who ran for U.S. president in 1884 and 1888, Belva Lockwood; he provides an eye-witness report on Oscar Wilde's attire during the British poet's United States speaking tour in celebration of aestheticism; he assesses the impact of women's entrance to the professions, the business world, politics, authorship, and suffrage; he closely reads Walt Whitman's poetry, especially the poems of the Calamus section of *Leaves of Grass*; and he writes his own poetry about "Love in the City," which happens outside the heterosexual matrix of the nuclear family, "in the street, standing in the dust / of saloons and public squares" (*Selected Writings*, 62–63). Unlike Frederick Douglass, who ran for office as Victoria Woodhull's vice-presidential candidate and who spoke regularly in defense of women's rights, Martí frequently associates the baneful effects of modernity with the new woman's frenetic, androgynous, chameleonic emergence into public space as a consumer and a political actor. Martí celebrated specific Cuban women for their contributions to the proindependence movement, women like Mariana Grajales, the mother of General Maceo and his brother, for the self-sacrificing gift of her sons to the revolution. But even his "Manifesto of Montecristi," which announced the objectives of the Cuban liberation movement and which he wrote in 1895 while passing through Santo Domingo en route to Cuba, did not announce women's suffrage in the new Cuba (and Cuban women would not gain access to the vote until 1934).

Martí responded to his isolation and economic need in 1885 by planning and undertaking several forms of infiltrative translation and by experimenting with writing from a woman's point of view. Turning to a genre consumed primarily by women, Martí published a serialized novel *Amistad funesta* (Baneful Friendship) under the female pseudonym Adelaida Ral, and he translated Helen Hunt Jackson's *Ramona*, both of which appear with prologues by him in all editions of his *Obras completas*. Economic necessity motivated both of these novels. The former, which he republished in book form with the title *Lucía Jerez*, was written ostensibly as a favor to his friend Adelaida Baralt in exchange for a paltry forty-four dollars (*Obras*, 18:191).[70] The novel depicts how female desire and artistic creativity wreak havoc on the home life of the principle male character, Lucía Jerez's cousin, Juan Jerez, who is patterned after Martí. Similarly, the translation project of *Ramona* acknowledges the power of women as writers and consumers of books, insofar as Martí sought to make money through its sales. A liberal plea for the Indian, Jackson's characters and narrative nevertheless reaffirm the conventional discourse of the blue-eyed, raven-haired Ramona as an exotic mestiza, daughter of a Scottish immigrant, Angus Phail, and an unnamed indigenous woman. Ramona happily embraces the Spanish culture and religion in the home of her unsympathetic guardian, Señora Moreno, an elite California widow and landholder. Escaping the señora's hostility toward her decision to marry the Indian Alessandro, a noble and talented sheep-shearer, Ramona flees with him into the mountains. After Anglo-American squatters burn Alessandro's town to the ground and shoot him dead in front of Ramona, the mestiza marries her foster brother, Felipe, and emigrates with him to Mexico.[71] Both *Ramona* and *Lucía Jerez* endorse traditional gender roles for women, while nevertheless portraying women in active, even dominating, roles.

Shortly after finishing *Lucía Jerez*, Martí's proposed project of regular articles on U.S. culture reached fruition and he began to send periodic correspondence to Mexico's *El Partido Liberal*. His contributions to this newspaper offer ambivalent assessments of the "extrememly curious...life" ("La Mujer Norteamericana," 84). This chronicle, in particular, conveys Martí's response to the unconventional modern women of whom, for whom he and in whose name he wrote in this period. Along with descriptions of women in the temperance movement, successful businesswomen, women voters, women lawyers, actresses, and women producers in theater, Martí's chronicles generalize about the "uglifying freedom" (libertad afeadora) of the North American woman, especially in comparison to the "enchanting dependence of our women" ("La Mujer Norteamericana," 84). In "La Mujer Norteamericana," as in his novel *Lucía Jerez*, Martí endorses the most conventional of gender roles for "his" women. Under the subheading "The Virile Character of the North American Woman and Its Cause," Martí speculates that the abandonment of U.S. women to their own resources in an unstable economy with limited options, along with the fragility of conjugal relations, contributed to this "individually useful," but collectively "baneful" phenomenon of "female virility" (*Otras crónicas*, 84). This discussion glosses the original title of the novel, *Amistad funesta*, in which the desiring, envious, and supposed friend, Lucía, becomes a monstrous murderer of the beautiful, innocent, and impressionable Sol del Valle.[72] The chronicle, like the novel, studies and exposes unconventional women, such as Lucia's infirm friend Ana, who creates strange paintings and appears to be dying of a wasting disease, possibly as a result of her dangerous creativity and "female virility."

New scholarship has broken decades of silence about Martí's ambivalence on issues of gender and sexuality, including his repressive responses to queer sexuality.[73] Following Frances Negrón-Muntaner's observation that Anzaldúa's border theory has been only selectively incorporated into cultural studies, we might interpret Martí's inability to fully confront "sexuality as a fundamental aspect of the lives of colonial subjects" as another—less laudable—way in which Martí anticipates the mainstream discussion of borders in American studies.[74] The long-standing critical silence about Martí's views of queer sexuality or female virility has perhaps permitted the greater recognition of Martí's anti-imperialist border writing in the mainstream fields of history, political science, and literary studies as they define transnational frames for thinking about race and nation. As Coco Fusco observes, leftists often resist "taking radicalism into the privacy of the bedroom"; most of Martí's writing on sexuality and gender exemplifies this tendency.[75]

On the other hand, Martí's portrait of women as a new and influential intellectual and social force exceeds the typical misogynist response to the "new woman." His study of some North American women informs Martí's embrace of androgyny in claiming that practices of femininity in U.S. national culture would be necessary to combat the increasingly autocratic tendencies of the emergent empire.[76] The United States' failure to incorporate adequately "the virtues that are feminine" (*Obras*, 12:154), argues Martí, abrogated, rather than expanded, the principles of the nation's mother—liberty. An androgynous balance between masculine and feminine elements of the spirit helps to secure liberty, Martí argues ("Graduation Day," *Selected Writings*, 156). This surprising openness to androgyny parallels Martí's increasingly radical position on the most prominent nineteenth-century working-class social movements. Martí's sympathetic portrait of one of these female activists, the unwavering mestiza or mulatta

Lucy Parsons, suggests that it may have been she who inspired him to translate—and revise—Helen Hunt Jackson's novel about an "arrogant mestiza" called Ramona (*Obras*, 24:205).

∾ ANARCHY UNDERLYING MARTÍ'S ANTI-IMPERIALISM: ON LUCY PARSONS AND "THE TERRIBLE DRAMA" OF THE HAYMARKET HANGINGS

Beside the José Martí Anti-Imperialist Tribunal in Havana—a large open-air performance space that faces the drab, fenced-in, U.S. Interest Section office building at one end of the city's famous seaside wall, el malecón—a statue of Martí cradles an infant child while accusingly pointing a finger at the office building and toward the island's northern neighbor. The location and nature of that statue make an apt figure for the question, upon what intellectual and political traditions do Martí's most radical anti-imperialist views stand? The anti-imperialism of figures like William James questioned the ability of the United States to assimilate mixed-race cultures, which were being annexed by the United States. Both proponents and opponents of U.S. imperialism frequently described their goals as a "fight for American manhood."[77] What then was Martí's position?

Although one typically irreverent Havana joke about the statue has Martí telling the infant, "There, hijo, is where to apply for your visa," the bronze sculpture's official message is anti-imperialist, and this position still manages to unite portions of a dispersed and increasingly diverse Cuban exile community with many nationals on the island. According to René Vázquez Díaz, a Cuban exiled in Sweden, Martí's anti-imperialism has the gravitational pull of "an imminent cyclone."[78] At the base of this representation of Martí in Havana are the names of popular leftist leaders in the United States who lost their lives while struggling for the rights of oppressed groups, including the anarchists who demonstrated in Haymarket, Chicago, and were punished with death for "crimes" that most legal scholars now argue they did not commit.[79]

What is the significance of commemorating anarchy at the base of a monument to a figure whom we have learned to think of primarily as the great father of the Cuban nation? If, according to the journalist and editor Lucy Parsons, anarchism is "the philosophy of a new social order based on liberty unrestricted by man-made law, the theory that all forms of government are based on violence—hence wrong and harmful, as well as unnecessary," how does the most radical late phase of Martí's ideas relate to critics of the nation-state and to the principles of anarchy?[80] While this question is too large to address here, I raise it to note that Martí's challenge to a sexualizing and racializing discourse in U.S. popular culture parallels the figure of anarchy underlying Martí's anti-imperialism. Like Anzaldúa's "mestiza consciousness," Martí's border writing ruptures the paradigms of both expansionist Pan-Americanism and masculinist nationalism from within the structures that articulated them in the late 1880s.

In its bronze sculpture, flags, and metal arches soaring over a large public forum, the Anti-Imperialist Tribunal stages the contact, exchange, and still unresolved border conflict between the United States and Cuba.[81] Antiracism, solidarity with U.S. working-class radicalism, and ambivalence toward unconventional gender and sexual practices informed Martí's commitments and biases. But during the years leading up to the formation of the Cuban Revolutionary Party in 1892, Martí brought his increasingly radical politics to bear on popular cultural forms that justified and spelled out new modes of U.S. expansion in the Western hemisphere. Helen Hunt Jackson's novel *Ramona* proposed for the United States a future return to the happy idylls of Spanish missionary colonialism. Similarly, *Buffalo Bill's Wild West Show* commemorated the heroism of the victors in a drama of expansion, as if U.S.–Indian conflicts existed only in the past. Martí's translation of each offers a dissenting reading. Shattering the imagined homogeneity of a fully assimilated "Anglo" community in the United States, his translations validate the claims of despised radical working-class spokespersons like Lucy Parsons.[82] His translations of the popular culture of the U.S. West project a dystopic future for the migrant Latino/a subject in terms of displaced native Americans, annexed Mexicans, lynched Italians, and fleeing African Americans, all of whom he shows to be excluded not just from political and economic power but also in many cases, from basic human rights. These translations show how newly whitened immigrants ascended into Anglo imperial privilege through the violent exclusion of politically and culturally different minorities. They disrupt the narrative of assimilation and unity by beginning to articulate Latinness as another sector among many racialized and excluded alterities in the United States.

If Helen Hunt Jackson's novel backfires in its desire to "help" the Indian because of its role in promoting the Dawes Act of 1887, even according to

sympathetic readings of the novel, Lucy Parsons represents an exemplary
alternative mestiza activist whose fearless conviction mobilized a large
social movement in defense of workers' rights in general. Seeing the limits
of the pristinely Catholic, "arrogant mestiza" at the center of the novel, and
desiring to challenge Mexican racism, Martí claims Lucy Parsons as another kind of mestiza. Martí's essay on Parsons challenges her demoniza-
tion in the mainstream press and celebrates her remarkable power as a
revolutionary spokeswoman.

Born Lucy Ella Waller in Waco, Texas, in 1853, Parsons gained notoriety
as a dark-skinned, African-, Mexican-, and Amerindian-descended anarchist leader, a newspaper editor, writer, and defender of workers' rights.[83]
Raised by a Mexican ranchero in Johnson County, Texas, and possibly the
child of a black mother and a Mexican father, Parsons sometimes used the
last name Gonzalez, spoke Spanish, experienced racism, and claimed indigenous and Mexican ancestry.[84] She pioneered the organizing of women
workers in Chicago by helping to found the Working Women's Union in
1879, and with her husband, Albert Parsons, she joined the Knights of
Labor. Dismayed by the ineffectiveness of liberal reform, she and her husband helped to organize the International Working People's Association in
October 1883. Lucy frequently contributed to the association's newspaper,
The Alarm, of which Albert was the editor. One of her most famous contributions was an incendiary address in 1884, "To Tramps," in which she
advised the "Unemployed, the Disinherited and the Miserable" to "Learn
the use of explosives!"[85] During the campaign for the eight-hour day in the
late 1880s, she spoke regularly on behalf of the anarchists who were facing
capital punishment in connection with the Haymarket bombing of 1886.
Albert Parsons, was among the accused who were eventually hanged on
charges of bombing, even though the prosecution and the defense agreed
that none of the anarchist defenders could have actually detonated an
explosive device.[86] Lucy Parsons figures in labor history as an audacious,
imaginative, and fearless "firebrand," who helped to lead innovative public
demonstrations and who advocated armed self-defense of African Americans and others who faced vigilante and police violence.

According to the mainstream New York press, Parsons was "the dusky
representative of anarchy," and lacked oratorical skill: she repeated herself
"half a dozen times" and "attempted to excite pity" by "acting" a part.[87]
Martí's description dissents from this assessment by focusing on Parsons's
ability to inspire awe and admiration among large working-class audiences

through her oratory. Reminiscent of detailed accounts of some of the North Americans he most admired, such as Wendell Phillips or Peter Cooper, Martí's interpretation of Parsons places her among the great orators of his time. Although the U.S. racialized Parsons by referring to her in pejorative descriptions as a "mulatta," Martí sought to counter the attack on Parsons and confirmed her belonging to his Mexican and Spanish-speaking readers' America. Describing her as both a "mulatta" and a "mestiza" of Indian and Mexican descent who spoke fluent Spanish and English, and detailing Parson's copper-colored skin, finely formed hands, wavy hair, and large, sparkling eyes, Martí's recategorization differentiates Parsons from most of the other North American women of whom he writes (*Otras crónicas*, 82). Neither a greedy husband-seeker, nor a bespectacled, puritanical bluestocking, like the women of Martí's early "Impressions of America" (*Selected Writings*, 35–36), Parsons did not identify with European ancestry, religion, or culture, nor did she practice the avid consumerism that many women did in the United States.

Martí's praise for Parsons's oratorical skill corresponds to his antiracist, proindigenous stance (and to his longing for a supportive wife who was willing to share both his economically unstable lot and his radical political commitments). Martí describes Parsons's superior oratorical skills in a way that only another highly skilled practitioner of the art can:

> [Parsons] speaks with a soft and sonorous voice, which appears to arise from her depths, and that moves the hearts of those who hear her speak. Why not say it? This woman spoke yesterday with the same spirit [brío] as the greatest orators. It is true that sorrow overflowed from the hearts of those who heard her speak. And the trembling auditorium is the sign of a triumphant orator. But in her case, the power of eloquence derives not so much from the natural art with which she regulates and accumulates its effect, as from the intensity of her conviction, whence eloquence always comes. Sometimes her words raise blisters, like a whip; suddenly, there is a comic outburst, which appears to have been gnawed with lips of bone, because it is so cold and hard. Without transitions—because the vastness of her anguish and her belief does not require them—she elevates *pathos* with amazing power and calls forth at will tears and sobs. There were moments when not a sound could be heard in the assembly except her inspired voice, which flowed slowly from her mouth, like spheres of fire, and the gasping of those who had stopped breathing momentarily in order to hear the sob in her throat. When this Indian and Mexican mestiza stopped speaking, all the heads were

inclined, as if in prayer upon the benches in church, and the room seemed to fill, like a field of wheat bending in the wind. . . . Everything in her appears an invitation to believe and to rise up. Her speech, in its total sincerity, is literary. Her doctrines wave like a flag: she does not ask for mercy for those condemned to death, for her own husband, but denounces the causes and the accomplices to the misery that leads men to desperation. (*Otras crónicas*, 82)

The rhetorical question "Why not say it?" and the emphasis on Parsons's gender and appearance convey Martí's sense that his observations violate common understandings of women, of anarchists, of Mexicans, and of Latinas. Perhaps his description disturbs even his own assumptions. The chronicle describes bearded men weeping, women standing on chairs and waving their handkerchiefs, and little girls—perhaps including Martí's own god-daughter Maria—lifting their small hands and shouting "Hurrah!" while perched on the shoulders of their fathers.

From this scene, the account rapidly shifts to an analysis of the "extremely curious" prominence of women in North American life. Almost grudgingly, the chronicler acknowledges the "genuine and absolute" victory of many virile women such as Parsons. He observes that North American women have weathered political combat, created and managed difficult enterprises, and intrepidly entered into the field of arts and letters. In keeping with his profound ambivalence, Martí notes that such women had not only become ugly in their freedom, but also "loveless" and "affectionless," because of the ridicule and ostracism heaped on them for playing unconventional roles (*Otras crónicas*, 84). Martí's attention to Parsons and to the anarchists suggests an unusual affinity with her queer relationship to the civilization that she so fervently sought to tear down and remake.

Attempts to understand Martí's increasing revolutionary militancy—which mobilized a large portion of the Latino migrant community on the East Coast before the end of the century—have rightly focused on Martí's change in reporting about the hanging of the Chicago anarchists in 1887. Martí's admiration for Lucy Parsons anticipates contemporary attempts by Rodolfo Acuña to reclaim her for a Chicano/a labor movement, by Robin D. G. Kelly and Paul Gilroy for a black radical internationalist tradition, and by Shelley Streeby for a transamerican cultural history in which women played a leadership role.[88] In the period following the Chicago anarchists' year-long trial, Cuban and Puerto Rican migrants in New York, New Jersey, and Florida transformed themselves into the organized force behind the movement for independence in 1895, which made possible Cuba's conditional independence in 1902. During the anarchist trial in 1886–87, Martí made an about-face in his public stance on the Haymarket anarchists, whose ideology was anathema in the United States and among South America's wealthy elites, in whose midst similar long-suffering, working-class mestizo and European immigrant workers mounted a defense of their class.[89] Anarchist ideas had an active following among Latino/a migrants in Havana and in South Florida. In order to tap this source of support, Martí faced—and largely met—the challenge of convincing this group to join the revolutionary separatist movement.[90] Recognizing the past and potential contributions of anarchists to the workers' movement (and to Cuba's liberation), Martí's chronicles for the Buenos Aires paper *La Nación* about the Haymarket debacle dramatically shifts from parroting mainstream antianarchist views in 1886 to critique of the state that condemned them to death and of the conditions that led them to engage in public protest in 1887.

Entitled "Un drama terrible" (1887), this chronicle validates the Chicago anarchists and their supporters' demands for a change in the social conditions that catalyzed the workers' protest.[91] In what amounts to a eulogy for the dead, the chronicle recreates with mournful ironic distance and surreal figures the public spectacle of the trial, the hangings of four anarchists, and the macabre suicide of Louis Lingg in his cell (he lit a cigar laced with dynamite). In "Un drama terrible," Martí added his pen to an outpouring of elegiac writing by poets throughout the world who claimed these silenced critics of imperial modernity as the inheritors of John Brown's legacy and as exemplars of America's most admirable revolutionary tradition.[92] The "terrible drama" of the Haymarket anarchist trial revealed the waning difference between alleged democracy and empire: "The police, proud in their wool jacket uniform, proud of their authority, and terrifying to the uneducated, beat and assassinate [the workers]. They are cold and hungry and they live in reeking shacks. America then is the same as Europe!" (*Obras*, 11:338; *Selected Writings*, 200, translation modified). Because of its similarity to the "mock trial held under mob pressure" in 1871 in Havana, under the Spanish imperial administration, and which resulted in eight Cuban medical students being "put to death amid frantic applause," the Haymarket trial demonstrated how little difference there was between the oppressive tactics of the imperial Spanish and North American judicial systems.[93]

∽ ON WATCHING THE CURIOUS PEOPLE WHO WANT
    TO KNOW WHAT IS INSIDE AN INDIAN TENT: MARTÍ
    ON *BUFFALO BILL'S WILD WEST SHOW*

Martí's radicalization responds to conditions on the ground in the United States, Cuba, Mexico, and Latin America, but also to the cultural narratives that disseminated imperial violence through popular heroes such as Jesse James or Buffalo Bill Cody. Pretending to serve as wholesome education for the masses (ranging from homeless shoe-shine boys to tourists whom Cody specifically invited at the Columbian Exposition in Chicago), Cody's show channeled class, racial, and even international tensions into the unifying project of Anglo imperial modernity. However, like the African-descended people of New Orleans who attended Cody's show and so identified with the Indians' struggle that they began to "mask" as Indians during Mardi Gras in 1885, Martí projected a dissenting reading of the prescribed "object lesson" of Cody's show, and sided with the victims of Anglo-American civilization.[94]

The eight-hour-day movement ended with the hanging of probably innocent people and thus Martí's "Un drama terrible" mourns their deaths and honors these immigrants' protest against the abuse of police power. By contrast, his border writing on Cody's *Wild West* ironically portrays the tragedy of immigrants becoming complicit with the state as imperial subjects. As Bernardo Callejas notes, the concurrent military subjugation of various Amerindian tribes (in which Cody performed as a scout and United States negotiator) is the condition of possibility for the exhibition of the Indian warriors.[95] Ethnographic scenes of "authentic" tribal life enabled the white imperial subject to distinguish its superior civilization and to safely explore the private life of the conquered. This white imperial subject defined itself in relation to the tribal Amerindians in the show, who were released into Cody's custody in return for agreeing to reenact a script that portrayed them as criminals.[96] The ritual of traveling to the *Wild West* venue in droves, sitting through hours of horse stunts, and applauding the reenactments of various battles with tens of thousands of others trained the imperial subject to see its privileged position as part of a natural course of events.[97]

Martí discusses this transformation of immigrants into imperialists in his chronicles with a tone of bafflement and horror. Not hesitating to spill each others' blood if necessary, as we saw in "Como se crea un pueblo nuevo en los Estados Unidos," working-class immigrants from Europe often competed with one another; but they also formed ranks while carrying out mob violence against workers of color. Spectacles such as *Buffalo Bill's Wild West Show* and the Columbian Exposition of 1893 enacted a drama in which unpaid, bonded, or colonized laborers figured as "wards" of the state.[98] Whereas Cody's *Wild West* narrates the defeat of native tribes, Martí's chronicle about it entitled "¡Magnifico espectáculo!" (Magnificent Spectacle!) exposes the show's transformation of multiethnic European working-class immigrants into full citizens in relation to the vanquished Indians (or others whom Cody subsequently inserted into the show). Martí's staging of this transformation differs from Cody's performance and from Frederick Jackson Turner's theory of European-immigrant re-generation on the frontier, because the narration adopts the point of view of the natives exhibited in the show.

This reversal of the show's dominant gaze occurs offstage, in the en-campment where showgoers could pay a separate admission to see "real Indians" in their "authentic" habitat.[99] Martí brings the often transparent ethnographic gaze onto center stage: "In the interior of their tents the warriors repose after their exercises, reclining silently in a circle around the edge of the canvas, watching the curious ones who want to know what the inside of an Indian tent is like as they crowd into the tent's opening" (*Obras*, 11:35). In this scene, the roles of ethnographer and "informant" are reversed, as the Latino American reader looks from *inside* the tent and alongside the Indian warriors at these gawking audience members. Whereas *Buffalo Bill's Wild West Show* made the Amerindians into a per-manent ethnographic exhibit and a precursor to the infamous Department M of the World's Columbian Exposition in 1893, also known as the Midway Plaisance, Martí's translation rubs against the grain of this apparatus for training imperial subjects.[100]

Martí's account of the warriors transforms the sensational and spec-tacular language of the show's propaganda.[101] Rather than rendering the Indians the stabilizing objects of a white gaze, Martí's chronicle makes the amateur tourist-anthropologist an object of the Indians' vision: "These are the penetrating eyes of one who lives his life standing up and in a state of alarm. . . . A basketful of eyes can be seen: they all look ahead [Se ve una cesta de ojos: todos miran de frente]" (*Obras*, 11:35). The chronicler recog-nizes the final authority of the natives as witnesses to the violence of expansion, the threat of which still leaves them perpetually on guard.

Groups of eyes meet the gaze of another group of eyes. The Spanish reflexive verb, "se ve" (it is possible to see) posits the mutual constitution of the
prying crowd and the seated warriors they have paid to see. Against the
dominant narrative's relegation of these warriors to curios in the dramatic
past of civilization, the natives here become producers of knowledge in the
process of remembering another future.

Several new biographies and memoirs extend the claims that Pahaska—
Buffalo Bill's Indian name, meaning "Long Hair"—was the noblest of
whites and a respected hero of the Indians, and that his show offered Native
Americans a means to represent and to continue to practice traditional
indigenous ways of life with dignity.[102] While it may be true that any
alternative to the restrictive and infantilizing conditions of the reservations
proved sufficiently attractive to lure many Amerindians to accept the Office
of the Interior's conditions for their performance in Cody's show, the show
required the principal leaders of the indigenous nations to enact and reiterate their defeat in daily performances designed by Cody and his copro-
ducers. The *Wild West Show*'s retelling of the incorporation and settlement
of the U.S. West became "America's national entertainment," as Martí calls
it in his chronicle, precisely insofar as it occluded the angle that Martí's
border writing brings into the foreground: the natives' subjugated but still
resistant insurgency in relation to U.S. expansion or annexation.

While Cody's drama portrays the natives as savage aggressors and the
fated losers, the chronicle shows the Indians killing time in silence between
acts. The description of these warriors evokes the banality of the show in
comparison to the history of violence that Cody's spectacle subsumes
within imperial nostalgia. When Martí translates the warriors for his reader,
he evokes the subjective frame, the positions of the bodies, and the controlled anguish of their imprisonment: "One lies recklessly with his head in
the palm of his hands, with the fierce abandon of a young god. Another, sub-
jecting his folded legs with both hands, rocks himself in a swing-like motion. . . . Another, seated on his heels, looks attentively, with his elbows
planted on his knees, and with his feather-crowned head buried in the palm
of his hands" (*Obras*, 11:36). This scene does not refer to the savage acts that
might excite the crowds. To the audience member accustomed to lurid gestures or spectacular feats, these watching Indians merely express the hebe-
tude of being "wards". The warriors' positions express nonverbally their
meditation on their current confinement and their unpredictable future.

In order to criticize Cody's narration of the United States' past, Martí's

"¡Magnífico espectáculo!" does not simply invert the binary of civilization and savagism. Rather, the chronicle dramatizes the coexistence of two interpretations of the events. In the penultimate section, a summary of the show produces radically divergent meanings, depending on who makes up the "nosotros" (we) that appears toward the end of this excerpt:

> And so one goes on seeing the absorbed fantasy, with the pleasure of a woman in love, the native happenings of that original and grandiose existence: so one witnesses in all the brilliance of truth the heartless combat between the natural owners [dueños naturales] of the country and the conquerors of [or from] the forest [conquistadores de la selva]; so the soul goes on calmly removing itself from the smallness and squalor of life as a citizen, —when a blood-curdling spectacle involuntarily moves one to stand up in one's seat, which makes one feel ashamed to stay and relax in the drawing rooms of life, when those who struggle in life's blood and guts [entrañas] are passing before us [nosotros], with the majesty of work and danger. (Obras, 11:42)

One way to read this passage is from the point of view of the civilizing spectators who view themselves as the "natural owners" and "natives" of the country. They accede to possession after their military representatives have neutralized outbreaks by aggressive, savage "conquerors of the forest." Distancing itself from the exaggerated rhetoric of sentimentalism and squalid details of realism, this passage portrays the consumer of literary mass culture—an enraptured woman—who is also a major producer and consumer of the novelistic genre out of which Buffalo Bill's character emerges. This "we" is made up of those who stand up involuntarily with the crowd to applaud the bravery of Cody and thus momentarily escape their drawing-room lives.

But the passage provides for another interpretation, from the perspective of the native warriors and of clandestinely insurgent colonial subjects. This group too considers themselves to be the natural owners of their lands, despite their defeat by those who invade and conquer the forest. Those who belong to this "we" stand in shame as they witness the defeat of their own or others' nations. Rather than watch these events passively, these distant witnesses to the border war by a common enemy feel compelled to take part in this struggle. The chronicle outlines the various contradictory subject positions that do not conform to a single, unified, "we." Representing an "alien" migratory presence in the audience, this counterreading of the Wild West breaks open the unity of an imperial "we" that the show attempts to produce. Housing a contradiction, the passage's unstable meaning reflects the diverse and conflicting viewpoints of Cody's audience. The passage represents a disunified collectivity that does not reside clearly on either one side or the other of the binary of savagery and civilization: the destabilizing border confounds the demarcation of *they* and *we*.

In this account, terms such as "lances nativos" (native scenes/weapons), "el fulgor de la verdad" (brilliance of the truth), "existencia original" (original existence), and "dueños naturales" (natural owners) signify in two directions. The interpretation of the subject of the first sentence, the one who "goes on seeing" this show, will depend on how the reader interprets the phrase "absorbed fantasy" (la absorta fantasía). On one hand, the subject may be seeing the show itself; on the other hand, the subject may be studying the "moving spectacle" (espectáculo estremecedor) of the entranced audience itself. Those enraptured spectators fall for the sentimental story "like a woman in love." Cody's "Wild West," the chronicle suggests, does not represent the past per se, but rather the production of imperial modernity. Martí's translation of the show releases alternative histories, without pretending to offer the final word on the interior world of the prisoners/performers.

The chronicle deploys ironic turns of phrase and shifts in voice to convey the instability of the chronicler's border subjectivity. The chronicler's bilingual cultural position makes these double meanings an effective way to evade Latin American censorship and to establish divergent readings. For example, the Spanish of Martí's description of Cody's feats juxtaposes the heroizing rhetoric that appeared in the show's advertisements with a withering critique of Cody's role in U.S. Indian policy. The chronicle appears at one point to celebrate Buffalo Bill, but at the same time it mimics the mercurial shift of Cody's friendship into betrayal:[103] "he, the strongest and most agile, the best horseman; he, the one who in times of combat directs Homeric harangues to the Indians that they enjoy; he who almost always manages to get them to loosen their grip so that they will let go of the tomahawk, and will sit in a circle and smoke the peace pipe; . . . he, Buffalo Bill, who appears to have been born in the saddle, and who has no equal in tracking, soothing, ridiculing, nor in governing Indians" (*Obras*, 11:40). The tone of this passage changes when the reader reaches the last two verbs. Cody's "ridiculing [them]" (burlarlos) and above all, "governing [of them]" (gobernarlos), that is, of his former foes and new-found friends, retrospectively alters the tone of the whole portrait. His Homeric speeches become wily rhetoric; his negotiation and peace treaties reek of duplicity. The final claim about his leadership ability and skill in the arts of government sounds like a puff for a poser. Mimicking the form of false friendliness, the rhetoric takes the reader in with praise only to betray these smiling phrases with a pair of biting words.

Although *Buffalo Bill's Wild West Show* was first performed in Nebraska in 1883 and toured extensively thereafter, one of its most prominent, lucrative, and well-attended venues was in Chicago, just outside the official grounds of the World's Columbian Exposition ten years later. Turner's lecture on the subject of the frontier, the spectacular performance of the *Wild West Show*, and the Exposition in honor of the four hundreth anniversary of Columbus's discovery all celebrated the introduction of European-American "law and order and progress" to a previously barbarous hemisphere.[104] The Columbian Exposition's "White City" and its ancillary exhibits belonged to a genre of "white supremacist entertainments" that promoted emulation of the U.S. model of progress.[105] Martí's translation fleshes out the role prescribed for new European immigrants in this White City while letting off steam on the Midway Plaisance or at Cody's *Wild West* exhibition. These entertainments, which have most often been read as part of genealogy of a U.S. racial system, appear in Martí's chronicles to perform the cultural work that also undergirded a hemispheric, Pan-American ideal.

ᏉᏇᎧ THE FOX FROM UP ABOVE AND THE FOX FROM DOWN BELOW: MARTÍ'S *RAMONA* AS A KEY TO MOBILIZING LATINO/A MIGRANT INSURGENCY

The popular representations of U.S. history in the West apologize for the violence of imperial modernity. Its U.S. interpreters would either hasten or reform, but would never stop expansion's movement forward in the tracks of history's slowly turning wheels. Helen Hunt Jackson and William Cody coincide in representing the American Indian as friendly "former foes," who must undergo assimilation to Anglo-America, or else be crushed. Both Cody's *Wild West Show* and Jackson's sentimental novel *Ramona* have entertained millions of North Americans and remain in the public eye today as part of the contested historical record of the U.S. West. By contrast, Lucy Parsons and A. K. Cutting—representing opposite programs—

proposed radical alternatives to a slow but ineluctable movement of white, Anglo domination. Parsons questioned the validity and durability of the civilization that squelched its critics and advocated the dismantlement of civilization in its current form. Although her speeches on behalf of anarchism have never received the widespread approbation that *Ramona* has, she reached a significant audience, insofar as her mass movement helped to change public opinion and convince the governor of Illinois, John Peter Altgeld, to pardon the anarchists.[106]

Like Parsons, Cutting enacted a dramatic attempt to peremptorily transform United States foreign relations with Mexico. His appeal to the masses reveals widespread endorsement of preemptive invasion among various sectors, but his methods threatened to unmask U.S. democracy's imperial character. Cutting's tactics undermined U.S. claims to modernity, democracy, and superiority to its Latin neighbors. Both Cutting's radical annexationism and Parsons's radical anarchism do not quite fit in the story that imperial modernity likes to remember and repeat about its origins. Gesturing to an alternative modernity, Martí's border writing excavates both Parson's unsettling critique and Cutting's attempt to provoke aggression in order to reveal the uncertainty of the U.S. empire's future.

Martí's translation of imperial modernity testifies to the violence with which it was inscribing itself in the American landscape, as it was "written by triumphant locomotives emerging from the bowels of the hills, over crypts, abysms, plains and canyons, inscribed with rifle bullets in the heads of buffalo and through the breasts of Indians" (*Otras crónicas*, 69). Similarly, he translated *Ramona* into Spanish at his own expense in order to write this history differently. The translation provides the key for deciphering a recurring metaphor for Latino/a insurgency, including Chicano/as and Californios/as on the West Coast, migrant Caribbean and Latin Americans on the East Coast, and anyone threatened with annexation, especially on and off the islands of Cuba and Puerto Rico. The translation of Jackson's novel introduces as "zorros" the displaced and fleeing natives of the states that had formerly been northern Mexico—whole communities the Anglo-American invaders sought to exterminate or send off the land. By "smoking an entire village out of their houses like foxes, including women and little children," this violence reduces prior inhabitants of American lands to the position of fleeing animals (*Obras*, 24:351). The image derives from Jackson's narrative of the historical destruction of the town of Temecula in southern California, which left her characters Alessandro and Ramona homeless, and drove Alessandro's father, Chief Pablo, to madness. Martí conceptualizes a Latino/a insurgency of natives and migrants through the translation of Jackson's narrative of Chicano/a annexation. Like his reports on African, Native, Asian, and immigrant workers, Martí's making of Chicano/as into an allegory for Latino/a insurgency looks forward to current theorizing of possible alliances among diverse communities and against an institutionalized Anglo-supremacism. This move anticipates discussions at the forefront of debates in African diaspora and Latino/a studies.[107] Martí's border writing emphasizes that such allegiances and alternative futures can arise in opposition to a white-identified imperial modernity.

Enigmatic references to zorros or foxes being shot in cold blood or driven from their land represent the agonizing future that would likely accompany Cuban, Puerto Rican, and further Mexican annexation. By alluding to similar violence toward other groups in the past, the image of these zorros flashes up in a moment of danger to illuminate and mobilize a broad base of Latino/a opposition to assimilation and to annexation. First appearing in the fall of 1889 and continuing through Martí's exhortation to Cubans to finally abandon their homes in Key West in 1894, the term "foxes" also refers to exiled, fleeing, and lynched people of color in California, Texas, Florida, and also other parts of the West. Martí's translation of Jackson is the intertext that sheds light on the description of white supremacists who avidly shot at the African American target "as if at a fox" (*Obras*, 12:336). It explains Martí's figuring the people who climbed upon their oxcarts and fled their burning homes in Texas, rather than be crushed under the "Juggernaut" of empire, as "rabid foxes, with their dead on their hindquarters" (*Obras*, 6:54). The translation of *Ramona* serves also as a textual bridge that illustrates connections between Texas "marauders" who entered black neighborhoods and shot into the doorways of homes, the invading whites who burned down pueblos in Texas and California, and the Anglo police and government officials who threw striking Cubans in jail in South Florida, in a concerted attempt to break up the independence movement:

> Were they, too, to be ousted, like the zorros of California or the last tejanos, from the town they had built by the product of their industry, and, more important, by their earnest and uncompromising patriotism! . . . "To Cuba!" says our whole soul, after this deceit in Key West, this brutal wound to our love and our illusions: to the only country in the world from which we shall not be chased away like the zorros from California and the tejanos from Texas! (*Obras*, 3:50–51; *Selected Writings*, 325)

A comparative imagination infuses this metaphor of the zorro that Esther Allen wisely leaves untranslated in her English translation of Martí's rousing speech to Cuban tobacco workers in Key West, two of whom had been thrown into jail on flimsy charges in the winter of 1893, and who were rumored to be at risk of being lynched.[108] According to Horatio S. Rubens, the young lawyer who represented the jailed Cubans and became the Cuban nation's legal representative in the United States up until the Armistice of 1902, this conflict between the Cuban tobacco workers and Anglo authorities in Key West sparked the Cuban revolution. Rubens interprets the collusion of North American judicial and economic authorities in Key West with tobacco factory owners and with the Spanish government as an attempt not only to break the tobacco workers' strike for higher wages, but as a plot to cow the Cubans and dissolve their movement (Rubens, *Liberty*, 21, 42). Martí's speech in the wake of these events, "To Cuba!," indicts the "frenzied hatred" of North Americans for the Latino/a community in Florida by mentioning the "South's barbaric lynchings" and "continual murders perpetrated by men in white masks in the Northeast" (*Selected Writings*, 327). The excerpt quoted above alludes to depredations by North American authorities in Florida upon a largely African-descended and integrated Latino migrant community. The reference to the Ku Klux Klan's activities in the North and the South enables Martí to distinguish Latino/as of all shades from U.S.-style white supremacism and from some Latin Americans' "yankeemania," or a treacherous belief in "blond superiority" (*En los Estados Unidos*, 1755; *Obras*, 6:55).

The reference to the terrorizing of Latino/as in Key West in the same terms that he applied to displaced African Americans, Amerindians, and Chicano/as, implies that in Martí's border writing all of these threatened and racialized groups shared a common structural position within imperial modernity. It suggests the extent to which Martí's concept of Cubans and Latino/as relied upon his comparative knowledge of other racializing discourses in the United States. The simultaneous allusion, in a letter to Serafín Bello in November 1889, to abuses against people of African descent, to exploited workers, and to peoples threatened by displacement through annexation suggests the triple conditions of class, race, and nationality that inform the positioning of Latino/as in the late nineteenth century (*Epistolario*, 2:159–60). These intersecting discourses inform the significance of the term "zorros" for interpreting the threat of an exodus in Florida or Cuba like that imposed by North Americans in Texas, California, and Oklahoma.

Intended both to create a viable source of income for Martí and to forge links among the various dispersed sections of his America, his translation of *Ramona* into Spanish became the pilot project of the transamerican publishing venture that Martí elaborated in letters to Mercado between 1885 and 1889. Mexicans and Argentines were the intended audience for the translation of *Ramona* because Mexico and Argentina were the principle countries in the Americas where friends with sufficient prestige and personal commitment could help Martí to launch the publishing venture.[109] Martí's *Ramona* and his chronicles concerning the imperial domestication of the U.S. West seek to outweigh the dominant U.S. discourse that preached incorporation within Anglo culture. Though Martí reveals little awareness of the rebellious and autonomous indigenous regions in the borderlands south of the Rio Bravo, he astutely questions the myth of Franciscan missions' singularly beneficial impact on the so-called "Mission Indians"; he also maintains an ironic distance from the Friends of the Indian in the United States and depicts the reservation system as a deadening political imprisonment.[110] Diverging from the original English-language novel, the Spanish-language translation of *Ramona* critically assesses Jackson's portrayal of Spanish imperialism as benign and of Anglo-American imperial expansion as an unavoidable fact. While Martí would approve Jackson's withering criticism of Yankee invaders as hounds, his *Ramona* goes further than Jackson's in lending much more credence to the viability and necessity of a militant revolutionary opposition within but also beyond the boundaries of the United States. This militancy would also buttress his America's capacity forcefully to hold the line against further U.S. expansionism.

Why does Martí choose to translate a novel that, in John M. González's astute reading, "mak[es] empire at home" by defining positions of power for Anglo-American women in a multicultural empire's administration and management ("The Warp of Whiteness," 456)? In speculating on this question, Susan Gillman argues that white reformist women's writing offered the Cuban a model for a twinned project of "rescuing the Indian and making a place for the Negro."[111] In this view, Martí's Cuba would bring together blacks and Indians, the Black Atlantic and the Spanish borderlands, abolitionist and Indian reform movements, and the geographically and historically segregated cultural regions and literary traditions of the U.S. South and the Southwest. This reading implies Martí's unqualified identification with Jackson (and Harriet Beecher Stowe) and simultaneously portrays Martí as an investor who made "Pan-American capital" out of U.S. sentimentalism ("*Ramona* in 'Our America,' " 99). While Gillman rightly notes Martí's personal investment in the translation of *Ramona*, as a means to make a living and "to make men," this collapsing of the space between Martí's and Jackson's *Ramona* misses Martí's differently weighted translation, his fierce animosity to the political project of Pan-Americanism, and his keen interest in addressing the complex position of the Afro-Latino/a Caribbean (as opposed to Gilroy's Anglophone Black Atlantic).[112] By making Cuba a nexus between historically segregated U.S. American discourses, this argument domesticates the foreignness that Martí's translation and his position as a Latino migrant with a revolutionary agenda adds to Jackson's English-language text. Recuperating the difference between the original and Martí's translation, let us consider how Martí's *Ramona* sets border writing against Pan-Americanism.

To miss the gap between the original and the translation of *Ramona*, a discrepancy that scholarship on Martí and Jackson has yet to consider fully, is to minimize differences between the location and investments of the white North American woman reformer from New England and the migrant Latino revolutionary. Martin Padget argues that Jackson's commitments as a reformer required that she deemphasize historical incidents of rebellion, such as the Cupeño leader Antonio Garra's 1851 attempt to unite various California indigenous groups into a force that might successfully attack and remove Anglo-American settlements through a strategic alliance with Mexicans.[113] Deemphasizing or erasing from the historical record the multiple incidents of small and large-scale resistance of Indians against either the Catholic missions or Anglo-American invaders corroborated Reformist arguments for a respectable incorporation of submissive victims and skilled workers who could and would adopt the dominant white culture effortlessly, if only given a respite from the United States' dishonorable dealings. Giving minimal narrative space to these historical acts of insurgence, the reform novel depicted "good" and docile Indians—of which Alessandro and Ramona are quintessential examples—whose godly characteristics made them ideal candidates for assimilation through vocational training and missionary discipline. This rhetoric of beneficial colonization reveals a telling parallel between the reform novel and the emerging discourse of Pan-Americanism. Both endorsed the extension of manifest destiny into former Spanish colonies in the name of a beneficent civilizing mission, in which the United States demanded that the conquered themselves sign "the decree of their irredeemable servitude."

For Martí and many other Latino/a migrants in this late period, militant self-defense and revolutionary anticolonial self-government represented the only viable option for the postcolonial, postslavery nations of Spain's former or crumbling colonies. Whereas Jackson's *Ramona* makes the idea of military resistance against Anglo settlement unthinkable, Martí's translation transforms the novel into a warning against identifying with or accommodation to either Spanish or Anglo-American governments. In dedications or letters to his friends and colleagues, he refers to the *Ramona* translation as an act of "prevision."[114]

The novel's principle indigenous character, Alessandro, inherits and reproduces a strategy of accomodationism that his grandfather and his father, Chief Pablo, taught him to obey, like all the other curses or blessings of Spanish priests, while growing up as servants and neophytes on southern California missions. Martí's translation changes the tone of the narrator in relation to Alessandro's and Chief Pablo's obedience. Jackson's narrator reports on the association that their people, the Temeculans, made between evil and reading and on Chief Pablo's attempt to help his son by raising him as a white, as if such positions represented logical, sensible decisions under "good" imperial or missionary government: "He [Alessandro] was a distant, cold boy, his own people of the Temecula village said. It had come, they believed, of learning to read, which was always bad. Chief Pablo had not done his son any good by trying to make him like white men. If the Fathers could have stayed, and the life at the mission have gone on, why, Alessandro could have had work to do for the Fathers, as his father had before him. . . . But that was 'in the time of the king'; it was very different now. The Americans would not let an Indian do anything but plough and sow and herd Cattle. A man need not read and write to do that." (Jackson, *Ramona*, 51). The passage suggests that whereas it had once made sense for Pablo to learn to read to forcibly assimilate his son to whiteness, the Anglos had cast that conclusion into doubt. In calling for reform, Jackson's novel suggests that the Anglos would need to encourage more humane assimilation education and exploitation by following the model of "good" prior colonization.

By contrast, Martí's narrator lends a sense of irony to viewing reading as a cause of Alessandro's situation and on par with assimilating to "whiteness":

> Decían los de Temecula que era frío y callado, lo que le vendría de leer, *por supuesto*: ¡leer trae males! ¡Pablo se había empeñado en criar a su hijo como un blanco! (*Obras*, 24:250)
>
> (The people of Temecula said that he was cold and quiet, which came from reading, *of course*: Reading brings on harm! Pablo had sought to raise his son as a white!) (Emphasis added)

The exclamation points and the interpolated phrase, "of course," change the tone. Whereas Jackson portrays the chief's self-doubt and resignation after having made the reasonable decision to make Alessandro "like white men," Martí adds exclamation points to suggest the narrator and reader's distance from the assimilated chief's views. Against Pablo's or the Temeculans' despair at having taught Alessandro to read, Martí's ironic exclamations suggest that reading skills may not be the cause of harm. This proposition appears here to be as absurd as the idea that an Indian chief would raise his son to identify with the conquering whites.

In both the original and Martí's translation, Chief Pablo and Alessandro faced exile and ruin due to the invasion of the Anglo-Americans. However, whereas Jackson's version narrates in a deadpan and detached voice an ineluctable tragedy, Martí's translation gives more space and words to describe the father and son's heartwrenching responses to this imminent possibility. Anglo squatters took over the indigenous pueblos that during Mexican secularization had become the property of Mexican military and civil officials, and Anglos often burned whole villages to the ground, as *Ramona* recounts. In preparation for conflicts over land, the advice of Father Peyri to Chief Pablo had been "above all, keep peace with the whites" (Jackson, *Ramona*, 52). In strenuously striving to obey the Spanish priest, Chief Pablo had urged, persuaded, and then commanded his people not to join a revolutionary movement to stop the invasion. Through this strategy of avoiding hostilities by joining with the invader, Pablo believed that he could maintain his community intact, albeit on lands deeded to Mexican citizens by the Catholic Church, and thus contingent upon the favor of landowners and the indigenous leaders' nonresistance.

In the post-1848 period, however, with the influx of Anglo-Americans, the prior verbal understanding came "to be held as of no value" and "not binding on purchasers of grants" (Jackson, *Ramona*, 52). A comparison of Martí's translation and Jackson's original reveals the translator's augmentation of the text by adding figurative language that comments on the strategy of accommodationism, to which the church and landowners instructed Indians to remain faithful. Jackson's text appraises Pablo's intelligence in recognizing his people's demise:

> But Pablo heard rumors, which greatly disquieted him, that such pledged and surveyed lines as these were coming to be held as of no value, not binding on purchasers of grants. He was intelligent enough to see that if this were so, he and his people were ruined. All these perplexities and fears he

confided to Alessandro; long anxious hours the father and son spent together, walking back and forth in the village or sitting in front of their little
adobe house, discussing what could be done. There was always the same
ending to the discussion,—a long sigh, and, "We must wait, we can do
nothing." (52–53)

By describing the reaction to the Anglos' invalidation of prior pledges and
surveyed lines with an objective documentary style that uncritically confirms the "intelligence" of adhering to the church's teachings of submission, Jackson's novel fails to capture the mortal significance of Pablo and
Alessandro's impending exile.

If Jackson associates native intelligence with the ability to see and accept
their people's ruin, Martí infuses this passage with embittered and alarmed
protest. His translation enriches the text by introducing a metaphor that
connotes useless or ineffective writing, a "letra muerta" (dead letter):

Pero ya Pablo venía oyendo que todo aquello era letra muerta para lo nuevos
compradores. ¡Perdidos, pues, como le dijo el Padre Peyri!: ¡sin sus tierras,
sin su pueblo, sin su capilla, sin sus casas!: ¡no era suyo lo suyo! Contaba
todas sus angustias as su hijo, con quien hablaba largas horas, ya en tristes
paseos por las siembras, que comenzaban a hablarle la lengua del adiós, ya
sentados meditando en lo que habrían de hacer, frente a su casa de adobe. Y
se paraba siempre en lo mismo: en suspirar, y en "Esperemos, no podemos
hacer nada!" (*Obras*, 24:251)

(But already Pablo had heard that all that [the unrecognized surveys and
pledges] was a dead letter for the new buyers. Lost, just as Father Peyri told
him! Without their lands, without their pueblos, without their chapel, without their houses!: What was theirs was not theirs! He recounted his anguish
to his son, with whom he spent long hours, now sadly walking through their
planted fields that had begun to speak to them the language of goodbye, and
other times meditating on what they should do in front of their adobe
house. And he always reached the same conclusion: with a sigh, and saying,
"Let's wait, we can do nothing!")

Martí's translation adds several sentences that hint at Chief Pablo's sense of
having been betrayed by his own accommodationism. After 1848, the prior
Mexican laws became a "letra muerta" and Father Peyri's advice became a
vile prediction, even though Pablo and his community had fully obeyed his
command to keep "peace with the whites." Rather than reporting Chief
Pablo and Alessandro's "intelligent" acceptance of their conquest by the

Anglo-Americans, Martí's version gives agonizing details of the displacement and of the significance of Alessandro's failure to protest or take up arms in self-defense. This metaphor of the "dead letter" suggests texts that only give up a bare, literal sense. It obliquely comments on Jackson's original bland description of the decimation of the village of Temecula. The metaphor also refers to the expiration of the unwritten agreements between the church and the Mexican landowners concerning lands inhabited by Luiseños such as Chief Pablo and Alessandro's group, which made the Anglos' destruction of villages "legal" or unpunishable. Martí's "dead letter" also refers to the now obsolete rhetoric of self-government by and for the people as a founding principle of the Anglo-American nation.

Whereas Jackson's *Ramona* minimizes the history of militant Indian insurrections against the Anglo invasion, Martí's translation underscores the significance and reach of indigenous revolts. In English, Pablo and Alessandro's position comes across as hopeless resignation. While in Jackson the Franciscans remain saintly figures in whose words and institutions Ramona admirably takes refuge, in Martí's version this very Catholic "gospel" of identifying with the invading European culture leads Pablo to an infuriating and patently erroneous failure to see his structural connections with other oppressed groups. Jackson refers off-handedly to "one time" when "some" tribes took up arms and Chief Pablo removed to Los Angeles so that "they might be identified with the whites" (52). By contrast, Martí's translation alludes to a missed and singular opportunity for Pablo and Alessandro to throw in their lot with other threatened indigenous and Mexican groups who sought to stop the Anglo-Americans' advance: "una vez que se alzaron unas tribus del Sur, y amenazaba una gran guerra india, se llevó a lo más de su gente con sus bueyes y ovejas a los Angeles" (once, when some tribes of the South rose up in protest, and threatened a great Indian war, he brought the majority of his people with oxen and sheep to Los Angeles) (*Obras*, 24:250). The translation expands Jackson's subjunctive phrase, "it looked as if there would be a general Indian war," to the past tense of a verb that does not specify whether an act was completed: they "threatened" a great Indian war. In the interstices of Jackson's text, Martí gives weight to the specter of insurgency that the original sought to minimize.

Many Cubans in exile considered Martí's unwavering commitment to his America's capacity and to the urgent need to prevent Cuban annexation to the American Union to be a form of madness. Similarly, we may read, in

Martí's translation, Alessandro's madness as an illegible political condition of insurgence, which the discourse of Indian reform transforms into a problem of mental hygiene. More than a merely psychological diagnosis of the "locoed" Indian—a term that Jackson imported from her documentary *Report on the Condition and Needs of the Mission Indians of California* (1883) to describe the condition of desperate and angry Indians in the novel—the translation denounces the insidious pact that Alessandro's own father had made with "perpetual and irredeemable servitude" by trusting the Spanish priests' advice rather than forming their own judgment and alliances.[115] In Martí's version, Pablo and Alessandro's greatest error lies in not entering the "great Indian war" and in remaining faithful to the Catholic father's prediction of their defeat.

Especially insofar as it preserved and fostered cross-class and cross-race alliances in the face of an imperial enemy, the idea of a unified Indian war echoes Martí's United States of South America that might value its indigenous, peasant, and African roots, hold empire at bay, and redefine modernity. By contrast, Jackson's original title for her novel, "In the Name of the Law," indicates a limited criticism of U.S. Indian policy from within the invading state's sovereignty, which depended on the incorporation or elimination of the possible spectral alternatives to it.[116] Jackson's *Ramona* could not imagine justice beyond the principles of tolerance, charity, and legal reforms within the expansionist empire, as articulated in the novel by the white woman caretaker of Alessandro and Ramona, Aunt Ri, who prefigures dimly a contemporary official multiculturalism.

If Jackson's novel's most daring appeal to justice is on behalf of reform and more effective assimilation through the evangelizing and training of a multicolored empire, the eloquent mestiza Lucy Parsons and her anarchist comrades articulated a contrasting "decentralization of power" that proved so threatening that the state responded by dramatically staging the anarchist hangings (*Otras crónicas*, 81). In keeping with his revised, sympathetic portrayal of the anarchists' position, Martí's translations work at crosspurposes to the agenda of "reform" in *Ramona*. The translation reveals a radically different interpretation of the long period of flight of the "arrogant mestiza" Ramona, first with her dark Indian lover Alessandro, and then with her equally dark Mexican foster-brother Felipe. Jackson's *Ramona* has given many readers to believe that Ramona's dream of raising Alessandro's and her daughter in Mexico suggests the novel's "death knell for her complex racial heritage" and a flight into Hispanic whiteness, where her comfortable class position as Felipe's wife and light coloring would enable her to escape the entrapping "bond of race" (Jackson, *Ramona*, 359). Martí's translation of this "bond of race" as "peligro de raza" (racial danger) (*Obras*, 24:500) projects onto Mexico his utopian imagining of an antiracist alternative to U.S. imperial modernity. That neither Mexico nor Cuba's elites came to share Martí's commitments and probably would never have accepted entirely the daughter of an Indian woman and an inebriated Scot into their ranks does not invalidate Martí's hope that a future Mexico might offer an alternative to the anti-immigrant, anti-Latino and antiblack imperialism that he had encountered in the United States.

❧ "THE LATIN PORTION OF NORTH AMERICA": LATINO AND U.S. RESPONSES TO PAN-AMERICANISM

Kentucky statesman Henry Clay's dream of Western hemispheric unity, progress, and modernization led by and modeled on the United States moved closer to fulfillment with the conference that brought representatives of seventeen American republics to Washington, D.C., in 1889–90. The International American Conference—which marks the origins of many Pan-American institutions such as the Organization of American States, the Inter-American Development Bank, and others that emerged from the Bureau of American Republics—failed in the short term, but nevertheless laid a foundation for its principal if unstated goal: "to secure the political and commercial ascendancy of the United States on this continent."[117] It planted the seeds of foreign policies and Pan-American institutions that continue to germinate and bear poisonous fruit. These objectives included reciprocity agreements to create a common customs union or a preferred trading area in the Americas; the creation of a system of arbitration of inter-American conflicts; government concessions to subsidize new inter-American transportation networks; and a single silver-based or mixed-base currency modeled on the Prussian zollverein, to be entitled "the Columbus." This Pan-American project also commissioned the culturally and politically significant erection of the White City at the World's Columbian Exposition that took place in Chicago three years later. Although marginal in diplomatic history—precisely because the conference, by most accounts, proved a debacle for the United States—the archives of these meetings spark new interest today because they mark the origins of cultural and political terms that have reshaped the field of American studies during the long twentieth century.

If today we speak of the literature and the culture of the United States to

refer more precisely to a nation-specific cultural field that used to monop-
olize the name "American," this nomenclature bears the traces of a late
nineteenth-century struggle to deter or alter the course of an empire in the
hemisphere. If the first Pan-American Conference and the International
Monetary Commission in 1891 failed to achieve any specific policy objectives beyond an intercontinental train and a clearinghouse of information
for U.S. investors in Latin America, Martí's translation of these events
invite readers back to records and minutes of these meetings to see a
genealogy of present debates. Because in Martí's view these meetings became an opportunity to define and "defend the independence of Spanish
America," wherein would lie the very "equilibrium of the world," the rhetorical skirmishes and ideological battles of Latin and U.S. American delegates reveal how a handful of "Latins" temporarily derailed "a people
raised in the hope of continental domination" (*Obras*, 6:63). The meetings
dramatically augmented Martí's clout and notoriety, and in this sense,
provided a context in which the organizations he associated with were able
to contravene the expected annexation of Cuba and to defer the fulfillment
of Clay's dream.

The adjectives "Latin" and "United States" arose in English and in Spanish more or less contemporaneously to specify a layered division between
North and South Americas, and between Anglo-Saxon and Latin cultures, a
fissure that became palpable during the sharp interactions occasioned by
the Pan-American conference of 1889–90 and the period when Martí
served as Uruguay's delegate to the International Monetary Commission in
1891. In addition to referencing divided political and cultural formations
within the Americas, the tension between these terms brings into focus a
border zone that is as cultural as it is territorial. The Latino/United States
binary transcends national boundaries—a fact that has become patently
clear in the past decade in the collaboration of the United States with
Mexican border police in cracking down on northward migration. This
binary first took on more than national significance as Pan-Americanism
came to threaten Latin American self-government and began to shape a
U.S. racial discourse concerning Latinness.

Martí's critical opposition to the Pan-American ideal becomes patent in
his sardonic chronicles on these 1889–90 meetings. It illuminates the
border essay "Madre América," which Martí presented to Latin American delegates in New York on December 19, 1889. His widely cited chronicles, "Congreso Internacional de Washington" (Washington's International

Congress) that details the history, elements, and tendencies of the meetings, judiciously leaves the term "America" out of the title, as Martí fiercely fought in his journalism and later in his diplomatic participation to rescue the word and the idea from distortion by its association with the "highway robbery" of Pan-Americanism (*Obras*, 6:46). The opening paragraph of the "Congreso Internacional" chronicle translates headlines from the U.S. press that euphorically construct the conference as a victory of "the Pan-Americans," who, by sending "Steamships to South America" and by chanting "Manifest Destiny," assumed that "Already the Gulf Is Ours" (*Obras*, 6:46). Presciently interpreting the first Pan-American Conference as an assertion of a new form of imperial domination in the hemisphere, Martí defines the historic encounter of leaders of America North and South as a catalyst for "Spanish America" to repeat its earlier struggle against Spanish imperial tyranny and declare its "second independence" (*Obras*, 6:46), this time from the United States.

The brainchild of Secretary of State James G. Blaine since his first tenure in the Garfield administration, the conference brought U.S. and Latin American delegates together for a six-month period of discussion and touring. Reports on the meeting by Martí and the Mexican diplomat and longtime U.S. resident Matías Romero used the terms "Latin" and "of the United States," in English and in Spanish, as modifiers to convey cultural tensions between groups during the meetings. The Latin delegates' contravening responses to U.S. proposals during the Pan-American conferences also played a determining role in redefining Latinness against U.S. racial stereotype and in opposition to an imperial project.

Romero, who acted as a temporary translator and peacemaker during the meetings, uses the term "Latin" to describe delegates who responded critically to U.S. delegates' comportment in relation to Latin American delegates. Sympathetic to the Republican administration that hosted the meetings, and a longtime business partner of Ulysses S. Grant, Romero published an account of the first Pan-American conference in which he explained and apologized for the Anglos' treatment of the Latins. Although Romero's essay strives to portray the Latins' reaction to the Anglos as hasty and hypersensitive to innocuous cultural misunderstandings, Romero's description acknowledges tension between what he calls the "two races" represented in the conference: "when they came in contact, the contrast was very apparent" ("The Pan-American Conference," 358).

Romero blames poor translation for the Pan-American Conference's failure to overcome the Latin delegates' suspicion of the United States' motives in extending the invitation in the first place. Problems in translating between cultures and languages occasionally devolved into "sharp answers, which provoked sharp retorts," which seemed to "threaten the success of the Conference" (361). Despite his appeal to racial difference, Romero shows how political dynamics during the conference occasioned month after month of divergences and misunderstandings, not only between North and South Americans but also between the host culture and a group he defines as "the Latin portion of North America." I take Romero's evocative phrase to refer to Mexico after 1848, of course, but the "Latin" inside the North must also allude to the Mexican-origin inhabitants of the states that formerly made up northern Mexico, or residents of the United States–Mexico borderlands.[118] Although the term "Latin" pertained in the 1880s above all to the territorially distinct countries south of the Rio Bravo and to the peoples of remaining Spanish colonies in Latin America, it also distinguished an incipient cultural formation characterized by its difference from dominant Anglo culture in the North.

This "Latin portion of North America" acquired meaning in the Anglo-dominant context of quotidian, ongoing, and often conflictive interactions of the delegates in Washington, D.C. The diplomatic Romero insinuates— in contrast to his objective of defending the North American government from accusations of racial disdain—that Latins encountered inhospitable treatment from U.S. delegates, however unintentional. Martí's chronicles note that the interactions between the "hybrid" postcolonials of Latin America and "blond" representatives of steamship companies (*Obras*, 6:47, 55) coincided with debates in the U.S. Congress concerning a project to expatriate North American blacks, "so that North American whites need not treat them as men and sit beside them on trains."[119] In keeping with the U.S. delegates' vantage point as wealthy investors with business interests in Latin America, postreconstruction practices of racial segregation of public spaces in Washington likely made some darker-skinned Latin delegates feel the stinging disdain of U.S. racial discourse during their stay. This mention of white supremacist assumptions at the highest levels of government suggests that the beliefs that gave rise to the imminent *Plessy v. Ferguson* decision were already shaping treatment of Latinos/as and people of African descent in the United States.

The ten U.S. delegates to the first Pan-American conference included many U.S. industrialists of the Gilded Age, investors in Latin America, and transportation tycoons—men with little or no knowledge of either diplomacy or the Spanish language. Among them were Andrew Carnegie, steel corporation owner and railroad investor; Charles Flint, member of the New York firm W. R. Grace, who helped to bungle negotiations during the War of the Pacific when the idea of a Pan-American conference first arose; William Hughes of the Ward steamship line; Cornelius Bliss, textile mill owner; Henry Gassaway Davis, coal mine and railroad owner; and Clement Studebaker, carriage and automobile manufacturer.[120] To criticize the Pan-American ideal articulated during the conference was to dissent from an economic project envisioned by the U.S.'s wealthiest and most powerful elite. That Blaine appointed businessmen rather than diplomats led some Latin delegates to "imagine that the [U.S. delegates'] selection was an act of disrespect to the Latin-American nations" (Romero, "The Pan-American Conference," 357). This lack of respect on more than one occasion took on a "more lively character, and sometimes went so far as to be personal" (362).

Although Romero blames the Latins' cultural hypersensitivity rather than U.S.-style racism or hemispheric antagonism for the heated conflicts that arose during the conference debates, his report in the *North American Review* nevertheless gives evidence of categorical disdain of the Anglos toward the Latins. As secretary of state and convener of the meeting, Blaine and several of his supporters in the conference nominated Blaine as president of the conference. The Argentine delegation remonstrated that Blaine was ineligible for the position because he was not an accredited and official participant in the conference. In order to reiterate publicly their opposition to Blaine's election, the Argentines did not sit quietly in their hotels. They donned top hats and rode with fanfare through the streets of Washington, in a highly public protest of the opening session during which Blaine was to be elected.[121]

Perhaps as a rebuke to the Latin delegates for refusing to cooperate by blessing Blaine's predetermined election, the U.S. delegates responded by failing en masse to show up to the meeting in which the conference's vice president, understood to be a Latin American, would take place. Romero comments that the incident generated ill-feeling among the Latin delegates: "[The North American delegates'] absence was considered by some of the Latin American delegates as an act of discourtesy, because they believed that a want of consideration had induced them not to assemble in

the same room, whereas the true reason was a desire to show consideration for their associates" (409). Despite Romero's placating defense of the
North Americans' reasons for absenting themselves, the collective decision
to avoid assembling in the same room with the Latin delegates suggests the
specter of segregation, which was only the most quotidian and visible form
of racial violence that characterized this era. It is quite possible that in the
conflict between U.S. and Latin American delegates, the shadow of race
crept across even the lightest-skinned, white-looking Latins, in the southern town of Washington, D.C.[122]

The Argentines led the opposition that foiled Blaine's plans for the Pan-
American Conference, and their political insubordination invested extra
significance in their cultural differences. According to Ernesto Quesada,
son of a leading Argentine diplomat who recused himself from the conference, the South American delegates incarnated a "Latin type," characterized by tropical urbanity, delicate courtesy, and careful cultivation, all of
which contrast sharply with the clumsy Anglo-Americans, whose frankness bordered on vulgarity, and whose self-assertion revealed certainty of
racial superiority. Introducing the slogan "America is for humanity," which
implicitly revises the slogan Martí cites ironically in one of his chronicles—
"America is for North Americans, because they are blond, broad-backed,
Anglo and strong" (*Obras*, 12:313)—the Argentines Manuel Quintana and
Roque Saenz Peña butted heads with one particularly hot-tempered delegate, the lawyer John Henderson, over the Latin American proposal to
eradicate the right to conquest in the hemisphere. Despite the conference's
stated goal of promoting peace in the hemisphere, both the United States
and Chile insisted upon preserving the right to conquest in the hemisphere, a right that would leave open the possibility of acquiring Cuba and
Puerto Rico.

This dawning awareness of the friction between Latino and Anglo America in the face of an expanding United States characterizes Martí's border
writing. In a letter from Martí to his U.S.-born Cuban disciple, Gonzálo
de Quesada y Aróstegui, he compares the Cuban-American cultural at-
tachment to Cubanness to cultural struggles in Montreal and California:
"French Canada neither wishes to be English nor North American: it wants
to be French. The Mexicans of California don't want to be of the United
States: they want to be Mexicans. You, raised from your roots in the colleges
of the North, . . . know the impossibility of accommodation, the futility and
banefulness of accommodation;—and you are Cuban."[123] *Ramona* in Span-

ish, along with other chronicles of border violence, sought to launch a popular educational campaign in Spanish to support militant regional self-defense of any Latin American nation, colony, or annexed territory that would resist unwanted intimacy with the powerful northern republic. Martí's translations of the bellicose "war fever" along the United States–Mexico border in 1886, of the psychic violence inflicted upon Amerindian and Chicano communities in California and Texas, of the state-sponsored hangings of outspoken radicals like the Chicago anarchists, and of the amnesia of urban easterners concerning the history of U.S. expansion represent the reactions of the dominated to imperial modernity. Each of these chronicles of the border predicts and warns against the threat of Pan-Americanism for Martí's America, and for the world.

Cross-Pollinating "Dust on Butterfly's Wings": Latina/o Writing and Culture Beyond and After Martí

> Yo puedo hacer, puedo hacer
> De esta desdicha una joya;
> (I can make, I can make
> my misfortune into a gem.)
> —**José Martí,** "[Yo puedo hacer . . .]," *Poesía completa*

❧ IN ORDER TO limn the different American modernity and early experiments in modernist literary form by Latino writers in the late nineteenth century, this book draws primarily on work by José Martí, who despite his migratory status and accented English enjoyed the privileges of masculinity, light-skin, and professional training. Detailed consideration of this ample corpus of major and minor texts was necessary in order to engage a long history of Martí criticism. This kind of in-depth work proved a condition for attempting to think about how Martí's translations recast fundamental concepts and methods in U.S.-based American studies. Focusing on a critically acclaimed major writer enables me to assume his work's literary significance, and to leverage that weight toward the book's larger claim: that we who work in the field of a new American studies should pay attention to Martí not only as a great Latin American modernist, but as a migrant Latino writer who reveals to us aspects of the United States not visible to readers in the United States widely. As Martí himself came to acknowledge, the strange savage beauty of his prose and poetry is not the single-handed creation of an individual author's genius, but the product of a struggle to formally convey a subaltern, postcolonial, and largely invisible condition. He perceives his condition through his work as a translator of English-language texts and of U.S. scenes in which he and his community have a place, but along the margins. Martí's consciousness of his position as a being part of a group he calls Latino, and the resulting small shimmering works of prose and poetry that he and others created in New York reveal a debt to spoken words that flit from mouth to mouth in public spaces like butterflies.

In an unfinished poem entitled "Polvo en alas de mariposas" (Dust on Butterfly Wings), he makes explicit the association of his poetry with the butterfly's flight:

Que mis versos vuelan	That my verses fly
Como mariposas	As butterflies do
Pequeñas e inquietas	Small and unquiet
	(*Poesía completa*, 513)

Carrying pollen from flower to flower, cross-pollinating and engender-ing fruit, Martí's poetry—*Ismaelillo* (1882), *Versos Sencillos* (1891) and his unpublished collection of "Versos Libres"—is the residue of the images he confronts in the city. Words and scenes that arrive in a strange tongue, sometimes marvelous, sometimes horrifying, became his muse: "Envilece, devora, enferma, embriaga / La vida de ciudad" (Villifies, devours, sickens, intoxicates / Life in the city).[1] The poet encountered profoundly mon-strous examples of humanity: "Conozco al hombre, y lo he encontrado malo" (I know man, and I have found him to be evil).[2] They constitute what the poet sees in an abyss largely unknown to others, which he tries to convey with discretion from behind a mask:

Es verdad. So la máscara discreta	It is true. Behind the decorous mask
Oculta su tormento el corazón:	He hides his tormented heart:
Nadie sabe el abismo que el poeta	No one knows the abyss the poet
En los dinteles de la vida vió.	Saw from the lintels of life.[3]

From the lintels of life—the support or border below which a window or door opens—the poet gazes into an untranslatable abyss. These lines sug-gest the double task of covering and revealing the tormented—yet carefully masked—responses of the poet's heart to what he observed that constitute the gems in his poetry.

While motivated by a desire to redress an oversight of Latino contributions in discussions of modernity and modernism and to explore the implications of this extra-national migrant condition, between languages and between cultures, the Martí-centered approach of this book nevertheless raises the question of whether his corpus of texts can be said to speak for a heterogeneous Latino group. Indeed, while many embraced Martí's leadership because of his antiracist, proindependence proposals and his curious poetic images, others did not. Nancy Raquel Mirabel provides convincing evidence for the conclusion that Martí's "writing, discussing, and expounding on the futility of racism, however, was not enough to alleviate racial tensions among Cubans in Tampa."[4] Martí proposed a utopian antiracism and a vision of a more equitable distribution of wealth in a decolonized Latin America. I have argued that we should not reduce this proposal—however unrealistic—to the more cynical and mainstream views of the Free Soilers, like Whitman, who wanted to limit the expansion of slavery but did not favor abolition or transracial social equality, and thus compromised the liberty we associate with his daring poetic forms. Even the philosophical rigors of Emerson, who denounced slavery and embraced abolition, became inadequate as a model for Martí, because Emerson's mountaintop thinking permitted him to remain aloof from the din, strife, and muck of working-class, immigrant, or racialized life in the city. Martí attributes to Emerson a description of a man "wallowing in the mire of dialectics" (pisoteando en el fango de la dialéctica) (*Obras*, 13:30; *Selected Writings*, 129). Given that thus far scholars have not been able to locate the original version of this "translation" in Emerson's works, we might read this as Martí's invention. This sentence that appears in quotation marks in the original ventriloquizes how he—or someone in his prostrate migrant Latino position—might be described by Emerson. Reading Emerson, Martí has the experience of seeing himself through the eyes of the Anglo, North American other and thus begins to see, and then theorize from his difference.

The focus on Martí also means that this book does not extensively treat the works of other Latino migrant writers to which I refer to in these pages, nor do I address (beyond the "mestiza" Lucy Parsons) what Latinas, many of whom were active leaders in their community, were saying, doing, and writing. A full discussion of the other late nineteenth-century Latina/o writers and artists, whose latent, invisible works we are in the process of recovering, translating, and interpreting, will fill the pages of future books. Martí's extensive correspondence and journalism will be a tool, as they point us to many other Latina/o writers, artists, and orators of his time. Nonetheless, nationalist and masculinist passions about Martí as founding father shapes the archive that this book recontextualizes. Although I put the archive to a slightly different use, that is, for interpreting Martí's contributions to a migrant Latino tradition, the social forces that produced that archive also structure silences in the narrative. The written legacies of the Afro-Cuban leader and organizer Paulina Pedroso, of Martí's indefatigable Venezuelan partner who provided the material basis for much of his eating and living in New York, Carmen Miyares, and the prolific and influential poetry of Lola Rodríguez de Tío, for example, await treatment.[5] Rather than seeing these women as significant for their support and annointing of the male hero—as Martí most often did—this research will need to define the specific contributions of Latina writing.

For U.S. Americanists to acknowledge a debt to Martí and to migrant Latino culture may be a first step, but the debt must then provoke an action. Acknowledgment might begin with paying attention to and incorporating Martí's redefinition of America. His usage "others" and abbreviates the United States, and thus with a small but trenchant act of renaming, rejects Latin America's incorporation into an Anglo-dominant hemisphere headed up by the United States. Martí began referring to the country by the abbreviated form "U.S." in 1891, in his polemical refusal to refer to it and its delegates during the Pan-American Conference as "American."[6] Thus, the increasingly common and logically necessary usage of the term "United States" or "U.S.," as opposed to the more capacious "United States of America" and the adjective "American," does not allow one nation to rhetorically subsume the others in the hemisphere.[7] Earlier, Martí prophetically warned his Honduran readers that the "pacific and provident señores of the U.S." would "come to have their whole *hacienda*" (*Obras*, 8:88) in the islands of the Caribbean. As a response to these developments, Martí fought and died for cultural and political recognition of his America. With an apt critique of U.S. national discourses that naturalize the chanciness of its boundaries into a manifest destiny, Martí helped launch an ongoing transamerican reflection on social and aesthetic decolonization in the Americas. To sever Martí's modernist writing from an uncompromising ethical critique of the United States' rapid advance toward imperialism is to miss a key insight of migrant Latino writing of the Gilded Age.

This book offers an analysis of José Martí's translations of U.S. culture and its imperial modernity at a specific time, in the first decade of the new millennium, when the United States continues to expand, with increasing bravura and violence. At the same time, inheritors of Martí's legacy struggle to keep in check this betrayal of an American revolutionary tradition by guaranteeing the status of Cuba and other Latin American countries as self-governing nations and by envisioning a region not subject to the directives of the United States. In the last communication that Martí sent to U.S. readers in 1895, he projects another United States that also might practice an alternative American modernity. Another United States might join with him in endorsing Cuba's self-government by the people who make up its largest, working-class, and multiracial majority: "The United States, for example, would prefer to contribute to the solidity of the liberty of Cuba, with sincere friendship for its independent people who love them, and will authorize their total freedom rather than become accomplices to a pretentious and useless oligarchy that only seeks from them to establish the local power of this class—which is in truth, the lowest of the island—over their fellow citizens who are the producers."[8] The term "oligarchy" in this passage references Martí's experience as a migrant and a worker who observed firsthand the attempts of the leaders of an extremely wealthy Gilded Age to form economic bonds, often through manipulation and corruption of government representatives, with the small, wealthy elites of Latin America's new republics. The "producers," with whom he hopes the United States might rather ally itself, comprise the large working class in which Martí included himself. That Martí divides colonial society into a pretentious oligarchy and a multiracial mass of producers reflects a sense of the social content that he would infuse into the revolution and into his Latino modernism. This passage, among those left out or partially translated in the English version of Martí's 1895 letter to U.S. readers, which appeared in the *New York Herald* on the day of his death, indicts a tendency in U.S. foreign policy to prop up governments that represent the interests of a small, wealthy, and usually European or U.S.-identified portion of the nation rather than its struggling majority. The passage appeals to the best tradition of revolutionary defense of liberty and popular self-government, values that Martí associates here with the United States' founding principles.

In the midst of increasing xenophobia and targeted policing of Spanish-speaking and brown-skinned migrants in the contemporary United States, I find transformative promise in this long-standing Latino critique of imperial modernity. At a time when migration from Latin America to the

United States has reached an all-time high and when Latinas/os have officially become the largest subculture in a United States that will no longer have a non-Hispanic white majority by 2050, this book invites us to acknowledge American studies' debts to the Latino migrant insights of Martí's work.[9] We have seen that Martí depicted the vulnerability of the Cuban migrant to cracker racism in Florida in terms of the longer history of Anglo attitudes toward Mexican, Asian, African, Native, and non-Anglo immigrant Americans. Within the increasingly militarized borders of the United States and across the globe, Latin Americans and Latino/as constitute a major American cultural force, and this power has provoked efforts to fragment and divide this group into factions and to foster divisions between non-white groups who will constitute the new majority. In this reading, Martí becomes a forerunner of this new America, and of the twelve million undocumented immigrants, over half of whom have come from Mexico.

For the hundreds of thousands of their supporters who marched in 2006 in some of the largest demonstrations in U.S. history to protest legislative proposals that would criminalize undocumented migrants and their supporters, Martí's poetic evocation of his distant, not yet existing country with "the night" might give voice to the unspeakable desire for something else besides the United States, to which they have had no choice but to migrate. The poet, in "beastly letters / that resemble swords" (letras fieras / Que parecen espadas), prefers death to incorporation into the United States.[10] Martí's political allegiances and cultural commitments traverse and transgress the boundaries of the United States, and thus demand new methods of transnational, and translational inquiry. Reading Martí within this migratory tradition indicates that this poetry of uprooting belongs to and honors noncitizens in a nation that has mostly refused to recognize them, their culture, and their labor. Martí's Latino migrant texts render nonsensical the notion that America originated with Europeans or Puritan culture, and questions its corollary, that all immigrants to the United States therefore should speak English and become U.S. citizens or else be deported.[11] Through careful attention to these translations, we may perceive the Latino American precursors who initiated, long ago, the critical response to empire that documents the emergence of other American modernities.

ꙮ PREFACE

1   Throughout this text *translation* refers to the action of transferring a text from one language into another. At the same time I use *translation* in a figurative sense to describe the transformation, alteration, and renovation that occurs in the process of rendering the cultural and historical events of a particular time—the U.S. Gilded Age—for Spanish-language readers of a distinct cultural, i.e., non-Anglo, background.

2   Alberto, *Informe contra mi mismo*, 111. Throughout this book, all translations from Spanish are mine, unless otherwise indicated.

3   Flaubert, *Bouvard and Pécechet*, 249; Anderson, *Imagined Communities*, 17; Benjamin, "On the Concept of History," sec. 7 (1940); Benjamin, *Walter Benjamin*, 4:392.

4   Alberto, *Informe contra mi mismo*, 107.

5   Ibid., 211; see also Cheah, "Given Culture."

6   Martí, "A Manuel Mercado, April 12, 1885," *Epistolario*, 1:299. The term "Latino" commonly refers to a set of practices that define the culture of Latin Americans and of people of Latin American descent living in the United States, as set out by Aparicio, "Latino Cultural Studies," 3–31, and Flores, "Latino Studies," 191–205. "Latin America" begins to refer to a New World geographical and cultural formation in 1856, when the Paris-based Colombian intellectual and political leader José María Torres Caicedo refers to "two Americas"—Latin or South America and "Saxon" or North America—in poetry and programmatic documents. According to Uruguayan philosopher Arturo Ardao, Torres Caicedo adapted the term from the French statesman Michel de Chevalier's notion of a "Latin race," which he proposed in 1836 to describe France's tutelary role in the New World, in opposition to the threatening spread of the "Saxon race" over the globe. Torres Caicedo and the Chilean Francisco Bilbao initiated the concept of a Union of Latin American states in response the aggressions of the United States against Mexico in 1845–48 and in particular against William Walker's U.S.-endorsed aggression against Nicaragua in 1855–56. See Ardao, *Génesis de la idea y el nombre de América Latina*.

7   Rojas, "Otro gallo cantaría," 13.

8   As Kadir notes, in "Defending America against Its Devotees," 30, students

of United States today have an acute responsibility to engage in a critical discussion of the United States and of its actions around the world.

9   Ette, *José Martí. Apostól, poeta, revolucionario,* 405–8.

10 Senate Committee on Foreign Relations, report to accompany Bill S. 497, "Making Appropriations to Facilitate the Acquisition of the Island of Cuba, by Negotiation" (Jan. 24, 1859), 35th Cong., 2nd sess., 1859, S. Rep. 351, 9.

11 Ette, *José Martí. Apostól, poeta, revolucionario,* 408.

❧ INTRODUCTION

1   By "Latino American," I suggest the broad group of immigrants and migrants, permanent and nonpermanent residents and their descendants, regardless of citizenship status, who may or may not speak and read Spanish in addition to English. Regarding this, see note 6 of the Preface.

2   On the effects of abolition, see Mirabal, "No Country But the One We Must Fight For," 63. According to Dvignan and Gann, *The Spanish Speakers in the United States,* 29, the number of Spanish-speaking immigrants increased from 8,731 during 1891–1900 to 27,935 during 1901–10.

3   This use of the verb to "provincialize" follows Dipesh Chakrabarty, in *Provincializing Europe,* 42–46, where he refers to a remaking of Europe's Enlightenment tradition from the margins in order to imagine the world as radically heterogeneous. To provincialize the center begins with attention to the incommensurability and opaqueness in between languages and cultural systems.

4   The journals *Representations, Radical History Review, Modern Language Notes, Modern Fiction Studies,* and *American Literary History* have all featured special issues that are dedicated to Martí's concept of "Our America," or to the idea of a hemispheric perspective, which since the 1990s has been influentially linked to Martí's key phrase. Note Belnap and Fernández's edited collection's subtitle, *José Martí's "Our America": From National to Hemispheric Cultural Studies* or Shukla and Tinsman's *Imagining Our Americas.*

5   Mignolo, *Idea of Latin America,* 90.

6   Throughout this book, in citing Martí's *Obras,* I refer to the twenty-eight-volume edition of his *Obras completas,* published in Havana by the Editorial de Ciencias Sociales (1963–75), with the abbreviation *Obras.* Occasionally, I cite the critical edition, published by the Casa de las Americas in Havana, including Roberto Fernandez Retamer and Pedro Pablo Rodriguez's critical edition of Martí's journalism, *En los Estados Unidos* (2003). In making translations, I have consulted and give page references to Esther Allen's English edition, *Selected Writings* (2002). I also cite Ernesto Mejía Sánchez's *Otras Cronicas de Nueva York* (1983).

7   To his Uruguayan friend Enrique Estrázulas, Martí describes himself as "a defrosted mountain, or as a tree without leaves" (*Epistolario,* 1:413); in a January 1892 letter responding to the Cuban commander Enrique Collazo

and three other Cubans who questioned Martí's sincerity and capacity because he had not fought in the Ten Years War, he describes his situation in
New York as a "cold corner": "And it is cold this corner, and not adequate for
visits" (*Epistolario*, 3:13).

8   Du Bois describes this gift in *Souls of Black Folk*, 2. See Stecopoulos's essay on
Johnson's conflicted relationship with U.S. empire and Latin America, especially when Johnson occupied the prestigious post of U.S. consul in Puerto
Cabello, Venezuela, and Corinto, Nicaragua, and facilitated an invasion of
several thousand Marines there in 1912 ("Up from Empire," 36), the same year
he anonymously published *Autobiography*.

9   James, *Holding Aloft the Banner of Ethiopia*, 239–47, describes the antiracist
practices of the proindependence tobacco worker communities in south
Florida under Martí's leadership.

10   Martí places this phrase in quotation marks. It echoes John T. Sprague's
rendition of the Seminole warrior Coacooche: "I saw the white man and was
told he was my enemy. I could not shoot him as I would a wolf or a bear; yet
like these he came upon me; horses, cattle, and fields, he took from me. He
said he was my friend, abused our women and children, and told us to go
from the land. Still he gave me his hand in friendship; we took it, whilst
taking it, he had a snake in the other; his tongue was forked; he lied, and
stung us" (Sprague, *The Origin, Progress and Conclusion of the Florida War*,
288–89).

11   The terms "empire" and "imperialism" refer in this argument to a state
power, most commonly a nation-state, and to its procurement of economic
and political control of foreign territories and/or resources through annexation, or through combined forms of economic, military, or cultural
pressure. Unlike colonialism, which relied on the establishing of a governing
outpost from the "mother" country, imperialism collaborates with local representatives of the nonelite or subaltern population in the concentration of
national wealth amongst the governing elite and transnational economic
interests.

12   Pease, "Global Dominance without Colonies."

13   Williams, *The Country and the City*, 37.

14   According to Jameson, *A Singular Modernity*, 31–32, prominent dates for the
origins of modernity in the singular include Europe's colonization of the New
World, the Protestant Reformation in England, the German invention of the
printing press, Descartes's cogito, the French Revolution, the European Enlightenment, capitalist industrialization, and secular and aesthetic responses
in Europe and the United States. See also Pratt's similar list in "Modernity
and Periphery," 24–25; Pratt, like Jameson, criticizes the open-ended definition of modernity in Western cultural history as extending from the sixth
century to the present.

15   Pratt exposes the whiteness of modernity in "Modernity and Periphery," 27.
She and Jameson challenge the universal aspirations and explanatory value of

this narrative. As a Latin American enthusiast of modernity, Sarmiento traveled to the United States in order to study and adopt its model for Latin America, as Ramos observes in "Saber del otro," 551–69. As Pratt notes, it was Argentina's cosmopolitan, modernizing President Sarmiento who followed the United States' example in launching campaigns of genocide of indigenous people in the pampas ("Modernity and Periphery," 36).

16 According to de Man, modernity "exists in the form of a desire to wipe out whatever came earlier, in the hope of reaching at last a point that could be called a true present, a point of origin that marks a new departure" ("Literary History and Literary Modernity," 148). Alonso associates "socioeconomic advancement" with European practices of modernity in *The Burden of Modernity*, 30.

17 See Hegel, *The Philosophy of History*, 83–87; and Hortense Spillers's reading of Hegel and of Martí's dissent from Hegel, in "Who Cuts the Border?" 1–2.

18 See Schelling, *Memory and Modernity*, 3, on modernity rising through the popular.

19 Pratt, *Imperial Eyes*, 6; Santiago, "The Space In-Between," 63. I am indebted to Eliana Ávila for pointing out the connection between Pratt and Santiago in her questions after my lecture at the International American Studies Conference, July 12–16, 2005, in Florianópolis, Brazil.

20 Fernando Ortiz, Rama, and Pratt refer to this inevitably two-way exchange between center and periphery as "transculturation." Besides mundane errors like tracing the origins of potatoes and tomatoes to Ireland and Italy, I am thinking here of transculturation as a Latin Americanization of the United States and its culture through the displacement caused by the North American Free Trade Agreement and the like. See discussion of transculturation in chapter 1.

21 This phrase derives from Sarlo, *Una modernidad periférica*.

22 Martí, "Flaubert's Last Work."

23 Flaubert, *Bouvard and Pécuchet*, 172.

24 Varela exemplifies a Latin American attitude toward the United States that Martí comes to challenge as a result of his experiences as a resident in New York. Varela believed "all [South American nations] turned their eyes toward the United States, to search there for a model for the new organization of modern nations" (*Democracia prática* 123).

25 Although Maribel Ortiz and José Eduardo González describe Angel Rama (and implicitly Martí) as invested in European-derived modernity and technique, I share Román de la Campa's view that Rama and Martí's theorizing of hybridity and transculturation clears a path for contemporary discussions of postcoloniality and empire in the Americas. See de la Campa, *Latin Americanism*, 66–70, 73–79, and 121–47.

26 Gaonkar, "On Alternative Modernities," 18.

27 Schwarz, "Pressupostos, salvo engano," 153, 155.

28 James, *The Black Jacobins*, 392, 401, 402.

29   Césaire, *Notebook of a Return to the Native Land*, 44; quoted James, *Black Jacobins*, 401.

30   In C. L. R. James's view, Martí and Maceo pertain to and do not transcend the Creole nationalism of Washington, Jefferson, and Bolívar (*Black Jacobins*, 394). I agree with Dalleo, who revises C. L. R. James's exclusion and traces a trajectory of tragic postcolonial intellectuals that includes Toussaint, Martí, James, and Scott ("Emplotting Postcoloniality," 137).

31   Fischer, *Modernity Disavowed*, 33.

32   Carr, "A Revolutionary Hero"; Ripoll, "Marx and Martí."

33   Ripoll, "Marx and Martí."

34   Ibid.

35   However, note that Varela defines his project for emancipation as a means to avoid damages to the white population only. See *El habanero*, xii.

36   On the antiannexationist and antiracist position of *El Mulato*, see Lazo, *Writing to Cuba*, 142–44, and David Luis Brown's forthcoming work. African-descended abolitionist masons such as Henry Highland Garnet, of whom Martí writes with admiration, opposed slavery and annexation. The transnational nature of slavery created bonds of solidarity between African-descended people in the North and in the islands of the Caribbean.

37   Lazo, *Writing to Cuba*, 75.

38   On Schomburg's cofounding of El Sol de Cuba with Martí and other West Indian and Hispanic Caribbeans, and on Schomburg's self-construction in between racial categories, as an Afro-Caribbean Prince Hall mason with an indigenous Taíno pen name, see Arroyo, "Technologies," 10, 17, 19.

39   Deschamps Chapeaux, *Rafael Serra*; Ripoll, *Patria*; Bueno, *José Martí y su periódico "Patria"*; and Tinajero, *El Lector de Tabaquería*.

40   See Brickhouse, *Transamerican Literary Relations and the Nineteenth-Century Public Sphere*, and Lugo-Ortiz, *Identidades Imaginadas*.

41   For example, the former Central Valley New York school principal who was to become the first president of the Cuban Republic, Tomás Estrada Palma, received from Martí the significant gift of a portrait of the fiery abolitionist Wendell Phillips. But Estrada ignored Wendell Phillips's model, just as he rejected Martí, Figueroa, and Serra's antiracist practices. See Guerra on Estrada in *The Myth of José Martí*. See Toledo, *Sotero Figueroa, Editor de Patria* on Figueroa's difficult marginality after Cuban independence. Lipsitz theorizes the financial and psychic wages of whiteness in *The Possessive Investment in Whiteness*.

42   Martí uses the evocative phrase "raza de la libertad" in a piece entitled "Escenas Newyorkinas," that appeared in *La América* in 1884, and which Cepeda recovered and reprinted.

43   Figueroa, *Patria*, 1, "we should not, nor do we want to resign ourselves to the complete absorption of our race by another one, for it does not seduce us to exchange for it, or to forget our language, customs, traditions, sentiments— all of which constitute our Latin American physiognomy" (no debemos ni

queremos resignarnos a la absorción completa de nuestra raza por otra que
no nos seduce hasta el punto de olvidar por ella idioma, costumbres, tradi-
ciones, sentimientos; todo lo que constituye nuestra fisonomía de pueblo
latinoamericano).

44 Medley, *We as Freemen*, recounts the history of a group of free men of color
in New Orleans who sought to fight Jim Crow restrictions by arranging for
Homer Plessy to "pass" in a whites-only carriage. They engaged in an act of
civil disobedience that prompted the Supreme Court to define the separate-
but-equal doctrine in the infamous *Plessy v. Ferguson* case of 1896.

45 In his letter to Mercado of July 6, 1878, Martí notes that in this period he "had
firmly decided to go to Peru" (*Epistolario*, 1:123).

46 Serra y Montalvo, "Ni Española ni Yankee," 125.

47 See Toledo, *Sotero Figueroa, Editor de Patria*, 92–105.

48 Serra y Montalvo, "Martí es la democracia," 273.

49 In "Libros de Hispanoamericanos y ligeras consideraciones," Martí asserts
that one America extends from the Río Bravo to Patagonia, "a Latino nation,
no longer conquering, as in Rome, but hospitable" (la nacion latina; ya no
conquistadora, como en Roma, sino hospitalaria), 8:319.

50 Foner, "Introduction," 30; Carr, "Reply to Carlos Ripoll," *New York Review of
Books* (Dec. 8, 1988); Pérez Cabrera, *Diego Vicente Tejera*, 23; on the anarchist
presence in the proindependence movement see Poyo, *"With All and For the
Good of All,"* 87–90.

51 Rodríguez, *Estudio sobre el origen*, 279, 281–82.

52 Ibid., 282.

53 Ibid., 280.

54 Saldívar, *Borderlands of Culture*; Gikandi, *Writing in Limbo*, 254; Baker, *Modernism and the Harlem Renaissance*; Schwarz, *A Master on the Periphery of
Capitalism*, 123.

55 Paz, *Children of the Mire*, 97.

56 On the inauguration of *Modermismo* in 1882, see Schulman, *Genesis del modernismo* (1966), and González and Schulman in *Martí, Darío y modernismo* (1969).

57 Schulman and Garfield dispute Octavio Paz's distancing of Latin American
modernism from Brazilian, French, and U.S. modernisms and posit modernity's origins in the New World (*Las entrañas del vacío*). Similarly, Aching,
The Politics of Spanish American Modernismo, contests the stereotype of modernism as apolitical and as different from later modernist practice.

58 Onís, "Martí y el modernismo," 157–58.

59 In addition to Aching, see Jrade, who defines modernismo as "Spanish America's first full-fledged intellectual response and challenge to modernity"
(*Modernismo, Modernity*, 137). On realism's political engagement as compared to modernism, see Larsen, *Determinations*.

60 Retamar, "José Martí: A Cuban for All Seasons," 8.

61 Shukla and Tinsman, eds., *Imagining Our Americas* (2007), based on a special
issue of *Radical History Review*; and Levander and Levine, *Hemispheric Amer-*

ican Studies. The anthologies use and elaborate on Martí's generative concept, but they devote very little time to Martí's own, voluminous, mostly untranslated, writings.

62 Manuel Sanguily, "De una entrevista," in Suárez León, *Yo conocí a Martí*, 158–59.

63 Wilson, "William Dean Howells' Unpublished Letters," 9–11.

64 Martí makes brief mention of Howells's novels, *Their Wedding Journey* (*Obras*, 21:281), *A Chance Acquaintance* (1873) (*Obras*, 12:113), and of a short story "Pordenone" (*Obras*, 21:351), but draws his judgment on realism in 1887, during the years when Martí read *Harper's* regularly and probably was familiar with Howells's "Editor's Study" (*Obras*, 11:360–61).

65 I adapt this definition of modernism from Said, "Representing the Colonized: Anthropology's Interlocutors" (*Reflections on Exile*, 293).

66 Recently both Jameson and Anderson have called attention to the neglect of Hispanic writer's role in the emergence of modernism: Anderson, *The Origins of Post-modernity*, 3; Jameson, *A Singular Modernity*, 100–101. When Jameson redresses his own privileging of the twentieth-century Latin American boom in his earlier essay entitled "Modernism and Imperialism" by calling attention to Ruben Darío's contributions, he unfortunately overlooks a well-established consensus regarding modernismo's emergence with Martí's influential prose in the 1880s, along with that of Mexican, Colombian, and Cuban contemporaries. Although Jameson mentions only Darío, Martí's prior initiation of modernist style profoundly influenced Darío and other modernist writers. Jameson criticizes the neglect of Latin American modernismo by citing two sources, both of which failed to alert him to Martí's earlier contributions: Chenot, "'Le *modernismo* hispano-americain'," and Calinescu, *Five Faces of Modernity*, 69–78.

67 Jameson, "Modernism and Imperialism," 51.

68 Martí, "El alzamiento de los trabajadores en los Estados Unidos"; I have taken the first descriptive subheading created by Martí to serve as the title of the article. Roberto Fernández Retamar notes that the date of publication is not March 29, as the text indicates, but May 29, which follows logically from the date that Martí associates with its composition: May 15, 1886. See also where Martí states in *La Opinión Nacional*, March 4, 1882: "the marvels of these times are such that neither to conceptualize or to narrate them fits in the mind of even a marvelous poet" (*Obras*, 13:48).

69 Ramos, *Divergent Modernities*, xxxv.

70 Shelley, "Defense of Poetry," quoted in Abrams, *The Mirror and the Lamp*, 333.

71 This phrase provides the title for a forthcoming anthology of Martí's and others' untranslated chronicles that I am preparing: "Small, Shimmering Works: An Anthology of Gilded Age Latino/a writing of New York and New Jersey."

72 Said, *Culture and Imperialism*, 189.

73 In the course of my research I discovered that my title *Translating Empire* also echoes that of Limón's brief and localizing response (in his "Translating Empire") to Kaplan's 2003 presidential address to the American Studies Association, on the perspective that Lieutenant General Ricardo S. Sanchez brought as commander of U.S. ground forces to the war in Iraq (Sanchez was originally from Rio Grande City, Texas). Unlike the twenty-first-century translation of empire from within the leadership of the U.S. military that depends on heavy recruitment from working-class youth of the Americas, especially Chicanos and Latinos, the late nineteenth-century Latino translations of empire that this book is concerned with assume a space after or beside the United States and its policy of preemptive military expansion.

74 My phrasing adapts Spivak's definition of "catachresis," a misuse of a word in that the sign's usage breaks with its proper sense ("Poststructuralism, Marginality, Postcoloniality and Value," 225).

75 See Derrida on the deconstructive tactic of lodging oneself within the structure in order to best dismantle it (*Writing and Difference*, 111; *Of Grammatology*, 24).

76 Martí, "The Patrick Henry of Cuba," *Equator Democrat*, November 24, 1892; summary in *Obras*, 28:341. This printed English summary offers only a guide to the original speech in English, which is not extant. It is likely that Martí spoke extemporaneously.

77 Ivan Schulman's life's work sets the United States on the course of acknowledging this debt. See especially his "La mirada desde el norte," 49.

78 Benjamin, "Paralipomena to 'On the Concept of History,'" 4:406.

79 Benjamin, "The Task of the Translator," 17–19.

80 Martí first refers to "nuestra América" (our America) in 1876 (*Obras*, 6:423), and he published several essays with this title before his most well-known and widely anthologized piece of 1891. See "Respeto a Nuestra América," *La América*, August 1883; *Obras*, 6:23–24; and "Nuestra América," *El Partido Liberal*, September 27, 1889; *Obras*, 7:349–53. See also other essays with references to "la América que no es nuestra," *Obras*, 8:35 and to "nuestras tierras latinas," 8:95; "la otra América," *Obras*, 6:34; "dos nacionalidades en América," *Obras*, 6:48–49; "las dos Américas," *Obras*, 6:53.

81 Martí's classmate José Ignacio Rodríguez, for example, adopted U.S. citizenship upon arriving in Washington, D.C., where he married and practiced law before becoming the official translator and staff member of the Bureau of American Republics. María Amparo Ruiz de Burton, the California writer, wrote about the elite class of former Mexicans who tended to intermarry with wealthy Anglos in hopes of preserving their status in opposition to both the Anglo "squatters" and their indigenous peons.

82 Miguel Tedín, Argentine delegate to the International American Monetary Commission of 1891, reflects on José Martí's profound knowledge of English and his "lack of inclination to speak it" ("José Martí," *La Nación*, December 1, 1909; reprinted in Suárez Léon, *Yo conocí a Martí*, 163). Martí describes his

English as "barbarous" in *Obras*, 22:284. He writes in a letter to Miguel Viondi of studying English with "tenacious fervor" in Madrid in 1879 (*Obras*, 20:272).

83 See Ripoll, "Martí en *The Hour*," in *Letras y huellas desconocidas*, 35–57. After 1882, Martí continued to write in English to support himself economically: according to Ivan Schulman's research, he produced under the pseudonym "M. de S." some three hundred articles in Charles Dana's *The Sun* between 1882 and 1895. See Schulman, *Genesis del modernismo*, 83.

84 Although the North American editor and publisher Charles Dana clearly admired Martí and was interested in the Cuban efforts to oust Spain, he was still capable of what Ruben Darío called a "dictatorial gesture": in Darío's meeting with Dana, Dana conducted the conversation in English and barely permitted Darío one or two monosyllables (Darío, "Charles A. Dana," 93).

85 Nietzsche, *Beyond Good and Evil*, frag. 230, 160.

86 Here I am drawing on one of Nietzsche's most influential readers, Michel Foucault, who makes this argument in *The Archeology of Knowledge*, 48.

87 Many U.S. and Latin American writers and translators who knew Martí personally —Charles (1898), Darío (1895), and Rubens (1932)—have called attention to Martí's important message for readers in the United States. Latin Americanist literary critics and translators Manuel Pedro González (*José Martí, Epic Chronicler* [1953]), Federico de Onís (Introduction [1954]), Mañach (*El Apóstal* [1950]), Mistral ("Preface" [1950]), Baralt (*Martí on the U.S.A.* [1966]), Foner ("Introduction" 1977), and Fernández Retamar ("José Martí" [1995]) have called for a U.S. readership of José Martí. U.S. Americanists and comparatists began to heed this call in the 1980s: Fountain (*José Martí and U.S. Writers* [2004]), Ballón (*Autonomía cultural* [1986]), Sommer ("Supplying Demand" [1986]), Oviedo (*La niña de Nueva York* [1989]), Belnap and Fernández (*José Martí's "Our America"* [1998]), Rodríguez-Luis (*Re-Reading José Martí* [1999]), and Montero (*José Martí* [2005]). José David Saldívar (*Border Matters* [1997], *The Dialectics of Our America* [1991]; see also 1990) especially carves out a field in which to conceptualize Martí's role in connecting the postcolonial spaces of the American borderlands. I build on this work by addressing the issues of language difference, translation, and comparative readings across migrant and diaspora traditions in the late nineteenth-century context. Other studies that have established Martí as a vibrant field for teaching and research in the United States include translations of two major Latin Americanist studies of Martí and modernity by Rotker, *The American Chronicles of José Martí* (2000; see also *Fundación de una escritura*, 1992), and Ramos, *Divergent Modernities* (2001; see also *Desencuentros de la modernidad en America Latina* [1989]); three new collections of essays: Pérez, *José Martí in the United States* (1995), Rodríguez, *José Martí y los Estados Unidos* (1998), and Font and Quiroz, *The Cuban Republic and José Martí* (2006); and studies that address Martí's relationship to the United States: Schulman, *Relecturas martianas* (1994), Rojas, *José Martí* (2001), Ballón

Aguirre, *Martí y Blaine* (2003), and Sarracino, *José Martí y el caso Cutting* (2003). Recent related studies by Gruesz (*Ambassadors of Culture* [2002]), Guerra (*The Myth of José Martí* [2005]), and Lazo (*Writing to Cuba* [2005]) address the historical periods preceding and succeeding Martí's exile in New York.

88   The editors note that the remaining three lines following this comment are unintelligible in *Obras*, 21:360. This comment nevertheless reveals Martí's uncanny foresight that his works would be published in English and French (and have been). Although it is impossible to know which target language he actually would have preferred, the notebook in which he recorded this comment also outlines a "symbolic tragedy of the present moment" and a "synthesis of American Civilization" in which Amerindian groups rise up against an "intervention from the North" (*Obras*, 21:359–60). The recurring refrain in these notes is "the Indian awakens." This comment suggests a desire for translation into a future language of America that is grounded in the continent's ancient civilizations and millennial history.

89   In a letter to Valdés Domínguez, Martí sends to his friend an article Martí published in New York concerning the Spanish government's apology for having killed by firing squad eight innocent Cuban medical students in 1871: "Blood of the Innocents," *New York Herald*, April 9, 1887; reprinted in *Obras*, 28:151–57.

90   Martí's literary translations include Helen Hunt Jackson, *Ramona*; Victor Hugo, *Mes fils* [*Mis hijos*]; Shakespeare, *Hamlet*; attempted translations of Longfellow and Poe; a lost translation of Thomas Moore's *Lalla Rooke*; and Theuriet, "Un idilio de Pascua," which appeared in *La Revista Ilustrada de Nueva York*, May 15, 1892. See de la Cuesta, *Martí, Traductor*; Suárez León, *José Martí y Víctor Hugo*; Llanes Abeijón et al., "La traducción martiana de un poema de Longfellow."

91   Moreiras points out that translation from a "less powerful" language into a "more powerful" one, as in the salient instance of my rendering of Spanish into English, puts into circulation a reductive sample of Latino/a or Latin American culture and identity (*The Exhaustion of Difference*, 21–22). For example, the travel writing of William Eleroy Curtis and Charles Dudley Warner, which I examine in chapter 5, engages in this sort of disfiguring cultural translation and prompts Martí's proposal of "infiltrative translation" to disarm these travel writings' potentially disastrous ideological effects. Although both Spanish and English languages are colonial in origin, I follow Cervantes-Rodríguez and Lutz, "Coloniality of Power," who argue that Spanish takes on the characteristics of subalternity in the historical context of Anglo-American domination of the hemisphere. I discuss this problem in my essay "Imperialism, Modernity and the Commodification of Identity."

92   Viswanathan warned about the difficulty of attempting to listen for the subaltern from within the dominant language: "How the native *actually* responds is so removed from the colonizer's representational system, his under-

standing of the meaning of events, that it enters into the realm of another history of which the latter has no comprehension or even awareness" (*Masks of Conquest*, 12). Translational thinking attempts to recognize and traverse the gap between this other history and the Anglo cultural system.

93   Porter, "What We Know That We Don't Know," 508.

94   Venuti, "The Translator's Invisibility," 181.

95   Saldívar, *The Borderlands of Culture*, 148. As is also true with regard to the ability to cross languages, the different levels of crossing borders is inflected by class, color, and gender; see Marcos's description, of travel to Mexico on foot, by bus, or by airplane, in *Our Word Is Our Weapon*, 61–67.

96   The most influential cultural theorist to associate Martí with Pan-Americanist ideas is Saldívar, *The Dialectics of Our America* (1991). Saldívar's work influenced a broad range of Americanist interpretations of Martí that describe him as an oppositional Pan-Americanist, ranging from Porter, "What We Know That We Don't Know," to essays by Pease and Gillman in Belnap and Fernández, *José Martí's "Our Americanism."* In 2001, President George W. Bush claimed Martí as a supporter of the ideas behind both Bushs' Free-Trade Area of the Americas. I do not presume that Saldívar and Bush share the same ideology. In both uses, however, "Pan-Americanist" expresses an Anglophone term from within the United States that Martí always characterizes negatively.

97   In a letter to his U.S.-born Cuban disciple Gonzalo de Quesada, October 29, 1889, Martí outlines this strategy of response to the U.S.'s "fraud or trick" (superchería) and to its enigmatic position in the Pan-American conference (*Epistolario*, 2:143).

98   A long-standing tendency to overlook or simplify opaque qualities of Martí's texts has to do with the history of Martí's translation into English. Prefaces and introductions to English versions have tended to marshal Martí for or against the current socialist government in Cuba. Revindicating the pre-Castro Martí who "belongs to the United States," Baralt situates his translation as a weapon to advocate a procapitalist position in a cold-war polemic and argues that Martí should be read as a "typical nineteenth-century liberal," and that Martí would never favor "anti-capitalist extremism" (Baralt, introduction to *Martí on the U.S.A.*, xiii). Foner, who has overseen the most extensive but also the most technically problematic translation of Martí's work, asserts that although "Martí was no socialist," he criticized human suffering under industrial capitalism (*Our America*, 30). Two recent translations of Martí clarify similarities and differences that cut across prior editorial agendas. Schulman emphasizes Martí's uncanny ability to mediate his "unstable, chaotic present" in the introduction to the *José Martí Reader*, and Roberto González Echevarría reads Martí's poetic form as a response to modernity (introduction to Esther Allen's translations). González Echevarría unfairly accuses scholarship emerging from Cuba's research institutions of "distort[ing] facts and texts to turn [Martí] into the unlikely herald of their doctrines" (x), but he rightly calls for critical alternatives to a long-standing

near-religious cult of Martí that throughout the twentieth century proved to be an obstacle to a sober and careful reading of his work. While I hope my readings contribute to desacralizing of the Martisian writ, I also recognize that any interpretation I make of Martí here in the United States must respond forthrightly to its nearly two centuries of struggle for control over the island's destiny.

99   Martí: "The geographic coincidence of living together in America does not oblige a political union, except in the mind of some degree candidate or recent graduate of high school" (*Obras*, 6:160; *Selected Writings*, 307, translation modified).

100 This phrase appears in Martí's reports on the Pan-American Conference, *Obras*, 6:56.

101 Because I share Murphy's view that American studies may miss the opportunity to imagine another America along the lines proposed by Martí if it thinks the Americas unilaterally within an Anglophone tradition, my book engages with multilingual Latin and U.S. American critical traditions. See Murphy, *Hemispheric Imaginings*, 155.

102 Martí disputes the assumed status of "native" by descendants of European immigrants who achieved wealth through taking over Mexican and indigenous land or by exploiting slaves. See my readings of U.S. popular culture in and about the U.S. West, in chapter 5.

103 Dimock, *Through Other Continents*, and Spivak, "World Systems and the Creole," both discuss "planetary" American literature.

104 Ngai, *Impossible Subjects*, 5.

105 In this same essay, Martí evokes the conditions on the "criminal ships" that brought "whipped and herded" Jewish immigrants who were fleeing, as Martí notes, the racism of Russian cities (*Obras*, 9:225). Martí knew the conditions of immigration in third-class steerage firsthand. Fermín Valdés Domínguez recalls Martí's disgust at the smell of filth and the food, which reminded him of the prison in Havana ("Ofrenda de hermano," 250–51; quoted in Ripoll, *Letras y huellas desconocidas de José Martí*, 10).

106 Rushdie, by contrast, claims that the "British Indian writer simply does not have the option of rejecting English" (*Imaginary Homelands*, 17).

107 Said, *Reflections on Exile*, 177, 184, 185.

108 See for example Martí's description of his neighbor's response to his attentions to her child: "Upon going up to my apartment I saw a little boy who reminded me of my own. I patted his head and bent down to kiss him. The little boy smiled, and the mother said to me brutally:—Get out of here, Señuritu! He is bunitu, eh? Ea! Go upstairs! And with this, my eyes were full of burning tears and my heart overflowing with a gentle perfume" (*Obras*, 21:114).

109 Martí ended up staying in New York for the long term after first trying unsuccessfully to make a life in Mexico, Guatemala, and Venezuela. His public intellectual commitment as an educator and journalist in these countries

chafed against the models of patronage employed by the modernizing generals Porfirio Díaz, Justo Rufino Barrios, and Antonio Guzmán Blanco.

110 Ramos, *Divergent Modernities*, 280, 281.

111 Besides spaces like boarding houses, migrant Latinos claimed and transformed islands within the Anglo-dominant public space of the city. For example, the Galician Mambí Félix de los Ríos recalled an encounter with Martí that led Ríos to become a volunteer in the fight for the island's independence: the meeting took place in the lobby of the Hotel América in New York where he stayed at Martí's suggestion. This space "was only for Latinos, although there was no difference in the service on each floor and one elevator served all the floors" (Ríos, "El tren de Martí," 152–53).

112 For literary depictions of Latino tropicalizations of the urban landscape, see Cotto-Thorner, *Tropicó en Manhattan*, and González, *En Nueva York y otras desgracias*; for contemporary analysis of Latino revitalization of inner cities, see Davis, *Magical Urbanism*; for a theoretical discussion of the phenomena of tropicalization, see Aparicio and Chávez-Silverman, "Introduction."

113 Mirabal, " 'Ser de aquí,' " 368, points to examples of Latino/a migrants in the late nineteenth century that show the limits and weaknesses of the "exile" model.

114 Levander and Levine offer a bibliographic history of this field's emergence, dating to 1990, in their "Introduction," 398–400, but they do not mention Sánchez's comprehensive four-volume hemispheric American literary history, *Historia comparada de las literaturas americanas*. See Kadir, "Defending America from Its Devotees," where he argues that the imperial policy of the United States demands that American studies reconceptualize its object from outside the United States using comparative methods and global perspectives.

115 Flaubert, *Bouvard and Pécuchet*, 170.

∾ CHAPTER 1

1 Fanon, *Black Skin White Masks*, 19; James, *Black Jacobins*, 402.

2 Gonzalo de Quesada y Miranda, Martí's U.S.-born Cuban disciple, identified the books on Martí's desk to have included Carlyle, Emerson, and Poe, while a Colombian friend who became close to him in 1891, Vélez, mentions Malebranche's *Treatise on Nature and Grace*, Marcus Aurelius's *Meditations*, Macaulay's *Essays*, and Marx's *Capital* as part of Martí's daily reading. The first list appears in Quesada, *Martí, periodista*, 95; the second list in Vélez, "José Martí," *Notas de Arte* (Colombia), August 15, 1910. Ripoll cites Vélez's 1910 chronicle in his introduction to Figueroa, *La verdad de la historia*, 8.

3 Saldívar, *Border Matters*; Fountain, *José Martí and U.S. Writers*; and Rodríguez, ed., *José Martí y los Estados Unidos* all lay the groundwork for thinking of Martí in these terms. Rojas, Fernández Retamar, García Marruz, Vitier,

and Marinello represent highlights and key points of tension within the Cuban Martisian tradition. Recent influential Latin Americanist interpretations include Rotker and Ramos. Ramos and Montero eloquently introduce the theme of Martí's position as a Latino in New York and constitute a point of departure for my own work.

4   Rodríguez, *Estudio histórico*. For more information on Luis Posada Carriles, see Tim Weiner, "Cuban Exile Could Test U.S. Definition of Terrorist," *New York Times*, May 9, 2005.

5   Belnap notes this affiliation in "Headbands, Hemp Sandals and Headdresses."

6   Veléz, "José Martí."

7   Said discusses this distinction between filiation and affiliation in *The World, the Text and the Critic*, 16–21.

8   James celebrates the cross-section of the globe's working class that was imprisoned with him on New York's port of entry, Ellis Island, as wielding a special firsthand knowledge of the contemporary world (*Mariners, Renegades and Castaways*, 152).

9   Martí's chronicle, "Carta de New York" with a section subtitled "un orador negro" (A Black Orator), *El Partido Liberal*, July 16, 1890, reprinted in *Otras crónicas*, 148–53, indicates that Martí knew of Du Bois, whom he describes as "a black man of energetic diction and illustrious appearance," who was selected to give Harvard's graduation speech (150).

10   Horatio Rubens, who acted as the legal representative of the Cuban Revolutionary Party beginning in 1893, remembers Martí working hours that often did not spare him time to dine: "[Marti] had an appalling capacity for hard work. He was magically sustained in his sheer nervous expenditures. His working day was 18 hours" (*Liberty*, 26, 32). Zacharie de Baralt recalls Martí as so hurried by his revolutionary tasks that he ran without his overcoat, like an arrow, into a freezing winter morning early in 1895 (in Suarez Leon, *Yo conocí a Martí*, 212).

11   Martí, *Epistolario*, 4:141.

12   Martí, "A Rafael María de Mendive," October 1869 (*Epistolario*, 1:13).

13   Burrel, "Martí," in Suarez Leon, *Yo conocí a Martí*, 29.

14   Martí published a fifteen-page prison narrative shortly after his arrival in Spain, *La República española ante la Revolución cubana*.

15   Hidalgo Paz, *Cronología*, 30.

16   Martí, *El presidio político en Cuba* (*Obras*, 1:45–75; *Selected Writings*, 9–18).

17   Gonzálo de Quesada y Miranda notes in *Martí, periodista*: "The father, believing he was protecting the future well-being of his son, was resolved to put an end to those juvenile illusions, which he fancied to be dangerous and absurd. Remembering his own difficult days as a military recruit, the uncomfortable crossing from the mother country to Cuba in a boat, the new and different life in a strange land with neither friends nor consideration, the Spanish policeman longed for a less precarious position for Pepe [Martí]. His mind was fixed on making the youth into a submissive colonial employee or

into a merchant complicit in the lucrative sale of products for an overseas market" (6).

18 For the talisman and the ring, see Tedín, "José Martí," 163; and Edelman y Pintó, "Recuerdos de Martí," 53.

19 According to Spivak's essay "Translation as Culture," 13, the process of the human subject's entry into language—of shifting from bodily objects to signs for them—may be imagined as a translation between inside and outside. The mother's body operates as a figure for the mother tongue, the original language, which must undergo translation in order to be communicable in a cultural system. Insofar as translation expresses the shift between outside and inside, between the poetic, bodily aspects that cannot be fully translated and the sign system that circulates more broadly, subjectivity arises through translation.

20 Martí, "Heredia," *El Economista Americano*, July 1888; *Obras*, 5:138.

21 Gikandi, *Maps of Englishness*, 49.

22 Martí, "Our America," *Selected Writings*, 293.

23 Contardi speaks of Martí as a "deportee" whose oblique relationship to nationality permitted him to acquire an "occult sense" of modernity and to make a home in modernist literary form, *José Martí: la lengua del destierro*, 8, 70.

24 I am suggesting that Martí's conception differs from the definition of modernity as a single, unfinished project of distinctly European origins, as articulated by Habermas in *The Philosophical Discourse of Modernity*.

25 See Ripoll's detailed research, upon which I draw here, "Martí en Nueva York: la primera visita," *Letras y huellas desconocidas*, 9–22; reprinted in Martí, *En los Estados Unidos*, 2050–57.

26 Valdés Dominguez, "Martí," 250–51; quoted in Ripoll, *Letras y huellas desconocidas*, 10. See also Martí's vivid description of the sordid conditions in which immigrants traveled to New York, which may well draw on his personal experience of steerage-class travel (*Obras*, 9:221–28).

27 *Passenger Lists of Vessels Arriving at New York*, 1820–97, microfilm roll 396: January 1–March 10, 1875 (Washington, D.C.: National Archives, 1958); quoted in Ripoll, *Letras y huellas desconocidas*, 11 n. 4.

28 González, *Crónica modernista hispanoamericana*, 82.

29 García Marruz, "Modernismo, modernidad y orbe nuevo," 17.

30 Martí, poem 30 of the *Versos sencillos* in *Poesía completa*, 255. According to Scott, *Degrees of Freedom*, 23, Africans were brought to Cuba illegally as late as 1867, and the slave trade was still in full operation in the 1850s, so it is quite possible that Martí had witnessed these scenes as a boy.

31 Martí, "Odio el mar" (I Hate the Sea), in *Selected Writings*, 66–69; *Poesía completa*, 102–4.

32 Martí envisions alliances between sons of master and man, of rich and poor, and the union of the peoples of America in *Obras*, 2:177.

33 See, for example, García-Canclini on hybridity and Cornejo-Polar on heterogeneity as an alternative to mestizaje and hybridity.

34   Glissant, *Caribbean Discourse*, 139, distinguishes an "estuary of the Americas" from the idea of a U.S.-owned American lake.

35   Martí, "A Manuel Mercado" (*Epistolario*, 5:250–51; *Selected Writings*, 347).

36   James, *Black Jacobins*, 410.

37   See for example, Toledo Sande's three-column appendix, in which it is possible to see where the translators added and suppressed passages. I refer to the abridging of a passage in which Martí alludes to the intervention of a foreign power in collusion with a former Cuban elite: "a foreign power that might unwisely offer to act as an intruder into the natural domestic struggle of the island, favoring its otiose oligarchy over the productive matrix of its population, as the French empire favored Maximilian in Mexico" ("Letter to the Editor of the *New York Herald*," 61). The English version makes no mention of this revelatory comparison of possible foreign intervention into Cuba's war of independence to the propping up of Maximilian in Mexico by the French empire. The English translation interpellates: "Cuba desires that the world may be able to carry its industries to that island, that the hidden treasures may be brought forth," thus introducing to the original the notion of external agents. The Spanish text indicates that Cubans should develop and be free to sell to whom and where they wish: "Cuba wants to be free so that men may realize on the island their full potential; so that the world may work there; and so that Cuba's hidden riches may be sold in the markets of America where her Spanish master prohibits the world from buying today" (53).

38   Martí, "Letter to the Editor of the *New York Herald*," 61.

39   I am thinking of the veterans along the U.S.-Mexico border who nearly invaded under A. K. Cutting's leadership in 1887 (see chapter 5), but I also have in mind the twentieth-century School of the Americas at Fort Benning, Georgia, renamed the Western Hemisphere Institute for Security Cooperation in 2001.

40   Published in the *New York Evening Post*, March 25, 1889; Martí's vindication, and the proannexationist pieces that prompted it, appeared in Spanish translation as a pamphlet entitled *Cuba y los Estados Unidos* (Cuba and the United States) (reprinted in *Obras*, 1:229–41).

41   Martí, "To the Director of *The Evening Post*," March 25, 1889 (*Epistolario*, 2:85). See chapter 5 for Martí's reactions to the arrogant travel writing to which he alludes here.

42   Martí, "Letter to the Editor of the *New York Herald*," 69.

43   Baldwin, *The Fire Next Time*, 20.

44   Among Martí's fragmentary writing is one that reveals Martí's damning opinion of such violations of other, less powerful nations' sovereignty: "No statesman worthy of the name will be found in this mighty republic wishing to cast on his name and on the name of his country, such a stain as the deprivation of the liberties, of the independence, the very existence of other peoples, of a free people for the mercenary interest of securing by force or

threats or of shrewdness—must rot from immoral shrewdness—the products that cannot anywhere else be sold" (*Obras*, 22:287).

45 Martí, "Escenas neoyorkinas," 215. Page references for this essay are to Cepeda's reprint. As a founding member of La Liga, Manuel de Jesús González recalls Martí lecturing on Washington, Bolívar, San Martin, Hidalgo, O'Higgins, Sucre, Páez, Morazón, and Toussaint L'Ouverture. See González, "El Maestro," 90.

46 Marx, *Eighteenth Brumaire*, 119; Martí, "Letter to Manuel Mercado (May 18, 1895)," in *Selected Writings*, 347.

47 Martí, "Escenas neoyorkinas," 217, 215.

48 I am grateful to Maria Caridad Pacheco of the Centro de Estudios Martianos for calling this publication to my attention.

49 Martí, "Letter to the Editor of the *New York Herald*," 52.

50 Foner calculates the loss as equivalent to some $58,000 dollars and three years of work in *The Spanish-Cuban American War and the Birth of American Imperialism (1896–1902)*, vol. 1, 3.

51 According to the *Diccionario de la Real Academia*, "crucero" has several meanings appropriate to this context. A crucero is also a flag-bearer or a ship designed for crossing bodies of water. Because flags and ships often represent a state or society in microcosm, this metaphor for the emerging island republic of Cuba brings to life the text's assertion of its place among the "nationalities of the planet" (orbe) ("Escenas neoyorkinas," 54).

52 Martí for example makes a note of Chinese explorer Hi-Lee, who preceded Europeans in traveling to the New World by ship (*Obras*, 21:377).

53 Martí warns in 1894: "The danger our society faces would be to concede to the entrenched colonial spirit, which will continue to sniff around the very roots of the republic, as if the government of the nation were the natural property of those who sacrifice least in her service, and who are more likely to offer her up to the foreigner" (*Obras*, 3:140).

54 See Isaacson, who translates Martí's official membership certificate in "José Martí y el Club Crepusculo."

55 "Fragmento traducido del discurso pronunciado en inglés, en el *Twilight Club*, de Nueva York, el 22 de Octubre de 1890," *El Porvenir*, October 29, 1890; reprinted in *Obras*, 28:340.

56 The publication history of Santiago's influential "O entre-lugar do discurso latinoamericano" merits a note. Santiago wrote the essay first in French, with the title "L'entre-lieu du discours latino-américain." At the suggestion of his host, Eugenio Donato, Santiago presented the lecture with the boldly Foucaultian title: "Naissance du sauvage: anthropophagie culturelle et la littérature du nouveau monde," on March 18, 1971. The State University of New York Press at Buffalo published it with the English title *Latin American Discourse: The Space-in-Between* in 1973. Finally, the text appeared in Santiago's mother tongue, Portuguese, translated by Santiago himself in a collection of essays entitled *Uma literatura nos trópicos* (1978). A retranslation of the Por-

tuguese into English appears in Santiago, *The Space In-Between*; parenthetical references in the text are to this edition.

57 Santiago, "Eça, autor de *Madame Bovary*," was first given as a lecture on April 30, 1970, at Indiana University. Santiago translated it into Portuguese for his 1978 volume of essays; it has recently been retranslated from the Portuguese by Ana Lúcia Gazzola and Gareth Williams in *The Space In-Between*, 39–52.

58 Significant exceptions are the essays in Rodríguez, ed., *José Martí y los Estados Unidos*.

59 Santiago, *The Space In-Between*, 30.

60 Ibid., 63.

61 Borges, "Pierre Menard," 45–55. Mignolo, "Human Understanding and (Latin) American Interests," 187–88, recognizes Santiago's important contribution in his discussion of transculturation and geohistorical locations.

62 Borges, "Pierre Menard," 53.

63 Ovid, quoted in "Pierre Menard," 50.

64 Borges, "Pierre Menard," 47. Menard's invisibility is augmented by a "resigned or ironic habit of propounding ideas which were the strict reverse of those he preferred" (52).

65 The U.S.-funded propaganda outlets, Radio and T.V. Martí, are two prominent examples of such institutions. See Anne Robbins, "Our Jam in Havana: This U.S. Station Does Not Rate in Cuba," *Wall Street Journal*, November 25, 1997.

66 Cervantes, *Don Quixote*, 78.

67 Borges, "Pierre Menard," 48.

68 Pratt, *Imperial Eyes*, 6.

69 While these assumptions, happily, are increasingly less well-founded, the normative position of English as the language of value in American studies persists.

70 Juan Gualberto Gómez, the Paris-born Afro-Cuban carriage maker who conspired on the island in coordination with Martí, notes that poverty provided protection for insurgents on the island: "For me, there have always been among my friends people in whom I could trust, and who because of their modest position or poverty—like mine—almost always failed to provoke the suspicion of the Spanish authorities" ("Martí y yo," 80).

71 Cervantes, *El Ingenioso Hidalgo Don Quijote de la Mancha*, 1:145; Cervantes, *Don Quixote*, 78. The passage to which Borges sends us begins with hilarious irony: "Now if any objection can be made against the truth of this history, it can only be that its narrator was an Arab—men of that nation being ready liars, though as they are so much our enemies he might be thought rather to have fallen short of the truth than to have exaggerated" (78).

72 Sommer, "José Martí, Author of Walt Whitman," 81. Whether by fate or by design, this reading follows Brazilian theorist Silviano Santiago's paraphrasing of the Borges's title, but does not include Santiago's 1970 essay "Eça, autor de *Madame Bovary*" among its extensive citations. Sommer's essay was revised and incorporated into an essay on Whitman in Latin America, "Freely

and Equally Yours, Walt Whitman," in *Proceed with Caution*, 35–60; an earlier version appeared as "Supplying Demand," 68–91. Sommer also explores the implications of Borges's "Pierre Menard" in "Plagiarized Authenticity," 130–55.

73 Santiago, *The Space In-Between*, 38.

74 Pratt, *Imperial Eyes*, 7.

75 Hardt and Negri's quotation of Martí's sentence, "Now is the time of furnaces, and only light should be seen," in the section of their "Alternatives within Empire," points to Martí's influence in the theorizing of empire without fully exploring Martí's fundamental contributions to theories of "empire" today. Martí wrote this sentence, which Ernesto "Che" Guevara quoted as an epigraph to his speech "Message to the Peoples of the World through the Tricontinental," in a letter to José Dolores Poyo, dated December 5, 1891 (*Obras*, 1:275). A phrase from Martí's sentence also became the title of an Argentine experimental film about the violence of cultural imperialism by Fernando Solanas and Octavio Getino (*La hora de los hornos*, 1966–67).

76 Martí, "Pueblos Nuevos" (New Nations), *Patria*, May 14, 1892; reprinted in *Escritos desconocidos de José Martí*, 211. I have modified the translation by Santí in " 'Our America,' the Gilded Age and the Crisis of Latin americanism," 190.

77 Schwarz, "Brazilian Culture: Nationalism by Elimination," 2–3.

78 Ibid., 6.

79 Ramos, *Divergent Modernities*, 278.

80 The work of Spivak, Young, and Scott exemplify this trend.

81 Schwarz, *A Master on the Periphery of Capitalism*, 119.

82 Ibid., 163.

83 See Lowe, "Towards a Critical Modernity"; Gilroy adapts the term "countermodernities" from Foucault, "What Is Enlightenment?" 39. See also Dussel, "Eurocentrism and Modernity," 65–66; and *El encubrimiento del otro*. This argument has a much longer history, dating to the 1930s, when O'Gorman's essay "Hegel y el moderno panamericanismo" responded to Herbert Bolton's and Lewis Hanke's arguments for a "greater America," in a debate that I discuss at length in my dissertation "American Alterities: Reading between Borders in José Martí's 'North American Scenes.' " See Fischer's critique, *Modernity Disavowed*. See also José David Saldívar's similar concept of "subaltern modernities" in Saldívar, "Foreword"; Ramos, *Divergent Modernities*, xiii; and Ramon Saldívar, *The Culture of the Borderlands*.

84 See Huntington's concern that bilingualism and other cultural retentions among Mexican and Latin American immigrants threaten the founding WASP cultural principles of the United States (*Who Are We?*, 256).

85 Mignolo, *The Idea of Latin America*, 45, 53, 97, draws on Gloria Anzaldúa and Frantz Fanon to define the colonial wound as shaping subjectivity. According to Mignolo, Martí's "Nuestra America" dissents from Latin American Creole emulation of Euope.

86 Spivak in *Other Asias* acknowledges this debt: "The title of my chapter is an

altered citation—an iteration—of Martí's" (217). By altering the citation she acknowledges the impossible "wish for a unified originary name" (220).

87 Spivak, *Death of a Discipline*, 25; Du Bois, *Souls of Black Folk*, 2.

88 Fernández Retamar, "Martí en su (tercer) mundo," in *Obras*, 2:38.

89 Spivak notes in an interview with Barlow that she spoke in Hong Kong as someone who has lived in the United States for forty-two years, although she retains an Indian passport and thus, like Martí, continues to "straddl[e] the gap" as a migrant. See Barlow, "Not Really a Properly Intellectual Response," 157; Spivak, *Other Asias*, 219.

90 Spivak, "Poststructuralism, Marginality, Postcoloniality and Value," 225.

91 In a striking parallel to C. L. R. James, Rama wrote *Transculturación* while he was teaching at the University of Maryland and wrestling with the INS over the secret grounds upon which his visa application had been denied.

92 Rama, *Transculturación narrativa en América Latina*.

93 Ibid., 20.

94 Ibid., 30.

95 See Benjamin's definition of the hack in his 1934 lecture at the Institute for the Study of Facism, "The Author as Producer," 229–30; and my essay on Martí's angst-ridden meditations on the hack in "Modernity, Imperialism and Commodification of Identity."

96 De la Campa makes a strong case for Rama's contribution of transculturation to postcolonial theory; attention paid to Bronislaw Malinowski's "discovery" of the concept while reading Ortiz often eclipses Rama's role. See *Latinamericanism*, 66–70.

97 *Imperial Eyes*, 6.

98 Rama, *Las máscaras democráticas del modernismo*, 64–65. Rama's long exile from Uruguay surely gave him an intimate knowledge of suitcases.

99 Nietzsche, *Beyond Good and Evil*, 146–47, fragment 223; and Rama, *Las máscaras democráticas del modernismo*, 80–83.

100 Williams, *The Politics of Modernism*, 45.

101 Rushdie, "Imaginary Homelands," 11. Cooppan cites Martí's passage in "W(h)ither Post-colonial Studies?" See *Obras*, 6:20; *Selected Writings*, 293.

102 Spivak, "Teaching for the Times," 484.

103 Tocqueville, *Democracy in America*, 1:28.

104 See Kanellos, *Herencia*, for numerous counterexamples.

105 Spivak, *Death of a Discipline*, 94–96.

106 Martí, "A Gonzalo de Quesada," April 1, 1895 (*Epistolario*, 5:140).

107 Spivak attributes this effect to "a literary understanding of language," which she analyzes in "Our Asias," an essay to appear in Angelina Yee's forthcoming edited collection, *Cultural Conflicts, Modernities, and Our Asias* (Hong Kong: Center for Cultural Studies, the Hong Kong University of Science and Technology), as referenced in Barlow, "Not Really a Properly Intellectual Response," 155.

∽ CHAPTER 2

1   De los Ríos, "El tren de Martí," reprinted in Suárez León, *Yo conocí a Martí*, 149.

2   Morejón, "Cuba's Deep Africanity," 938.

3   Díaz Quiñones, "Martí," 2147.

4   Vico, *The New Science*, 96.

5   Anderson, *Imagined Communities*, 43–47.

6   Robert E. Park's study *The Immigrant Press and Its Control* defends the legitimacy of controlling the immigrant press, in order to "emphasize immigrant heritages congenial to ours, . . . [and] to hasten [the immigrant press's] development into an instrument of Americanization" (448). Park claims that "foreign-language papers are frequently agencies of Americanization in spite of themselves," especially insofar as they feature advertising of American goods (449–50). Park effectively proposes to make the immigrant press into a tool of assimilation and eventual loyalty to U.S. law, order, and ideology.

7   Rodríguez notes that Martí continued to publish in *La América* in 1884 and even in 1887, but the final date and conditions of Martí's stepping down as editor of the magazine remain unknown. Martí associates the enterprise's demise with the arrival of a new editor, the Colombian Santiago Pérez Triana. Pérez Triana's role in the Latino American community in New York merits further investigation, as he was also the founding president of the Sociedad Literaria Hispanoamericana of New York. See Rodríguez's discussion of Martí's involvement with *La América* in *De las dos Américas*, 194–215.

8   See Ramos, *Desencuentros de la modernidad*, 88–89; Rotker, *American Chronicles*, 33 (note that Rotker's translators misconstrued the title of the magazine as "*Las Américas*"); Rodríguez, *De las dos Américas*, 193–215.

9   Ramos defines Martí as a translator who negotiates "conflicting discourses" including technical or nonliterary and literary writing in his analysis of "Brooklyn Bridge," *Divergent Modernities*, 175.

10 Benjamin, "The Task of the Translator," 19.

11 Silva Gruesz notes that in 1872, when Juan Manuel Mestre became a coeditor, the magazine merged with *La América Ilustrada*, and J. C. Rodrigues replaced Frank Leslie as publisher, with offices in the New York Times building (*Ambassadors of Culture*, 191).

12 José Ignacio Rodríguez served as secretary and translator to Pan-American conferences of 1889–91, and became the principal U.S. government employee of the Washington-based Bureau of American Republics. Despite Martí's admiration for Rodríguez as a young adult, Martí and Rodríguez became nemeses as the former advocate of Cuban independence increasingly made arguments for Cuban annexation to the United States. Unlike Rodríguez, the Sellén brothers, who were veterans of the Ten Years War, maintained close relations with Martí, and Francisco Sellén eventually returned to Cuba, where he died in 1907.

13 Each of these writer-translators merits further research. Essays by José Ignacio Rodríguez published in Cuba's rich collection of periodicals include "La
despedida de la nodriza africana," *El Artista* 1 (Havana, 1848): 174; "Botánica,"
Brisas de Cuba 1 (Havana, 1855): 384–87, 425–27, 461–64, 465–72; "El desem-
barco de los puritanos," *El Palenque Literario* 1 (Havana, 1877): 112–14; "Las
escuelas gratuitas," *Cuba Literaria*, 5th ser., 1 (1862): 89–95. Antonio Sellén
published over fifty translations, original poems, and articles in Cuban and
exile newspapers, including "Elegia, de Gautier, Teophile," *Cuba Literaria*,
2nd ser., 1 (1862): 242; "Literatura contemporaria: Henry Heine," *Revista
Habanera* 2 (1861): 226–31; and "Literatura extranjera: poesia de la Lituania,"
El Cesto de Flores (Havana, 1856): 33–34. Similarly, the catalogue in the José
Martí National Library in Havana lists over forty articles and translations
by Francisco Sellén, in Cuban and exile journals, which include "Goethe,
Johann Wolfgang von, 'Mi diosa,'" *Floresta Cubana* (1856): 311; "Gautier,
Theophile, 'Las Palomas,'" *El Kaleidoscopio* (1859): 32; "A una flor marchita.
Recuerdo a . . . ," *Cuba Literaria* 2 (Havana, 1862): 15–16; and "En la barricada
(Paris 1871), Poesía," *El Palenque Literario* 4 (1883): 279. Drafts of some of
them appear in Rodríguez's manuscript collection, which is housed in the
Library of Congress of the United States.
14 According to Enrique Trujillo, Enrique Piñeyro was recognized as the most
eminent literary critic of Hispanoamerica in 1892, at which time he resided in
Paris. See Trujillo Navarrete, *Album de "El Porvenir."*
15 Silva Gruesz, *Ambassadors of Culture*, 191–92.
16 This definition appears in the introductory note to an essay entitled "Cuadros
de costumbres," *El Mundo Nuevo*, June 25, 1871, 23.
17 In "Los Estados Unidos del Sud antes y despues de la guerra," *El Mundo
Nuevo*, October 10, 1871, 2, the U.S. South figures as a vice-filled culture in
need of immigration and modernization from and by the North.
18 Karl Marx parodies the attitude of the "parliamentary republic" of Louis
Bonaparte, who with avowed class terrorism considered the working-class
revolutionaries a "vile multitude," in his "Address to the General Council of
the International Working Men's Association," *The Civil War in France*, 55.
19 *El Mundo Nuevo*, May 25, 1871.
20 Martí calls the attention of readers of his "Sección constante" in *La Opinion
Nacional* (Caracas) to Tourgée's journal, noting its "Pan-Americanist" orientation (*Obras*, 23:237). In commenting on an article entitled "The Seal of 'Our
Continent,'" *Our Continent*, February 22, 1882, Martí carefully describes the
journal's masthead, in which the "O" of the title encircles one of Columbus's
ships, and the "O" of the cover encloses an Aztec hieroglyphic.
21 "Americanism vs. Anglicism," *Our Continent*, February 15, 1882, 8.
22 Henry Clay, House of Representatives, *The Annals of Congress*, 15th Cong., 1st
Sess. (December 1, 1817–April 20, 1818), 1492. See Moore's celebratory discussion of Clay's vision in "Henry Clay and Pan-Americanism."
23 See the article entitled "American English," *Our Continent*, March 15, 1882, 45.

24 "Our Name," *Our Continent*, February 15, 1882, 15.

25 "American English," *Our Continent*, March 15, 1882, 75.

26 Martí comments on the contradictions of the magazine, *Our Continent*, which denounces any European intervention in Yankee life, on the one hand, and on the other hand, features only the literati of the United States, celebrates the Quaker as the principal founding fathers, and reprints the British poetry of Oscar Wilde in its first issue. Martí aptly describes Tourgée's Yankee sentiments: "The director of the newspaper is a politician of note, who has become famous for his novel in which he defends the supremacy of the northern States in those of the South" (*Obras*, 23:237).

27 Marín, "Martí," 28–29. For Martí's attempt to counterbalance the overwhelmingly celebratory conception of Columbus in 1893, see his references to Columbus as pirate, thief, and cowardly prevaricator in "Galería de Colón" (*Obras*, 5:204). See also Martí's discussion of the Chinese arrival in the New World prior to Europeans (*Obras*, 10:267).

28 Martí's New Worldism in this early phase embraces the entire American continent, including the United States. In a notebook entry that Martí's editors date between 1878–1880, and thus during the first months of his temporary residence in New York or in Venezuela, Martí identifies a North American poet—scholars suspect Ralph Waldo Emerson—with a radical American renovation of inherited poetic forms. In this, his earliest probable reference to Emerson, Martí attacks the dulling, saccharine effect of inherited conventional poetics. His comment singles out one "venerable American" poet's ability to do away with such hackneyed, conventional verse forms (*Obras*, 21:137). Although he initially associated Emerson with an exemplary rejection of European-derived poetic forms that the majority of his northern and southern contemporaries dutifully imported and imitated, he adjusted this assessment upon taking up residence in New York, as I argue in chapter 3.

29 "Sucursal de la Agencia Americana," *La América* 1.1 (April 1882): 3.

30 See the discussion of the term "Latin race" (raza latina) in note 6 of the Preface.

31 In an advertisement for La Agencia de Turistas de New York, Martí describes the experience of desire that these widely disseminated catalogues generate in Latin America: "In leafing through catalogues of furniture, books, mechanical objects, fashion circulars, and advertisements of one thousand kinds that U.S. manufacturers distribute throughout Latin America, who has not longed to possess some of the finished products of North American industry? What mother has not longed to buy for her children some of these beautiful little outfits or elegant hats that they sell in certain times of the year, just as if she had access to the bazaars of 23rd or 14th Streets, or the discount centers of 6th Avenue or 8th Avenue?" ("La Agencia de Turistas de Nueva York," *La América*, January 1884; *Obras*, 28:218).

32 The breadth of distribution suggests this magazine's influence. According to the second issue, May 1882, *La América* had agents in thirteen cities in Cuba,

six cities in Puerto Rico, four cities in Santo Domingo, four cities in Mexico, five countries in Central America, five cities in Venezuela, five cities in Colombia, two cities in Ecuador, four cities in Peru, one city in Bolivia, three cities in Chile, three cities in Argentina, one city in Uruguay, and two cities in Spain. Cuba's central role in the distribution and reception of North American technology through this magazine and through Enrique Valiente's American Agency suggest the island's preeminence as commercial entrepôt for the emergent North American empire, during the final phases of Spanish control. A commission house is a firm that buys and sells only for customer accounts and not for its own account.

33   The agency represented some nineteen firms in Cuba alone, including, for example, Colgate and Marvin Safe Company. Martí gives this description of the cyclopean modernity that overproduces and then renders itself obsolete: "Uncle Samuel, the American nation, spins on his heels with restlessness and with signs of illness, between his wool-weaving factories that now do not sell even a quarter of what they used to—or of arms factories, mounted in order to produce much more than the armies naturally consume—of machinery factories, that because of the price of iron, or because they have produced more than is necessary, lie in lazy inactivity, dissimulating their poverty or working at a loss, sad and decomposing, like a hungry Cyclops. This is the problem: the hunger of a Cyclops" (*Obras*, 10:413). See González for a discussion of "surplus capital and peaceful conquest" in *Culture of Empire*, 19–21.

34   *La America* 1.1 (April 1882). The only extant holding of this beautifully illustrated magazine's three-year run is in the Instituto de Literatura y Lingüística in Havana, Cuba (formerly the library of the Sociedad Económica de Amigos del Pais), though the August 1882 and February 1883 issues are missing. I am grateful to Pedro Pablo Rodríguez, director of the Centro de Estudios Martianos for facilitating my access to this rare document.

35   The early issues of this magazine include translations from *The Scientific American*, *American Agriculturist*, and *The Canadian Horticulturist*. A translation of Darwin's last work, *The Formation of Vegetable Mould, through the Action of Worms*, appears early on, which Martí's notebooks indicate that he was familiar with and may have translated.

36   *La America* 1.1 (April 1882): 2.

37   *Obras*, 5:367–68; *Obras*, 20:387; *Obras*, 5:211–12. Castro-Palomino may have been the "agile and verbose" secretary of General Antonio Maceo whom Martí mentions in his war diaries of 1895 (*Obras*, 19:228). He likely returned to his wife, Lilla, and his daughter, Virginia, in Hoboken, New Jersey, where he continued to work as an editor, clerk, correspondent, and translator until his death there, sometime between 1900 and 1905. See García Pascual, *Entorno martiano*, 60–61. Castro-Palomino Sr.'s obituary in the *New York Times*, July 19, 1889, 5, indicates his relatively long residence in the United States and gives reason to believe he probably had greater fluency in English and greater relative economic stability than Martí. I am grateful to research assistance from Jeffrey González concerning Castro-Palomino in Hoboken, New Jersey.

38   In a similar spirit, the magazine's lead story in the first issue portrays a giant mobile lamp invented by a French army officer, which was exhibited at the Paris Exhibition of 1871. It endorses the expansionist—and frankly militaristic —trajectory of modernization under the auspices of European enlighten-ment. "Aparato portatíl de luz electrica" (Portable Apparatus for Electric Light), *La América* 1.1 (April 1882): 1.

39   See Martí's "Apuntes para los debates sobre 'El idealismo y el realismo en el arte,'" reprinted from manuscript notes, *Obras*, 19:409–31.

40   "Trigo y maíz" (Wheat and Corn), *La América*, June 1883; *Obras*, 28:249. See also "Una indicación de '*La América*,'" which reports on an enthusiastic reader's proposal to organize a Hispanic American Exposition where Latin American books translated into English, framed paintings, theoretical studies and little known mechanical improvements would be displayed, so that these inventions and products might not disappear without the acknowledgment they deserve (*La América*, November 1883; *Obras*, 8:362–64).

41   See for example, Martí's article on U.S. companies' violations of the "Ley de los Estados Unidos para la exportación del aceite de kerosene" (U.S. Law on the Exportation of Kerosene) (*Obras*, 28:540–41), in which he notes that violators of the 1872 law were selling thousands of gallons of inexpensive but very dangerous oil that was prone to explode because of its low grade. Eager to promote appropriate technology, *La América* identified easy-to-assemble products with simple repairs, which prove essential in the torrid climates where mechanical parts tend to corrode or break more frequently. In one article, Martí gives a detailed account of Borgner and O'Brien's especially strong fire-resistant bricks, thus sharing this technology with his readers, in "Industrias americanas: fábrica de ladrillos refractarios de retortas de arcilla" (*La América*, November 1883; *Obras*, 28:199–204).

42   Martí wrote subjective, critical reflections on Paris under the Amerindian pseudonym Anahuac during the same time that Henry James was sending chronicles to America about Paris. Martí explicitly refuses to offer an "objec-tive" report. See Martí, "Variedades de Paris," *La Revista Universal*, March 9, 1875; *Obras*, 28:15–19; García Marruz, "Un articulo desconocido de Martí."

43   Martí, "Los propósitos de '*La América*,' bajo sus nuevos proprietarios" (The Purposes of *La América* under Her New Proprietors), *La América*, January 1884; *Obras*, 8:266. The pun on the title of the magazine speaks to Martí's polemical repossessing of America through his journalism and through his political action.

44   Similarly, in Martí's view, modern poetry—as he enacts it in his "Versos libres" and his dream of writing an "Ode to the City"—must mediate and grapple with the contradictions of temporal and spatial location. In one fragment, Martí plans his ode to New York city: "ODE—to the city. A modern city, so that it will last. Gather, like fragments of marble that endure, the most marvelous characteristics of a city of these times. New York, the best type. . . . Factories. Masses. The Mills Building" (*Obras*, 22:306). In another, Martí plans to insert his times into poetic form: "In a poem: my time: factories,

industries, evils and peculiar greatness: the transformation of the old world and the preparation of a new world" (*Obras*, 18:291). Elsewhere, Martí describes the screeching of car axles as a new lyre, which in turn produces a new poetic sound (*Obras*, 9:338).

45 "Los propósitos de '*La América*,'" in *Obras*, 8:268; *Selected Writings*, 140, translation modified.

46 Martí uses these terms strategically and relatively and does not refer to essential, immutable, or scientific "racial" qualities. Rodrígo Lazo makes a similar argument regarding the use of these and other racializing terms in *Writing to Cuba*, 157.

47 *La América* featured, for example, discussions that emphasized Latin American creativity in technology and the need to disseminate it in the north (*Obras*, 8:439). Martí notes a Hispanic inventor of a patented idea, and Hispanic students who occupy places of prominence in their graduating classes. He notes that the largest train ever produced in the United States and destined to assist in the clearing out of the Panama Canal, is named "El Gobernador," a term that derives from what Martí calls "our less powerful lands" (*Obras*, 8:395). Martí notes with vehemence and irony that this train, which was large enough to carry a gigantic white circus elephant to Central America, bears a name that derives from the lands and cultures invaded by the United States. "El Gobernador" is also the title of Martí's article in *La América*, April 1884; *Obras*, 8:395–96.

48 "Repertorios, revistas y mensuarios literarios y científicos de Nueva York," *La América*, February 1884; *Obras*, 13:428–34.

49 "La América grande," *La América*, August 1883. See related discussion of the "Evening of Emerson," in chapter 3, where Martí uses the verb *entreverse* to describe reflection on his America's future amidst the din and cultural ruins of U.S. cities.

50 See "El Puente de Brooklyn," *La América*, June 1883; *Obras*, 9:423–32. See Ramos's close reading of this chronicle in *Divergent Modernities*, 160–86.

51 Martí, "Jonathan y su continente," *El Partido Liberal*, February 7, 1889; *Obras*, 12:153.

52 Some examples of this informational propaganda as a supplement to paid advertisement in the magazine include "La fábrica de locomotoras de Baldwin: Sres. Burnham, Parry, Williams & Co., Propietarios," *La America*, July 1884; *Obras*, 28:240–42; "Devoe & Co.," *La America*, June 1884; *Obras*, 28:233–39; "The American Watch Company, De Waltham," *La America*, April 1884; *Obras*, 28:228.

53 Martí compares reading bulletins of the Electric Light Company to reading the *Thousand and One Arabian Nights* ("Nuevo aparato eléctrico," *La América*, September 1883; *Obras*, 28:267–68).

54 See Edmond François Valentin About's farce, *Le nez d'un notaire* (The Notary's Nose) (1862).

55 Laraway, "José Martí and the Call of Technology," 290–301.

56 See Souvestre, *Le monde tel qu'il sera* (*The World as It Shall Be*).

57 In 1871, after his sentence for political crimes was commuted to exile rather than forced labor, Martí notes his horror at the death penalty (*Obras*, 21:22–23).

58 The metaphor of a violent stampede appears in "Repertorios, revistas y mensuarios": "the pawing of the ground, the extending of claws, the half-turns to the right and left, the denuding, the fatigue, the stampede of modern life" (*Obras*, 13:429).

59 Baudelaire, *The Painter of Modern Life*, sec. 13; Benjamin, "Paris of the Second Empire in Baudelaire," 23–25, 30, 44–50; Foucault, "What Is Enlightenment?" 40–41.

60 Baudelaire singled out Poe's "anti-American" sensibility as a basis for his interest in translating him, as Duquette notes in "The Tongue of an Archangel," 23.

61 Loynaz, *Bestiarium*, 20–21.

62 Martí's notebooks reiterate the idea of each unity being made up of hetero-geneity (*Obras*, 21:255). See Rama's discussion in "José Martí en la dialéctica de la modernidad," 133–34.

63 Derrida, *Writing and Difference*, 220.

64 Martí mentions all of these last names in the letter to Gonzalo de Quesada written in the Dominican Republic that is known as his literary testament; "A Gonzalo de Quesada," April 1, 1895 (*Epistolario*, 5:138–41).

65 Wendell Phillips's pamphlet points out the contradiction of the United States' failure to acknowledge the Cuban belligerents in order to preserve rela-tions with the Spanish monarchy. *The Cuban Question and American Policy* was published in both Spanish and English. See also Manuel de Quesada's ignored plea for recognition of the Cuban belligerents, addressed to President Ulysses S. Grant, *Manifesto de Cuba a los Estados Unidos*.

66 Cooper's phrase is quoted by Southworth, "Peter Cooper's Great Work," 28, which apppeared just after Martí's correspondence dated April 9, 1883, pub-lished June 3, 1883. Emphasis is Cooper's.

67 Phillips and other U.S. abolitionists, such as the African American Henry Highland Garnet, carried out transamerican campaigns to abolish slavery, because like Martin Robison Delany, they recognized the transnational net-works of this institution and formed parallel social movements to advocate for still enslaved Caribbean peoples. Delany declares that Africans in the Americas should all be interested in and should see the struggle of Afro-Cubans as their own ("Annexation of Cuba," 165). For evidence of Martí's endorsement of black abolitionism, see Martí's essay "Henry Garnet, notable orador negro" (Henry Garnet, Notable Black Orator) in *Obras* 13:235–36.

68 In Martí's literary testament, he requests that his portrait of Wendell Phillips be given to Tomás Estrada Palma, who was to become the party's delegate and the first president of the Cuban nation.

69 Martí used this figure several times: of Cooper, asking questions of the abyss, and of Darwin (*Obras*, 15:38): "with a fixed gaze and a scrutinizing hand, not eaten by a yearning to know what the future holds, he bends over the earth

with a serene spirit, to ask from whence it comes. . . . As far as the construction of worlds, there is no better way to know how to do it than by asking the worlds themselves" (*Obras*, 15: 380).

70 Martí's laudatory articles on abolitionist orator Wendell Phillips in *La América* and *La Nación* of February 1884 evince a desire to unmask, by directly addressing the U.S. reading public, the United States' betrayal of the revolutionary legacy. In May 1884, as editor of *La América*, Martí informs readers that Curtis (the former editor of *Putnam's*, *Harper's*, and *Harper's Bazaar*, who also knew Ralph Emerson, Nathaniel Hawthorne, and Margaret Fuller) had sent a note of appreciation for *La América's* article on Wendell Phillips, published a few months earlier. Martí translated and published part of this note from Curtis: "It is with great pleasure that I note that your appreciation of the great orator in no way differs from my own" (*Obras*, 13:55). This comment on a heretofore lost literary exchange indicates that Martí's work on Phillips circulated outside the Hispanophone community (perhaps at Martí's initiative) in established North American intellectual circles, and may well have inspired Curtis while he was preparing his April 1884 eulogy for Phillips. See Curtis, *Wendell Phillips*.

71 "These books have been my vice and my only luxury," Martí wrote to Gonzalo de Quesada at the end of his life (*Epistolario*, 5:141). Martí's notebooks are full of titles of books that he planned to purchase. In the midst of his final preparations for the clandestine entry into eastern Cuba, Martí records in the last entry of his Haitian diary the generosity of a "black gentleman of Haiti," the bookseller who sent him the books he requested but refused to accept his two-peso note (*Selected Writings*, 380). See also Martí's note to himself: "Book to buy:—'Modern Thinkers'—by Van Buren Denslow—Ll. D. Sketches of Eminents [*sic*] philosophers" (*Obras*, 21:224).

72 Although Martí managed to visit Paris, meet Sarah Bernhardt, and translate a Victor Hugo short story into Spanish after earning his law degree in Spain, his travels largely conformed to the political exigencies of deportations due to his anticolonial commitments and limited funds.

73 Fabian, *Time and the Other*.

74 *La República* (Honduras), July 1886; *Obras*, 8:21.

75 "Longfellow," *La Opinion Nacional* (Venezuela), March 22, 1882; *Obras*, 13:226.

76 See Rojas's study of Martí's "impossible books," in *José Martí*, 109, in which he notes that Martí aspired to authorship on the scale of a Victor Hugo, a Goethe, or—I might add—an Emerson.

77 Rojas, "La republica escrita," 56.

78 Some of these notes were published in an essay entitled "Curiosidades americanas," reprinted in *En los Estados Unidos*, 1112–13.

79 Gonzalo de Quesada, "Martí y su amor a los libros," in *Facetas de Martí*, 202.

80 Jitrik usefully observes that the rise of the author cannot be separated from the role of the bourgeois individual in capitalist culture. See his "El sistema modernista (o rubendariano)," 55.

81   In addition to Martí's earlier account, I draw these terms from R. R. Bowker's seventh installment on "The Printed Book," which appeared in a series entitled "Great American Industries," *Harper's Monthly Magazine*, July 1887, 165–88. Martí explicitly mentions with disdain the novels edited by *Harper's*, calling them spineless and imitative (*Obras*, 13:424).

82   Martí, "Libros americanos," *La América*, November 1883; *Obras*, 13:422.

83   In Ripoll's research into the 1884 conflict between Martí, Antonio Maceo, and Máximo Gómez, he notes that General Gómez responded in his diary to Martí's criticism: "In addition to the miserable shortage of material resources, there is, and it is worse, a scarcity of manly resolution—there is even a fear of a revolutionary dictatorship. Could there be a more ingenuous or effeminate way of thinking? Is it possible to cite a revolution that has not had its dictatorship?" (Ripoll, *Diario*, 193; quoted in *José Martí: letras y huellas desconocidas*, 94).

84   Martí, *Epistolario*, 1:280.

85   Hidalgo Paz, *Jose Martí, 1853–1895*, 107–9.

86   After Porfirio Díaz took power, Martí fled México. Several of Martí's letters to Manuel Mercado from this period between 1876 and 1878 refer to Martí's economic instability. Martí struggles economically in the United States, but his greater mental anguish derives from the fact that he can earn sufficient wages as a writer only by living in the United States. This limitation is due in part to economic conditions and political censorship of the press in Latin American countries where he lived. For example, Martí notes in a letter to Mercado of March 8, 1878: "In elemental countries, in the intellectual sphere, the life of virtuous men is very difficult" (*Epistolario*, 1:113). See Martí's verse account of a printing press in Mexico: "De noche, en la imprenta" (At Night, at the Press), *Poesía completa*, 394.

87   Rafael Castro-Palomino Jr., *Cuentos de hoy y mañana*. This rare booklet is available in the Library of Congress. Ripoll discusses this pamphlet in *José Martí, the United States and the Marxist Interpretation of Cuban History*, 68.

88   Castro-Palomino, "Algunas palabras del autor" (Some Words from the Author), *Cuentos de hoy y mañana*, ii.

89   As evidence of Castro-Palomino's leadership roles, I rely on correspondence from Enrique Trujillo to José Ignacio Rodriguez, November 20, 1889 (Manuscript Division, Library of Congress). Cf. Enrique López Mesa, *La comunidad cubana de New York*, 40. It would have complicated Martí's position at *La América* to alienate the well-established Castro-Palomino and to generate a schism in the relatively small and heterogeneous migrant community in New York. After penning this prologue and during his association with *La América*, Martí, the professionally trained but economically precarious recent migrant, assumed the presidency of a charitable organization (the Cuban Aid Society) that secretly raised war funds for the independence movement in 1884. Shortly thereafter, Martí broke off ties with Gómez. But, three years later when Martí returned to proindependence organizing in 1887, he shared a speaker's platform with Castro-Palomino. Their collaboration, although

not intimate, continued in a spirit of respect and without apparent conflict through 1895 (*Obras*, 20:500). As Martí took leadership roles in revolutionary organizations, Castro-Palomino continued to maintain his position in the same organizations. Martí and Castro-Palomino cosigned a letter to Civil War veteran leader Juan Arnao and to General Máximo Gómez in late 1887 to invite the latter to be the military leader of a reactivated proindependence movement that the exiles proposed to fund. Castro-Palomino's name appears on the masthead as assistant editor of Enrique Trujillo's *El Avisador Hispano-Americano* (Spanish-American Advisor), a newspaper to which Martí was occasionally invited to contribute. Castro-Palomino was the secretary of the Sociedad Literary Hispano-Americana in 1888 and in 1893, and Martí served as president of this literary society in 1890–91. The evenings of poetry, lectures, and dancing sponsored by this organization brought the two into regular contact, suggests Sotero Figueroa's note on Castro Palomino's reading at a December 12, 1890, *velada* (evening of poetry, speeches, and dance) (*Obras*, 20:376). The leadership of the Sociedad Literaria Hispano-Americana appears also in the Spanish-language edition of *Godoy's Guide World's Fair Chicago*, 40–41.

90   For example, Castro-Palomino is not included in the comprehensive *Diccionario de Literatura Cubana*.

91   The Venezuelan printer Manuel M. Hernández crafted an exquisite volume for the poetry. A rare copy of this volume may be found in the Sala Cubana in Havana's Biblioteca Nacional "José Martí."

92   The 1871 revolution, in his view, began as a reasonable movement for municipal self-government against the centralized power of Versailles, but the masses spoiled this effort: "afterwards, the desperate masses overflowed and took advantage of the movement" (*Cuentos*, 50). Similarly, the mine with its four hundred workers and fifty professionals degenerated quickly, from singing the Marseillaise together in early scenes of the story to violent fighting amongst the workers. La Chimère and Unthunlich decide to reinstate their ownership of the mine after the collective government instituted "free love" (31), or more precisely, the rule that women should exist as common rather than private property. At that point, the members of the experiment began to kill one other or abandon the enterprise.

93   Castro-Palomino cites Spencer, *Illustrations of Universal Progress*; quoted 14 n. 1.

94   Castro-Palomino cites Jules Verne by name and mentions also Jacolliot, *Voyage au pays de la Liberté*, and Laboulaye (pseud. René Lefebvre), *Paris in America*. Jacolliot's novel parallels Castro-Palomino's second story in that it spotlights a repentent ex-Communard who comes to embrace North American capitalism and liberty. Similarly, Laboulaye, the intellectual sire of the Statue of Liberty project and France's leading interpreter of the United States, abhorred the Paris Commune of 1871, according to his biographer. See Gray, *Interpreting American Democracy in France*, 37. Laboulaye's widely translated and immensely popular *Paris en Amérique* (1863) relocates Paris to a New

England village in which a free press, education, and liberal institutions protect against revolutions in the Jacobin tradition.

95 In 1884, Martí reviewed Spencer's critique of socialism, *The Coming Slavery*, in which Spencer attributes poverty to the indolence and moral worthlessness of the socially marginal: "They [i.e., the impoverished] are simply good-for-nothings, who in one way or other live on the good-for-somethings, vagrants and sots, criminals and those on the way to crime, youths who are burdens on hard-worked parents, men who appropriate the wages of their wives, fellows who share the gains of prostitutes. . . . There is a notion . . . that all social suffering is removable and that it is the duty of somebody or other to remove it. Both of these beliefs are false" (Spencer, *The Coming Slavery*, 1–2).

96 Castro-Palomino may be the implied nibbler in this short and sharp critique, entitled simply "Spencer," in which Martí likens the British sociologist to a "mendrugo roído de ratones" (a crust of bread gnawed by rats) (*Obras*, 15:388).

97 See Fischer's discussion in *Modernity Disavowed*, 107–28, of the Cuban Creole elite's views of black insurgents and its disavowal of radical antislavery in the early nineteenth century.

98 This debate was republished in a rare volume edited by Trujillo, *La evolución y la revolución* (17), available in the Sala Cubana at Havana's Biblioteca Nacional "José Martí."

99 Yúdice emphasizes the role of imperialism as a constitutive framework for avant-garde aesthetics. He also criticizes the northern European Atlantic bias that has limited awareness of avant-garde responses to imperialism beyond Europe ("Rethinking the Theory of the Avant-Garde from the Periphery," 59).

100 For a similar critique of copies of colonial education, see "Educación de aula" (Classroom Education), *La América*, October 1883; *Obras*, 28:195. Martí proposes to his readers books that every modern person should read in "Hechos Notables" (Notable Facts), *La América*, September 1883; *Obras*, 8:413). He endorses strong tactics to persuade workers to learn to read and write in "Fuera perezosos" (No lazies allowed), *La América*, January 1884; *Obras*, 28:221. Martí takes the wisdom of a worker as a most useful source for imagining how to transform the colonial educational system in "Sabio consejo de un trabajador" (Wise Words from a Worker), *La América*, November 1883; *Obras*, 28:212–13. Martí praises the decision of Tomás Suri to learn to read and write at the age of seventy, so as to be able to meet the requirements for achieving the third order, as stipulated by his African secret society. Suri's decision to pursue literacy coincided with a move on the part of the secret society to set up a school and to stop playing African drums. Martí neither endorses nor condemns this abandonment of drums in the society; his chronicle focuses on the society's valuing of literacy for its members ("Una orden secreta de africanos," *Patria*, April 1, 1893; *Obras*, 5:324–25).

101 Macaulay, "Indian Education," 729.

102   Williams, *Keywords*, 76–82.
103   As Ramos demonstrates in his cultural history of the nineteenth century, the modern Latin(o/a) American intellectual (unlike the Latin American *letrado*) increasingly occupied a position outside the state. See his *Divergent Modernities*, 64; quotation of Martí is from *Obras*, 21:369.
104   Spivak's comments on my reading of this passage in 1999 illuminate my discussion of it here. See her discussion of this passage in *Death of a Discipline*, 94–96.

❧ CHAPTER 3

1   Montero, *José Martí*, 117.
2   Lizaso, "Emerson visto por Martí," 35; Montero, *José Martí*, 106. See Shuler, "José Martí, su crítica de algunos escritores norteamericanos," 175.
3   Buell, *Emerson*, 350 n. 36.
4   Ballón Aquirre quotes in extenso the American Adam passage from Emerson's journal no fewer than three times in *Autonomía cultural americana: Emerson y Martí*, 16, 137, 179.
5   I refer to Roy Harvey Pearce, Perry Miller, and R. W. B. Lewis. Both Rama, "La dialéctica de la modernidad en José Martí," 150, and Molloy, "His America, Our America" (265) comment on how Martí articulates the fantasy of self-generation without mediation of the female body, in terms reminiscent of the British romantics: "Nació en sí mismo. Hijo de sí mismo" (He gave birth to himself. Son of himself)" (*Obras*, 21:162).
6   See Díaz Ruiz, "Presentación," *Lecturas norteamericanas de José Martí*, xii; Fountain, *José Martí and U.S. Writers*, discusses Emerson and Martí as "kindred souls," 27.
7   Santiago, "Latin American Discourse: The Space In-Between," and "Eça, autor de *Madame Bovary*," in *The Space In-Between*, 31, 63.
8   Ballón Aguirre, *Autonomia cultural americana*, 66. John Englekirk also claims Martí's prominent role in establishing Emerson's influence in Latin America in "Notes on Emerson in Latin America."
9   Martí, *Obras*, 21:163.
10   Emerson's essay "John Brown" attributes the origin of Brown's values to his being a "fair specimen of the best stock in New England" (Emerson, *Complete Works*, 11:261).
11   Emerson, *Complete Works*, 11:91; quoted in Dallal, "American Imperialism UnManifest," 56.
12   Emerson, "Fate," in *Conduct of Life*, 36; quoted in Sommer, "A Vindication of Double Consciousness," 167.
13   Emerson, "Race," in *English Traits*, 50. See Castillo, " 'The Best of Nations?' " 100–111.
14   Emerson, "The Poet," and "Nature," in *Selections from Ralph Waldo Emerson*, 236, 44.

15 Emerson, *Complete Works*, 1:346, 366. On Emerson and the Young Americans, see Harrison, *Agent of Empire*, 27–51.

16 See Martí's "Escenas neoyorkinas," in which a collectivity of "those from
below . . . advance shoulder to shoulder"; the quotation is from page 215 of
Cepeda's article in *Santiago*.

17 Emerson, "The Poet," in *Selections*, 240, 224.

18 Emerson, "The Transcendentalist," in *Selections*, 195.

19 Emerson, "Self Reliance," in *Selections*, 152, 148, 155; "The American Scholar,"
in *Selections*, 75.

20 Martí's editor at *La Nación* of Buenos Aires, Bartolomé Mitre y Vedía, explains his need to censor Martí's criticism of the United States in order to sell
newspapers. See "De Bartolomé Mitre y Vedía," in Garcia Pascual, ed., *José
Martí: destinatorio*, 109. In 1882, Martí's editor explicitly threatened to censor
any aspect of Martí's correspondence that "might suggest erroneously that
the newspaper had opened a campaign of denouncing the United States as a
political body, social entity or commercial center, by ignoring the great les-
sons that this immense grouping of men gives every day to humanity" (*Martí
destinatorio*, 108). Because of his dependence on freelance journalism as
a principle source of income, he would have no choice but to mask his criticism or divergence from U.S. authors accordingly.

21 Borges, "On William Beckford's *Vathek*," in *Selected Non-Fictions*, 239.

22 Memmi, *Colonizer and the Colonized*, 123.

23 Zeno Gandia, "Cómo conocí a un caudillo," 213–14.

24 I am referring to the master/slave dialectic in Hegel's *Phenomenology of
Mind*, which in Gilroy's gloss is "relational" (53). The Russian-born, Berlin-
educated Alexandre Kojève developed the notion of the master's disavowed
dependence upon the slave in his 1933–39 lecture series on Hegel (*Introduction to the Reading of Hegel*). Sibylle Fischer's gloss on Kojève's reading of
Hegel shows how translation plays a key role in Kojève's theorizing of relation
as revolution. Although Fischer privileges revolutionary antislavery projects
over the cultural vernaculars studied by Gilroy, both aim to bring into focus
the slave's perspective on modernity in their reinterpretations of Hegel. I am
interested in how the divide between colonizer and colonized structures
consciousness and gives rise to a revolutionary translation. See Gilroy, *The
Black Atlantic*, 51–58; Fischer, *Modernity Disavowed*, 24–38; Kojève, *Introduction to the Reading of Hegel*, 29–30.

25 Emerson, "The Transcendentalist," *Selections*, 204; "double consciousness"
reappears in the late essay "Fate," *Selections*, 351.

26 Saldívar notes Ramos's role in constructing a U.S. Latino/a migratory parallel
to the Black Atlantic in his preface, xxiv–xxviii; Gillman emphasizes Martí's
parallel construction of a transnational Americanism in "*Ramona* in 'Our
America,'" 105–6. My reading builds upon Ramos's argument and differs from Gillman's in that it shows Martí's explicit critique of the pan-
Americanism that has emerged from the United States.

27 Martí's October 1884 letter to Máximo Gómez reminded the general that it was impossible to run a civil society like a military camp. See discussion in chapter 2. In November 1884, Martí rhetorically asks his Mexican confidante, Manuel Mercado: "Why topple a foreign tyranny in order to put in its place, with all the prestige of a triumph, our own?" (*Epistolario*, 1:285).

28 This figure also appears among Martí's typed fragments, *Obras*, 22:306.

29 See Adams on Martí's Coney Island in *Side Show, USA*.

30 Emerson, "Nature," in *Essays*, 3:196; quoted in Martí, *Obras*, 21:408 and 19:370.

31 See Martí's alarmed observation of "what may be the gravest change that the United States has experienced since the war": "It involves nothing less than the preparation of a pacific and decisive occupation of Central America and of adjacent islands through a system of commerical treaties and other conventions" (*La Nación*, February 22, 1885; reprinted in *Obras*, 8:87).

32 Giles, "The Parallel Worlds of José Martí," 187.

33 Giles: "In this light, Martí's most pressing concern seems to be not so much imperialism, but globalization and displacement. As someone who was himself traversing national frontiers continually and who felt most at home, paradoxically, among exiles, Martí employed contradiction not as a method merely of subversion but as an engaged way of intimating how every situation and social organization could be looked at from a different point of view. . . . If the most compelling part of Emerson's writing is its plausibility, its willing accommodation of neoplatonic ideas to a politics of everyday experience, perhaps the most striking aspect of Martí's life and work is its ultimate impossibility" ("The Parallel Worlds of José Martí," 187–88).

34 See references to and descriptions of the "Evening of Emerson" at *Obras*, 21:387 and in *Obras*, 22:323.

35 Ballón, *Autonomía cultural*, 31; Fountain, *José Martí and U.S. Writers*, 41; Montero, *José Martí*, 121.

36 Martí, *Obras*, 22:323; Montero, *José Martí*, 121; translation modified.

37 Although García Pascual indicates that this letter has never been recovered, Martí received several notes of appreciation from Adriano Páez, Colombian literary critic and the editor of *La Pluma* of Bogotá and other magazines. The first accompanied his publication of a translation of Martí's unsigned essay, originally written in French for Dana's *The Sun*. A Spanish-language translation appeared in *El Repertorio Colombiano* (February 1881) and was reprinted also in Caracas. Only in September 1881 does Páez discover and reveal Martí to be the author of the essay, after having mistakenly identified the author as a Catalunyan revolutionary in exile. In December 1881, Páez published a prefatory note identifying the author as "one of the most brilliant writers of our time." The note was designed to accompany Martí's first publication in *La Nación* of Buenos Aires, July 15, 1882, reprinted in Rodríguez and Fernández Retamar's edition of Martí's journalism (Martí, *En los Estados Unidos*, 203–6). According to Ripoll, Martí's writing had sparked a sensation among Latin

American readers even earlier, in response to a Spanish-language translation of an essay on modern Spanish poetry, which appeared to great acclaim in Bogota. See Ripoll, *Letras y huellas desconocidas,* 73.

38   Martí's selection of these particular memories has motivated speculation that María Mantilla may have been his biological daughter; see Oviedo, *La niña de Nueva York.*

39   García Pascual credits *El Porvenir,* November 22, 1897, for this information about the donation of Páez's library (*Entorno martiano,* 189).

40   Martí, *En los Estados Unidos,* 204.

41   Martí, in "Emerson," asks: "Why must a man envy the sacred sufferings, the childbearing of a woman? For a thought, in the agony of its birth and the joy that follows, is a child" (*Selected Writings,* 120).

42   Borges characterizes Thomas Carlyle's romantic theory in *On Heroes, Hero-Worship and the Heroic in History* as fascist. Although he notes Emerson's debts to Carlyle, he insists on the vast distance between Emerson's monism and Carlyle's "plebian vices and virtues" (see his prologue to his translation of Emerson's *Representative Men,* in *Selected Non-Fictions,* 414, 417).

43   Gould, *Grand Old Party,* 63.

44   Morgan, *From Hayes to McKinley,* 56.

45   "Carta de Nueva York," *La Opinión Nacional* (Venezuela), March 22, 1882; *Obras,* 9:270.

46   *La Nación,* November 6, 1884; *Obras,* 10:93–98.

47   *La Nación,* February 22, 1885; *Obras,* 8:90.

48   Kinzer analyzes the tactics of U.S.-backed overthrow of local regimes by a combination of economic policies, military shows of force, and diplomatic pressure, beginning with the overthrow of the local government by descendants of U.S. missionaries in Hawaii in *Overthrow.*

49   *La América,* April 1884; *Obras,* 13:265.

50   Muzzey, *James G. Blaine,* 206.

51   Already in 1875, the United States implemented such a reciprocity treaty in Hawaii, which Great Britain described as a "virtual protectorate" that removed any "diplomatic obstacle to our annexation of Hawaii in case the sentiment there and in the U.S. should favor such a move" (Muzzey, *James G. Blaine,* 392).

52   Crapol, *James G. Blaine,* 79.

53   See Blaine's address to the U.S. Senate, "Chinese Immigration to the Pacific Slope," on the Republican endorsement of the view of Chinese inadmissability to citizenship rights (*Political Discussions,* 222). This volume also contains essays on the "Peace Congress," on the need to arbitrate in the Peru-Chile conflict, and on the defense of "impartial" suffrage principally as a means to undermine Democratic party power—not white supremacy—in the South.

54   See Blaine's arguments that the Chinese represent a "form of servile corruption, in some aspects more revolting and corrupting than African slavery. . . .

Practical statesmanship would suggest that the Government of the United states should avoid the increase of race troubles, and that nothing but sheer recklessness will force upon the American population of the Pacific slope the odious contamination of the lowest grade of the Chinese race. It may be attempted; but, in my judgment, it will lead to direful results, in which violence and murders and massacres will be terribly frequent" (*Political Discussions*, 239, 245).

55   See Tchen's reading of Nast's ambivalent "defense" of the Chinese against Blaine's rabid anti-Chinese attacks (Tchen, *New York before Chinatown*, 205–6). Blaine's argument in the "Letter to the Editor of the *New York Tribune*" on the corrupting influence of Chinese immigration of February 1879, came to define the bipartisan consensus on the Chinese as fundamentally alien and threatening to Anglo-Saxon Christian values. Tchen reveals a surprising kinship between abolitionist Wendell Phillips and Blaine, citing Phillips's racist epithets toward the Chinese (*New York before Chinatown*, 184). It is important to note in this context that Wendell Phillips directed racist epithets toward the Chinese even as he defended Cuba. See Tchen, *New York before Chinatown*, 184. Martí deeply admired Phillips, but managed not to reproduce this sort of anti-Asian rhetoric.

56   According to the *New York Herald* of January 27, 1882, two of Blaine's ministers to Peru, Mr. Hurlbut and Mr. Christiancy, proposed various means for annexing or making a protectorate of Peru. See Ballón's thorough critique of the United States' meddling in the War of the Pacific in *Martí y Blaine*.

57   Martí reiterates his critique of electoral fraud and describes in detail a scene in which a party employee "purchases" a vote in the November 1884 elections (*Obras*, 10:110).

58   *The Nation* observes that Blaine floated the idea of buying Cuba for $500 million as a vote-gaining strategy (June 26, 1884, 537); quoted in Ballón (*Martí y Blaine*, 270). Martí brags about throwing out of his house a representative of Blaine's electoral campaign who approached him about purchasing the Cuban immigrant vote in the 1884 presidential election for $4,000, according to Carlos A. Aldao's anecdote in Suárez Léon, *Yo conocí a Martí*, 14.

59   For an analysis of Johannes Keppler's 1880 centerfold illustration "The Chinese Invasion," in *Puck's* magazine, which helped cast the bipartisan racial stereotype of Chinese as alien invaders, see Tchen, *New York before Chinatown*, 214–18.

60   Aldrey, "A Martí, May 3, 1882," in García Pascual, *Martí destinatorio*, 98. Rotker notes that the Venezuelan dictator who forced Martí to leave Venezuela in 1881, Antonio Guzmán Blanco, frequently published letters on his views of the nation in *La Opinión Nacional* (Rotker, *The American Chronicles of José Martí*, 37). By way of explanation for terminating his relationship with *La Opinión Nacional*, Martí writes to a friend in Venezuela: "In the last letter from J. Luis [Aldrey's son], it seemed to me that this consideration came

dangerously close to disappearing" ("A Diego Jugo Ramirez," June 10, 1882, *Epistolario*, 1:232).

61   As Rotker notes, Martí's "Emerson" has "little to do with the institutionalized and recognized 'Mr. Emerson' " who dominated the pages of the press during this period (*The American Chronicles of José Martí*, 94). Rotker's reading emphasizes Martí's affinity with Emerson's disdain for the materialist mainstream of U.S. society.

62   Fernández Retamar quotes Bolívar's dictate that "our nation is not European nor North American, but a mixture of Africa and America rather than an emanation of Europe," in *Calibán and Other Essays*, 10.

63   Lee, *The City in Which I Love You*, 83. See Partridge, "The Politics of Ethnic Authorship," 103–26.

64   Emerson, *The Journal and Miscellaneous Notebooks*, 378–79; quoted in Partridge, "The Politics of Ethnic Authorship," 116.

65   In *Autonomía cultural americana* Ballón describes Emerson's and Martí's interactions taking place in "un océano común bilingüe" (a common bilingual ocean) (54) or an "entretejido bilingüe" (bilingual web) (33), figures cited by Montero as demonstrating "necessary" intellectual preparation for Martí's war diaries and for his death in Dos Rios, in Montero's chapter entitled "Bilingual Emerson" (*José Martí*, 105). I agree that this labor of translation and linguistic border crossing enables Martí to focus his revolutionary project. Yet Ballón's influential images of free-flowing bilingualism, expressed in the repeated claim that "it doesn't matter whether it is in English or Spanish" (*Autonomía cultural americana*, 172, 175), minimize cultural tensions, linguistic hierarchies, and untranslatability across the barriers that divide these borderlands. In raising language as a site of disjuncture rather than free flow, I do not propose to return to a neat division of the two Americas. José David Saldívar remapped this idea in "Nuestra América's Borders" and reminds the reader of the presence of Hispanophone America in the North even as Anglophone America was stretching south and westward.

66   Wald, "Fabulous Shadows," 839.

67   Pratt, "Modernity and Periphery," 21–47.

68   Young writes: "Deconstruction, we might say, therefore, has itself been a form of cultural and intellectual decolonization, exposing the double intention separating the rational method from its truth" ("Deconstruction and the Postcolonial," 199).

69   De Man, "Review of Harold Bloom's *Anxiety of Influence*," 273.

70   Cheah, *Spectral Nationality*, 129. Spivak has long suggested Martí represents a postcolonial critic, as I discuss in chapter 1.

71   Ballón, *Lecturas norteamericanas*, 23.

72   Banquo prefigures the late Martí, who is plagued by betrayals within and from outside of the party. See Rodríguez's discussion of these references to Banquo in *De las dos Américas*, 233–75.

73   Derrida, *Specters of Marx*, 105.

74   Martí's assessment of Emerson seems less radical, given that it resonates with
      a lecture on Emerson given by his fellow Cuban philosopher José Enrique
      Varona in 1884. As a leader in the Partido Autonomista (Autonomist Party),
      an adherent of local self-government within a Spanish colonial framework,
      and an opponent of the proindependence movement until after 1895, Varona
      affiliated culturally as a European in terms of race, language, and political
      theory. Unlike Martí, Varona uncritically placed all of America in a tutelary
      relationship to Europe ("Emerson," in *Seis conferencias*, 151); nevertheless
      Martí concurs with Varona's estimation of Emerson insofar as he "puts into
      relief, with singular perspicuity, the infrequently visible similarities between
      the idealist Emerson and his market-oriented nation" (*Economista Ameri-
      cano*, January 1888; *Obras*, 5:119). See Varona, "Emerson," originally read
      before the Nuevo Liceo de la Habana, March 13, 1884, published in *Seis
      conferencias*, 149–85.

75   Tzu-kuei, "Rock Springs Incident," 358.

76   Two versions of this manuscript on Emerson, both partially typewritten,
      appear among Martí's fragmentary writing. The least complete has been
      reprinted in *Obras*, 22:156–57. A longer version that repeats the exact phras-
      ing of the former appears along with Martí's other philosophical fragments
      in *Obras*, 19:353–56.

77   Fountain reaches this conclusion in the only other scholarly analysis of the
      manuscript fragments for Martí's second essay on Emerson of which I am
      aware: "At one point the Cuban writer seemed almost envious of Emerson's
      independence in his work. . . . [I]n writing about the way ideas come to a
      writer, Martí could have been referring to himself as well as to Emerson" (*José
      Martí and U.S. Writers*, 36).

78   I am not thinking here of the dialectal, minor-language remaking of the
      major in a strict sense, for Martí only rarely writes in English and rarely
      writes in creolized patois to capture other minor uses of language. See De-
      leuze and Guattari, *A Thousand Plateaus*, 104–5.

79   See, for example, the image of the man who buries his sword in the depths of
      the sun in "Maestros ambulantes," *Obras*, 8:290.

80   Allen and I both revise Baralt's translation, which appears in *Martí on the
      U.S.A.*, 40–52. Baralt attaches the pen to a writer (who does not appear in the
      original) and inserts the phrase "as if he," which both genders and eliminates
      the trembling movement of the verb. This interpretation makes Martí's sen-
      tence into a seeming choice between a writer and a priest. In my translation, I
      have tried to preserve the undecidability of the synecdoche *pen*, so that the
      pen could be the figure for the sinning minister at the same time that it is a
      figure for the writer of the chronicle. Martí seems to be alluding to Emerson's
      own vacillation between pastor and writer, which ultimately led him to aban-
      don the ministry in 1838, on the occasion of his "Harvard Divinity School
      Address." This ambiguity pertains also to Martí, whose iconization as a na-
      tional hero, apostle, and a martyr has often covered over his contributions as

a writer, and who himself sees writing as shameful and effeminate compared to heroic action. Yet Martí manages to zigzag between words and actions without ever abandoning either.

81   A condor is a South American hawk of religious significance in Andean culture. Its strength and size (it has a ten-foot wingspan) enable it to fly in the high Andes.

82   In "Civilization," Emerson creates the figure that Martí revises here: "Hitch your wagon to a star. Let us not fag in paltry works which serve our pot and bag alone" (*Collected Writings*, 7:30).

83   Such desire concurs with his investment in patriarchal procreation and in prescriptions for feminine subordination within a heterosexual matrix. See Beauregard, "La feminización del héroe moderno," 135–51.

84   James, "Ralph Waldo Emerson," 596.

85   Juan Clemente Zenea's poem, "En Greenwood," identifies his exilic postwar grief with the absence of "[his] plaintive palms" (557). In an 1878 letter to José Joaquin Palma, Martí denounces the colonial tendency to imitate foreign models: "Trocar las palmas por los fresnos . . . vale tanto, ¡oh, amigo mío! tanto como apostatar" (To trade palms for ash trees . . . is the same, my friend, the same as becoming an apostate) (*Obras*, 5:96). In his "Discurso en Cayo Hueso," December 25, 1891, Martí describes the Cuban people as "displaying its nostalgia in cold lands that lack the fire of our sun and the dignity of our palm" (*Obras*, 4:289).

86   Figueredo, "Recuerdos de Marti," 137–57.

87   Bacon, "Of Friendship," 141.

88   Vélez, "José Martí."

89   Brook Thomas suggests that Josiah Strong's bestselling expansionist and evangelical tract *Our Country* (1885) may be another possible source for Martí's phrase ("Turner, Martí, a Home on the Range," 285). However, Martí's far more significant engagement with Emerson's work points to the latter, who uses the identical phrase in "Fate," *Selections*, 331.

ᢙ CHAPTER 4

1   Stuart Merrill was a young visitor from France at the event as he describes in "Walt Whitman," 55–57. "A Tribute from a Poet: Walt Whitman Tells of Lincoln's Death," *New York Times*, April 15, 1887, 1, gives details about the event and reprints Whitman's speech.

2   Whitman, "Song of Myself," sec. 52, in *Leaves of Grass*, 77. The two epigraphs to this chapter that are by Whitman come, respectively, from his articles "Mr. Gallantin's Plan of Settling our Dispute with Mexico" *Brooklyn Daily Eagle*, December 2, 1847 (quoted in Garza, *Walt Whitman*, 193); and "The Spanish American Republics," *Brooklyn Daily Eagle*, September 10, 1858 (reprinted in Whitman, *I Sit and Look Out*, 162–63).

3   Marti's earliest commentary on Whitman demonstrates his wariness toward

Whitman's unencumbered expansiveness: "the effrontery of his rhymes, the daring of his thoughts and the easy self-confidence—verge on a lack of respect" ("Sección constante," *La Opinión Nacional*, November 15, 1881; *Obras*, 23:81).

4   Martí, "El poeta Walt Whitman," in *Obras*, 13:141; *Selected Writings*, 193, translation modified.

5   The appearance of a kind of divinity is repeated in the opening paragraph of an unattributed news report of the period: "The poet, without honor as some say, in his own country, was the picture of wise old age, and as he read his story to some of the best wits and minds of the time, he was not unlike a seer with his disciples at his feet." See "The Grey Bard's Lecture."

6   "The Good Gray Poet Is White Now." According to Reynolds's description of the reception, "Whitman was seated on a plush chair of red velvet. Known and unknown bigwigs strutted by, greeting him enthusiastically" (*Walt Whitman's America*, 555).

7   Justin Kaplan summarizes the event and claims Martí attended the lecture (*Walt Whitman*, 29). Scholars at the Centro de Estudios Martianos doubt Kaplan's claim. See *Anuario del Centro de Estudios Martianos* 4 (1981): 431–32.

8   Whitman's comment to John Johnston, as quoted in Basler's introduction to *Memoranda During the War and Death of Abraham Lincoln*, 40.

9   Martí, *Obras*, 13:140 and 13:138; *Selected Writings*, 192, 190, emphasis added. The latter quotation translates Whitman in "Song of Myself," sec. 24: "Divine am I inside and out; and I make holy whatever I touch or am touch'd from" (*Leaves of Grass*, 46).

10 As a student of law and philosophy in the 1870s, Martí observed the corruption and calculation of the United States and imagined an alternative nation of his own that would oppose the death penalty and yet would never go to mass (*Obras*, 21:16). By the late 1880s, Martí's secularism had already met with explicit criticism from the Venezuelan editor Fausto Teodoro Aldrey, who also discouraged Martí's acerbic observations about the United States. Aldrey's prescription illuminates Martí's choice to portray Whitman as a priest: "it is recommended that your future writings have an Ultramontanes flavor. After all, it is the general character of this little land; the so-called priests *dominate, impose, and flay* and it is inconvenient to clash with them" (*José Martí: Destinatorio*, 76, emphasis in the original). Martí writes his essay on Walt Whitman for Argentine and Mexican newspapers several years later, but most likely without having forgotten this pressure to tailor his writing to the church's powerful agenda.

11 Said, *Reflections on Exile*, 131; *Musical Elaborations*, 55.

12 I refer to Sarmiento's letter to Paul Groussac, a French journalist and man of letters, in which he invites Groussac to translate Martí, but also criticizes Martí for his southern perspective. Sarmiento also chastises Martí: "I want Martí to give us less Martí, less Latino, less Spaniard and less South American and a bit more of the Yankee, the new model of modern man, the son of that

liberty whose colossal statue he has made us admire next to that hanging bridge in Brooklyn, which appears to resemble Niágara falls in size" (quoted in Gonzálo de Quesada, *Martí periodista*, 107).

13 Martí, "A la raiz," *Patria*, August 26, 1893; reprinted in *Obras*, 2:377–80.

14 Ibid., 379.

15 Martí, "El poeta Walt Whitman," (*Obras*, 13:139; *Selected Writings*, 191). I diverge from Allen's translation, which renders the pronoun "él" as Whitman—"he looks upon that which suffers inside him"—and thus encloses the drama of this suffering inside that North American poet.

16 Molloy's careful reading notes that Martí's translation of "City of Orgies" from the Calamus section leaves out the line that would require the translator to acknowledge his own homoerotic desire: "Offering response to my own" (*Leaves of Grass*, 107).

17 Martí's cryptic annotation is fascinating as a gloss on the image that lies at the heart of "El poeta Walt Whitman" of an imperial Whitman atop a Roman chariot. In Martí's essay "Alea jacta est," published December 7, 1876, the final month of his residence in Mexico (*Obras*, crit. ed., 2:283–84), Martí ascribes to the Mexican dictator Porfirio Díaz the characteristics of Julius Caesar and describes him as a smiling statue floating on a sea of Mexican blood. Martí contrasts Porfirio's leadership style to his vision, in which the revolution has a broad base among the people.

18 Behdad, *A Forgetful Nation*, 94.

19 Mir, "Contracanto a Walt Whitman," *Hay un País en el mundo*, 52.

20 Whitman, "As I Ebb'd with Ocean of Life," in *Leaves of Grass*, 213.

21 Pratt, "Modernity and Periphery," 26.

22 Whitman, "A Broadway Pageant," sec. 2, in *Leaves of Grass*, 204–5.

23 Ibid., 204; Martí, *Obras*, 13:132.

24 It is notable that Martí does not refer to Whitman as an American poet in this quotation from an essay entitled "Nuestra América," published in *El Partido Liberal* (September 27, 1889), two years before his more famous essay of that title; reprinted in *Obras*, 7:351. See also Martí's comment in "El poeta Walt Whitman": "Words of our language can be found on every page in his book" (*Obras*, 13:142; *Selected Writings*, 194).

25 Alegría, *Walt Whitman in Hispánoamerica*. Similarly, Manuel Gomez-Reinoso concludes his brief reading of Martí on Whitman by stating: "All that [Martí] said of the North American prophet and *Leaves of Grass*, and all that he said of himself, leads us to affirm that they are one in spirit" ("Martí and Whitman," 47–48). For similar conclusions, see Doumont, "Notas para un estudio del 'Whitman' de José Martí," and Garcia, "José Martí y Walt Whitman," 75–88.

26 Alegría, "Whitman in Spain and Latin America," 73. As Enrico Mario Santí points out in "The Accidental Tourist," Alegría initiated the study of Whitman in Berkeley, in the heyday of the Pan-Americanist ideology of the Roosevelt era. Eugene Bolton packed lecture halls with courses whose themes echoed his

1932 presidential address to the American Historical Association, "The Epic of Greater America," and defended Pan-American unity as a resource to aid the United States in its fight against the Axis powers. In presenting this thesis at the State Department in 1939, Bolton advocated training of students in inter-American studies for jobs at the Organization of American States, administering the "good neighbor policy."

27 For a critique of this sublimationist reading, see Quiroga and Salessi, "Errata sobre la erótica," 123–34.

28 Whitman's prudish contemporaries pushed Whitman's poetry to the margins of U.S. literature due to its "cynical instances of indecent exposure" and vowed to "keep *Leaves of Grass* out of the way of students." The first phrase is from Oliver Wendell Holmes, "Over the Teacups," 388–89; James Russell Lowell made the second comment in M. A. DeWolfe Howe, ed., *New Letters of James Russell Lowell* (New York: Harper, 1932): 115–16, quoted in Kaplan, *Walt Whitman*, 26. Complying with this groundswell of moral judgment, Emerson timidly retracted his initial letter of affirmation and tried unsuccessfully to coax Whitman to revise an overly frank discussion of heterosexual acts in "The Children of Adam" section (Reynolds, *Walt Whitman's America*, 540).

29 Binns elaborates on Whitman's mistress and illegitimate mulatto offspring in *A Life of Walt Whitman*, 51; Kaplan, *Walt Whitman*, 19, 142–43. Holloway reads Whitman's frankness and militancy about sexuality as primarily informed by a "desire to increase the number of happy marriages by teaching a modern pride in oneself" (introduction to *I Sit and Look Out*, 30).

30 Martí's translation even enriches the text with graphic sexuality. Whitman's onanistic invitation to the sea to "dash" him with "amorous wet" appears in Spanish as the more explicitly sexual "penetrate me" (penétreme) (Whitman, *Complete Poetry and Selected Prose*, 40; *Obras*, 13:138). See Molloy on Martí's homoerotic fascination and paranoid heterosexism in "His America, Our America."

31 Erkkila and Grossman's volume of essays that emerged out of the Whitman Centennial Celebration in 1992, *Breaking Bounds*, portrays Whitman's poetics, public presentation, and ideology as transgressive, liberating, and emblematic of the unrealized potential of the United States. Kaplan's biography reveals Whitman's tortured self-policing in response to an emergent criminalization of homosexuality. In the decades before the emergence of the "homosexual" as a criminalized subject in public discourse with Oscar Wilde's 1895 "sodomy" trials, Whitman alters or destroys manuscripts, changes "him" to "her" in his journals or substitutes a code for a man's initials as protection against the panic of literary historians.

32 Moon, *Disseminating Whitman*, 13.

33 Smith, *Virgin Land*, and Anderson, *The Imperial Self*.

34 Whitman, "1855 Preface," *Leaves of Grass*, iv; quoted in Moon, *Disseminating Whitman*, 116. Harrison notes Whitman's association with O'Sullivan, who

coined the phrase "manifest destiny" and was a founding member of the annexationist movement that mimicked the rhetoric of Emerson's essay, the "Young Americans" (*Agent of Empire*, 48). O'Sullivan introduced the phrase "manifest destiny" in his essay "The Great Nation of Futurity," published in *United States Magazine and Democratic Review*, where Whitman also published stories and sketches.

35 Smith, *Virgin Land*, 48; quoted in Moon, *Disseminating Whitman*, 114.

36 Arac's provocative critique of nationalist American studies ("Whitman and the Problems of the Vernacular") constitutes a significant exception to the nationalist frame of much Whitman criticism up until recently. Arac criticizes Anglo-Saxonist and nationalist definitions of the vernacular in U.S. American studies so as to include Whitman along with Baudelaire as developers of a mixed literary journalism that Arac calls "city-writing," a form that also encompasses Martí's *crónicas* and his poetry about the city in the 1880s and 1890s. Arac's redefinition of the vernacular to recover its association with the subjugated and alien suggests a connection between Martí and Baudelaire as innovators in writing against capitalist modernity (see Contardi, *Jose Martí*). It also reconfirms yet another distinction between Martí and Whitman, as the latter wrote "with his age" (Arac, 58) while the former critically opposed its dominant trends.

37 Folsom, "Lucifer and Ethiopia," 45–95.

38 Whitman, *Prose Works*, 2:762; Traubel, *With Walt Whitman in Camden*, 2:283; both quoted in González, *Walt Whitman*, 177–79; and in Reynolds, *Walt Whitman*, 136. The passages excavated by González have become part of the textual basis for the acknowledgment of Whitman's formative role in elaborating manifest destiny beyond momentary "lapses" (Reynolds, *Walt Whitman's America*, 35; Reynolds, *Walt Whitman*, 147).

39 Whitman, "The Gem of the Antilles," *Brooklyn Daily Times*, January 12, 1858; reprinted in *I Sit and Look Out*, 157.

40 González, *Walt Whitman*, 10; Gruesz, *Ambassadors of Culture*, 108. González notes in his preface that he received a ten-month dissertation fellowship from the U.S. embassy in Mexico and spent additional years pursuing his research just across the U.S.-Mexico border in Laredo, Texas. Despite this support and the publication of his research, González's reading has remained marginal compared to Alegría's assessment of Whitman and his readers in Latin America.

41 Whitman, "Our Territory on the Pacific," *Brooklyn Daily Eagle*, July 7, 1846; reprinted in González, *Walt Whitman*, 183–84.

42 Similarly, when asked about L'Ouverture, the Haitian paragon of self-government and liberty, Whitman reportedly replied to his friend John Burroughs: 'I don't believe that nigger existed" (Burroughs, quoted in Barrus, *Whitman and Burroughs*, 335.

43 Editorials in the *New York Tribune* questioned the U.S. policy of military aggression toward Mexico, and thus incited the *Brooklyn Daily Eagle* editor's

militarism. To suggest that the United States may have wrongly initiated the war, or that it may have been abusing its power or revealing its corruption in administering the conquered territory constitutes "treason," according to Whitman's "Abetting the Enemy," *Brooklyn Daily Eagle*, November 16, 1846; reprinted in González, *Walt Whitman*, 185–86. In matters of war, wrote Whitman, "the past is the past. As to the origin of the war, and the way it came to be a war, and all that, argument and discussion would be both useless and unprofitable" (Whitman, "Mr. Gallantin's Plan of Settling Our Dispute with Mexico," *Brooklyn Daily Eagle*, December 2, 1847; quoted in González, *Walt Whitman*, 193).

44   Whitman, "The Most Bloodless War Ever Known," *Brooklyn Daily Eagle*, December 16, 1846; quoted in González, *Walt Whitman*, 187, emphasis in the original.

45   Whitman argues that the middle passage and enslavement signified an improvement for Africans: "had their forefathers remained in Africa, and their birth occurred there, they would now be roaming Krumen or Ashanteemen, wild, filthy, paganistic—not residents of a land of light, and bearing their share, to some extent, in all its civilizations," in "[Slavery]," *Brooklyn Daily Times*, July 17, 1857; reprinted in *Uncollected Poetry and Prose*, 2:9. Martí specifically contests this line of argument in his rewriting of Sarmiento's portrayal (in Sarmiento, *Civilización y barbarié*) of Latin America as barbarian and in need of European civilization. Ramos examines Martí's criticism of Sarmiento's identification with European civilization rather than with American civilizations (*Divergent Modernities*, 251–67).

46   Whitman, "Prohibition of Colored Persons," in *I Sit and Look Out*, 90.

47   González, *Walt Whitman*, 10.

48   "Democracy," says González, "would be the political instrument that the United States would perfect and through which it would be able to dominate the world. . . . The love of friends, 'adhesiveness,' would realize this union, and would become the basis of a de-secularized religion, in which the poet occupies the role of the high priest" (*Walt Whitman*, 169).

49   Whitman reserved a special disgust for "foreigners who scream in their horrible language," a comment that condemns the foreigners' bilingualism and disapproves of their failure to completely assimilate to Anglo culture (*Walt Whitman of the New York Aurora*, 57–58).

50   Whitman, "Song of Myself," sec. 16, in *Leaves of Grass*, 39; Martí, *Obras*, 13:138.

51   Martí appraised Stedman as a "good critic" in 1882 (*Obras*, 9:18) and again in his 1883 essay on Emerson (*Obras*, 13:13). Mayorga Rivas also mentions Stedman's essay on Whitman in "El poeta Walt Whitman," 7.

52   According to an article from *Patria* from 1893, Whitman is the "most Creole poet" ("poeta más criollo") of the United States, who in conversation with bus fare collectors, gathers wisdom from the book of life. See Martí, "Juntos, y el secretario," *Patria*, May 21, 1892; reprinted in *Obras*, 1:451.

53   Stedman, "Walt Whitman," 56, 53, 62.

54   Darío recollects the impact of Martí's prose in his autobiography: "He wrote a profuse prose full of vitality and color, plasticity and music. Through it shined the cultivation of the Spanish classics and knowledge of all literatures ancient and modern. And above all, was the spirit of an elevated and marvelous poet" (*La vida de Ruben Darío*, reprinted in Suárez León, *Yo conocí a Martí*, 42).

55   When Darío visited New York in the 1890s, he encountered Martí in the midst of heated revolutionary activities. Martí invited Darío to attend his lecture, and brought him up on stage to a burst of applause. They had embraced each other in a dark hallway, right before Martí was to begin his lecture: "I found myself in the arms of a small-bodied man, with an illuminated face, and a voice sweet yet dominating at the same time, which said to me just one word: 'Son!' " In a mysterious act of recognition, Martí recorded Darío's affinity as a reader and writer and bound himself to the younger man with a metaphor that Martí had previously loaded with erotic feeling in his *Ismaelillo* (1882).

56   Darió, "Walt Whitman," in *Azul*, 175.

57   In a neglected contribution to comparative American literary history, resonantly entitled "Las relaciones literarias interamericanas," the erudite and encyclopedic Mexican scholar Ernesto Mejía Sánchez quotes from Manuel Pedro González's unpublished manuscript of 1953 on page 53. The essay provides convincing evidence that Darío had read Whitman's verse, either in Francisco Gavidia's 1889 translations, which appeared in *El repertorio salvadoreño* or in a volume of verses that he brought with him to Chile in 1886. Mejía Sánchez has transformed our knowledge of Martí by excavating numerous chronicles from *El Partido Liberal* that had not been previously collected. In keeping with his meticulous standards, he cites the Chilean A. Mauret Caamaño's remembrances of the period: "In the final days of a sumptuous tropical spring, in or near the year 1886, a young Nicaraguan [i.e., Darío] embarked for Chile. In this traveler's desk drawer was his only treasure: a book of Walt Whitman's verses" (*Ramillete de reflexiones* [Madrid: 1917], quoted in "Las relaciones literarias interamericanas," 54. Mejía Sánchez's article also correctly locates the other of Darío's sources: Sarracine's essay appeared in *La nouvelle revue*, May 1, 1888, and was reprinted in Sarracine's essay collection *La renaissance de la poésie anglaise (1789–1889)* [Paris: Perrin, 1889]. Harrison S. Morris translated it into English and Whitman's literary executors republished it as *In re Walt Whitman*, ed. Horace Traubel et al. (Philadelphia: D. McKay, 1893). Darío's poem indicates that the response of Latin American readers to Whitman's imperialism was not to stop reading Whitman's poetry or prose, but to study his powerful rhetoric all the more carefully.

58   Darío, "José Martí," 197–99.

59   Henríquez Ureña quotes Darío's 1888 definition of modernism in relation to a Mexican writer, Ricardo Contreras, quoted in *Breve historia de modernismo*, 156–57.

60   Schulman and González, *Martí, Darío y el modernismo*.

61   Menéndez y Pelayo, *Historia de la poesía hispanoamericana*, 285.

62   Although Derusha and Acereda trace Darío's articulation of Hispanoamerican alarm to 1898 in their translators' introduction to Darío, *Songs of Life and
Hope*, 31, Darío's sonnet raises this concern earlier, in conjunction with the
negotiation of trade agreements by the United States with Latin American
countries, and with the disturbing Pan-American conference of 1889–90,
which Darío read about in Martí's chronicles.

63   Mayorga Rivas, "El poeta Walt Whitman," 7–8. In his comments on Darío,
Martí, and Whitman, Mejía Sánchez lamented that *La Revista Ilustrada de
Nueva York* had been lost to posterity. However, Schulman and Chamberlain
recovered and preserved a nearly complete run of *La Revista Ilustrada*, which
is available in the Special Collections of the University of Kansas. See their
biographical comment on Mayorga Rivas, in which they describe him as
contributing seventy-three signed articles—more than any other contributor.
They also note his national classification as Salvadoran, because during his
lengthy residence in that country he founded the biweekly *Repertorio del
diario de El Salvador* and compiled a major anthology of Salvadoran poetry,
the three-volume *Guirnalda salvadoreña*. See Schulman and Chamberlain, *La
Revista Ilustrada de Nueva York*, 26–27.

64   In this fascinating fragmentary letter of May 1894, Martí acknowledges the
death of Mayorga Rivas's brother José María, who was also a poet. The letter
calls for laurels and flags for the young revolutionary poet, who died in a
battle on behalf of Honduran independence. The letter also fatefully projects
Martí's forthcoming death not only for the "solitary star," but also on behalf of "our peoples," whom Martí describes in terms that foreshadow the
Peruvian writer, José Maria Arguedas: "la América indohispánica" (Indo-
Hispanic America) (*Epistolario*, 4:135–36).

65   Exactly one year later, Martí's revised version of that speech appeared as
"Nuestra América" in the *La Revista Ilustrada de Nueva York* (January 1891).

66   On the connection between journalism and verse, see Grossman, *Reconstituting the American Renaissance*, 86.

67   Whitman, "Prohibition of Colored Persons," *Brooklyn Daily Times*, May 6,
1858; reprinted in *I Sit and Look Out*, 89–90.

68   Whitman, "Song of Myself," in *Leaves of Grass*, 48.

69   Ibid., 64.

70   Martí, "Cartas de Martí: Estados Unidos de América," *La Nación*, September
15, 1883; reprinted in *Anuario del Centro de Estudios Martianos* 24 (2001): 8.

71   Whitman, "Starting from Paumanok," in *Leaves of Grass*, 16.

72   Whitman, "A Broadway Pageant," in *Leaves of Grass*, 205.

73   Whitman, "Mr. Gallantin's Plan of Settling Our Dispute with Mexico";
quoted in González, *Walt Whitman*, 193–94.

74   Benjamin, *Illuminations*, 261.

75   Whitman, "Democratic Vistas," in *Leaves of Grass*, 770.

76   *Obras*, 13:136; *Selected Writings*, 188, translation modified. The last sentence

roughly translates Whitman's verse: "I laugh at what you call dissolution, / And I know the amplitude of time" ("Song of Myself," in *Leaves of Grass*, 42).

77   In addition to the views expressed in my epigraphs to this section, Whitman affirms the need for slavery in Brazil and Cuba, "for Cuba and Brazils [*sic*] are not the West." In the same article, we learn that slavery continues to exist in Cuba, Brazil, and the United States because of divine mandate: "Has not God seen fit to make [the slave], and leave him so?" in Whitman, "[Slavery]," *Brooklyn Daily Times*, July 17, 1857; reprinted in *Uncollected Walt Whitman*, 2:9–10; quoted in Garza, *Walt Whitman*, 176.

78   Benjamin, *Illuminations*, 263.

79   "Song of Myself," in *Leaves of Grass*, 64, "On women fit for conception I start bigger and nimbler babes. / (This day I am jetting the stuff of far more arrogant republics.)."

80   According to the Real Academia Española, the phrase "dejar caer" may connote a dissembled intention, an unexpected introduction, or a careless insinuation. A fragment in a notebook of Martí's from around 1886 suggests that he saw Whitman's beard as a figure for the tendency of Whitman's verse to be caught up in its own circular movement: "The verse of W. Whitman—of the beard in which he gets rolled up" (*Obras*, 21:279).

81   The earliest version of Sommer's essay appeared as "Supplying Demand," 68–91. A slightly different version appeared as "José Martí, Author of Walt Whitman," 77–90. A third, revised version was incorporated into a chapter entitled "Freely and Equally Yours, Walt Whitman," in *Proceed with Caution*, 35–60.

82   Sommer, "Supplying Demand," 86, 68, 78–79, 74–75.

83   Ibid., 83.

84   Sommer, "José Martí," 82.

85   Ibid., 78.

86   One frustrated reader who has engaged Whitman and Martí, George B. Handley, swerves abruptly toward a conclusion that rejects Sommer's indeterminate open-endedness and instead implies that Martí endorses Whitman's views: "Must we always assume that Martí is winking, or would it be arguable that Whitman's naïve imperialism seduced Martí?" ("On Reading South in the New World," 536). In response to Sommer, Handley delivers a Martí firmly allied with Whitman's agenda of Free Soil extension, "ambivalen[t] about Latin America itself" and complicit with Whitman's antipathy toward *mestizaje*, toward the U.S. South, and toward black citizenship. Collapsing the distinction between Whitman and Martí, Handley's essay supposes that "their [Whitman's and Martí's] views for possibilities for solidarity across national lines are compromised in significant ways, not least of which is the disappearance of the U.S. South and other such liminal spaces that challenge the racial, geographical and national boundaries upon which such inter-American solidarity is premised" (527). Handley rightly observes Whitman's investment in a "whites only" model of continental expansion that

resonates with contemporary demands for more secure borders to keep Latin "foreigners" out of America. Handley notes serious problems with the U.S.-led Pan-Americanism that builds on Whitman's mid-century rhetoric. I differ from Handley insofar as he depicts Martí as unaware of the spaces between U.S. empire and European-identified Creole nationalism, for this is the very location from which Martí challenges Whitman's vision of America. See Handley, "On Reading South in the New World," 521–44.

87 José Limón coined the phrase "the greater South" at the "Bastards of Imperialism: 1848, 1898, 1998" conference held at Stanford University in 1998, and he continues to conduct research in this area, according to his comments in Schmidt, "Concluding Roundtable," 171–94. Martí's interesting comparison of the U.S. South—as an independent entity with its spirit and its problems, especially the threat of the North's conquistador-style impositions—and Latin America in 1890 prefigures similarities between these regions that U.S. scholars continue to explore (*Obras*, 13:395). See Cohn's teasing-out of these interconnections with regard to the high modernist period in *History and Memory in the Two Souths* and *Look Away!*

88 Whitman, "Democratic Vistas," in *The Portable Walt Whitman*, "In vain do we march with unprecedented strides to empire so colossal, outvying the antique, beyond Alexander's, beyond the proudest sway of Rome," 404.

89 The parallel between Grady's rhetoric and Martí's is striking. In a speech to the Bay State Club of Boston, 1889, Grady complains about how a state funeral for a southerner featured only imported manufactures: "The South didn't furnish a thing on the earth for that funeral but the corpse and the hole in the ground. There they put him away and the clods rattled down on his coffin, and they buried him in a New York coat and a Boston pair of shoes and a pair of breeches form Chicago and a shirt from Cincinnati, leaving him nothing to carry into the next world with him to remind him of the country in which he lived, and for which he fought for four years, but the chill of blood in his veins and the marrow in his bones" (*The New South*, 133). See Martí's similar complaint in "Nuestra América" (*Obras*, 6:20; *Selected Writings*, 293). In 1890, Martí gives a caveat about Grady's failure to respond adequately to the depredations of southern whites upon blacks before he applauds the lifelong efforts of Grady as an orator and newspaper editor who denounced the plundering by northern capitalists of the U.S. South (*Obras*, 13:390–99).

90 See for example, Ripley's travel narrative *From Flag to Flag*. Of these North American residents of Cuba, Martí notes in 1871: "Look at the martyrs of our revolution. Tell me if there is among them one North American" (*Obras*, 21:16).

91 See the manuscript, not included in the *Obras*, in which Martí answers the rhetorical question: "Would you marry your daughter to a black man?" Martí answers in the affirmative, explaining that "the fusion of the two races has happened and it will continue to happen. . . . The marriages between the two races will begin among those whose work keeps them together. Those who sit together every day at the same desk are more likely to choose their compañera there." In "Para los Escenas," 2, Martí's logic does not acknowledge

female desire, but it does indict the hypocrisy of relegating interracial sex to illegitimacy. Although Ferrer's earlier essay "Silence of the Patriots" makes an astute challenge to the effects of Martí's anti-racist doctrine during the first republic, her book envisions the redefinition of Cuban nationalism to accommodate an anti-racist critique articulated by Martí and his corevolutionaries in the 1880s and 1890s. See her *Insurgent Cuba*, 234.

92 See Pérez, *On Becoming Cuban*, 91.

93 The Martiniquan philosopher and novelist Edouard Glissant includes Martí in a list of Caribbean heroes celebrated at the 1976 meeting of Carifesta (*Caribbean Discourse*, 67). Glissant honors Martí by using his terminology, especially a reference to "Other America" (115) in the sense Martí gave to that phrase in 1889: to speak of Americas that are not the United States (*Obras*, 6:34). For a reading that emphasizes Martí's identification with French Caribbean *creolité*, see Plummer's essay on the parallels between Martí and the Haitian antiracist Antenor Firmin, "Firmin and Martí at the Intersection of Pan-Americanism and Pan-Africanism," 210–27. For connections between Martí, Kamau Brathwaite, and Glissant's Caribbean aesthetics, see Dalleo, "Another 'Our America.' "

94 Martí's translators have not helped to remedy this logic. The 1999 *José Martí Reader* translates Martí's historicizing conception of ethnic, racial, and national difference—"la consecuencia peculiar de la distinta agrupación histórica" as "the peculiar outcome of the different historical groups" (172). This translation reduces the substantive formed from the verb *agrupar* to the immobile plural noun "groups." It replaces the complicated relationship between the historical clustering of people and the consequences of such clustering with a teleological, or perhaps even theological "outcome." Preventing Martí's text from unsettling the long-standing tradition of attaching raced subjects to particular places or circumscribing their futures to nefarious "outcomes" in the United States, the translation actually makes Martí into a spokesperson for the very tendency to construct rigid racial categories that his writing repeatedly denounces. Randall's republished translation of "The Truth about the United States" reads: "It is a fact that in those Southern states of the American Union where there were Negro slaves, those Negroes were predominantly as arrogant, shiftless, helpless and merciless as the sons of Cuba would be under conditions of slavery" (*José Martí Reader*, 173). The translation radically revises the subject of the largest subject-verb clause of the sentence: "El carácter dominante" (the dominant character) becomes "those Negroes." The interpretation ascribes the dominant character of the U.S. South to the *dominated* group. Yet the adjectives more logically suggest the characteristics of slave *owners* rather than those who sweated under their lash. This translation erroneously inserts the Cuban into the position of the racist who blames blackness for white racism. Allen's 2002 translation remedies this problem by using the phrase "the predominant character of the people" rather than "Negroes."

95 Whitman, "Children of Adam," sec. 7, in *Leaves of Grass*, 85.

96   Sánchez-Eppler, *Touching Liberty*, 57.

97   Both Gruesz and Grossman study the racial implications of Whitman's so-
     journ in New Orleans and draw conclusions about Whitman's reliance upon
     figures of slavery. See Grossman, *Reconstituting the American Renaissance*,
     162–83, and Gruesz, *Ambassadors of Culture*, 134–35.

98   "Song of Myself," sec. 21, in *Leaves of Grass*, 45.

99   Menéndez y Pelayo, *Historia de la poesía hispanoamericana*, 258. My trans-
     lation follows Sibylle Fischer's in *Modernity Disavowed*, 92. See her analysis
     of Plácido's excoriation by white Cuban Creole national discourse in which
     Plácido figures as an abject remnant of Haiti-inspired radical antislavery, the
     suppression of which became a condition for the emergence of the integra-
     tionist Creole nation. Despite his failure to grapple with Toussaint L'Ouver-
     ture's significance in the history of American revolutions, Martí comments
     on the lack of knowledge about Aponte's conspiration (*Obras*, 22:247); he
     planned to write a book on Plácido comparing him to Horace, as a revolu-
     tionary poet (*Obras*, 18:281) and he collaborated in a commemorative "Noche
     de Plácido" (*Obras*, 20:359) along with members of the Afro-Antillian
     League. All of this suggests his divergence from a frankly colonial attitude
     toward Plácido and toward black antislavery insurgency.

100 J. A. Saco, quoted in Delany, "Annexation of Cuba," 164.

101 *Congressional Globe*, 29th Cong., 2nd Sess., App., 317–18, quoted in Reynolds,
     Walt Whitman's America, 123.

102 David Wilmot, "Speech of Mr. Wilmot of Pennsylvania, Restriction of Slav-
     ery in the New Territories, House of Representatives, August 3, 1848," re-
     printed in *The National Era* 2, August 17, 1848, 145.

103 Both Martí and Whitman may be indebted to Emerson for this comparison
     of the "sovereign" and his "valet," which Emerson makes in "Self Reliance," in
     Selections, 164. Mark Twain sets up a similar comparison between the mas-
     ter and his valet, except that the two are changelings, in *The Tragedy of
     Pudd'nhead Wilson and the Comedy of those Extraordinary Twins* (1894).

104 Among Martí's typed fragments there is a call for this sort of close reading of
     the sense of each word in which this essay engages: "This is how languages are
     constructed: putting in each word mountains of meaning" (*Obras*, 22:308).

105 Martí applauds the rejection of livery in the White House, a decision made
     "as if to condemn these Anglomaniac rogues of New York, who only yester-
     day rolled barrels through the streets, dug mines or fished for trout, and now
     direct their homes with all sorts of courtly practices, and people their stair-
     wells and doorways with lackeys in shoes with buckles, silk socks and tight-
     fitting red jackets" ("El 'Century Magazine,'" *La América* [April 1884]; *Obras*,
     13:436).

106 "Fiestas de la Estatua de la Libertad," *La Nación*, January 1, 1887; *Obras*, 11:99.

107 See Cheah, "Given Culture," 290–328.

108 Otero, *Impresiones y recuerdos*, 114. Rodríguez Otero indicates that the visit
     began in New York on July 2, and featured train travel through the eastern

states. He cites statistics from the 1884–85 school year. In order for him to publish his essay the following year, the latest he could have traveled is the summer of 1886.

109   The long tradition of misrepresentations of Martí includes the Hollywood picture *Santiago* (1956; directed by Gordon Douglas), about the Cuban-Spanish–United States War, in which Martí (played by Ernest Sarracino) is cast as an overweight, slaveholding, and proannexation filibusterer. See Colón's critique of the film, "Hollywood Rewrites History," 81–84.

110   Martí responds with biting irony to this statement's vague allusion to his past: "And now it just remains for me to beg you not to become angry with me because I don't accept as precisely mine the words 'whatever may be my past.' In this, yes, your memory, so affectionate with me, was unfaithful to you, because it has never occurred to me to think about myself when it comes to the things of my homeland, except to work for her well-being from here as my strength permits" (*Epistolario*, 2:32).

111   The Puerto Rican doctor Manuel Zeno Gandía recounts an anecdote of his first meeting with Martí in Madrid in April 1871, after Martí was released from a Havana prison. Saying that he wanted to know if Zeno Gandía would find him worthy of a handshake, given that Martí had been wronged by his Spanish captors and yet had not responded, Martí took Zeno Gandía aside, removed his jacket, and showed him his bare back. A terrible scar from a whipping had produced an ulcerated wound, traversing his entire back. Martí explained that he had received the whipping when he refused the orders of a driver in the prison. Seeing this eighteen-year-old's unbowed indignation, Zeno Gandía remembers that he exclaimed: "You are worthy of the respect of men and worthy of repayment in due time!" (Zeno Gandía, "Como conocí a un caudillo," 213–14).

112   "A Ricardo Rodríguez Otero," *El Avisador Cubano*, May 16, 1888; reprinted in *Epistolario*, 2:31–32. On Martí's conflict with Rodríguez Otero, see Lizaso, *Martí, Místico del Deber*, 252–53.

113   Cruz, "Una de las más sorprendentes creaciones martianas," 134.

114   Martí, "Un artículo desconocido de Martí: ¿A los Estados Unidos?" *La Doctrina de Martí*, August 15, 1897.

∾ CHAPTER 5

1   Martí describes scenes of harassment and ridicule in the Murray Hill Hotel in his notebooks, where "one lives in the United States as if subject to blows. People speak and it seems like they are waving a fist in front of one's eyes" (*Obras*, 21:399; *Selected Writings*, 287, translation modified).

2   See Matsumoto and Allmendinger, *Over the Edge*, and Gutierrez and Orsi, *Contested Eden*, for essays that privilege indigenous and environmentalist perspectives on Spanish and Anglo conquest and that critically assess the victors' version of "California settlement."

3   Steele Mackaye, playwright and from 1886 creator of Cody's stage machinery and script, used this phrase as the title for the *Wild West Show* that played in Madison Square Garden in New York City, according to Warren, *Buffalo Bill's America*, 256. In the United States, *Ramona* is one of the great all-time best-sellers. In 1885, it sold 21,000 copies, and by 1900 readers had purchased more than 74,000 copies. It was owned by 68 percent of U.S. libraries in 1893, and was one of only three contemporary novels to be owned by more than half of the public libraries in the United States (Moylan, "Materiality as Performance," 225).

4   Russell notes that Sitting Bull and the Sioux were billed as "Foes in '76—Friends in '85" (316). See DeLyser, *Ramona Memories*, on the tourist industry that grew up in the wake of Jackson's *Ramona*.

5   Slotkin, *Gunfighter Nation*, 83; quoted in Streeby, *American Sensations*, 3.

6   See Conway, "José Martí frente al Wild West de Buffalo Bill," 131; and Gillman, "*Ramona* in 'Our America,'" for interpretations of Martí as identified with Cody and Jackson.

7   I allude to two terms from an essay by American diplomatic historian David M. Pletcher, "commercial expansionists" and "American economic expansionism," which he uses to refer euphemistically to imperialism without mentioning annexation or colonization ("Rhetoric and Results," 93, 96).

8   Lewis, *Main Currents in Caribbean Thought*, 299.

9   Turner, in "Significance of the Frontier in American History" (1893), describes wars with Indians and expansion westward in terms of natural evolution and flows. He predicts that the American intellect will continually demand a wider field for its exercise (228). Struggles with Indians consolidated a "composite" white nationality and introduced civilization (203). By contrast, on November 16, 1889, Martí writes to his coconspirator Serafín Bello—who like Martí was born in Cuba and resided for many years in the Unted States—of his concerns regarding the global expansionism of the United States and the tenor of discussions at the Pan-American conferences: "Powerful ambition has very subtle methods, and it would be necessary that you were here [in New York], and even if you were, you might not see clearly enough to understand the damage caused by the baneful hope—slyly seconded by our own, through interest or fanaticism—that some good for Cuba will come from a Congress of American nations where, due to large and incredible ill fortune, there are more who are disposed to help the government of the United States to take control of Cuba than there are those who understand that their own tranquility and the reality of their independence will disappear if they allow the key to the other America to fall into these foreign hands. The hour has arrived for this country, pressed by protectionism, to make public its latent aggression; and as they dare neither to gaze at Mexico nor Canada, they make eyes at the islands of the Pacific and of the Antilles, at us" (*Epistolario*, 2:160).

10 According to Bolton's letter to the Committee on History and Education for

Citizenship in the Schools, his historical method contributes to "better relations with Hispanic America, to the unity of interests of the nations of this
hemisphere and to our own growing need of foreign markets where we may
compete to advantage against the great mercantile powers in the world" (May
26, 1919, Bolton Papers; quoted in Magnaghi, *Herbert Bolton and the Historiography of the Americas*, 55).

11 Collazo, "José Martí," 32.

12 Martí, "De Washington: La comedia de *El Senador*" (*El Partido Liberal*,
March 6, 1891, 1; reprinted in *Otras crónicas*, 170); Lloyd and Rosenfeld, *The
Senator*, 19, 41, 66–67. During the first months of the meeting, the annexation
of Cuba appeared in the news and in informal conversations amongst the
delegates as inevitable and necessary, according to Marquez Sterling, *Martí,
ciudadano de América*, 266–68.

13 "De Washington: La comedia de *El Senador*," *Otras crónicas*, 170.

14 Aparicio, "Latino Cultural Studies," 20. Gaspar de Alba specifies the debts of
sexuality, postcolonial, and diaspora studies to Anzaldúa's work in "Crop
Circles in the Cornfield," vi.

15 In an essay entitled "Hegel y el moderno panamericanismo," that appeared in
English as "Do the Americas Have a Common History?" in a volume of that
same title edited by Lewis Hanke, Edmundo O'Gorman problematizes Herbert Bolton's 1932 address to the American Historical Association, "Epic of
Greater America." Bolton celebrated Pan-American unity as a political, economic, and ideological resource for the United States. For example, in the late
1930s, Bolton was instrumental in promoting the Good Neighbor Policy at
the University of California; in 1937, the university formed the Committee on
International Relations and sponsored lectures promoting Wilson's Good
Neighbor Policy. O'Gorman notes that Bolton's Pan-Americanism reduces
the cultural history of each part of the Americas by explaining all of them in
terms of a predetermined geographic unity, what O'Gorman calls in the
English translation a "geographic hallucination" (in Hanke, *Do the Americas
Have a Common History?*, 109). O'Gorman's essay extends Martí's 1889 indictment of the Pan-American ideal as a "geographic morality" (*Obras*, 6:56,
160; *Selected Writings*, 307). See a discussion in Fox, "Commentary," 640.
My reading problematizes Fox's inclusion of Martí in a genealogy extending
from Bolívar to Bolton that assumes an "inter-American 'we'" ("Commentary," 641). Although Martí's "we" extends beyond a single nation's borders, it should not be confused with "inter-American" or "Pan-American"
projects.

16 See Acuña, *Occupied America*, and Silva Gruesz, "The Gulf of Mexico System
and the 'Latinness' of New Orleans."

17 Flores, "Latino Studies," 198; Aparicio, "Latino Cultural Studies," 20.

18 Saldívar, *Border Matters*, xiii.

19 Anzaldúa, *Borderlands / La Frontera*, 25.

20 Saldívar, *Border Matters*, xiii, 183.

21   Anzaldúa cites the Nahuatl definition of "nepantla" as "a space between two bodies of water, [or] the space between two worlds," and then extends the metaphor to associate this location with "a way of reading the world." This "space between" implies possibilities of transformation: "a stage that women and men, and whoever is willing to change into a new person and further grow and develop, go through" (*Borderlands*, 237, 113).

22   Gutierrez Jones, *Rethinking the Borderlands*, 118.

23   Anzaldúa grounds her Chicana identity in the Indian woman's history of resistance (*Borderlands*, 43). Limerick juxtaposes the realism of Anzaldúa's late twentieth-century definition with Turner's late nineteenth-century usage (Limerick, "The Adventures of the Frontier in the Twentieth-Century," 68, 90).

24   Hegel, *The Philosophy of History*: "But America is hitherto exempt from this pressure, for it has the outlet of colonization constantly and widely open, and multitudes are constantly streaming into the plains of the Mississippi. By this means the chief source of discontent is removed, and the continuation of the existing civil condition is guaranteed," 86.

25   Anzaldúa, *Borderlands*, 119.

26   Turner, *Early Writings*, 187, 228. Whereas Turner concurs with the Italian economist Achille Lora that the United States, or Turner's America, "has the key to the historical enigma which Europe has sought for centuries in vain" (qtd. in "Significance of the Frontier," 198), Martí declares that "No yankee or European book could furnish the key to the Hispanoamerican enigma" ("Nuestra América," 20; *Selected Writings*, 293–94).

27   In a chronicle dated September 30, 1889, entitled "El problema negro" (The Black Problem), Martí describes violent, daily attacks by blond (rubios) armed men on black communities, and mocks the view of small-footed, silky-bearded "gentlemen" of the cities who complain that "all the blacks are ungrateful, for in twenty years of this amiable treatment they do not show love for their former masters, nor do they want to learn the arts and sciences that they have no place to show off nor cultivate, nor do they frequent the schools where the teachers are paid by the same folks who applaud, favor and encourage the persecution and butchery [*carnicería*]" (*Obras*, 12:335). The phrase "naturalistic organicism" is from Thomas, "Frederick Jackson Turner, Martí and a Home on the Range," 283.

28   Martí, "El asesinato de los italianos" (The Lynching of the Italians), *Obras* 12:493–99; and "Un Pueblo Quema a un Negro" (A Town Sets a Black Man on Fire), *En los Estados Unidos*, 1505–7.

29   Irwin, "*Ramona* and Postnationalist American Studies," 545.

30   Rivero, "Fronterisleña," 342.

31   See Behar, introduction to *Bridges to Cuba*, 12. See also Negrón-Muntaner's analysis of Behar's collection as indebted to Gloria Anzaldúa.

32   Behar, introduction, 18.

33 Martí, "México y los Estados Unidos," *La Nación*, September 18, 1886, 694.

34 Flores and Yúdice, "Living Borders / Buscando América," 224.

35 De la Cuesta, "La crítica de las traducciones de Martí en Cuba," 1–2.

36 Collazo, "José Martí," in *Yo conocí a Martí*, ed. Suárez León, 36.

37 Rafael Merchan to José Ignacio Rodriguez, October 24, 1895, Papers of José Ignacio Rodriguez, Library of Congress Manuscript Collection.

38 Sellén, *Poesías*.

39 Ibid., 16.

40 Renan, "What Is a Nation?" 11.

41 Martí, *Obras*, 12:203. This chronicle appears in translation as "The Oklahoma Land Rush," in Martí, *The America of José Martí*, 121–35.

42 White, "Frederick Jackson Turner and Buffalo Bill," 54.

43 *New York Herald*, February 12, 1889, 4. This article cites Blaine's principal arguments as to why the United States should and could conveniently annex Cuba.

44 José Martí published a pamphlet with translations of his "vindication of Cuba" along with two proannexationist articles, "Shall We Take Cuba?" (*The Manufacturer*, March 16, 1889) and "A Protectionist View of Cuban Annexation," *New York Evening Post*, March 21, 1889, to which he responded. The pamphlet along with Martí's response entitled *Cuba y los Estados Unidos* were published by *El Avisador Hispano-Americano* in 1889.

45 Warner, "Mexican Notes: Morelia and Patzcuaro," *Harper's Monthly* 75 (1887): 287. Martí translates and analyzes excerpts of this essay in "México en los Estados Unidos: sucesos referentes a México," *El Partido Liberal*, July 7, 1887; reprinted in *Obras*, 7:50–57. See my analysis of this translation in "José Martí between Nation and Empire," 123–24.

46 James, *The American Scene*, 91.

47 Martí, "Los Asuntos Hispanoamericanos en Washington," (Hispano-American Affairs in Washington), *La Nación*, August 31, 1890; Wells, *A Study of Mexico*, 3–6. Wells refers to the burgeoning of travel writing by visitors who took advantage of the comforts of the newly established train service.

48 Wells, *A Study of Mexico*, 4, 22.

49 Curtis, *Capitals of Spanish America*, 5, 1.

50 Martí, "Crónica no publicada," dated August 2, 1886; in Sarracino, *Caso Cutting*, 147.

51 Martí, "México en los Estados Unidos," *El Partido Liberal*, June 23, 1887; rpt. in *Obras*, 7:50–57.

52 Martí, "Crónica no publicada," dated August 2, 1886, in Sarracino, *Caso Cutting*, 123, 144.

53 Martí uses this phrase in the cover letter addressed to Manuel Mercado, which accompanied his first of six chronicles on the Cutting case. See "A Manuel Mercado," August 2, 1886 (*Epistolario*, 1:344–45; my emphasis).

54 Sarracino, *José Martí y el Caso Cutting*, 19.

55 A. K. Cutting, "Card of Reconciliation with Emigdio Medina," *El Paso Her-*

ald, June 20, 1886; rep. in "The Case of Mr. Cutting: Particulars of His Arrest by the Mexican Authorities," *New York Times*, July 25, 1886.

56   Governor John Ireland's letter to the editor of the *New York Herald* dated August 12, 1886, claims that Cutting did not appeal to him. But his letter does affirm that although Cutting may have been found guilty under Mexican law, "the people and the government of the United States can never submit to such rule of law" (reprinted in *National Police Gazette*, August 28, 1886).

57   See U.S. Department of State *Report on Extraterritorial Crime and the Cutting Case*, and *Case of the American A. K. Cutting*. Representative Hitt's testimony that Cutting "scornfully refused to give bail and said he would stay" appears in *Congressional Record*, 49th Cong., 1st Sess., vol. 17, part 8 (August 4, 1886), 8008.

58   Because the source of my verb is an 1886 article related to the investigation of Cutting's imprisonment with the subtitle "A Queer Story," which appeared in the *New York Police Gazette*, "queer" has the pre-1920s sense of strange, odd, eccentric, counterfeit, or other than normal. It references the verb "to queer" or "to banter, to puzzle, to spoil, to put into an unfavorable position, or to thwart," according to *Webster's New Twentieth-Century Dictionary*.

59   Arthur George Sedgwick was a lawyer, editor, essayist, and great-grandnephew of Catharine Maria Sedgwick; he worked at *The Nation* (1872–84) and the *New York Evening Post* (1881–85) and was a longtime neighbor of the William Henry James household in Cambridge, Massachusetts, until he moved to New York in 1872.

60   "[Sedgwick] said: . . . if the investigation develops that in this or in any previous case American citizens have been wronged, the people of America can rest assured that the Government will take a firm stand, and if war is found to be unavoidable, then, without the slightest hesitation, war will be declared" (reprinted in *New York Times*, August 20, 1886).

61   See Avila, "Diplomacia and interes privado," and Parra, "Cónsules y empresarios," on the collusion of U.S. and Mexican diplomats in U.S. expansion into Mexico.

62   Roosevelt lists the preparations for war: "the organization of a troop of cavalry in our district, notifying the Secretary of War that we were at the service of the Government, and being promised every assistance by our excellent chief executive of the Territory, Governor Pierce. Of course the cowboys were all eager for war, they did not much care with whom; they were very patriotic, they were fond of adventure, and to tell the truth, they were by no means averse to the prospect of plunder" (*Ranch Life and the Hunting-Trail*, 109).

63   Quesada y Miranda, *Así fue Martí*, 26–27.

64   Plochet, "Los ojos de Martí," in Suárez León, *Yo conocí a Martí*, 146–47.

65   Martí, *Versos sencillos*, 30–31, translation modified.

66   Martí, "A Manuel Mercado," March 29, 1889 (*Epistolario*, 2:97).

67   The editor of the five-volume *Epistolario*, Luis García Pascual, speculates that

this allusion might refer to *El Latino Americano*, the Spanish-language New York magazine of fiction and fashion, where Martí's novel *Amistad funesta* was serialized in 1885. See García Pascual's footnote 2 to Martí's letter to Mercado of April 12, 1885 (*Epistolario*, 1:299).

68 Anzaldúa, *Borderlands*, 25.

69 Ibid., 102; Behar, introduction to *Bridges to Cuba*, 12. For a fuller discussion of Martí's contradictory positions on gender and sexuality, see Lomas, "Redefining the American Revolutionary."

70 While Martí took only seven days to write his novel *Lucía Jerez*, which appeared under the pseudonym "Adelaida de Ral," the translation of Helen Hunt Jackson's Indian reform novel demanded several months of work during the summer of 1887. According to Félix Iznaga, his secretary at the time, Martí dictated the translation aloud at breakneck speed while pacing back and forth with *Ramona* in hand. The translation manuscripts for *Ramona* and for Hugh Conway's anticommunist novel *Called Back* [*Misterio*], which Appleton had hired him to translate, went straight to the printer with only minor revisions, based on Martí's oral dictation. Gimeno, "Reminiscencias de José Martí," 72.

71 Venegas, "Erotics of Racialization," 76.

72 Martí, *Lucía Jerez*, 206.

73 Martínez, *Martí*; Molloy, "His America, Our America"; and Montero, *José Martí*.

74 Negrón-Muntaner observes this quality in contemporary American Studies' appropriations of Anzaldúa and offers a critique of Mignolo's stripping of gender from the border ("Bridging Islands," 276).

75 Fusco, "El diario de Miranda," 211.

76 Montero, *José Martí*, 58. Martí discusses Mrs. Jewel in "Un pueblo quema a un negro," *El Partido Liberal*, March 5, 1892; reprinted in *Otras crónicas*, 188–89.

77 James, "Address at the Annual Meeting of the New England Anti-Imperialist League"; Hoganson, *Fighting for American Manhood*.

78 Vázquez Díaz makes this observation in an interview with Martínez: "Contradictions, Pluralism, and Dialogue," 237.

79 Eight anarchists were arrested, one committed suicide in jail, three were acquitted or gained a commutation of life sentences, and the State of Illinois hung four in 1887 on unsubstantiated charges of having thrown a bomb. Legal scholars and historians concur that the widely publicized and irregular trial deviated from principles of fair judicial procedure.

80 Parsons, "The Principles of Anarchism," in *Lucy Parsons*, 38. For a study that examines Cuban anarchism in the period leading up to and after the war of independence, see Shaffer, *Anarchism and Countercultural Politics*.

81 Pérez emphasizes contact and proximity between North American and Cuban culture as developmental factors in both societies in *On Becoming Cuban*, 27–32, even though the two nations don't share a land boarder.

82 Parsons, "Our Civilization: Is it Worth Saving?" *The Alarm*, August 8, 1885; rpt. in *Lucy Parsons*, 44–45.

83 Acuña, *Occupied America*, 194.

84 Parsons, "Address in London;" quoted in Streeby, "Labor, Memory and the Boundaries of Print Culture," 415–16.

85 Ashbaugh reprints this essay in her biography of Parsons.

86 Avrich, *The Haymarket Tragedy*.

87 "Socialists and Anarchists: They Listen to one of Mrs. Lucy Parson's Familiar Speeches," *New York Times*, November 5, 1886, 2; "Lucy Parsons Talks: Preaching Anarchy in the Streets of Cleveland," *New York Times*, October 16, 1886, 5; "Mrs. Parsons Arrives: How the Notorious Anarchist Looks and Talks," *New York Times*, October 17, 1886, 9.

88 Acuña, *Occupied America*, 194; Kelly, "Lucy Parsons," 910; Gilroy, *The Black Atlantic*, 18; Ahrens, "Lucy Parsons," 8; Streeby, "Labor, Memory, and the Boundaries of Print Culture," 407–8.

89 Armas, "La obra literaria de José Martí en 1887," 84, 87; Callejas, "1887," 149; Cantón Navarro, "José Martí y los mártires de Chicago," 33–44.

90 Poyo, *"With All, and for the Good of All."*

91 Martí opposed anti-immigrant xenophobia and called for the uprooting of the causes of the injustice against which the anarchist movement protested: "The anarchist need not be extirpated, but the root cause of anarchism, which is the intolerable abuse of unjust privileges" (*Obras*, 12:365).

92 Boudreau, "Elegies for the Haymarket Anarchists," 320.

93 An English-language article by Martí offers an oblique commentary on the Chicago trial of the anarchists under way in 1887 and looks forward to the eventual apology and commutation of the sentences that Illinois governor Altgeld would issue. Martí's "Blood of the Innocents" (*New York Herald*, April 9, 1887), which announces the Spanish apology and vindication of innocence of eight Cuban medical students who were charged with defiling the grave of the loyalist Spanish newspaper editor Gonzalo Castañon, is reprinted in *Obras*, 28:151–54. See Valdés Dominguez, *Tragedy in Havana*, which traces the efforts of Martí's childhood friend to secure the vindication of his fellow first-year medical students.

94 Smith, "Buffalo Bill and the Mardi Gras Indians," 20.

95 Callejas refers to "Mágnifico espectáculo," in "1887" (175). According to Rennert, after negotiating on behalf of the United States during the Ghost Dance affair, Cody took nineteen native leaders hostage in 1891 and brought them with him to Europe to perform in his show (10).

96 In Judith Butler's gloss on Althusser's theory of subjection, ideology constitutes the subject's willingness to accept guilt in exchange for an identity. Returning to Althusser's famous instance of the policeman who hails a suspect and thus occasions the subject's self-constitution as a guilty party by simply turning around, Butler asks: "How and why does the subject turn, anticipating the conferral of identity through the self-ascription of guilt? . . . It is important to remember that the turn toward the law is not necessitated by the hailing; it is compelling in a less than logical sense, because it promises

identity" (*Psychic Life of Power*, 107–8). In Buffalo Bill's show, the law mandates civilization's inevitable triumph over savagery, and helps to consolidate the preexisting "less than logical" interpretation of westward expansion as a necessary evil, carried out by guilty subjects. When showgoers respond to the hailing by the *Wild West* narrative, they recognize themselves as guilty, in exchange for the civilized identity conferred by the show. The promise of identity is bound up with violent yet unavoidable civilizing of savagism. The civilized subject thus self-ascribes guilt and gains an imperial identity.

97   Ambrose Park in south Brooklyn, the venue for *Buffalo Bill's Wild West Show* in New York in 1894, boasted seating for twenty thousand people (Rennert, 26).

98   See Martí, "El indio en los Estados Unidos," *La Nación*, October 25, 1885, reprinted in *Obras*, 10: 319–27, where he describes the reservation system as vile, insofar as it "apaga su personalidad" (shuts off their personality) by curtailing freedom of movement and removing the Indians' means of self-sufficiency. Martí denounced the U.S. belief that it has a right to all lands and all seas, and to place other peoples under their tutelage (*Obras*, 12: 239–40).

99   Brasmer notes that in 1886 Salsbury set up the quarters of the natives in the hall over the entrance to the Gardens and labeled the area "The Indian Encampment." Cf. Blair, 9.

100   See, for example, the account given by the autonomist Manuel Pichardo in his travel narrative of the Chicago Exposition and New York, which caricatures both the grotesque cultures of the Midway Plaisance and the antiannexationist figure as a "hard-hitting Creole" who venerated Martí and who savagely pounded his hand on a table in a New York hotel while protesting the difficulty of being an "immigrant Latino" (*La ciudad blanca* [1893], 100, 221).

101   For example, the program notes for *Buffalo Bill's Wild West Show* of 1884 offers this description of a Pawnee encampment under the title "A Wild and Fascinating Sight": "At a little distance from the teepees, a great brush fire darted its lurid tongues of flame up into the black dome of night. Around the fire, in wildest contortions and gesticulations—expressive by a sort of rude but very vigorous pantomime of the incidents of combat with the Sioux—leaped, danced, stamped, crouched, writhed, and wielded their weapons, two score Pawnee braves. Hoarse guttural exclamations burst from their lips, and they seemed half frenzied with the excitement of the war dance" (n.p.). Note how the writer suggests a parallel between the fire's mysterious "tongues" and the Pawnees' "guttural exclamations." This scene communicates threatening tensions among different tribes, perhaps as a substitute for the unsavory memory of conflict with the U.S. government.

102   O'Connor, *Buffalo Bill, the Noblest Whiteskin*; Carter, *Buffalo Bill Cody*, 287; Moses argues that Indians sought the right to work in Wild West shows so as to earn money and to get away from the restrictive surveillance of missionaries and Indian agents. Cody never sided with the Indians' right to rebellion, however, and often in his correspondence with the Department of the Inte-

rior he observed that by taking Indians on tour they could not form part of rebellious movements on the reservations (Moses, *Wild West Shows and the Images of American Indians*, 110–11). According to Bridger, *Buffalo Bill and Sitting Bull*, Cody befriended and represented the Lakota with the dignity they deserved: "finally, an important white man had appeared to inform the world of their desperate situation," 319.

103 Cody, in fact, quit the show briefly in the 1890s in order to represent the U.S. government in negotiations just prior to the massacre at Wounded Knee.

104 The 1893 program from *Buffalo Bill's Wild West and Congress of Rough Riders of the World*; quoted in White, "Frederick Jackson Turner and Buffalo Bill," 10.

105 Rydell, *All the World's a Fair*, 5–6.

106 Altgeld, *The Chicago Martyrs*.

107 See, for example, West, "On Black-Brown Relations," and the debate between Aparicio, "Jennifer as Selena," and Gaspar de Alba, "The Chicana/Latina Dyad."

108 Rubens, *Liberty*, 17.

109 See documents related to the establishment of an editorial business in December 1886 in which Martí was administrator and major shareholder (Martí, *Papeles de Martí*, 3:107–9).

110 Martí refers to the "not always praiseworthy methods of the Franciscan friars," in "Un libro del norte sobre las instituciones españolas en los Estados Unidos que fueron de México" (A Book of the North on the Spanish Institutions in the United States That Were Once Mexican) (*Obras*, 7:61) On the condition of Indians on reservations, Martí writes: "The Indian is dead under this ignoble system, which extinguishes his personality" (*Obras*, 10:323; *Selected Writings*, 160).

111 Gillman, "*Ramona* in 'Our America,' " 103.

112 As early as March of 1886, Martí proposed the idea of a publishing venture whereby his editorial contacts in Argentina and Mexico would help him fund, promote, and distribute books that are "vital and useful" for Latin American readers, much as Appleton had done with Martí's previous translation of Hugh Conway's anticommunist thriller *Called Back* [*Misterio*]. See Martí, *Epistolario*, 1:324; *Epistolario*, 1:395–400.

113 Padget, "Travel Writing, Sentimental Romance, and Indian Rights Advocacy," 854. See Phillips, *Chiefs and Challengers*, 20–46, on Garra's rebellion.

114 For example, in Martí's handwritten dedication of a copy of *Ramona* to Elías de Losada, editor of *La Revista Ilustrada de Nueva York*, Martí describes the motivations for translation as "gratitude and prevision" (*Obras*, 28:504).

115 Helen Hunt Jackson and Abbot Kinney, *Report on the Condition and Needs of the Mission Indians of California, Made by Special Agents Helen Hunt Jackson and Abbot Kinney, to the Commissioner of Indian Affairs*, rpt. in Jackson, *A Century of Dishonor*.

116 Agamben, *State of Exception*, 88.

117 Romero, "The Pan-American Conference," 356. Healy defines the goal of the Pan-American Conference to be "the creation of a pan-American trading bloc headed by the United States and potentially excluding Europe," which Latin delegates successfully prevented from becoming reality. Healy describes the results of the meetings as "limited," and notes that by the time it adjourned, the conference had really only established a Washington, D.C., clearinghouse of commercial information for investors in Latin America, the Bureau of American Republics, and gained publicity for other Pan-American projects, including an intercontinental railroad to bring Texas into contact with Chile (*James G. Blaine and Latin America*, 158–59).

118 Romero, "The Pan-American Conference," 407.

119 *La Nación*, March 20, 1890; *Obras*, 6:75.

120 McGann, *Argentina, The United States and the Inter-American System*, 130–31; Quesada, *Primera Conferencia Panamericana*, 6–7; Flint, *Memories of an Active Life*.

121 Quesada, *Primera Conferencia Panamericana*, 7.

122 Homer Plessy's infraction of riding in a "whites only" car in a New Orleans train in 1892 led to the Supreme Court's legalization of segregation in public spaces for at least sixty years.

123 Martí, "Carta a Gonzalo de Quesada," in prologue to Quesada, *Primera ofrenda* (1892); rep. in *Obras*, 5:195.

❧ CONCLUSION

1 "[Envilece, devora . . .]," *Poesía completa*, 129.

2 "[Yo sacaré lo que en el pecho tengo]," *Poesía completa*, 168.

3 "[Es verdad . . .]," *Poesía Completa*, 436.

4 Mirabal, "Más que negro: José Martí and the Politics of Unity," 58.

5 See Hewitt, "Paulina Pedroso and Las Patriotas of Tampa," and Sarabia, *La Patriota del Silencio*.

6 Martí, "Conocimientos internacionales," *La América*, September 1883.

7 In his reporting on the Pan-American Conference Martí refers to "the relations of the United States with the other American peoples" and to "the United States in America" rather than to the United States of America (*Obras* 6:53). The National Archives of the United States at College Park, Maryland, hold the manuscript of Martí's "Original Report of the Committee on the Proposition of the Delegates of the United States," in which Martí uses the abbreviation "U.S.," in his Spanish and English versions. See Records of the International American Monetary Commission, Box 930, MS dated March 30, 1891.

8 Martí, "Letter to the Editor of the *New York Herald*," 61.

9 See Felicia R. Lee's problematic animalizing metaphor of a horse race: "Last week the Census Bureau announced that the Hispanic population had jumped to roughly 37 million. For the first time, Hispanics nosed past blacks (with 36.2

million) as the largest minority group in the United States." *New York Times*, February 3, 2003, A1, and Davis, *Magical Urbanism*, 8.

10   Martí, "Al Extranjero (To foreign)," *Poesías completas*, 128.

11   See Noble, *Death of a Nation*, which makes this claim through a critique of the Anglo-Protestant monopolization of America.

BIBLIOGRAPHY

〜 NEWSPAPERS

La América, New York, New York
El Avisador Cubano, New York, New York
El Avisador Hispano-Americano, New York, New York
Brooklyn Daily Times, Brooklyn, New York
Brooklyn Daily Eagle, Brooklyn, New York
La Doctrina de Martí, New York, New York
La Economista Americano, New York, New York
La Edad de Oro, New York, New York
Harper's Monthly, New York, New York
The Hour, New York, New York
El Latino Americano, New York, New York
The Manufacturer, Philadelphia, Pennsylvania
El Mundo Nuevo / La América Ilustrada, New York, New York
La Nación, Buenos Aires, Argentina
The Nation New York, New York
New York Evening Post, New York, New York
New York Herald, New York, New York
New York Times, New York, New York
New York Tribune, New York, New York
New York World, New York, New York
North American Review, Boston, Massachusetts
La Opinión Nacional, Caracas, Venezuela
Our Continent, Philadelphia, Pennsylvania
El Partido Liberal, México, D.F., México
Patria, New York, New York
La Pluma, Bogotá, Colombia
El Porvenir, New York, New York
El Repertorio Colombiano, Bogotá, Colombia
La República, Tegucigalpa, Honduras
La Revista Ilustrada de Nueva York, New York, New York
La Revista Universal, México, D.F., México
Scribner's Monthly, New York, New York

The Sun, New York, New York
Wall Street Journal, New York, New York
Washington Post, Washington, D.C.

❧ BOOKS AND JOURNAL ARTICLES

About, Edmond. *Le nez d'un notaire*. Paris: Michel Lévy Fréres, 1862.

Abrams, M. H. *The Mirror and the Lamp: Romantic Theory and the Critical Tradition*. New York: Oxford University Press, 1953.

Aching, Gerard. *The Politics of Spanish American Modernismo*. Cambridge: Cambridge University Press, 1997.

Acosta-Belén, Edna, and Carlos E. Santiago. "Merging Borders: The Remapping of America." In *Latino Studies Reader*, ed. Antonia Darder and Rodolfo P. Torres, 29–42. London: Blackwell, 1998.

Acuña, Rodolfo. *Occupied America: The Chicano's Struggle toward Liberation*. San Francisco: Canfield Press, 1972.

Adams, Rachel. *Side Show, USA*. Chicago: University of Chicago Press, 2001.

Adorno, Theodor W. "Commitment." In *Aesthetics and Politics*, by Theodor Adorno et al., trans. Francis McDonagh, 177–95. London: Verso, 1977.

——. "The Essay as Form." In *Notes to Literature*, ed. Rolf Tiedemann, trans. Shierry Weber Nicholsen, 1:3–23. New York: Columbia University Press, 1991.

Agamben, Giorgio. *State of Exception*. Trans. Kevin Attell. Chicago: University of Chicago Press, 2005.

Ahrens, Gale. "Lucy Parsons: Mystery Revolutionist, More Dangerous than a Thousand Rioters." Introduction to Parsons, *Lucy Parsons: Freedom, Equality & Solidarity*, 1–26.

Alberto, Eliseo. *Informe contra mí mismo*. Mexico City: Alfaguara, 1997.

Alegría, Fernando. *Walt Whitman in Hispánoamerica*. Mexico City: Colección Studiuum, 1954.

Atgeld, John Peter. *The Chicago Martyrs: the famous speeches of the eight anarchists in Judge Gary's court, October 7, 8, 9, 1886, and reasons for pardoning Fielden, Neebe and Schwab*. San Francisco: Free Society, 1899.

Alonso, Carlos J. *The Burden of Modernity: The Rhetoric of Cultural Discourse in Spanish America*. Oxford: Oxford University Press, 1998.

Anderson, Benedict. *Imagined Communities: Reflections on the Origin and Spread of Nationalism*. London: Verso, 1983.

Anderson, Perry. *The Origins of Postmodernity*. London: Verso, 1998.

Anderson, Quentin. *The Imperial Self*. New York: Knopf, 1971.

Anzaldúa, Gloria. *Borderlands / La Frontera: The New Mestiza*. 2nd ed. San Francisco: Aunt Lute Books, 1987.

Aparicio, Frances R. "Jennifer as Selena: Rethinking Latinidad in Media and Popular Culture." *Latino Studies* 1 (2003): 90–105.

——. "Latino Cultural Studies." In *Critical Latin American and Latino Studies*, ed. Juan Poblete, 1–31.

Aparicio, Frances R., and Susana Chávez-Silverman. Introduction to *Tropicalizations: Transcultural Representation of Latinidad*, ed. Frances R. Aparicio and Susana Chávez-Silverman, 1–17. Hanover, N.H.: University Press of New England, 1997.

Arac, Jonathan. "Whitman and the Problems of the Vernacular." In *Breaking Bounds*, Erkkila and Grossman eds., 44–61.

Ardao, Arturo. *Génesis de la idea y el nombre de América Latina*. Caracas: Centro de Estudios Latinoamericanos Rómulo Gallegos, 1980.

Armas, Emilio de. "La obra literaria de José Martí en 1887." *Universidad de la Habana* 232 (1982): 83–92.

Arroyo, Jossiana. "Technologies: Transculturations of Race, Gender and Ethnicity in Arturo A. Schomburg's Masonic Writings." *Centro Journal* 17.1 (spring 2005): 5–25.

Ashbaugh, Carolyn. *Lucy Parsons: American Revolutionary*. Chicago: Charles H. Kerr, 1976.

Avila, Alfredo. "Diplomacia and interes privado: Matías Romera el Soconusco y el Southern Mexican Railroad, 1881–83." *Secuencia: Revista de Historia y Ciencias Sociales* 38 (May–Aug. 1997): 51–76.

Avrich, Paul. *The Haymarket Tragedy*. Princeton, N.J.: Princeton University Press, 1984.

Bacon, Francis. "Of Friendship." In *Essays*. New York: Oxford University Press, 1985.

Baker, Houston A. *Modernism and the Harlem Renaissance*. Chicago: University of Chicago Press, 1987.

Baldwin, James. *The Fire Next Time*. New York: Dell, 1962.

Ballón Aguirre, José C. *Autonomía cultural americana: Emerson y Martí*. Madrid: Editorial Pliegos, 1986.

———. *Lecturas norteamericanas de José Martí: Emerson y el socialismo contemporáneo (1880–1887)*. Mexico City: Universidad Autónoma de México, 1995.

———. *Martí y Blaine en la dialéctica de la Guerra del Pacífico (1879–1883)*. Mexico City: Universidad Nacional Autónoma de México, 2003.

Baralt, Luis A. Introduction to *Martí on the U.S.A.*, ed. and trans. Luis A. Baralt, xi–xxxi. Carbondale: Southern Illinois University Press, 1966.

Barlow, Tani E. "Not Really a Properly Intellectual Response: An Interview with Gayatri Spivak." *Positions* 12.1 (2004): 139–63.

Barrus, Clara. *Whitman and Burroughs: Camarades*. Boston, Mass.: Houghton Mifflin, 1931.

Basler, Roy P. Introduction to *Memoranda During the War and Death of Abraham Lincoln*, ed. Roy Basler. Bloomington: Indiana University Press, 1962.

Beauregard, Paulette Silva. "La feminización del héroe moderno y la novella en *Lucía Jérez y el hombre de hierro*." *Revista de crítica literaria latinoamericana* 36.52 [Lima] (2000): 135–51.

Behar, Ruth, ed. *Bridges to Cuba: Puentes a Cuba*. Ann Arbor: University of Michigan Press, 1995.

Behdad, Ali. *A Forgetful Nation: On Immigration and Cultural Identity in the United States.* Durham, N.C.: Duke University Press, 2005.

Belnap, Jeffrey. "Headbands, Hemp Sandals, and Headdresses: The Dialectics of Dress and Self-Conception in Martí's 'Our America.'" In Belnap and Fernández, *José Martí's "Our America,"* 191–209.

Belnap, Jeffrey, and Raul Fernández, eds. *José Martí's "Our America": From National to Hemispheric Cultural Studies.* Durham, N.C.: Duke University Press, 1998.

Benjamin, Walter. *Illuminations.* Trans. Harry Zohn. New York: Schocken Books, 1986.

———. "Paralipomena to 'On the Concept of History.'" In *Selected Writings,* 4:401–11.

———. "The Paris of the Second Empire in Baudelaire." In *Selected Writings,* 4:3–92.

———. "The Task of the Translator." Trans. Harry Zohn. In *The Translation Studies Reader,* ed. Lawrence Venuti, 15–25. London: Routledge, 2000.

———. *Selected Writings.* 4 vols. Ed. Michael W. Jennings, trans. Edmund Jephcott. Cambridge, Mass.: Harvard University Press, 2003.

Binns, Henry Bryan. *A Life of Walt Whitman.* London: Methuen, 1905.

Blaine, James G. *Political Discussions: Legislative, Diplomatic and Popular, 1856–1886.* Norwich, Conn.: Henry Bill Publishing, 1887.

Blair, John G. "Blackface Minstrels and *Buffalo Bill's Wild West*: Nineteenth-century Entertainment Forms as Cultural Exports." In *European Readings of American Popular Culture,* eds. John Dean and John-Paul Gabilliet, 3–12. Westport, Conn.: Greenwood Press, 1996.

Blouët, Paul [pseud. Max O'Rell], and Jack Allyn, *Jonathan and His Continent (Rambles through American Society),* trans. Madame Paul Blouët. New York: Cassell, 1889.

Borges, Jorge Luis. "The Argentine Writer and Tradition." Trans. Esther Allen. In *Selected Non-Fictions,* ed. Eliot Weinberger, 420–27. New York: Penguin Books, 1999.

———. "Pierre Menard, Author of Don Quixote." In *Ficciones,* trans. Anthony Bonner, 45–55. New York: Grove Press, 1962.

———. *El otro, el mismo.* Buenos Aires: Emecé, 1969.

Boudreau, Kristen. "Elegies for the Haymarket Anarchists." *American Literature* 77 (June 2005): 319–47.

Bowker, R. R. "Great American Industries." *Harper's Monthly Magazine* (July 1887): 165–88.

Brasmer, William. "The Wild West Exhibition: A Fraudulent Reality." In *American Popular Entertainment: Papers and Proceedings of the Conference on the History of American Popular Entertainment,* ed. Myron Matlaw, 207–14. Westport, Conn.: Grenwood Press, 1979.

Brickhouse, Anna. *Transamerican Literary Relations and the Nineteenth-Century Public Sphere.* Cambridge: Cambridge University Press, 2004.

Bridger, Bobby. *Buffalo Bill and Sitting Bull: Inventing the Wildwest.* Austin, Tex.: University of Texas Press, 2002.

Browne, Jefferson B. *Key West: The Old and the New.* St. Augustine, Fl.: Record Company, 1912.

Buell, Lawrence. *Emerson.* Cambridge, Mass.: Harvard University Press, 2003.

Bueno, Salvador. *José Martí y su periódico "Patria."* Barcelona: Puvill Libros, 1997.

Burrel, Julio. "Martí." In Suárez León, *Yo conocí a Martí,* 28–29.

Butler, Judith. *The Psychic Life of Power: Theories of Subjection.* Stanford: Stanford University Press, 1997.

Cadava, Eduardo. *Emerson and the Climates of History.* Stanford: Stanford University Press, 1997.

Calinescu, Matei. *Five Faces of Modernity: Modernism, Avant-Garde, Decadence, Kitsch, Postmodernism.* Durham, N.C.: Duke University Press, 1987.

Callejas, Bernardo. "1887: un año clave en la radicalización martiana." *Anuario del Centro de Estudios Martianos* 2 (1979): 149–90.

Campa, Román de la. *Latin Americanism.* Minneapolis: University of Minnesota Press, 1999.

Canton Navarro, José. "José Martí y los mártires de Chicago." *Islas* 75 (May–August 1983): 33–44.

Carr, Raymond. "A Revolutionary Hero." *New York Review of Books* 35.12 (July 2, 1988): 26–28.

Carter, Robert A. *Buffalo Bill Cody: The Man Behind the Legend.* New York: Wiley, 2000.

Castillo, Debra. *Redreaming America: Toward a Bilingual American Culture.* Albany: State University of New York Press, 2005.

Castillo, Susan. " 'The Best of Nations?' Race and Imperial Destinies in Emerson's *English Traits.*" *Yearbook of English Studies* 34.13 (2004): 100–11.

Castro-Palomino, Rafael, Jr. *Cuentos de hoy y mañana: cuadros políticos y sociales.* New York: Imprenta y Librería de N. Ponce de Leon, 1883.

———. *Preludios.* New York: Imprenta y Librería de N. Ponce de Leon, 1893.

Césaire, Aimé. *Notebook of a Return to the Native Land.* Trans. Clayton Eshleman and Annette Smith, eds. Middletown, Conn.: Wesleyan University Press, 2001.

Cervantes, Miguel de. *Don Quixote.* Trans. J. M. Cohen. New York: Penguin, 1950.

———. *El ingenioso hidalgo Don Quijote de la Mancha.* Ed. Luis Andrés Murillo. Vol. 1. Madrid: Editorial Castalia, 1978.

Cervantes-Rodríguez, Ana Margarita, and Amy Lutz. "Coloniality of Power, Immigration, and the English-Spanish Asymmetry in the United States." *Nepantla: Views from South* 4.3 (2003): 523–60.

Chakrabarty, Dipesh. *Provincializing Europe: Postcolonial Thought and Historical Difference.* Princeton, N.J.: Princeton University Press, 2000.

Charles, Cecil. *Tuya, other verses and translations from José Martí.* New York: J. E. Richardson, 1898.

Cheah, Pheng. "Given Culture: Rethinking Cosmopolitical Freedom in Transnationalism." In *Cosmopolitics: Thinking and Feeling beyond the Nation,* 290–328. Minneapolis: University of Minnesota Press, 1998.

———. *Spectral Nationality.* New York: Columbia University Press, 2003.

Chenot, Beatriz. " 'Le *modernismo* hispano-americain.' " *Modernités* 6 (1991): 29–48.

Chevigny, Bell Gale, and Gari LaGuardia, eds. *Reinventing the Americas: Comparative Studies of the Literature of the United States and Spanish America.* Cambridge: Cambridge University Press, 1986.

Cohn, Deborah N. *History and Memory in Two Souths: Recent Southern and Spanish American Fiction.* Nashville, Tenn.: Vanderbilt University Press, 1999.

Collazo, Enrique. *Cuba independiente.* Havana: La Moderna Poesía, 1900.

———. "José Martí." In *Yo conocí a Martí,* ed. Suárez León, 30–37.

Colón, Jesús. "Hollywood Rewrites History." In *A Puerto Rican in New York and Other Essays,* 81–84. New York: Monthly Review Press, 1982.

Contardi, Argentina. *Jose Martí: La lengua del destierro: crónica y tradición moderna.* Rosario, Colombia: Universidad Nacional de Rosario Editora, 1995.

Conway, Christopher. "José Martí frente al Wild West de Buffalo Bill: frontera, raza y arte en la civilización y barberie norteamericana." *Hispanic Journal* 19.1 (spring 1998): 129–42.

Cooppan, Vilashini. "W(h)ither Post-colonial Studies? Towards the Transnational Study of Race and Nation." In *Postcolonial Theory and Criticism,* ed. Laura Chrisman and Benita Parry, 1–35. Cambridge: D. S. Brewer, 2000.

Cotto-Thorner, Guillermo. *Trópico en Manhattan.* San Juan: Editorial Occidente, 1951.

Crapol, Edward P. *James G. Blaine: Architect of Empire.* Wilmington, Del.: Scholarly Resources, 2000.

Cruz, Mary. "Una de las más sorprendentes creaciones martianas: 'El Poeta Walt Whitman.' " *Anuario Martiano* 11 (1988): 130–39.

Cuesta, Leonel-Antonio de la. *Martí, traductor.* Salamanca: Universidad Pontificia de Salamanca, Cátedra de Poética "Fray Luis de León," 1996.

Curtis, George W. *Wendell Phillips: A Eulogy Delivered before the Municipal Authorities of Boston, April 18, 1884.* New York: Harper, 1884.

Curtis, William Eleroy. *Capitals of Spanish America.* New York: Harper, 1888.

Dallal, Jenine Abboushi. "American Imperialism UnManifest: Emerson's 'Inquest' and Cultural Regeneration." *American Literature* 73.1 (2001): 47–83.

Dalleo, Raphael. "Another 'Our America': Rooting a Caribbean Aesthetic in the work of José Martí, Kamau Brathwaite and Edouard Glissant." *Anthurium: Caribbean Studies Journal* 2.2 (2004), http://scholar.library.miami.edu/anthurium/volume—2/issue—2/dalleo-another.htm.

———. "Emplotting Postcoloniality: Usable Pasts, Possible Futures and the Relentless Present." *Diaspora: A Journal of Transnational Studies* 13.1 (spring 2004): 129–40.

Darío, Ruben. *Azul.* Tegucigalpa: Editorial Guaymuras, 1993.

———. "Charles A. Dana." In *Ruben Darío: Poetic and Prose Selections,* 91–93. Boston: D. C. Heath, 1931.

———. "José Martí." In *Los raros,* 193–203. 1896. Buenos Aires: Editora Espasa-Calpe Argentina, 1952.

———. *Songs of Life and Hope.* Trans. Will Derusha and Alberto Acereda, eds. Durham, N.C.: Duke University Press, 2004.

Darwin, Charles. *The Formation of Vegetable Mould, through the Action of Worms.* London: Faber and Faber, 1966.

Davis, Mike. *Magical Urbanism: Latinos Reinvent the US City.* Rev. and exp. ed. London: Verso, 2001.

Delany, Martin. "Annexation of Cuba," *North Star* (April 27, 1849). In *Martin R. Delany: A Documentary Reader*, ed. Robert S. Levine, 164–65. Chapel Hill: University of North Carolina Press, 2003.

———. *Blake, or the Huts of America.* Ed. Floyd J. Miller. Boston: Beacon Press, 1970.

Deleuze, Gilles, and Félix Guattari. *A Thousand Plateaus: Capitalism and Schizophrenia.* Trans. Brian Massumi. Minneapolis: University of Minnesota Press, 1987.

DeLyser, Dydia. *Ramona Memories: Tourism and the Shaping of Southern California.* Minneapolis, Minn.: University of Minnesota Press, 2005.

De Man, Paul. "Literary History and Literary Modernity." In *Blindness and Insight: Essays in the Rhetoric of Contemporary Criticism*, 142–65. Minneapolis: University of Minnesota Press, 1983.

———. Review of Harold Bloom's *Anxiety of Influence*. In *Blindness and Insight*, 267–76. 2nd ed. Minneapolis: University of Minnesota Press, 1983.

Derrida, Jacques. *Of Grammatology.* Trans. Gayatri Chakravorty Spivak. Baltimore, Md.: Johns Hopkins University Press, 1974.

———. *Specters of Marx: The State of the Debt, the Work of Mourning and the New International.* Trans. Peggy Kamuf. New York: Routledge, 1994.

———. *Writing and Difference.* Trans. Alan Bass. Chicago: University of Chicago Press, 1978.

Deschamps Chapeaux, Pedro. *Rafael Serra y Montalvo: obrero incansable de nuestra independencia.* Havana: Unión de Escritores y Artistas de Cuba, 1975.

Díaz Quiñones, Arcadio. "Martí: La guerra desde la nubes." In Martí, *En los Estados Unidos*, 2129–48.

Díaz Ruiz, Ignacio. "Presentación." In José Ballón, *Lecturas norteamericanas de José Martí: Emerson y el socialismo contemporaneo (1880–1887)* (José Martí's North American Lectures: Emerson and Contemporary Socialism). Mexico City: Universidad Autónoma de México, 1995.

Dimock, Wai Chee. *Through Other Continents: American Literature across Deep Time.* Princeton, N.J.: Princeton University Press, 2006.

Domínguez, Fermín Valdés. "Ofrenda de hermano." *Revista Cubana* 29 (July 1951–December 1952): 237–87.

Dominguez, Teofílo. *Figuras y figuritas: ensayos biográficos.* Tampa, Fl.: Imp. Lafayette Street, 1899.

Doumont, Monique. "Notas para un estudio del 'Whitman' de José Martí." *Anuario de filología* 8–9 (1969–70): 199–212.

Du Bois, W. E. B. *The Souls of Black Folk.* New York: Dover Publications, 1994.

———. "The Souls of White Folk." In *W. E. B. DuBois: A Reader*, ed. David Levering Lewis, 453–65. New York: Henry Holt, 1995.

Duignan, Peter J., and L. H. Gann, *The Spanish Speakers in the United States: A History.* Lanham, Md.: University Press of America, 1998.

Duquette, Elizabeth. "The Tongue of an Archangel: Poe, Baudelaire, Benjamin." *Translation and Literature* 12.1 (2003): 18–40.

Dussel, Enrique. *1492. El encubrimiento del otro: hacia el origen del "mito de la modernidad: conferencias de Frankfurt.* Santa Fé de Bogotá: Ediciones Antropos, 1992.

——. "Eurocentrism and Modernity (Introduction to the Frankfurt Lectures)," *boundary 2* 20.3 (1993): 65–76.

Edelman Pintó, Federico. "Recuerdos de Martí." *Diario de la Marina*, May 22, 1927. Reprinted in Suárez León, *Yo conocí a Martí*, 52–56.

Emerson, Ralph Waldo. *Centenary Edition of the Complete Works of Ralph Waldo Emerson.* 12 vols. Ed. Edward Emerson. Boston, Mass.: Houghton, Mifflin, 1903–4.

——. *The Conduct of Life.* Boston: Ticknor and Fields, 1860.

——. *Emerson's Anti-Slavery Writings.* Len Gougeon and Joel Meyerson, eds. New Haven, Conn.: Yale University Press, 1995.

——. *English Traits.* Boston, Mass.: Houghton, Mifflin, 1888.

——. *The Journal and Miscellaneous Notebooks of Ralph Waldo Emerson.* Vol. 11. Ed. William H. Gillman et al. Cambridge, Mass.: Harvard University Press, 1961.

——. *Representative Men.* Ed. Pamela Schirmeister. New York: Marsilio Publishers, 1995.

——. *Selections from Ralph Waldo Emerson: An Organic Anthology.* Ed. Stephen E. Whicher. Boston, Mass.: Houghton Mifflin, 1957.

——. "The Young American" (lecture, Mercantile Library Association, Boston, February 7, 1844); *The Dial*, May 1844.

Englekirk, John. "Notes on Emerson in Latin America." *PMLA* 76.3 (1961): 227–32.

Erkkila, Betsy, and Jay Grossman, eds. *Breaking Bounds: Women and American Cultural Studies.* Oxford: Oxford University Press, 1996.

Ette, Ottmar. "Apuntes para una Orestiada americana: José Martí y el diálogo intercultural entre Europa y América Latina," *Revista de Crítica Literaria Latino-americana* 2.24 (1986): 137–46.

——. *José Martí, apóstol, poeta, revolucionario: una historia de su recepción.* Trans. Luis Carlos Henao de Brigard. Mexico City: Universidad Nacional Autónoma de México, 1995.

Fabian, Johannes. *Time and the Other: How Anthropology Makes Its Object.* New York: Columbia University Press, 1983.

Fanon, Frantz. *Black Skin, White Masks.* Trans. Charles Lam Markmann. New York: Grove Weidenfeld, 1967.

Fernández Retamar, Roberto. "A un siglo de cuando José Martí se solidarizó con los mártires obreros asesinados en Chicago." *Universidad de la Habana* 232 (1988). 59–70.

——. *Calibán and Other Essays.* Trans. Edward Baker. Foreword by Fredric Jameson. Minneapolis: University of Minnesota Press, 1989.

——. "Martí en su (tercer) mundo." In *Obras*, vol. 2: *Introducción a José Martí*, 13–80. Havana: Editorial Letras Cubanas, 2001.

——. "José Martí: A Cuban for all Seasons." Trans. Maria Arana-Ward. *Washington Post Book World* (May 14, 1995): 8.

——. "Sobre 'Ramona' de Helen Hunt Jackson y José Martí." In *Mélanges à la memoire d'André Joucla-Ruau*, 2:699–705. Provence: Editions de l'Université de Provence, 1978.

Ferrer, Ada. *Insurgent Cuba: Race, Nation, Revolution, 1868–1898.* Chapel Hill: University of North Carolina Press, 1999.

——. "The Silence of Patriots: Race and Nationalism in Martí's Cuba." In Belnap and Fernandez, *José Martí's "Our America,"* 228–49.

Figueredo, Bernardo. "Recuerdos de Martí." Transcribed by Cintio Vittier and Fina García Marruz. *Anuario Martiano* 3 (1971): 137–57.

Figueroa, Sotero. "La Independencia de Puerto Rico." *Patria*, no. 1 (March 14, 1892): 1. Reprinted in Meléndez, *Puerto Rico en Patria*, 147–56.

——. "Calle la pasión y hable la sinceridad." *La Doctrina de Martí*, September 16, 1896; October 2, 1896; November 10, 1896; November 30, 1896; December 30, 1896; February 15, 1897; March 2, 1897. Reprinted in *Anuario Martiano* 6 (1976): 192–224.

Fischer, Sibylle. *Modernity Disavowed: Haiti and the Cultures of Slavery in the Age of Revolution.* Durham, N.C.: Duke University Press, 2004.

Flaubert, Gustave. *Bouvard and Pécuchet.* Trans. A. J. Krailsheimer. New York: Penguin Books, 1976.

Flint, Charles R. *Memories of an Active Life: Men, and Ships, and Sealing Wax.* New York: G. P. Putnam's Sons, 1923.

Flores, Juan. "Latino Studies: New Contexts, New Concepts." In *Critical Latin American and Latino Studies*, ed. Juan Poblete, 191–205.

Flores, Juan, and George Yúdice. "Living Borders / Buscando América: Languages of Latino Self-Formation." *Divided Borders: Essays on Puerto Rican Identity*, 199–224. Houston, Tex.: Arte Público Press, 1993.

Folsom, Ed. "Lucifer and Ethiopia: Whitman, Race, and Poetics before the Civil War and After." In *A Historical Guide to Walt Whitman*, ed. David S. Reynolds, 45–96. Oxford: Oxford University Press, 2000.

Foner, Philip S. Introduction to *Our America: Writings on Latin America*, ed. Philip Foner, trans. Elinor Randall, with additional translations by Luis A. Baralt, Juan de Onís, and Roslyn Held Foner, 11–68. New York: Monthly Review Press, 1977.

——. *The Spanish-Cuban American War and the Birth of American Imperialism (1896–1902).* 2 vols. New York: Monthly Review Press, 1972.

Font, Mauricio A., and Alfonso W. Quiroz, eds. *The Cuban Republic and José Martí: Reception and Use of a National Symbol.* Lanham, Md.: Lexington Books, 2006.

Foucault, Michel. *The Archeology of Knowledge and the Discourse on Language.* Trans. Sheridan Smith. New York: Pantheon Books, 1972.

——. "What Is Enlightenment?" In *The Foucault Reader*, ed. Paul Rabinow. New York: Pantheon Books, 1984.

Fountain, Anne. *José Martí and U.S. Writers.* Gainesville: University Press of Florida, 2003.

Fox, Claire. "Commentary: The Transnational Turn and the Hemispheric Return."
    American Literary History (July 2006): 638–46.
Franklin, Jane. *Cuba and the United States: A Chronological History.* Melbourne:
    Ocean Press, 1997.
Fusco, Coco. "El Diario de Miranda / Miranda's Diary." In *Bridges to Cuba*, ed.
    Behar, 198–216.
Gagnier, Regenia. "A Critique of Practical Aesthetics." In *Aesthetics and Ideology*,
    ed. George Levine, 264–82. New Brunswick, N.J.: Rutgers University Press, 1994.
Gaonkar, Dilip Parameshwar. "On Alternative Modernities." In *Alternative Moder-
    nities*, ed. Dilip Parameshwar Gaonkar, 1–23. Durham, N.C.: Duke University
    Press, 2001.
Garcia, Enildo A. "José Martí y Walt Whitman: literatura, libertad y democracia."
    Circulo: Revista de cultura 25 (1996): 75–88.
García Canclini, Nestor. *Culturas híbridas: estrategias para entrar y salir de la mo-
    dernidad.* Mexico City: Grijalbo, 1990.
García Marruz, Fina. "Un artículo desconocido de Martí." *Anuario martiano* 2
    (1970): 111–19.
———. "Modernismo, modernidad y orbe nuevo." *Anuario del Centro de Estudios
    Martianos* 14 (1991): 16–34.
García Pascual, Luis. *Entorno martiano.* Havana: Casa Editora Abril, 2003.
———, ed. *José Martí: destinatorio.* Havana: Casa Editora Abril, 1999.
Gaspar de Alba, Alicia. "The Chicana/Latina Dyad, or Identity and Perception."
    Latino Studies 1 (2003): 106–14.
———. "Crop Circles in the Cornfield: Remembering Gloria E. Anzaldúa (1942–
    2004)." *American Quarterly* 56.3 (2004): iv–vii.
Gikandi, Simon. *Maps of Englishness: Writing Identity in the Culture of Colonialism.*
    New York: Columbia University Press, 1996.
———. *Writing in Limbo: Modernism and Caribbean Literature.* Ithaca, N.Y.: Cornell
    University Press, 1992.
Giles, Paul. "The Parallel Worlds of José Martí." *Radical History Review* 89 (spring
    2004): 185–90.
Gillman, Susan. "*Ramona* in 'Our America.' " In Belnap and Fernández, *José Mar-
    tí's "Our America,"* 91–111.
Gilroy, Paul. *The Black Atlantic: Modernity and Double Consciousness.* Cambridge:
    Harvard University Press, 1993.
Gimeno, Patricio. "Remini scencias de José Martí." In Suárez León, *Yo Conocí a
    Martí*, 67–74.
Glissant, Édouard. *Caribbean Discourse: Selected Essays.* Trans. J. Michael Dash.
    Charlottesville: University Press of Virginia, 1989.
Godoy's Guide: World's Fair Chicago. New York: E. Lockwood, 1893.
Gómez, Juan Gualberto. "Martí y yo." In Suárez Léon, *Yo conocí a Martí*, 75–82.
Gomez-Reinoso, Manuel. "Martí and Whitman." *West Hills Review: A Walt Whit-
    man Journal* 3 (1981–82): 47–48.
Gonzalez, John M. "The Warp of Whiteness: Domesticity and Empire in Helen
    Hunt Jackson's *Ramona*." *American Literary History* 16.3 (2004) 437–65.

González, José Eduardo. "Dialectics of Archaism and Modernity: Technique and Primitivism in Angel Rama's *Transculturacion narrativa en América Latina*." In *Primitivism and Identity in Latin America: Essays on Art, Literature and Culture*, Erik Camayd-Freixas and José Eduardo González, eds., 89–107. Tuscon: University of Arizona Press, 2000.

González, José Luis. *En Nueva York y otras desgracias*. Río Piedras, Puerto Rico: Ediciones Huracán, 1981.

González, Manuel Pedro. *José Martí, Epic Chronicler of the United States*. Chapel Hill: University of North Carolina Press, 1953.

González, Manuel J. "El Maestro." In Suárez León, *Yo conocí a Martí*, 87–91.

González de la Garza, Mauricio. *Walt Whitman: racista, imperialista antimexicano*. México: Colección Málaga, 1971.

González Echevarría, Roberto. Introduction to Martí, *Selected Wrtitings*.

González-Pérez, Aníbal. *La crónica modernista hispanoamericana*. Madrid: Ediciones José Porrúa Turanzas, S.A., 1983.

——. *Journalism and the Development of Spanish American Narrative*. Cambridge: Cambridge University Press, 1993.

González Veranes, Pedro N. *La personalidad de Rafael Serra y sus relaciones con Martí*. Havana: Imp. E.U.S.A., 1943.

"The Good Gray Poet Is White Now: Walt Whitman's Welcome by His Friends in Madison Square Theater." *The Sun*, April 15, 1887: 1.

Gould, Lewis L. *Grand Old Party: A History of the Republicans*. New York: Random House, 2003.

Grady, Henry Woodfin. *The New South, and Other Addresses*. Ed. Edna Henry Lee Turpin. New York: Haskell House, 1969.

Gray, Walter D. *Interpreting American Democracy in France: The Career of Edouard Laboulaye (1811–1883)*. Newark: University of Delaware, 1994.

"Grey Bard's Lecture, The." *New York World*, April 15, 1887.

Grossman, Jay. *Reconstituting the American Renaissance: Emerson, Whitman and the Politics of Representation*. Durham, N.C.: Duke University Press, 2003.

Gruesz, Kirsten Silva. *Ambassadors of Culture: The Transamerican Origins of Latino Writing*. Princeton, N.J.: Princeton University Press, 2002.

——. "The Gulf of Mexico System and the 'Latinness' of New Orleans." *American Literary History* 18.3 (fall 2006): 468–95.

——. "Translation: A Key(word) into the Language of America(nists)." *American Literary History* 16.1 (spring 2004): 85–92.

Guerra, Lillian. *The Myth of José Martí: Conflicting Nationalisms in Early Twentieth-Century Cuba*. Chapel Hill: University of North Carolina Press, 2005.

Guevara, Ernesto. "Mensaje a los pueblos del mundo a través de la Tricontinental" (Message to the Peoples of the World through the Tricontinental). *Tricontinental*, special supplement April 16, 1967. Reprinted in Ernesto "Che" Guevara, *Obras completas: escritos y discursos*, vol. 9, 355–72. Havana: Editorial de Ciencias Sociales, 1977.

Gutierrez, Rámon A., and Richard J. Orsi, eds. *Contested Eden: California before the Gold Rush*. Berkeley: University of California Press, 1998.

Gutiérrez-Jones, Carl. *Rethinking the Borderlands: between Chicano Culture and Legal Discourse*. Berkeley: University of California Press, 1995.

Habermas, Jürgen. *The Philosophical Discourse of Modernity: Twelve Lectures*. Trans. Frederick Lawrence. Cambridge, Mass.: MIT Press, 1987.

Handley, George B. "On Reading South in the New World: Whitman, Martí, Glissant and the Hegelian Dialectic." *Mississippi Quarterly: The Journal of Southern Cultures* 56.4 (fall 2003): 521–44.

Hardt, Michael, and Antonio Negri, *Empire*. Cambridge, Mass.: Harvard University Press, 2000.

Harrison, Brady. *Agent of Empire: William Walker and the Imperial Self in American Literature*. Athens: University of Georgia Press, 2004.

Hegel, Georg Wilhelm Friedrich. *Phenomenology of Mind*. Trans. J. B. Baillie. New York: Harper and Row, 1967.

——. *The Philosophy of History*. Trans. J. Sibree. New York: Dover Publications, 1956.

Henríquez Ureña, Max. *Breve historia del modernismo*. Mexico: Fondo de Cultura Económica, 1954.

Hewitt, Nancy A. "Paulina Pedroso and Las Patriotas of Tampa." In *Spanish Pathways in Florida, 1492–1992*. Ann Henderson and Gary Morminom, eds., 258–79. Sarasota, Fla.: Pineapple Press, 1991.

Hidalgo Paz, Ibrahim. *José Martí, 1853–1895: Cronología*. Havana: Centro de Estudios Martianos, 2003.

Hoganson, Kristin. *Fighting for American Manhood: How Gender Politics Provoked the Spanish-American and Philippine American Wars*. New Haven, Conn.: Yale University Press, 1998.

Holloway, Emory. Introduction to Whitman, *I Sit and Look Out*, 3–30.

Holmes, Oliver Wendell. "Over the Teacups." *Atlantic Monthly* 66 (September 1890): 388–89.

Huntington, Samuel. *Who Are We? The Challenges to American Identity*. New York: Simon and Schuster, 2004.

Irwin, Robert McKee. "Ramona and Postnationalist American Studies: On 'Our America' and the Mexican Borderlands." *American Quarterly* 55.4 (December 2003): 539–67.

Isaacson, William D. "José Martí y el Club Crepusculo." *Archivo José Martí* 15 (January–June 1950): 112–18.

Jackson, Helen Hunt. *A Century of Dishonor: A Sketch of the United States Government's Dealings with Some of the Indian Tribes*. 1885; Norman: University of Oklahoma Press, 1995.

——. *Ramona*. New York: Signet Classic, 1988.

Jacolliot, Louis. *Voyage to the Country of Liberty: Communal Life in the United States*. Ed. Paul Douglas. Trans. George McCool. Lewiston, N.Y.: Edwin Mellon Press, 2007.

James, C. L. R. *The Black Jacobins*. New York: Vintage, 1963.

——. *Mariners, Renegades and Castaways: The Story of Herman Melville and the World We Live In*. 1953; Hanover, N.H.: University Press of New England, 2001.

James, Henry. *The American Scene*. 1907; New York: Penguin, 1994.

———. "Ralph Waldo Emerson: Review of 'A Memoir of Ralph Waldo Emerson' by James Elliot Cabot." In *Major Stories and Essays*, 594–615. New York: Literary Classics of the United States, 1999.

James, William. "Address at the Annual Meeting of the New England Anti-Imperialist League," in *Report of the Fifth Annual Meeting of the New England Anti-Imperialist League*. Boston: New England Anti-Imperialist League, 1903.

James, Winston. *Holding Aloft the Banner of Ethiopia: Caribbean Radicalism in Early Twentieth-Century America*. London: Verso, 1998.

Jameson, Fredric. "Modernism and Imperialism." In Terry Eagleton, Fredric Jameson, and Edward W. Said, *Nationalism, Colonialism, Literature*, 43–68. Minneapolis: University of Minnesota Press, 1990.

———. *A Singular Modernity: Essay on the Ontology of the Present*. London: Verso, 2002.

Jitrik, Noe. "El sistema modernista (o rubendariano)." In *Nuevos asedios al modernismo*, ed. Ivan A. Schulman, 51–61. Madrid: Taurus, 1987.

Johnson, Barbara. "Writing." In *Critical Terms for Literary Study*, 2nd ed. Frank Lentricchia and Thomas McLaughlin, eds., 39–49. Chicago: University of Chicago Press, 1995.

Johnson, James Welden. *The Autobiography of an Ex-Coloured Man*. 1912. New York: Vintage Books, 1989.

Jrade, Cathy. *Modernismo, Modernity and the Development of Spanish American Literature*. Austin: University of Texas Press, 1998.

Kadir, Djelal. "Defending America against Its Devotees." In *How Far Is America from Here? Selected Proceedings of the First World Congress of The International American Studies Association, 22–24 May, 2003*, 13–34. Amsterdam: Editions Rodopi, 2005.

Kanellos, Nicolás, ed. *Herencia: The Anthology of Hispanic Literature of the United States*. Oxford: Oxford University Press, 2002.

Kaplan, Amy. "Violent Belonging and the Question of Empire Today." Presidential address to the American Studies Association, October 17, 2003. *American Quarterly* 56.1 (2004): 1–18.

Kaplan, Justin. *Walt Whitman: A Life*. New York: Harper Collins, 1980.

Kelly, Robin D. G. "Lucy Parsons." In *Black Women in America: An Historical Encyclopedia*, ed. Darlene Clark Hine. Brooklyn, N.Y.: Carlson, 1993.

Kinzer, Stephen. *Overthrow: America's Century of Regime Change from Hawaii to Iraq*. New York: Henry Holt, 2006.

Klammer, Martin. *Whitman, Slavery and the Emergence of "Leaves of Grass."* University Park: Pennsylvania State University Press, 1994.

Kojève, Alexandre. *Introduction to the Reading of Hegel: Lectures on the Phenomenology of Spirit*. Ed. Allan Bloom, trans. James H. Nichols Jr. Ithaca, N.Y.: Cornell University Press, 1969.

Kristal, Efraín. *Invisible Work: Borges and Translation*. Nashville, Tenn.: Vanderbilt University Press, 2002.

Kronick, Joseph. "Emerson and the Question of Reading/Writing." *Genre* 14.3 (fall 1981): 363–81.

Laboulaye, Edouard. *Paris in America.* Trans. Mary Booth. New York: Charles Scribners, 1863.

Laraway, David. "José Martí and the Call of Technology in 'Amor de ciudad grande." *Modern Language Notes* 119.2 (2004): 290–301.

Larsen, Neil. *Determinations: Essays on Theory, Narrative, and Nation in the Americas.* New York: Verso, 2001.

Lazo, Rodrigo. *Writing to Cuba: Filibustering and Cuban Exiles in the United States.* Chapel Hill: University of North Carolina Press, 2005.

Lee, Li-Young. "The Cleaving." In *The City in Which I Love You.* Rochester, N.Y.: BOA Editions, 1990.

Lewis, R. W. B. *The American Adam: Innocence, Tragedy and Tradition in the Nineteenth Century.* Chicago: University of Chicago Press, 1955.

Levander, Caroline F., and Robert S. Levine. "Introduction: Hemispheric American Studies." *American Literary History* 18.3 (2006): 397–406.

——, eds. *Hemispheric American Studies.* Rutgers, N.J.: Rutgers University Press, 2008.

Levine, Robert S. *Martin R. Delany: A Documentary Reader.* Chapel Hill: University of North Carolina Press, 2003.

Lewis, Gordon K. *Main Currents in Caribbean Thought: The Historical Evolution of Caribbean Society in Its Ideological Aspects, 1492–1900.* Baltimore, Md.: Johns Hopkins University Press, 1983.

Limerick, Patricia Nelson. "The Adventures of the Frontier in the Twentieth Century." In *The Frontier in American Culture: An Exhibition at the Newberry Library, August 26, 1994–January 7, 1995: Essays by Richard White and Patricia Nelson Limerick*, ed. James R. Grossman, 66–102. Chicago: Newberry Library, 1994.

Limón, José. "Translating Empire: The Border Homeland of Rio Grande, Texas." *America Quarterly* 56.1 (March 2004): 25–32.

Lipsitz, George. *The Possessive Investment in Whiteness: How White People Profit from Identity Politics.* Philadelphia, Pa.: Temple University Press, 1998.

Lizaso, Félix. "Emerson visto por Martí." *Humanismo* (September 23, 1954): 35.

——. *Místico del deber.* Buenos Aires: Editorial Losada, 1945.

Llanes Abeijón, Manuel, et al. "La traducción martiana de un poema de Longfellow." *Islas* 79 (September–December 1984): 15–25.

Lloyd, David Demarest, and Sydney Rosenfeld. *The Senator.* 1889. New York: Feedback Theatrebooks and Prospero Press, 1996.

Lomas, Laura A. "American Alterities: Reading between Borders in José Martí's 'North American Scenes.'" Ph.D. dissertation, Columbia University, 2001.

——. "Between Nation and Empire: Latino Cultural Critique at the Intersection of the Americas." In *The Cuban Republic and José Martí: Reception and Use of a National Symbol*, ed. Mauricio A. Font and Alfonso W. Quiroz, 115–27. Boston, Mass.: Lexington Books, 2006.

——. "Imperialism, Modernity and the Commodification of Identity." *Journal of Latin American Cultural Studies.* 9.2 (Aug. 2000): 193–212.

——. "Redefining the American Revolutionary: Gabriela Mistral on José Martí." *Comparative American Studies* 6.3 (September 2008): 241–64.

Lopez, Michael. "De-Transcendentalizing Emerson." *ESQ: A Journal of the American Renaissance* 34.1–2 (1988): 77–139.

——. "Emerson and Nietzsche: An Introduction." *ESQ: A Journal of the American Renaissance* 43.1 (1997): 1–35.

——. *Emerson and Power: Creative Antagonism in the Nineteenth Century.* DeKalb: North Illinois University Press, 1996.

López Mesa, Enrique. *La comunidad cubana de New York: Siglo XIX.* Havana: Centro de Estudios Martianos, 2002.

Lowe, Lisa. "Towards a Critical Modernity." *Anglistica* 4.1 (2000): 69–89.

Lowell, James Russell. *New Letters of James Russell Lowell.* Ed. M. A. DeWolfe Howe. New York: Harper, 1932.

Loynaz, Dulce María. *Bestiarium.* Havana: Editorial José Martí, 1993.

Lugo-Ortíz, Agnes. *Identidades imaginadas: biografía y nacionalidad en el horizonte de la guerra (Cuba 1860–1898).* San Juan: Editorial de la Universidad de Puerto Rico, 1999.

Macaulay, Thomas Babington. "Indian Education: Minutes of the 2nd of February, 1835." In *Macaulay: Prose and Poetry,* ed G. M. Young, 719–30. London: Rupert Hart-Davis, 1952.

Magnaghi, Russell M. *Herbert Bolton and the Historiography of the Americas.* Westport, Conn.: Greenwood Press, 1998.

Mañach, Jorge. *El Apóstol.* 1933; Havana: Editorial de Ciencias Sociales, 2001.

Marcos, [Subcomandante]. *Our Word Is Our Weapon: Selected Writings.* Ed. Juana Ponce de León. New York: Seven Stories Press, 2001.

Marín, Francisco Gonzálo. "Martí." In *En la arena: poesías.* Manzanillo, Cuba: Editorial el Arte, 1944.

Marinello, Juan. *Once ensayos martianos.* Havana: Comisión Nacional de la Unesco, 1965.

Marquez Sterling, Carlos. *Martí, ciudadano de América.* New York: Las Américas Publishing, 1965.

——. "Martí y la Conferencia Monetaria de 1891." In *Discursos leídos en la recepción pública del Dr. Carlos Márquez Sterling, Academia de la Historia de Cuba.* Havana: Imprenta "El Siglo XX," 1938.

Martí, José. "El alzamiento de los trabajadores en los Estados Unidos" (The Uprising of the Workers in the United States). *El Partido Liberal,* May 29, 1886. Reprinted in *Otras Crónicas de Nueva York,* 19–31. Reprinted in *En los Estados Unidos,* 600–608.

——. *The America of José Martí.* Ed. Federico de Onís. Trans. Juan de Onís. New York: Noonday Press, 1954.

——. "El asesinato de los italianos." *La Nación,* May 20, 1891. Reprinted in *En los Estados Unidos,* Fernández Retamar and Pedro Pablo Rodriguez, eds., 1484–88, and in *Selected Writings,* 296–303.

——. "Asuntos Varios." *El Partido Liberal*, January 11, 1887. Reprinted in *Otras Crónicas*, 96–99.

——. "Emerson." Reprinted in *Obras completas*, Editorial de Ciencias Sociales edn., 13:15–30. English translation in *Selected Writings*, 116–29.

——. *En los Estados Unidos: periodismo de 1881–1892*. Ed. Roberto Fernández Retamar and Pedro Pablo Rodríguez. Havana: Casa de las Américas, 2003.

——. *Epistolario*. 5 vols. Ed. Luis García Pascual and Enrique H. Moreno Pla. Havana: Editorial de Ciencias Sociales, 1993.

——. "Escenas neoyorkinas." *La América* (c.1884). Reprinted in *El Triunfo* (Havana) (September 5, 1884); and in Rafael Cepeda, "José Martí: otro artículo desconocido," *Santiago: Revista de la Universidad de Oriente* 46 (June 1982): 205–18.

——. *Escritos desconocidos de José Martí*. Ed. Carlos Ripoll. New York: Eliseo Torres and Sons, 1971.

——. "Exposición de productos americanos." In *Obras completas*, Editorial de Ciencias Sociales edn., 8:366–68.

——. "Flaubert's Last Work." *New York Sun*, July 8, 1880. Reprinted in *Obras completas*, Editorial de Ciencias Sociales edn., 15:203–9.

——. "Honduras y los extranjeros." *Patria*, December 15, 1894. Reprinted in *Obras completas* 8:35–36.

——. Letter to the Editor of the *New York Herald* ("The Letter from the Cuban Leader"). English version, May 19, 1895. Spanish version, *Patria*, June 3, 1895. Reprinted in *Epistolario*, 5:205–25, and in Toledo Sande, "José Martí contra *The New York Herald*," 49–72.

——. *Lucía Jerez*. Ed. Carlos Javier Morales. Madrid: Ediciones Cátedra, 1994.

——. "Maestros ambulantes." *La América*, May 1884. Reprinted in *Obras*, 8:288–92. Trans. "Wandering Teachers." In *José Martí Reader: Writings on the Americas*, Deborah Shnookal and Mirta Muñiz, 46–50. Melbourne: Ocean Press, 1999.

——. "México y los Estados Unidos." *La Nación*, September 18, 1886. Reprinted in *En los Estados Unidos*, 694–97.

——. "La Mujer Norteamericana." *El Partido Liberal*, November 7, 1886. In *Otras Crónicas*, 79–86. Reprinted in *En los Estados Unidos*, 737–42.

——. "Nuestra América." *El Partido Liberal*, January 30, 1891. In *Obras completas*, Editorial de Ciencias Sociales, 6:13–23.

——. *Obras completas*. 28 vols. Havana: Editorial de Ciencias Sociales, 1963–65. Page references are to the second edition, 1975.

——. *Obras completas*. Critical edition. Cintio Vitier, Fina García-Marruz, and Emilio de Armas, eds. Vols. 1–2. Havana: Casa de las Americas, Centro de Estudios Martianos, 1983–85.

——. *Otras crónicas de Nueva York*. Havana: Centro de Estudios Martianos, 1983.

——. *Papeles de Martí* (Archivo de Gonzalo de Quesada). 3 vols. Ed. Gonzalez de Quesada y Miranda. Havana: Imprenta "El Siglo XX," 1933–35.

——. "Para las Escenas." *Granma*, January 28, 1978, 2. Reprinted in *Casa de las Americas* 219 (2000): 5–6.

——. *Poesía completa*. Critical edition, Cintio Vitier, Fina García-Marruz, and

Emilio de Armas, eds. Mexico City: Universidad Nacional Autónoma de México, 1998.

———. "El poeta Walt Whitman." *El Partido Liberal*, May 17, 1887. Reprinted in *Obras completas*, Editorial de Ciencias Sociales edn., 13:129–43, and in *Selected Writings*, 183–94.

———. *El presidio político en Cuba*. Madrid: 1871. Reprinted in *Obras completas*, Editorial de Ciencias Sociales edn., 1:45–75; and excerpted in *Selected Writings*, 9–18.

———. Prólogo a *El Poema Niágara* de Juan Antonio Pérez Bonalde, i–xxv. Reprinted in *Obras completas*, Editorial de Ciencias Sociales edn., 7:223–38, and in *Selected Writings*, 43–51.

———. "Un pueblo quema a un negro." *Otras crónicas de Nueva York*, 186–89. Reprinted in *Selected Writings*, 310–13.

———. *La República española ante la Revolución cubana*. Madrid: Imprenta de Segundo Martínez, 1873.

———. *Versos sencillos / Simple verses*. Trans. with intro. by Manuel A. Tellechea. Houston, Texas: Arte Público Press, 1997.

———. "A Vindication of Cuba." *Evening Post*, March 25, 1889. Reprinted in *Selected Writings*, 263–67.

———. *Selected Writings*. Ed. and trans. Esther Allen. New York: Penguin, 2002.

Martínez, Mayra Beatriz. *Martí: eros y mujer (revisitando el canon)*. Havana: Letras Cubanas, 2005.

Martínez, Elena M. "Contradictions, Pluralism and Dialogue: An Interview with René Vázquez Díaz." In *Bridges to Cuba*, ed. Ruth Behar, 232–40.

Marx, Karl. *Eighteenth Brumaire of Louis Bonaparte*. New York: International Publishers, 1963.

———. "Letters to Dr. Kugelmann on the Paris Commune." In Marx and Lenin, *The Civil War in France*.

Marx, Karl, and V. I. Lenin. *The Civil War in France: The Paris Commune*. New York: International Publishers, 1968.

Matsumoto, Valerie J., and Blake Allmendinger, eds. *Over the Edge: Remapping the American West*. Berkeley: University of California Press, 1999.

Mayorga Rivas, Román. "El poeta Walt Whitman." *La Revista Ilustrada de Nueva York*, June 1890, 7–8.

McGann, Thomas F. *Argentina, the United States, and the Inter-American System: 1880–1914*. Cambridge, Mass.: Harvard University Press, 1957.

Medley, Keith Weldon. *We as Freemen: Plessy vs. Ferguson*. Gretna, Louisiana: Pelican Publishing, 2003.

Mejía Sánchez, Ernesto. "Las relaciones literarias interamericanas: el caso Martí-Whitman-Darío." *Casa de las Américas* 7 (1967): 52–57.

Meléndez, Edgardo. *Puerto Rico en "Patria."* Río Piedras: Universidad de Puerto Rico, Decanato de Asuntos Académicos, 1996.

Memmi, Albert. *The Colonizer and the Colonized*. Trans. Howard Greenfeld. Boston, Mass.: Beacon Press, 1967.

Merrill, Stuart. "Walt Whitman." Trans. John J. Espey. *Walt Whitman Newsletter* 3.4 (December 1957): 55–57.

Mignolo, Walter D. "Human Understanding and (Latin) American Interests—The Politics and Sensibilities of Geohistorical Locations." In Ray and Schwartz, *Companion to Post-Colonial Studies*, 180–202.

———. *The Idea of Latin America*. Malden, Mass.: Blackwell, 2005.

———. *Local Histories / Global Designs: Coloniality, Subaltern Knowledges and Border Thinking*. Princeton, N.J.: Princeton University Press, 2000.

Miller, Perry. *The American Puritans: Their Prose and Poetry*. New York: Doubleday, 1956.

———. *Errand into the Wilderness*. Cambridge, Mass.: Belknap Press of Harvard University Press, 1956.

Mir, Pedro. *Hay un país en el mundo y otras poemas de Pedro Mir*. Santo Domingo, Dominican Rep.: Ediciones de Taller, 1982.

Mirabal, Nancy Raquel. " 'No Country But the One We Must Fight For': The Emergence of an Antillean Nation and Community in New York City (1860–1901)." In *Mambo Montage: The Latinization of New York*, ed. Agostin Laó-Montes and Arlene Dávila, 57–72. New York: Columbia University Press, 2001.

———. "Más que negro: José Martí and the Politics of Unity." In *José Martí in the United States*, Louis A. Pérez Jr., ed., 57–69.

———. " 'Ser de aquí': Beyond the Cuban Exile Model." *Latino Studies* 1 (2003): 366–82.

Mistral, Gabriela. "On Jorge Mañach." In prologue to Jorge Mañach, *Martí: Apostle of Freedom*. Trans. Coley Taylor, xiii–xvi. New York: Devin-Adair, 1950.

Molloy, Sylvia. "His America, Our America: José Martí Reads Whitman." In *Breaking Bounds*, Betsy Erkkila and Jay Grossman, eds., 83–91.

Montero, Oscar. *José Martí: An Introduction*. New York: Palgrave, 2005.

Moon, Michael. *Disseminating Whitman: Revision and Corporeality in* Leaves of Grass. Cambridge, Mass.: Harvard University Press, 1991.

Moore, John Bassett. "Henry Clay and Pan-Americanism: An Address Delivered before the Kentucky State Bar Association at Frankfort, KY, on July 8, 1915," *Columbia University Quarterly* 17.4 (September 1915): 346–62.

Morales, Carlos Javier. "La americanización de la literatura en el pensamiento de José Martí." *CIEFL Bulletin*, new ser, 7.1–2 (June–Dec. 1995): 39–47.

Moreiras, Alberto. *The Exhaustion of Difference: The Politics of Latin American Cultural Studies*. Durham, N.C.: Duke University Press, 2001.

Morejón, Nancy. "Cuba and Its Deep Africanity." *Callaloo* 28.4 (2005): 933–51.

Morgan, H. Wayne. *From Hayes to McKinley: National Party Politics, 1877–1896*. Syracuse, N.Y.: Syracuse University Press, 1970.

Morrison, Toni. "On the Backs of Blacks." In *Arguing Immigration: Are New Immigrants a Wealth of Diversity . . . or a Crushing Burden?*, ed. Nicolaus Mills, 97–100. New York: Simon and Schuster, 1994.

Moylan, Michele. "Materiality as Performance: The Forming of Helen Hunt Jackson's *Ramona*." In *Reading Books: Essays on the Material Text and Literature in*

America, ed. Michele Moylan and Lane Stiles, 223–47. Amherst: University of Massachusetts Press, 1996.

Murphy, Gretchen. *Hemispheric Imaginings: The Monroe Doctrine and Narratives of U.S. Empire.* Durham, N.C.: Duke University Press, 2005.

Moses, L. G. *Wild West Shows and the Images of American Indians, 1883–1933.* Albequerque, N.M.: University of New Mexico Press, 1996.

Muzzey, David Saville. *James G. Blaine: A Political Idol of Other Days.* New York: Dodd, Mead, 1934.

Negrón-Muntaner, Frances. "Bridging Islands: Gloria Anzaldúa and the Caribbean." *PMLA* 121.1 (January 2006): 272–78.

Newfield, Christopher. *The Emerson Effect: Individualism and Submission in America.* Chicago: University of Chicago Press, 1996.

———. "The Next Secretary of State Casts Longing Eyes on Cuba: Shall We Buy the Island? Mr. Blaine on the Advisability of Making the Purchase." *New York Herald*, February 12, 1899, 4.

Ngai, Mae M. *Impossible Subjects: Illegal Aliens and the Making of Modern America.* Princeton, N.J.: Princeton University Press, 2004.

Nietzsche, Friedrich. *Beyond Good and Evil.* Trans. Marianne Cowen. South Bend, Ind.: Gateway Editions, 1955.

Noble, David. *Death of a Nation: American Culture and the End of Exceptionalism.* Minneapolis: University of Minnesota Press, 2002.

O'Connor, Richard. *Buffalo Bill, the Noblest Whiteskin.* New York: G. P. Putnam's Sons, 1973.

O'Gorman, Edmundo. "Do the Americas Have a Common History?" Trans. Angel Flores, *Points of View*, no. 8. Washington, D.C.: Pan-American Union, Division of Intellectual Cooperation, 1941. Reprinted in *Do the Americas Have a Common History? A Critique of the Bolton Theory*, ed. Lewis Hanke, 103–11. New York: Knopf, 1964.

———. "Hegel y el moderno panamericanismo," *Universidad de la Habana* 8.22 (January–February 1939): 61–74.

———. *La invención de América: el universalismo de la cultura de Occidente.* Mexico City: Fondo de Cultura Económica, 1958.

Onís, Federico de. *Antología de la poesía española e hispanoamericana, 1882–1932.* 1934; New York: Las Americas Publishing, 1961.

———. Introduction to José Martí, *The America of José Martí: Selected Writings*, ed. Federico de Onís, trans. Juan de Onís, vii–xiii. New York: Noonday Press, 1954.

———. "Martí y el modernismo." In *Antología crítica de José Martí*, ed. Manuel Pedro González, 155–66. Mexico City: Publicaciones de la Editorial Cultura, 1960.

Ortíz, Fernando. "Cuba, Martí and the Race Problem." *Phylon* 3.3 (1942): 253–76.

Ortiz Marquez, Maribel. "Utopía y crítica cultural: a propósito de Rama y Martí." *Revista de Estudios Hispánicos* 30.1 (2003): 167–79.

O'Sullivan, John L. "The Great Nation of Futurity." *United States Magazine and Democratic Review* (November 1839): 426–30.

Otero, Ricardo Rodríguez. *Impresiones y recuerdos de mi viaje a los Estados de Nueva York, Nueva Jersey y Pennsylvania*. Sagua la Grande, Cuba: n.p., 1887.

Ouillon, Juliette. "La discriminación racial en los Estados Unidos vista por José Martí." *Anuario Martiano* 3 (1971): 9–94.

Oviedo, José Miguel. *La niña de Nueva York: una revision de la vida erótica de José Martí*. Mexico City: Fondo de Cultura Económica, 1989.

Packer, Barbara. *Emerson's Fall: A New Interpretation of the Major Essays*. New York: Continuum, 1982.

Padget, Martin. "Travel Writing, Sentimental Romance, and Indian Rights Advocacy: The Politics of Helen Hunt Jackson's *Ramona*." *Journal of the Southwest* 42.4 (2000): 833–76.

Park, Robert E. *The Immigrant Press and Its Control*. Westport, Conn.: Greenwood Press, 1922.

Parra, Alma. "Cónsules y empresarios, expresión local del expansionismo estadounidense hacia fines del siglo XIX." *Secuencia: Revista de Historia y Ciencias Sociales*. Nueva época 48 (September–December 2000): 171–82.

Parsons, Lucy E. *Lucy Parsons: Freedom, Equality & Solidarity Writings and Speeches, 1878–1937*. Ed. Gale Ahrens. Afterword by Roxanne Dumbar-Ortiz. Chicago: Charles H. Kerr, 2004.

Partridge, Jeffrey F. L. "The Politics of Ethnic Authorship: Li-Young Lee, Emerson and Whitman at the Banquet Table." *Studies in the Literary Imagination* 37.1 (spring 2004): 103–26.

Pascual, Luis García. *Entorno Martiano*. Havana: Casa Editora Abril, 2003.

Paz, Octavio. *Children of the Mire: Modern Poetry from Romanticism to the Avant-Garde*. Trans. Rachel Phillips. Cambridge, Mass.: Harvard University Press, 1991.

Pearce, Roy Harvey. *The Continuity of American Poetry*. Princeton, N.J.: Princeton University Press, 1961.

Pease, Donald. "Emerson, *Nature*, and the Sovereignty of Influence." *Boundary 2* 8.3 (spring 1980): 43–74.

——. "José Martí, Alexis de Tocqueville and the Politics of Displacement." In *José Martí's "Our America*," Belnap and Fernández, eds., 27–57.

——. "U.S. Imperialism: Global Dominance without Colonies." In *Companion to Post-Colonial Studies*, Ray and Schwartz, eds., 203–20.

Pérez Cabrera, José Manuel. *Diego Vincente Tejera: Escritor y patriota*. Havana: Academia de la historia de Cuba, 1948.

Pérez, Louis A., Jr., ed. *José Martí in the United States: The Florida Experience*. Tempe: Arizona State University, ASU Center for Latin American Studies, 1995.

——. *On Becoming Cuban: Identity, Nationality and Culture*. New York: Ecco Press, HarperCollins, 1999.

Phillips, Dana. "Nineteenth-Century Racial Thought and Whitman's 'Democratic Ethnology of the Future.'" *Nineteenth-Century Literature* 49.3 (December 1994): 290–94.

Phillips, George Harwood. *Chiefs and Challengers: Indian Resistance and Cooperation in Southern California*. Berkeley: University of California Press, 1975.

Phillips, Wendell, and Plutarco González y Torres. *The Cuban Question and American Policy, in the Light of Common Sense.* New York: Biglow, 1869.

Picon-Garfield, Evelyn, and Ivan Schulman. *"Las Entrañas del Vacío": Ensayos sobre la modernidad hispanoamericana.* Mexico City: Ediciones cuadernos americanos, 1984.

Pichardo, Manuel S. *La Cuidad Blanca: Crónicas de la Exposición Colombina de Chicago.* Preface by Enrique José Varona. Havana: Biblioteca de "El Fígaro," 1894.

Pletcher, David M. "Rhetoric and Results: A Pragmatic View of American Economic Expansionism, 1865–98." *Diplomatic History* 5 (spring 1981): 93–105.

Poblete, Juan, ed. *Critical Latin American and Latino Studies.* Minneapolis, Minn.: University of Minnesota Press, 2003.

Porter, Carolyn. "What We Know That We Don't Know: Remapping American Literary Studies." *American Literary History* 6 (1994): 467–526.

Poyo, Gerald E. *"With All, and for the Good of All": The Emergence of Popular Nationalism in the Cuban Communities of the United States, 1848–1898.* Durham, N.C.: Duke University Press, 1989.

Pratt, Mary Louise. *Imperial Eyes: Travel Writing and Transculturation.* London: Routledge, 1992.

——. "Modernity and Periphery: Toward a Global and Relational Analysis." In *Beyond Dichotomies: Histories, Identities and the Challenge of Globalization,* ed. Elisabeth Mudimbe-Boyi. Albany: State University of New York Press, 2002.

Quesada, Ernesto. *Primera Conferencia Panamericana.* Buenos Aires: Imprenta Schenone, 1919.

Quesada, Manuel de. *Manifesto de Cuba a los Estados Unidos.* New York: n.p., 1873.

Quesada y Miranda, Gonzalo de. *Así fue Martí.* Havana: Gente Nueva, 1977.

——. *Facetas de Martí.* Havana: Editorial Trópico, 1939.

——. *Martí, periodista.* Havana: Imprenta y Papelería de Rambla, 1929.

Quiroga, José, and Jorge Salessi. "Errata sobre la erótica, or the Elision of Whitman's Body." In *Breaking Bounds,* Betsy Erkkila and Jay Grossman, eds., 123–32.

Rae, John. *Contemporary Socialism.* New York: C. Scribner, 1884.

Rama, Angel. "La dialéctica de la modernidad en José Martí." In *Estudios Martíanos: Seminario José Martí,* 129–97. Río Piedras: Editorial Universitaria, Universidad de Puerto Rico, 1974.

——. *Las Máscaras Democráticas del Modernismo.* Montevideo, Uruguay: Fundación Angel Rama, 1985.

——. "Saber del Otro: Escritura y oralidad en el Facundo de D. F. Sarmiento." *Revista Iberoamericana* (April–June 1988): 551–69.

——. *Transculturación narrativa en América Latina.* Mexico City: Siglo Veintiuno, 1982.

Ramos, Julio. *Desencuentros de la modernidad en America Latina: literatura y política en el siglo XIX.* Mexico City: Fondo de Cultura Economica, 1989.

——. *Divergent Modernities: Culture and Politics in Nineteenth-Century Latin America.* Durham, N.C.: Duke University Press, 2001.

——. "Trópicos de la fundación: poesía y nacionalidad en José Martí." In *José Martí y los Estados Unidos*, ed. Pedro Pablo Rodríguez, 133–42. Havana: Centro de Estudios Martianos, 1998.

Ray, Sangeeta, and Henry Schwartz, eds. *Companion to Post-Colonial Studies*. London: Blackwell, 2000.

Renan, Ernest. "What Is a Nation?" In *Nation and Narration*, ed. Homi K. Bhaba, trans. Martin Thom, 8–22. New York: Routledge, 1990.

Rennert, Jack. *100 Posters of Buffalo Bill's "Wild West."* New York: Darien House, 1976.

Reynolds, David S. *Walt Whitman*. Oxford: Oxford University Press, 2005.

——. *Walt Whitman's America: A Cultural Biography*. New York: Knopf, 1995.

Ríos, Félix de los. "El tren de Martí: memorias de un Gallego Mambí, en el 140 aniversario del natalicio de José Martí." In Suárez Léon, *Yo conocí a Martí*, 148–54.

Ripley, Eliza McHatton. *From Flag to Flag: A Woman's Adventures and Experiences in the South During the War, in Mexico, and in Cuba*. New York: D. Appleton and Company, 1889.

Ripoll, Carlos. *Letras y huellas desconocidas*. New York: Eliseo Torres and Sons, 1976.

——. *José Martí, the United States, and the Marxist Interpretation of Cuban History*. New Brunswick, N.J.: Transaction Books, 1984.

——. "Marx and Martí." *New York Review of Books* 35.19 (December 8, 1988): 60.

——. *Patria: el periódico de José Martí*. New York: Eliseo Torres and Sons, 1971.

——. "Prólogo." In Sotero Figueroa, *La Verdad de la Historia*, ed. Carlos Ripoll, 5–9. San Juan: Instituto de Cultura Puertorriqueña, 1977.

Rivero, Eliana S. " 'Fronterisleña,' Border Islander." In Behar, *Bridges to Cuba / Puentes a Cuba*, 339–44.

Rodríguez, José Ignacio. *Estudio histórico sobre el origen, desenvolvimiento y manifestaciones prácticas de la idea de la anexión de la isla de Cuba á los Estados Unidos de América*. Havana: Imprenta La Propaganda Literaria, 1900.

Rodríguez, Pedro Pablo. *De las dos Américas: aproximaciones al pensamiento martiano*. Havana: Centro de Estudios Martianos, 2002.

——. *José Martí y los Estados Unidos*. Havana: Centro de Estudios Martianos, 1998.

Rodríguez-Luis, Julio, ed. *Re-Reading José Martí (1853–1895) One Hundred Years Later*. Albany: State University of New York Press, 1999.

Rojas, Rafael. *José Martí: la invención de Cuba*. Madrid: Editorial Colibri, 2001.

——. "La republica escrita." *Union: Revista de Literatura y Arte* 9 (October–December 1997): 49–56.

Romero, Matías. "The Pan-American Conference." *North American Review* 151 (1890).

Roosevelt, Theodore. *Ranch Life and the Hunting-Trail*. 1899. Ann-Arbor, Mich.: University Microfilms, 1966.

Rotker, Susana. *The American Chronicles of José Martí: Journalism and Modernity in Spanish America*. Trans. Jennifer French and Katherine Semler. Hanover, N.H.: University Press of New England, 2000.

———. *Fundación de una escritura: las crónicas de José Martí.* Havana: Editorial Casa de las Américas, 1992.

Rowe, William, and Vivian Schelling. *Memory and Modernity: Popular Culture in Latin America.* New York: Verso, 1991.

Rubens, Horatio S. *Liberty: The Story of Cuba.* 1932. New York: Arno Press, 1970.

Rubin, Joseph J., and Charles H. Brown. *Walt Whitman of the New York Aurora, Editor at Twenty-Two, A Collection of Recently Discovered Writings.* State College, Pa.: Bald Eagle Press, 1950.

Rushdie, Salman, *Imaginary Homelands and Other Essays: Essays and Criticism, 1981–1991.* London: Granta Books and Viking Penguin, 1991.

Russell, Don. *The Lives and Legends of Buffalo Bill.* Norman: University of Oklahoma Press, 1960.

Rydell, Robert. W. *All the World's a Fair.* Chicago: University of Chicago Press, 1984.

Sadowski-Smith, Claudia, and Claire Fox. "Theorizing the Hemisphere: Inter-Americas Work at the Intersection of American, Canadian, and Latin American Studies." *Comparative American Studies* 2.1 (2004): 5–38.

Said, Edward W. *Musical Elaborations.* New York: Columbia University Press, 1991.

———. *Reflections on Exile and Other Essays.* Cambridge, Mass.: Harvard University Press, 2003.

———. *The World, the Text and the Critic.* Cambridge, Mass.: Harvard University Press, 1983.

Saldívar, José David. *Border Matters: Remapping American Cultural Studies.* Berkeley: University of California Press, 1997.

———. *The Dialectics of Our America: Genealogy, Cultural Critique and Literary History.* Berkeley: University of California Press, 1991.

———. Foreword to Ramos, *Divergent Modernities,* xi–xxxiv.

Saldívar, Ramón. *The Borderlands of Cultures: Américo Paredes and the Transnational Imaginary.* Durham, N.C.: Duke University Press, 2006.

Sánchez, Luis Alberto. *Historia comparada de las literaturas americanas.* 4 vols. Buenos Aires: Editorial Losada, 1973–76.

Sánchez-Eppler, Karen. *Touching Liberty: Abolition, Feminism and the Politics of the Body.* Berkeley: University of California Press, 1993.

Sanguily, Manuel. "De una entrevista." 1912. Reprinted in Suárez León, *Yo conocí a Martí,* 157–61.

Santí, Enrico Mario. "'Our America,' the Gilded Age, and the Crisis of Latin-americanism." In Belnap and Fernández, *José Martí's "Our America,"* 179–90.

Santiago, Silviano. *Una literatura nos trópicos.* São Paulo: Editora Perspectiva, 1978.

———. *The Space In-Between: Essays on Latin American Culture.* Ed. Ana Lúcia Gazzola. Durham, N.C.: Duke University Press, 2001.

Santos Moray, Mercedes. "Aproximación a la narrativa de José Martí." *Revista de literatura cubana* 2.3 (1984): 99.

Sarabia, Nydia. *La Patriota del Silencio: Carmen Miyares.* Bogotá, Columbia: Quebecor World Bogotá, S.A., 2001.

Sarlo, Beatriz. *Una modernidad periférica: Buenos Aires 1920 y 1930*. Buenos Aires: Ediciones Nueva Visión, 1988.

Sarmiento, Domingo Faustino. *Civilización y barbarié: vida de Juan Facundo Quiroga*. Ed. Raimundo Lazo. Mexico City: Editorial Porrúa, 1998.

Sarracine, Gabriel. *La renaissance de la poésie anglaise (1789–1889)*. Paris: Perrin, 1889.

Sarracino, Rodolfo, *José Martí y el caso Cutting: ¿extraterritorialidad o anexionismo?* Havana: Centro de Estudios Martianos, 2003.

Schmidt, Peter. "Concluding Roundtable: Post-Colonial Theory, the U.S. South and New World Studies." *Mississippi Quarterly* 57.1 (2003–2004): 171–94.

Schulman, Ivan A. *Genesis del modernismo: Martí, Nájera, Silva, Casal*. Mexico City: Colegio de México, 1966.

———. "La mirada desde el norte: Martí y los Estados Unidos." *Anuario del Centro de Estudios Martianos* 24 (2001): 48–64.

———. *Nuevos asedios al modernismo*. Madrid: Taurus, 1987.

———. *Relecturas martianas: narracion y nación*. Amsterdam: Rodopi, 1994.

Schulman, Ivan A., and Evelyn Picon Garfield. *"Las entrañas del vacío": ensayos sobre la modernidad hispanoamericana*. Mexico City: Ediciones Cuadernos Americanos, 1984.

Schulman, Ivan A., and Vernon A. Chamberlin, eds. *La Revista Ilustrada de Nueva York: History, Anthology and Index of Literary Selections*. Columbia: University of Missouri Press, 1976.

Schulman, Ivan A., and Manuel Pedro González. *Martí, Darío y el modernismo*. Madrid: Editorial Gredos, 1969.

Schwarz, Roberto. "Brazilian Culture: Nationalism by Elimination." In *Misplaced Ideas*, ed. and trans. John Gledson. London: Verso, 1992.

———. *A Master on the Periphery of Capitalism*. Trans. John Gledson. Durham, N.C.: Duke University Press, 2001.

———. "Pressupostos, salvo engano, de 'Dialética da Malandragem.' " In *Que horas são? Ensaios*. São Paulo: Companhia das Letras, 1987.

———. *Ao vencedor as batatas*. 1977; São Paulo: Duas cidades/Editora 34, 2000.

Scott, David. *Conscripts of Modernity: The Tragedy of Colonial Enlightenment*. Durham, N.C.: Duke University Press, 2004.

Scott, Rebecca J. *Degrees of Freedom: Louisiana and Cuba after Slavery*. Cambridge, Mass.: Belknap Press of Harvard University Press, 2005.

Sellén, Francisco. *Poesías*. New York: A. Da Costa Gomez, 1890.

Serra y Montalvo, Rafael. "Martí es la democracia." In *Ensayos políticos*. 1892. Reprinted in *Anuario del Centro de Estudios Martianos* 5 (1982): 272–74.

———. "Ni Española ni Yankee." *La Doctrina de Martí*, January 30, 1898. Reprinted in *Rafael Serra, patriota y revolucionario, fraternal amigo de Martí*, 124–25. Havana: Oficina del Historiador de la Ciudad de la Habana, 1959.

Shaffer, Kirwin R. *Anarchism and Countercultural Politics in Early Twentieth-Century Cuba*. Gainesville: University Press of Florida, 2005.

Shelley, Percy Bysshe. *Shelley's Literary and Philosophical Criticism*. Ed. John Shawcross. London: H. Frowde, 1909.

Shukla, Sandhya, and Heidi Tinsman, eds. *Imagining Our Americas: Towards a Transnational Frame.* Durham, N.C.: Duke University Press, 2007.

Shuler, Esther E. "José Martí, su crítica de algunos escritores norteamericanos." *Archivo José Martí* (Havana) 16 (1950): 164–92.

Slotkin, Richard. *Gunfighter Nation: The Myth of the Frontier in Twentieth-Century America.* Norman: University of Oklahoma Press, 1998.

Smith, Henry Nash. *Virgin Land: The American West as Symbol and Myth.* Cambridge, Mass.: Harvard University Press, 1950.

Smith, Jon, and Deborah Cohn. *Look Away! The U.S. South in New World Studies.* Durham, N.C.: Duke University Press, 2004.

Smith, Michael P. "Buffalo Bill and the Mardi Gras Indians." In *Mardi Gras, Gumbo and Zydeco: Readings in Louisiana Culture,* Marcia Gaudet and James C. McDonald, eds., 16–25. Jackson: University Press of Mississippi, 2003.

Sommer, Doris. "José Martí, Author of Walt Whitman." In Belnap and Fernández, *José Martí's "Our America,"* 77–90.

——. "Plagiarized Authenticity: Sarmiento's Cooper and Others." In *Do the Americas Have a Common Literature?,* ed., Gustavo Pérez-Firmat, 130–55. Durham, N.C.: Duke University Press, 1990.

——. *Proceed with Caution, When Engaged by Minority Writing in the Americas.* Cambridge, Mass.: Harvard University Press, 1999.

——. "Supplying Demand: Walt Whitman as the Liberal Self." In Chevigny and LaGuardia, *Reinventing the Americas,* 68–91.

——. "A Vindication of Double Consciousness." In Ray and Schwartz, *Companion to Post-Colonial Studies,* 165–79.

Southworth, Alvan S. "Peter Cooper's Great Work." *Frank Leslie's Popular Monthly* (July 1883): 28.

Souvestre, Émile. *The World as It Shall Be.* Originally published as *Le monde tel qu'il sera,* Paris, 1846. Ed. I. F. Clarke, trans. Margaret Clarke. Middletown, Conn.: Wesleyan University Press, 2004.

Spencer, Herbert. *The Coming Slavery and other Essays.* New York: Humboldt Publishing, 1888.

——. *Illustrations of Universal Progress.* New York: D. Appleton, 1878.

Spillers, Hortense J. "Introduction: Who Cuts the Border? Some Readings on 'America.'" In *Comparative American Identities: Race, Sex, and Nationality in the Modern Text,* ed. Hortense J. Spillers, 1–25. New York: Routledge, 1991.

Spivak, Gayatri Chakravorty. *Death of a Discipline.* New York: Columbia University Press, 2001.

——. *Other Asias.* Malden, Mass.: Blackwell, 2008.

——. "The Politics of Translation." In *Destabilizing Theory,* ed. Michelle Barrett and Anne Phillips, 177–200. Stanford: Stanford University Press, 1992.

——. "Poststructuralism, Marginality, Postcoloniality and Value." In *Literary Theory Today.* Ithaca, N.Y.: Cornell University Press, 1990.

——. "Teaching for the Times." In *Dangerous Liaisons: Gender, Nation and Post-*

Colonial Perspectives, ed. Anne McClintock, Aamir Mufti, and Ella Shohat. Minneapolis: University of Minnesota Press, 1997.

———. "Translation as Culture." *Parallax* 6.1 (2000): 13–24.

———. "World Systems and the Creole." *Narrative* 14.1 (2006): 102–12.

Sprague, John T. *The Origin, Progress and Conclusion of the Florida War.* New York:
D. Appleton, 1848.

Stecopoulos, Harilaos. "Up from Empire: James Walden Johnson, Latin America,
and the Jim Crow South." In *Imagining Our Americas*, Shukla and Tinsman, eds.,
34–62.

Stedman, E. Clarence. "Walt Whitman." *Scribner's Monthly* 21.1 (November 1880):
47–64.

Steiner, George. *After Babel: Aspects of Language and Translation.* Oxford: Oxford
University Press, 1992.

Stepan, Nancy. *The Hour of Eugenics: Race, Gender and Nation in Latin America.*
Ithaca, N.Y.: Cornell University Press, 1991.

Streeby, Shelley. *American Sensations: Class, Empire, and the Production of Popular
Culture.* Berkeley: University of California Press, 2002.

———. "Labor, Memory, and the Boundaries of Print Culture: From Haymarket to
the Mexican Revolution." *American Literary History* 19.2 (2002): 406–33.

Strong, Josiah. *Our Country: Its Possible Future and Its Present Crisis.* New York:
American Home Missionary Society, 1885.

Suárez León, Carmen, ed. *José Martí y Víctor Hugo: en el fiel de las modernidades.*
Havana: Centro de Investigación y Desarrollo de la Cultura Cubana Juan Marinello, 1997.

———. *Yo conocí a Martí.* Santa Clara, Cuba: Ediciones Capiro, 1998.

Tchen, John Kuo Wei. *New York before Chinatown: Orientalism and the Shaping of
American Culture, 1776–1882.* Baltimore: Johns Hopkins University Press, 1999.

Tedín, Miguel. "José Martí." *La Nación*, December 1, 1909. Reprinted in Suárez
León, *Yo conocí a Martí*, 163.

Thomas, Brook. "Frederick Jackson Turner, José Martí and Finding a Home on the
Range." In *José Martí's "Our America,"* Belnap and Fernández, eds., 275–92.

Tinajero, Araceli. *El lector de tabaquería: Historia de una tradición cubana.* Madrid:
Editorial Verbum, 2007.

Tocqueville, Alexis de. *Democracy in America.* 2 vols. Trans. Henry Reeve, Francis
Bowen, and Phillips Bradley. New York: Vintage Books, 1945.

Toledo Sande, Josefina. *Sotero Figueroa, editor de Patria: apuntes para una biografía.*
Havana: Editorial Letras Cubanas, 1985.

Toledo Sande, Luis. *Cesto de llamas: biografía de Martí.* Havana: Editorial Pueblo y
Educación, 1998.

———. "José Martí contra *The New York Herald: The New York Herald* contra José
Martí." *Anuario del Centro de Estudios Martianos* 10 (1987): 21–72.

Traubel, Horace. *In re Walt Whitman.* Philadelphia: D. McKay, 1893.

———. *With Walt Whitman in Camden.* Vol. 2. 1912; New York: Rowman and Littlefield, 1961.

"A Tribute from a Poet: Walt Whitman Tells of Lincoln's Death." *New York Times*, April 15, 1887: 1.

Trujillo, Enrique Navarrete, ed. *Album de "El Porvenir."* Vol. 3. New York: Imprenta "El Porvenir," 1892.

———. *Apuntes históricos; propoganda y movimientos revolucionarios Cubanos en los Estados Unidos desde Enero de 1880 hasta febrero de 1895.* New York: Tip. de "Porvenir," 1896.

———, ed. *La evolución y la revolución: artículos publicados en "El Avisador Cubano."* New York: Hernandez's Printing and Translating, 1888.

Turner, Frederick Jackson. "The Significance of the Frontier in American History." 1893. In *The Early Writings of Frederick Jackson Turner*. Ed. Everett E. Edwards. Madison: University of Wisconsin Press, 1938.

Tzu-Kuei, Yen. "Rock Springs Incident." *Chinese Studies in History* 8.3 (spring 1974): 51–66. Reprinted in *Chinese on the American Frontier*, ed. Arif Dirlik, 355–65. Lanham, Md.: Rowman and Littlefield, 2001.

U.S. Department of State. *Report on Extraterritorial Crime and the Cutting Case.* Washington, D.C.: Government Printing Office, 1887.

U.S. Embassy (Mexico). *Case of the American A. K. Cutting: Latest Notes Exchanged between the Legation of the United States of America and the Minister of Foreign Relations of the Republic of Mexico.* Washington, D.C.: Judd and Detweiler, 1888.

Valdés Dominguez, Fermín. "Martí: ofrenda de hermano." *Revista Cubana* 29 (July 1951–December 1952): 237–87.

———. *Tragedy in Havana: November 27, 1871.* Ed. and trans. Consuelo E. Stebbins. Gainesville: University Press of Florida, 2000.

Varela, Félix. *El Habanero: papel politico, científico y literario.* Miami: Ediciones Universal, 1997.

Varela, Luis A. *Democracia práctica: estudio sobre todos los sistemas electorales: propuestos para dar representación proporcional a las mayorías y minorías.* Preface by D. Emilio Castelar. Paris and Mexico City: Libreria de A. Bouret e hijo, 1876.

Varona, Enrique. *Obras completas.* Vol. 1. Havana: Edición Official, 1936.

———. *Seis conferencias.* Barcelona: Gorgas y Cía, 1888.

Vélez, Román. "José Martí." *Notas de Arte* (Colombia), August 15, 1910.

Venegas, Yolanda. "The Erotics of Racialization: Gender and Sexuality in the Making of California." *Frontiers* 25.3 (2004): 63–89.

Venuti, Lawrence. "The Translator's Invisibility." *Criticism* 28.2 (1986): 179–212.

Vico, Giambattista. *The New Science.* Trans. Thomas Goddard Bergin and Max Harold Fisch. Ithaca, N.Y.: Cornell University Press, 1968.

Viswanathan, Gauri. *Masks of Conquest.* New York: Columbia University Press, 1989.

Vitier, Medardo. "La obra político-social (primera parte)." In Varona, *Obras.*

Wald, Priscilla. "Fabulous Shadows: Rethinking the Emersonian Tradition." *American Quarterly* 50.4 (December 1998): 831–39.

Warner, Charles Dudley. "Mexican Notes: Morelia and Patzcuaro." *Harper's Monthly Magazine* (July 1887): 283–91.

Warren, Louis S. *Buffalo Bill's America: William Cody and the Wild West Show*. New York: Alfred A. Knopf, 2005.

Wells, David A. *A Study of Mexico*. New York: Appleton, 1887.

West, Cornel. "On Black-Brown Relations." In *Cornel West Reader*, 499–513. New York: Basic Civitas Books, 1999.

White, Richard. "Frederick Jackson Turner and Buffalo Bill." In *The Frontier in American Culture*, ed. James R. Grossman, 6–65. Berkeley: University of California Press, 1994.

Whitman, Walt. *Complete Poetry and Selected Prose*. Ed. James E. Miller Jr. Boston, Mass.: Houghton Mifflin, 1959.

———. *I Sit and Look Out: Editorials from the Brooklyn Daily Times*. Ed. Emory Holloway and Vernolian Schwarz. New York: Columbia University Press, 1932.

———. *Leaves of Grass and Other Writings*. Ed. Michal Moon. New York: W. W. Norton, 2002.

———. *The Portable Walt Whitman*. New York: Penguin, 2004.

———. *Prose Works*. Vol. 2, *Collect, and other prose*. Ed. Floyd Stovall. 1892; New York: New York University Press, 1964.

———. *Uncollected Walt Whitman*. New York: P. Smith, 1932.

Williams, Raymond. *The Country and the City*. New York: Oxford University Press, 1973.

———. *Keywords: A Vocabulary of Culture and Society*. New York: Oxford University Press, 1976.

———. *The Politics of Modernism: Against the New Conformists*. Ed. Tony Pinkney. London: Verso, 1989.

Wilmot, David. "Speech of Mr. Wilmot of Pennsylvania, Restriction of Slavery in the New Territories, House of Representatives, August 3, 1848." *The National Era* 2 (August 17, 1848): 132.

Wilson, Howard A. "William Dean Howells's Unpublished Letters about the Haymarket Affair." *Journal of the Illinois State Historical Society* 56 (1963): 5–19.

Young, Robert J. C. "Deconstruction and the Postcolonial." In *Deconstructions: A User's Guide*, 187–210. London: Palgrave, 2000.

Yúdice, George. "Rethinking the Theory of the Avant-Garde from the Periphery." In *Modernism and Its Margins: Reinscribing Cultural Modernity from Spain and Latin America*, ed. Anthony L. Geist and José B. Monleón. New York: Garland, 1999.

Zacharie de Baralt, Blanche. *El Martí que yo conocí*. New York: Las Americas Publishing, 1967.

Zenea, Juan Clemente. "En Greenwood." In *Herencia: An Anthology of the Hispanic Literature of the United States*, ed. Nicolás Kanellos. New York: Oxford University Press, 2002.

Zeno Gandia, M. "Cómo conocí a un caudillo" (How I Met a Leader). In Suárez León, *Yo conocí a Martí*, 213–14.

LAURA LOMAS is an assistant professor of English literature and American Studies at Rutgers University.

LIBRARY OF CONGRESS CATALOGING-IN-PUBLICATION DATA

Lomas, Laura
Translating empire : José Martí, migrant Latino subjects, and American modernities / Laura Lomas.
p. cm. — (New Americanists)
Includes bibliographical references and index.
ISBN 978-0-8223-4342-4 (cloth : alk. paper)
ISBN 978-0-8223-4325-7 (pbk. : alk. paper)
1. Martí, José, 1853–1895—Criticism and interpretation. 2. Martí, José, 1853–1895—Political and social views. 3. Martí, José, 1853–1895—Influence. 4. Spanish American literature—20th century—History and criticism. I. Title. II. Series.
PQ7389.M2Z722 2008
864'.5—dc22   2008028479